RACE INTO SPACE
The Soviet Space Programme

RACE INTO SPACE
The Soviet Space Programme

BRIAN HARVEY

ELLIS HORWOOD LIMITED
Publishers · Chichester

Halsted Press: a division of
JOHN WILEY & SONS
New York · Chichester · Brisbane · Toronto

First published in 1988 by
ELLIS HORWOOD LIMITED
Market Cross House, Cooper Street,
Chichester, West Sussex, PO19 1EB, England
The publisher's colophon is reproduced from James Gillison's drawing of the ancient Market Cross, Chichester.

Distributors:

Australia and New Zealand:
JACARANDA WILEY LIMITED
GPO Box 859, Brisbane, Queensland 4001, Australia

Canada:
JOHN WILEY & SONS CANADA LIMITED
22 Worcester Road, Rexdale, Ontario, Canada

Europe and Africa:
JOHN WILEY & SONS LIMITED
Baffins Lane, Chichester, West Sussex, England

North and South America and the rest of the world:
Halsted Press: a division of
JOHN WILEY & SONS
605 Third Avenue, New York, NY 10158, USA

South-East Asia
JOHN WILEY & SONS (SEA) PTE LIMITED
37 Jalan Pemimpin # 05–04
Block B, Union Industrial Building, Singapore 2057

Indian Subcontinent
WILEY EASTERN LIMITED
4835/24 Ansari Road
Daryaganj, New Delhi 110002, India

© **1988 B. Harvey/Ellis Horwood Limited**

British Library Cataloguing in Publication Data
Harvey, Brian, *1953–*
Race into space.
1. Soviet space flight to 1980
I. Title
629.4′1′0947

Library of Congress Card No. 88–11956

ISBN 0–7458–0437–3 (Ellis Horwood Limited)
ISBN 0–470–21099–0 (Halsted Press)

Typeset by Heather FitzGibbon, Fleet
Printed in Great Britain by Unwin Bros., Woking

Table of Contents

Foreword

Almost everyone knows that the Space Age began when the Russians launched their first artificial satellite, Sputnik 1. The date was 4 October 1957. Since that time, the Soviets have achieved an impressive list of 'firsts': the first true astronaut (or cosmonaut) was Yuri Gagarin; the first spacewalk was achieved by Alexei Leonov; the Russians were the first to soft-land a vehicle on the Moon, and the first to obtain photographs from the hostile surface of Venus, to mention just a few. Yet they have sent no men to the Moon, and they have had their failures too.

The American space programme has been open — one might almost say, wide open. That of the USSR has not. Even with the present climate of *glasnost* there is much that is not common knowledge. Brian Harvey has undertaken a tremendous amount of research, and in this book he presents his findings in a way which is both authoritative and readable. Even if you consider yourself an expert, you will find here facts that you did not previously know. This is both a fascinating story and a detailed historical account.

Patrick Moore

Preface

MIR

Look up at the clear skies of night now, for they have changed. Thirty years ago, the night sky was a canopy of tiny pinpoints of light, interrupted only when the trail of a fiery meteor blazed across the firmament. But little else moved as the galaxy slowly rotated through the heavens until it disappeared in the onrush of dawn.

It is different now. Every night – sometimes earlier, sometimes later – a bright star, dazzling as Venus, will rise slowly in the west. It is too silent and too swift to be an aircraft. In four to five minutes it will sail overhead, quite noiselessly, and describe a giant arc across the sky, to set in the east, lost in the horizon's glow.

It is the Soviet space station Mir circling the Earth, the first real home in space, symbol of how humankind has now left behind the gravitational bonds of our planet. Not that Mir's vigil is a silent one: a listener with a citizen's band receiver can pick up the routine chatter as each team of cosmonauts passes overhead and reports in to the ground.

Every few weeks the sharp observer will notice a smaller speck of light following after Mir, faster, more hurried. It will be a smaller space freighter flying supplies up to the station, chasing Mir in a lower, quicker orbit. And from time to time, a spaceship can be seen dropping down from Mir, sending cosmonauts home, back with the results of months of research.

And, on dark nights unspoilt by moonlight or city lights, the observer will spot another space station, much further up, more slowly traversing the sky. It is the old disused space station Salyut 7, veteran of the early 1980s, in high orbit. And, if you look carefully, little pinpoints of light will cross the sky, north to south, east to west, some quickly, some slowly, some flashing, some tumbling: sometimes the sky is alive with rockets and satellites passing over. Not all, by any means, will be Russian, but well over half will be, a tribute to one nation's effort to conquer space over thirty years.

MYSTERY

To many in Europe and north America, it comes as a genuine mystery that a country like the Soviet Union should invest so much of its material resources in the conquest of the cosmos. To a country that experiences routine difficulties in agricultural production, refrigeration, and meeting consumer needs, sending stations into orbit and spaceships to Mars seems like an extravagant form of self-indulgence.

Yet to judge the Soviet space programme purely in terms of economic choices would be a mistake. The concept of exploring space has been a theme of Russian scientists since the nineteenth century. In their own day, these scientists attracted their predictable share of derision, but they never doubted that it could be done — one day:

Konstantin Tsiolkovsky, who designed atomic spaceships in pre-revolutionary Petrograd.

Yuri Kondratyuk, who described orbiting space stations in the 1920s.

Friedrich Tsander, who penned the outlines of a space shuttle in the 1930s.

Of course the factors that led the Soviet Union into space in the 1950s had little to do with gratifying the whims of romantic savants; more mundane and perhaps less noble considerations played their part too. The drive for military supremacy, the desire to demonstrate technological prowess, the celebration of postwar economic advance — these were the real factors that put the first man into space and sent the first rockets to the Moon and Venus.

But as in the story of the sorcerer's apprentice, the race into space declared so recklessly by the Kremlin conjured up a trial of strength that was to overwhelm those who had once been the masters: for it provoked President Kennedy's challenge to go for the Moon, a challenge well beyond the capacities of Nikita Khrushchev, his political successors, and the divided rocket design institutes. The lunar spaceships fell behind schedule, hastily assembled superboosters blew up, and the new Soyuz spaceship on which so many hopes had rested entered a dizzying spin on its first flight to kill its pilot, the doomed Vladimir Komarov.

So decisive, so crushing, was the USSR's defeat in the Moon race in 1969 that a nation less committed to the long-term exploration of space might well have abandoned its efforts there and then. Instead, the victory of Apollo forced the Soviet Union back to first principles and the building of space stations. This was what, after all, the theoreticians from Tsiolkovsky onward had always said should be done first. By the late 1970s, Russians were flying in space for half a year at a time, and by the late 1980s a permanent home in space, the Mir, had been set up. Modules were docked together, parted, reformed, and refuelled. Ironically, these years of solid achievement went virtually unremarked outside the Soviet Union itself.

FILLING IN THE BLANK PAGES

The new Soviet leader, Mikhail Gorbachev, who from his own accession in 1985 quickly contributed his own authority to accelerating the expansion of the space programme, made an early pledge to 'fill in the blank pages of Soviet history'. Yet much of the space programme remains a series of blank pages. *Glasnost* has given us live television of manned launches, user manuals for rocket boosters, technical details of current missions, and the names and photographs of Yuri Gagarin's young colleagues — but not much else.

We still don't know much about Russia's Moon plans, how they changed and how they evolved and how they ultimately collapsed. We still know little about the lunar cabins that flew in secrecy. Cosmonauts appear and disappear in old photographs. Two space stations fell out of the sky in the early 1970s, their debris accompanied by implausible explanations. Designers lurk in the background — the brilliant Glushko, the elusive but influential Vladimir Chalomei. Other experts speak delphically of missions planned, contemplated, and sometimes abandoned. The Soviet space shuttle even now has an experimental flight history that has tested to the limit the powers of aviation detectives.

Yet for all its mystery, its eeriness, its secrecy, the Soviet space programme has become an industry in its own right. Its contribution to economic development has been considerable — it has acted as the cutting edge of technological development, despite Western descriptions that erroneously portray Soviet technology as crude and even antiquated. Earth resources, observations, materials processing in orbit, communications sputniks and weather-forecasting satellites have brought economic gains quantifiable in millions of roubles. The giant space centres of Plesetsk and Baikonour employ armies of workers. The Soviet military benefit from reconnaissance satellites, electronic ferrets, and satellite hunter-killers that put Soviet military science on a par with America's star wars. No study of the Soviet Union as a modern industrial society should ignore the very major investment represented by the space programme — its use of resources, its allocations of energy, labour and skilled workers, and its place in the planning of the Soviet economy.

This book is a serious attempt to record and assess these human and technical events, and place them in their historical and contemporary perspective. Finally, it looks to the future.

The building of the Mir station in the 1980s, the construction now of a new generation of sophisticated booster rockets, projected flights to the asteroids and Mars, all these point to the Soviet Union making an unambiguous effort to reclaim the high ground of spaceflight as the world nears the third millennium. The race into space may now be over: the conquest of the solar system could be about to begin.

ACKNOWLEDGEMENTS

I wish to express my thanks to John Mason and Beverley Coates for their assistance in compiling the Record of Soviet Manned Space Missions (Appendix C) and in organising the photographs and captions.

All photographs reproduced by courtesy of the Novosti Press Agency, London and the Soviet Academy of Sciences, Moscow.

1

Beginnings (to 1955)

Russia's exploration of space began in a small village called Izhevskoye near the city of Ryazan 200 km southeast of Moscow. On 17 September 1857 a small boy was born. His father, Eduard Tsiolkovsky was a forest ranger and he named his son Konstantin. Konstantin was a bright active child until he was ten, when one disaster followed another. He was struck down by scarlet fever and he became almost totally deaf. For three years his mother nursed him and despite his affliction taught him to read and write and manage at boys' high school. Then, when he had reached thirteen, she died suddenly.

Konstantin Tsiolkovsky's life is not only the story of one man's effort to cope with a terrible disablement. For despite it he became a self-taught scientist, a practical person, and a theoretician of space flight. He was the one person who inspired the idea of a Russian spece programme from the very beginning. Without him, it might never have happened at all.

By the age of 14, Tsiolkovsky was well able to read and he read books endlessly. It was one thing he was able to do, deprived as he was of the normal channels of human contact and communication. Financially supported by his father, he moved to Moscow when he was 16, rented rooms, and spent days and days in the city's public libraries. By 17, he had begun to master higher mathematics, differential calculus, and spherical trigonometry.

After three years in Moscow, Tsiolkovsky took up a teaching post in Kaluga, a town just southwest of Moscow. In the Tsar's Russia it was probably the most obvious career for him. His life was hard and he found deafness a terrible torment. He even designed tin funnels as hearing aids so that he could try to pick up what people were saying.

Konstantin Tsiolkovsky, the man who was the inspiration for the Soviet space programme. In the year the Wright brothers made their first flight, he wrote of liquid fuel rockets, soft landings on other planets and the colonization of space.

In 1883, in the course of the long summer school holidays, Tsiolkovsky turned his mind to something which had obsessed him — travel through space. We do not know where the inspiration came from and history gives us no clue. It may have been his deafness which while depriving him in so many ways also made him contemplative and, ironically, all the more imaginative.

Free space, his book from 1883, took the creative leap from the earth-bound solid practical world to that of fantasy, yet without cutting scientific corners. He described what a human being would see and experience if flying around the earth in a space ship. He would be weightless; and he would get up there by a 'reactive' interplanetary ship with a rocket engine using spherical projectiles fired by an on-board cannon. Gravity and weightlessness intrigued Tsiolkovsky. He rigged up devices that could create zero gravity on the ground, and a primitive centrifuge to test overloading, which he verified using chicken and mice. They could stand loads of six gravities ($6G$) but died at $10G$ — just like humans would [1].

Free space was followed by *On the Moon* (1887) and *A dream of Earth and sky* (1895). In the latter he described how a small-shaped Moon or artificial Earth satellite could be launched and circle the Earth at an altitude of 270 km.

It would be a mistake to regard Tsiolkovsky as simply a Russian equivalent of the French novelist Jules Verne, inspired by him though he was. He was also an inventor. He designed and built a wind tunnel in his home to study air resistance, and designed a monoplane aircraft with a gasoline engine, enclosed cockpit, autopilot and retractable landing gear.

1903 was a famous year. In South Carolina the Wright brothers made the first flight of an aeroplane. Tsiolkovsky — still a teacher in Kaluga - produced his most important paper called 'Exploring space with reactive devices'. In it he spelt out the advantages of rocket flight and of liquid-fuelled rockets; and he explained how it might be possible to soft-land on other planets. Eventually he predicted, poetically, 'people will ascend into the expanse of the heavens and found a settlement there'.

The house in which Konstantin Tsiolkovsky lived and worked at Kaluga, a town to the southwest of Moscow.

His ideas gained ground and won gradual acceptance as time went on. His paper was taken by the Petrograd journal *Scientific Review* and printed in 1911. By then his mind had moved on. In the same year he proposed that, owing to the possible inefficiency of liquid-fuelled rockets, some kind of atomic power would have to be considered for really distant space journeys!

PROBING THE ATMOSPHERE

In 1911 he made his most famous and often-quoted prophecy.

> Mankind will not remain forever on the Earth. In pursuit of light and space he will timidly at first probe the limits of the atmosphere and later extend his control throughout the solar system.[2]

Tsiolkovsky found some kind of financial security when in 1918 the new Revolutionary Government awarded him a pension for the rest of his life. He went on writing, to produce in 1924 *Cosmic rocket trains*, advocating multistage rockets in which one used the thrust gained by a lower stage to go on to ever greater altitudes. He then designed a 'stellar ship' — complete with closed ecocycle to resupply itself with air and plants and water. His spaceship designs would be conventional enough today in any technical journal dealing with future space travel: but liquid-fuel engines, solar batteries, wheel-shaped space stations, all these were part of his thinking sixty years ago. In the same year the Government republished all his old works.

In his later days, his home in Kaluga became a place of pilgrimage. Inventors, designers, journalists, aviators, scientists beat their path to Tsiolkovsky's door. The now-old, bearded, hollow-chested prophet lived in a two-storied house with a veranda where he sat out to reflect in the summer. Books, manuscripts, an odd globe were piled in his study. In his declining years there were similarities to the last old newsreel pictures of Tolstoy a generation earlier.

Konstantin Tsiolkovsky's health gave way in August 1935. Newspapers carried accounts of his collapse and his subsequent death in September 1935. In his will he bequeathed all his papers to the Communist Party of the Soviet Union.

His home was at once turned into a national museum and since then it has been a shrine and a tourist attraction. An obelisk has been erected as has a shining 20 m high silvery rocket against a bronze bust of his figure. Tens of thousands see it every year. In 1954 the Tsiolkovsky Gold Medal was struck, to be awarded every three years to the most outstanding contributor to space flight.

REVOLUTIONARY GOVERNMENT

On 16 April 1917, Vladimir Lenin returned from years of exile to the Finland Station in Petrograd. In the course of the year Russia slipped into greater and greater chaos, the result both of the war with Germany and of revolutionary conditions at home that would certainly have developed even if there had been no war abroad. The Bolshevik Party was the only one with sufficient will and determination and, while others talked and argued, the Party seized power in October 1917. Opposition parties were dissolved in 1918, civil war broke out soon after; and it was not until 1921 that a Communist Bolshevik Government was firmly established.

In the West, the whole period is regarded as an age of darkness, terror and oppression. Lenin died in 1924, worn down by an earlier assassination attempt which left him weakened and partially paralysed. Stalin gradually emerged as the new strong man, particularly after the expulsion of Trotsky in 1928. The purges and the terror began in 1936, and lasted until Stalin's death in 1953, interrupted only by the war with Germany in 1941—45.

The purges wreaked havoc on Russia's space programme, as we shall see. But the Revolutionary Government also provided conditions under which it could begin and develop in the first place. These considerations are important and are often neglected.

First, the Soviet Government was a new social experiment. It was an explicitly Marxist regime, deriving its inspiration from Karl Marx and his social theories. Economic progress was a central tenet of Marxism — as countries modernized, social change became rapid, and the relationships between people and machines were transformed. Marx in his writings — he was as much a historian as a philosopher — made considerable efforts to describe the speed and effect of these changes.

Marx's belief in the inevitability of change in industrial, economic and political relationships was matched by an equally strong belief in the ability of individuals, organizations and social classes to change these relationships. An organized working class could hasten a revolution that was inevitable and make it happen sooner rather than later; such a Government could build Communism quickly or slowly. As he himself said:

Hitherto philosophers have only described history: the point however is to change it.[3]

An established Soviet Government could and therefore should use its power consciously to do certain things. Its philosophy was therefore radically different from, say, the United States, where the conventional wisdom was that the *less* government there was, the better.

There were then few philosophical inhibitions holding back Soviet- and Government-sponsored scientific endeavours. Marx's materialist philosophy did not stop at national frontiers: humankind's desire to control his environment extended indefinitely. Certain Biblical insights which set God's natural world (up there), apart from man's sphere of influence (down here) were not part of Marx's thinking. Human control over all creation was central to his philosophy.

For the entire period until the late 1940s, the Soviet Government was not only a socialist state: it was the only one. The eyes of the world were very much on it. Supporters were quick to focus on its achievements; sceptics and those hostile were quick to find fault. The Soviet Government was very conscious of its role. Its failure to survive could well mean that socialists everywhere would lose faith in the basic validity, feasibility and desirability of Marxist government. So from the beginning it had a sense of its own destiny, which it has still not lost.

Not only was it a social experiment that could succeed, it had to succeed. Furthermore, proof of its success was its ability to develop faster and quicker than its capitalist rivals. In the early 1960s Khrushchev was to make much of the inevitability of the success of socialist science. That is later, but the seeds of the idea go back to the 1920s.

Scientific achievement soon became an acid test of the validity of socialism. The USSR simply had to progress faster and further — its science was unsullied by the profit motive or the corruptions of commercialism, and it was open to all citizens in a socialist society to be great scientists. Science became part of the trial of strength between capitalism and socialism, just like the figures of industrial and agricultural output, literacy, the numbers of doctors per thousand, coal output per pithead, and so on.

The USSR started out in the 1920s with many disadvantages compared to the United States, and in effect started from behind, with lower levels of literacy, education, industrialization and agriculture. Indeed, in the 1920s the Americans ran aid programmes to the USSR to help combat famine.

SYMPATHETIC TO SCIENCE

The new Soviet Government was one sympathetic to science and scientists. The explanation is not hard to find. Tsarist Russia was both an aristocracy and an autocracy and there was little place in it for people of moderate or few means, like scientists. The February 1917 Revolution was very much a middle-class one, carried out by a middle class that had been denied power or influence. Scientists, thinkers, educators, teachers had found little encouragement in the Tsar's time. There was little access to higher education for training, but plenty of police harrassment and censorship. Scientists looked to the new Government for help: it in turn needed their support to carry out its plans of modernization.

An interesting footnote to this is the story of Nikolai Kibilachich. Independently of Tsiolkovsky he drew up ideas for jet engines in the late 1870s and early 1880s. He devised a heavier-than-air flying platform, propelled by a rocket whose engine swivelled or gimballed [4]. But he was also a revolutionary and he was executed for designing a bomb that killed the Tsar.

His writings were impounded immediately — his last drawings were made in the condemned cell the night before he was hanged — and did not see the light of day until August 1917. They were then published at once.

The Soviet Government from 1918 on was anxious to secure, maintain and develop the goodwill of the scientific community. Its plans were ambitious and were pursued at a reckless pace throughout the 1920s and 1930s: they included electrification, air transport, heavy industry, a modern defence force, full employment and the ending of illiteracy.

For all these reasons, practical and philosophical, and the historical relationship between scientists and revolutionaries, the Soviet Government had a benign attitude towards science, scientists and designers. Rocketeers were not excluded. Tsiolkovsky (as previously mentioned) was in 1918 awarded a substantial life's pension. His writings were published by the Government presses. On his 75th birthday in 1932 the Government awarded him the 'Red Banner of Labour' and a special session of the Academy of Sciences was called to honour him.

It is instructive to compare the different Governmental attitudes to space travel. Right up to the late 1950s, western Governments were uninterested and sceptical, insofar as they spent any time thinking about it at all, which they did not. They tolerated scientists like Goddard in the United States and the British Interplanetary Society in Britain. Yet in the USSR 'officialdom' was behind the space effort from the start: the Soviet sense of destiny meant that it was only a question of *when* it all came true, not *if*.

Two theoreticians from the 1920s stand out: Frederick Tsander and Yuri Kondratyuk. Frederick Tsander (1887–1933) was an engineer from Riga Polytechnic in Lithuania, and was directly inspired by Tsiolkovsky. In his designs he attempted to combine rockets

Friedrich Arturovich Tsander was an engineer who was directly inspired by Tsiolkovsky. His designs were the forerunners of the modern space shuttle; his spaceship took off like a plane but utilized rocket power once the air became too thin for aerodynamic lift. He tested a liquid-fuelled rocket in 1933.

Yuri Vasilyevich Kondratyuk wrote about space travel between 1916 and 1929. He described multi-stage rockets, the use of solar energy for power and orbiting space stations.

and aircraft. His spaceship would take off and ascend like a plane but rocket power would be used once the air became too thin to use. In his designs are the antecedents of the space shuttle. In the midst of testing a 50 kg liquid-fuel rocket in 1933 he went down with typhoid fever and died. But he had already made his mark both as a designer and builder of small rockets and as a theoretician. His obsession was flight to Mars and he even did a schedule of a manned journey there. He ended it with the resounding words: 'One day we *shall* fly to Mars!' [5].

Yuri Kondratyuk wrote on space travel between 1916 and 1929, composing *The conquest of interplanetary Space*. His book described exactly that: his rockets were multi-staged and utilized solar energy. He described orbiting space stations, landing stages as a base for lunar takeoff (like the American Lunar Module) and return to Earth by atmospheric braking.

Writing on space travel in the 1920s had reached such a pitch that in 1929 a Professor Rynin was able to publish a nine-volume encyclopedia called *Space travels* summarizing all the main papers, ideas and concepts of the day.

ORGANIZING THE ROCKET EFFORT

The 1920s were a time when rocket and space organizations sprouted everywhere: a Society for the Study of Interplanetary Communications (OIMS, 1924); a Kiev Society for the Study and Conquest of Space (1925); and, to top it all, 1927 saw the first-ever exhibition of 'interplanetary machines'. It was held for three months in Moscow. Foreign exhibitors came from Britain, the USA (Goddard), France, Germany and Austria. The exhibits included designs, models, drawings, pictures and even a mockup spacesuit.

The seriousness with which 'amateur' space scientists took themselves was matched by officialdom. In April 1924 a Jet Propulsion Section was established in the Zhukovsky Military Air Academy. Its first tasks included a competition to launch a rocket that would fly 100 km; and it had a journal called *Raketa* which would, it proclaimed, 'distribute information on interplanetary navigation'. Its work was linked to a body with the cumbersome title of TsAGI (Central Institute of Aerohydrodynamics). TsAGI was a technical institute, and its rocket designs, whilst originally inspired by the needs of the Red Air Force, were later central to the space programme.

By the mid 1920s, all the major components of the Soviet space programme were in place: an Air Academy which trained test pilots; the prestigious E.N. Bauman Technical Institute which trained design engineers; a band of amateurs and visionaries; a Jet Propulsion Department; the TsAGI Technical Institute; and the Soviet Academy of Sciences. No other country was able to achieve such a potent combination of these different elements for some time [6].

It was a mixture that could be devastatingly successful, but there were flaws. Having a responsibility to Government (and in part inspired by Government) meant that it could be manipulated for political purposes, or, worse still, closed down if the Government's attitude turned sour. It was, quite clearly, far from a monolith, but a combination of different institutes, organizations and groups. They could just as easily pull apart as pull together.

GIRD, GDL AND RNII

The Soviet space programme produced its first hardware in the 1920s and it came from two groups with the awkward names of GIRD and GDL. Both started under the auspices of the most senior military man in the Soviet Union — the young, ambitious and ultimately doomed Marshal Tukhachevsky.

The Gas Dynamics Laboratory (GDL) was set up in Leningrad in 1927. Within five years it had produced a 20 kg thrust liquid-fuel rocket on a test stand. Conventionally enough, it ran on liquid oxygen and gasoline. By 1933 GDL was achieving thrust levels of 300 kg. Thousands of static tests were made: the engines had variable thrusts and achieved rates of efficiency that the West did not match till the 1950s. The burn marks from these early tests are still there — in the old Petropavlovskaya Fortress, the only safe site the experimenters could find. The roar from the fortress as the static tests went on startled passing citizens and probably mystified them too.

GDL also saw the breaking-in of Russia's foremost engine designer: Valentin Glushko. He was still influencing rocket designs in the 1980s [7].

GIRD was a larger but parallel organization functioning in Moscow at the same time. Composed of TsAGI scientists, GIRD (or Group for the Study of Reaction Propulsion) set up at 19 Sadovo-Spasskaya St near Moscow's city centre in 1932. It always saw itself as a national, not just a Moscow, organization, and its founder was Sergei Korolov, later known as the 'Chief Designer'.

GIRD's claim to lasting fame was that it designed and flew the first modern liquid-fuelled rocket in the USSR. The '09' rocket, as it was called, was 2.5 m long, weighed 17 kg divided equally between payload and fuel, and went up on 17 August 1933. Korolov lit the fuse himself. Its successor, GIRD-X, achieved the height of 4000 m four months later: still impressive as a black needle hurtling skywards on the jerky black-and-white film of the time. Tsander was designer.

Marshal Tukhachevsky, not one to waste time, was impatient of delays caused by the division of effort between the GDL in Leningrad and the GIRD in Moscow. So in 1933 he ordered these merged as the RNII (Scientific Rocket Research Institute). Two of his deputies, Ivan Kleimenov and G.E. Langemak, ran it along with Korolov.

The merger of 1933 led to an abrupt change of direction. The liquid-fuel rocket programme was abruptly halted, and emphasis was switched to winged rockets. Korolov in particular was involved in fitting rocket motors to gliders and there are many pictures from this time showing him in flying gear with gliders in the background. This abrupt change of track — it is glossed over in the histories of the period — was a portent of things to come. Liquid-fuel rockets simply disappeared out of the biographies and narratives at their most promising stage. After the success of GIRD-X it is hard to believe that the scientists can have been happy about this. The most mundane explanation is probably the most likely one. Tukhachevsky saw in winged rockets, rocket gliders and rocket planes a more likely weapon of war and that was where his first loyalty lay.

THE TERROR

On 11 June 1937, Marshal Tukhachevsky was arrested on Stalin's orders. He and seven other generals were shot in a prison yard later that night. It heralded a ferocious purge of the armed forces: 35 000 were shot, half the entire officer corps of the Red Army. An equally ruthless purge of the Communist Party itself had begun the previous year. Stalin's purges had broken on the USSR, occasioned by a suspected conspiracy against him and exacerbated by Stalin's own paranoia. Steeped in the Tsarist tradition of authoritarian rule, Stalin was also motivated by the desire to have an administration blindly loyal to himself [8].

Soviet rocket development was hit as much as any other sector of Russian society [9]. The rocket programme, simply and for no other reason than that Tukhachevsky had taken it under his wing, became automatically suspect. His two deputies in RNII, Langemak and Kleimenov, were shot in 1938. They were not the only people who were involved at the time whose official biographies stop in 1938 or thereabouts.

The official histories of the programme from around 1937 are sketchy. Very few precise dates are given. There were some glider tests, an occasional rocket test, quite a few military-related tests. As the danger of German attack grew so too did tests of ground-to-ground missiles and small rockets that could be fired from planes. But the histories are murky, imprecise. We catch only glimpses, compared to the wealth of light and detail of the GIRD and GDL years. This is nowhere more true than in the cases of the two personalities who subsequently emerged as the leaders of the space programme — Korolov and Glushko.

KOROLOV

Korolov never actually existed officially until after his death in January 1966. Krushchev simply could not bear the thought of the attention lavished on Soviet space successes from 1957 on being divided between himself and anyone else. All that we were permitted to know was that there was a 'Chief Designer' beavering away somewhere in the background.

Plenty is known of Korolov now — except for the grim years during the purges. There is good evidence that Korolov himself spent some time in the camps and was lucky to live at all. The adulation bestowed upon him after he died — and many biographies have been published since 1966 — contains only hints of how much was missed. Certainly the Soviet space programme was never the same again after he went, and much of the drive seemed to go out of it. One wonders if his biographers knew, but dared not say, that he might have lived longer but for the hard years of the camps.

Sergei Korolov was a Ukrainian, born in 1906. He developed a fascination with aircraft, went to Kiev Polytechnic, and (far from easy) got into the Moscow Higher Technical School. Some of its students were in GIRD, and this was Korolov's link to rocketry. A chance to visit Tsiolkovsky in 1929 converted him.

Korolov then made a living as an aircraft designer in the Tupolev design bureau. His connection with Tupolev may even have saved him during the purges. He was a versatile designer and took on board everything from gliders to sports planes to rocket fighters. He trained to be a pilot himself.

Once noticed, like his later rival, the equally young von Braun in Germany, his rise was rapid. In 1932 he became leader of GIRD's design and production section. In 1934 the Soviet Ministry of Defence published *Rocket flight in the stratosphere*, which he wrote. In the following year he sat in the passenger seat of a rocket glider he had designed himself. It made a test flight in tow from Moscow to the Crimea.

The purges that followed Tukhachevsky's arrest and execution set Russia's space programme back many years. The young Korolov — he was only 30 — was locked away in prison in Moscow. His rocket experiments came under suspicion. After a lengthy interrogation he was sent in a boxcar off to Siberia [10]. After many days the train reached the Pacific coast. Korolov spent some time at a seaport staging post before being transferred to the terrible Kolyma goldmines, from which most never returned. He was there for a year. In 1938 he was suddenly transferred back to Moscow, and put in a special prison, called a *sharashka*. It was a guarded complex, combined with a form of house arrest. His duties were to design aircraft, rocket-propelled gliders, and military hardware. Tupolev, it transpired, had saved him and got him out of Kolyma. Had he stayed he would probably have succumbed to the cold and the hard labour.

Hitler struck east in 1941, invading Russia. Within four months he was close to Moscow. Under guard — lest he should join the Nazis — Korolov was transferred back eastwards to the relative safety of Omsk, beyond the Urals. The engineer in charge was Valentin Glushko — one of the few early engineers not victim to Stalin's suspicions.

VALENTIN GLUSHKO

Glushko was a contemporary of Korolov — they were born in the same year — and if Korolov can be credited with the grand design of the later space programme, Glushko was the man who designed the engines. He is the last of the pre-1966 personalities about whom we know anything at all. Like many of the others he had been inspired by Tsiolkovsky: they had indeed corresponded when he was 15 and Tsiolkovsky 67.

Glushko was not simply an engine designer. His wider interest was evident when at 16 he had published *The conquest of the Moon* and at 18 *Station beyond the Earth*. His real

In 1927 the Gas Dynamics Laboratory was established in Leningrad and it was here that one of Russia's foremost rocket engine designers, Valentin Petrovich Glushko, produced his first prototypes. Glushko was still influencing Soviet rocket design in the 1980s.

expertise remained engine design. In 1931 he designed and static tested his first engine, the ORM-1, the first proper liquid-propellant rocket engine. By 1933 he had developed a technique of regenerative cooling which ensured that liquid-fuel engines could fire for a long duration without overheating. In 1936 he developed the first throttleable liquid-fuel engine.

WAR

How Glushko survived the purges we do not know. Undoubtedly scientists helped one another as much as they could. Those who were above board probably insisted that they could make no further progress until so-and-so was released. Glushko officially states that 'on my application' Korolov rejoined his design bureau from 1942 to 1946 [11]. Both even received awards in the Kremlin in 1945, the Order of the Red Banner of Labour.

Wartime Soviet rocket development followed a very different, and less exciting, track than in Germany. Most of the effort went into thrust-augmentation rockets that could be fitted to conventional fighter aircraft like the Yak 9d and the MiG-3.

Again, the reasons for this development are unclear. No effort was made or permitted to develop long-range rockets, even though they could have been sent in the direction of Berlin. Since the flight of the GIRD-X in 1933 the technology had been there. It is probably simply that priority was given to short-term projects that could be of immediate benefit to proven aircraft.

Glushko's group did not return from the isolation of east of the Urals until after 1944 — even though the tide of battle had turned long before. When it did, the group was shattered to learn of the progress made by the Germans during the war.

THE A-4

When the Germans retreated westwards they abandoned the Peenemünde station on the Baltic sea coast. The Russians immediately realized what a treasure trove they had stumbled across. Peenemünde was a real rocket range and its prize exhibit, the A-4, a real rocket.

The A-4 was the result of a strange project that combined the desire of the German rocketeers, led by von Braun, to conquer space and the desire of Adolf Hitler to produce a wonder-weapon that would reduce London to rubble and turn the tide of the war. The A-4 was 14 m high, weighed 12.8 tonnes at launch, and was the first operational rocket.

On the autumn day of 3 October 1942, von Braun's A-4 lifted off the sandy Baltic launch site, curved over gently into a clear blue sky, and disappeared out of sight. Tracking showed it went as high as 85 km and splashed down 190 km away. Programme Director Dornberger turned to von Braun: 'Do you realise what we have accomplished today? Today the spaceship was born!, [12].

The A-4 was larger, more powerful and sophisticated than anything that had gone before, and by generations. The military version of the A-4, called the V-2, was swiftly put to military use by Hitler against Britain. 1115 were fired. 3000 civilians died. Von Braun's team was no less ambitious than Dornberger had indicated The Peenemünde team flew a winged A-4b. Its range, employing aerodynamic skip over the atmosphere, was no less than 595 km. The two-stage A-10 was to fly 5000 km and could have hit New York [13].

An undignified scramble was the only way one could describe the efforts of the Russians and Americans to get hold of the A-4 hardware and the scientists who designed it. After Sputnik, the Americans fostered the rumour that they had somehow got the 'wrong' Germans and the Russians had got the right ones [14]. In fact, the more talented ones went to the West [15].

POSTWAR

Although the Russians took Peenemünde, von Braun and his colleagues arranged and, in some cases, tried desparately to ensure, that they were captured by the Americans. The British were not interested in rocketry, so did not come into consideration. Von Braun tipped off the Americans as to the whereabouts of the A-4 components, parts, and designs. Enough parts for 100 A-4s were found and shipped off to the United States. They were soon blasting off from the White Sands deserts in New Mexico to von Braun's delight and the US Army engineers' amusement. When the Russians asked for their share of A-4 parts, the Americans crated them tractor parts.

The Russians took a full year to get their act together in terms of dealing with the A-4. In August 1946, Glushko arrived in Germany, with Korolov under guard, to examine the A-4, more than a year after the war was over. Both attended a British-sponsored launch of an A-4 (Operation Backfire) [16]. Some left-over A-4 parts were collected and shipped off to Russia, and in October 1946 several German scientists were rounded up and put on a train to Moscow. Korolov himself remained in Germany until February 1947.

Three things happened next. First, Stalin gave his approval for a rocket programme. He gave permission for A-4s to be tested, and for Soviet rockets to be built, based on the A-4. Wingless rockets were once again back in business.

Second, a launching site was located. An isolated place near a railhead was what was sought — isolated because it was not a public programme and because failures should not crash down on populated areas. The railhead would help with transport. Another consideration was that there should be good launching conditions — sunny, cloudless skies in other words. A point was selected on a bend in the river Volga in the southeast. It was later called the Volgograd station, and was near the small town of Kapustin Yar (in translation the words mean 'cabbage patch').

Third, the Germans. They were split into different design groups. They were never integrated into the main Soviet design teams. They checked the Russian designs and double-checked the theoretical findings. It was all done by correspondence and they never met their opposite numbers. They were packed home in 1952.

1947 saw the Soviet rocket programme resume the forward momentum it had lost in 1937 — briefly at least at this stage. The designers were reshuffled and Korolov moved to the No. 1 spot. Glushko, for reasons not yet known, was relegated to giving lectures to students at Kazan University and the Bauman Institute. Korolov was put in charge of testing the German A-4s which were fired off from the Volgograd station throughout 1947.

Now Glushko disappears from the historical records. In the endless rewriting of Soviet postwar history, he always came off a poor second, even though there is good reason to believe he played a central role in rocket design into the 1970s. But all the glory went to Korolov. In 1974, Soviet science writer Boris Belistsky made a brave attempt to rehabilitate Glushko: 'Because of the sensitive nature of his contribution he did not receive his share of public acclaim at the time' [17]. We are left to guess why. It remains a mystery.

STALIN'S LAST YEARS

Russia's A-4 tests did everything expected of them. The first one went up on 30 October 1947 and flew 281 km. About 11 were fired altogether. The chief designer from the Peenemünde group, Helmut Gröttrup, was permitted to go to Kapustin Yar to watch.

But once again the spectre of the purges was to return to haunt these new developments. Police surveillance and imprisonment were never far away and their frequency increased as Stalin's life drew toward its end. He determined to hold on to his authority — there was no question of 'retiring' — and he grew more and more distrustful of his subordinates. Some of them may indeed have been guilty of jockeying for position for the day when Stalin would be gone.

Korolov was sent back to the *sharashka* in 1948. For how long, we do not know. A person very like Korolov was described in *First Circle* by novelist Solzhenitsyn. It was probably him. But Korolov's limited imprisonment this time did not have as destructive an effect on rocket development as in the more dangerous years of 1937 to 1942.

After the first batch of A-4s were dispatched, Korolov developed an improved version called the 'Pobeda' (Victory) missile. It had two purposes. First, it became the basis of the Soviet rocket corps and its main medium-range ballistic missile. Although the

'Pobeda' did not turn up publicly until the 1957 Red Square parade, it was the Rocket Corps' mainstay for many years. The first rocket division was formed in 1950.

Second, the 'Pobeda' was used extensively as a geophysical rocket to explore the atmosphere. Throughout 1949–52, nosecones were sent up as high as 100 km with instruments aboard. Korolov however wanted to take this a stage further by flying biological capsules. There was a lengthy debate as to what sort of animals would fly in space and which would be able to give the most accurate prediction as to how humans might respond. Rabbits, mice, reptiles were all considered. Eventually the rocketeers settled on dogs. Canines had the advantage of being small in size and weight. They had to be even-tempered and mongrels were chosen in preference to purebreds. 24 dogs were selected by Korolov's teams of zoologists. They were given extensive tests in small capsules, in aircraft, in vibration chambers and in centrifuges. Eventually they were fired aloft on the 'Pobeda' rockets. Initially they were in pressurised cabins. Then they were fitted with spacesuits and helmets. Cameras in the nosecone filmed their reactions to the strains and stresses of liftoff. On one flight the dog Albina was sent 85 km high. It was such a high altitude that she took a whole hour to parachute down.

Another psychological barrier to space flight was thereby passed. After these tests, new possibilities began to open out. Stalin died at last in March 1953. The shadow over Korolov lifted at once and the prison camps began to open. New and ambitious political leaders moved to the top.

2

Sputnik (1955–57)

At this stage — the period after the death of Stalin in 1953, and the election of Dwight Eisenhower to the Presidency of the United States — it is instructive to look at the relative advantages of both sides in the developing space race.

Both the United States and the USSR had been impressed by the German wartime rocket effort. Both had tested the A-4 after the war and realized its potential. The scientists and engineers involved saw that orbital flight by more powerful rockets was within sight. Both countries had basic launch sites — Kapustin Yar and White Sands. The question at this stage was: could the engineers persuade their political superiors that orbital satellites were possible or desirable? Could they establish a scientific space programme that would not be hijacked purely for military purposes? In both countries the engineers did succeed in persuading their political masters of both these things. In the end, America's divided organization cost it a race it would otherwise have won. But it is remarkable that any satellite was launched at all before 1958 because few people had any idea what it could be used for.

Science fiction writer Arthur C. Clarke put forward one concise idea of the precise function of unmanned Earth-orbiting satellites. That was in 1945. In *Wireless World*, Arthur C. Clark suggested that satellites in an orbit of 36 000 km, orbiting the earth once every day (and thereby appearing to be stationary) could act as transmitters in the sky for world radio broadcasting.

THE IDEA OF AN EARTH SATELLITE

There were a few studies available about early small Earth satellites and they had received only limited circulation. Most had been made independent of each other and not knowing about each other.

In 1945 the American Navy Bureau of Aeronautics had carried out a preliminary study of an artificial Earth satellite, as did the US Army Air Force in 1946.

The RAND Organization in 1948 suggested that satellites could demonstrate a nation's technological and political superiority. A more precise study was made by the British Interplanetary Society (BIS) in 1951 when a paper was read at one of its meetings called 'Minimum satellite vehicles'. A small payload, put up by a three-stage rocket, was proposed.

Little if any of this came to public notice at the time, even though the RAND study was released by the Secretary of State for Defence. In fact, America's space effort would have remained dormant for many years to come but for the intervention of, ironically, a Russian emigré and nephew of the composer Rachmaninoff. Alexander Satin was Chief Engineer to the Office of Naval Research in Washington DC (ONR). He had a general brief of keeping up-to-date with technological developments. Satellites aroused his curiosity, but nothing more. After his arrival in London one foggy night in November 1952, he located Arthur C. Clarke and was taken aback by the BIS paper on minimum satellite vehicles. This paper was critical, for it bridged the gap between the fantasies of the space dreamers with their large-wheeled space stations and the actuality of what the rockets of the day were capable of achieving. The BIS satellite was deliberately small. When Satin brought the paper to von Braun, the German reckoned that existing military hardware, if suitably modified, could get a 2.2 kg payload up to orbit, and no more.

Satin spent the next two years working hard trying to persuade his colleagues to accept some kind of minimum satellite scheme. The admirals were brought around. The ONR was brought around. The Defence Department was persuaded. 'Project Orbiter' was born. This was to be Wernher von Braun's project. He would convert the US Army's existing Redstone rocket, add solid-propellant upper stages, and a 7 kg satellite could make it to orbit. Von Braun and Satin's Orbiter project combined maximum use of existing hardware and the greatest possible speed.

President Eisenhower gave his public approval to 'Project Orbiter' on 15 July 1955. The satellite would probably have got into orbit within 18 months had not a subsection of the same Office of Naval Research not intervened. Its own Naval Research Laboratory (NRL) persuaded the Secretary of State for Defence (who in turn persuaded Eisenhower) to adopt instead its own project called 'Vanguard'.

'Vanguard' would also be a small satellite. It would be based on the Viking rocket, a descendant of the A-4; an Aerobee second stage; and a new third stage. It would be much more sophisticated than Redstone and use pivotal mounting engines. The advantages were that it used new technology and could be dressed up as a civilian rather than a military project. The disadvantage — not then apparent — was that it would take time. President Eisenhower approved 'Vanguard' in place of 'Project Orbiter' on 9 September 1955. The Americans were already too late [1].

THE DECISION TO BUILD SPUTNIK

Even before Stalin's death, there were straws in the wind about Soviet space intentions. In October 1951 Designer Tikhonravov stated that the creation of an Earth satellite was

In October 1951 Soviet designer Mikhail Klavdievich Tikhonravov stated that the creation of an artificial Earth satellite was a feasible proposition: only six years later the Russians launched Sputnik 1.

feasible. On 27 November 1953, Alexander Nesmeyanov of the Academy of Sciences announced that a satellite was a real possibility [2]. The following year, Korolov, now fully rehabilitated in the post-Stalin thaw, wrote in a scientific journal of the case for work to begin on an artificial Earth satellite: 'In my view it would be timely and advisable at this present moment to organize a research division to pioneer a satellite and more thoroughly analyse the range of related problems, [3].

On 9 January 1955, a group of scientists, inspired by Korolov's paper, met to promote the project. They persuaded the Praesidium of the Academy of Sciences to mail several hundred scientists the following terse instructions: 'Please comment on the use of artificial Earth satellites. What do you think they could carry? What experiments do you think could be conducted? [4]. The answers varied. Some were positive, some negative. Some said they would be no use at all. 'Fantasy: I visualize a space shot in the year 2000' was one reply.

It seems, in retrospect, that neither the Academy of Sciences nor their political decision-makers were much interested in replies: they had already made up their minds. On 15 April 1955, the Academy of Sciences set up a 'Permanent Commission for Interplanetary Travel', and gave this body with such an all-embracing title the modest task of developing an Earth satellite. A week later, a team of design scientists was formed. Events began to move with increasing rapidity.

BAIKONOUR COSMODROME

Six weeks later, on 31 May 1955, the first sod was turned on the USSR's first purpose-built cosmodrome and space centre. That was probably too glamourous a title at the time

— the construction workers lived in tents, shacks and caravans, and that was about all they had to start with. The decision to locate at Baikonour had been taken in 1954. Thirty construction workers arrived on 12 January 1955.

There were several reasons for the move from Kapustin Yar, or, to be more accurate, for something different from Kapustin Yar. First, it was too near to the Turkish border. American radar and listening posts now installed there knew virtually everything that was going on. Second, the USSR was anxious to test the new A booster ordered for the rocket forces. The A booster was to be the first intercontinental rocket, a 'city buster', capable of reaching America. A big new site was needed. Third, a place had to be found away from civilian areas — both for reasons of safety and secrecy. Kapustin Yar was close to relatively populated areas on the lower Volga river.

From the point of view of getting satellites into orbit, southerly locations were desirable. Baikonour was about as near to the equator as they could get, and that was worth a 4 per cent payload bonus compared to launching from Kapustin Yar.

Baikonour was a flat desert area. It had indeed been used by the Tsars as a place of exile and in 1830 they had exiled there one Nikifor Nikitin for 'making seditious speeches about flying to the moon' [5]. The area designated for rocket development was adjacent to the Moscow—Tashkent railway line, near the old town of Tyuratam (Baikonour itself is a long way away to the north. It is no more than a railhead). It was a place of harsh climates. Metres of snow covered the steppe in winter from October to March. The winds howled and blizzards were frequent. In summer there was long scorching desert heat and the ground was bleak yellow and stony brown. Only in April was it attractive when the snow melted and the flowers thrust their way upward and blossomed for their all-too-short days.

Tyuratam old town was eventually to grow into a thriving metropolis — a 50 000-strong science city alternately called Leninsk and Zvezgorod (Star City). That was later. North of the railhead went up, in record time, launching pads, assembly buildings, liquid oxygen production centres, tracking and control centres, power grids, hangars and an industrial area. By 1956 a rudimentary launch centre was in place and the first pad was completed on 4 March 1957. At the time, the pad was one of the world's largest engineering achievements. The foundation pit was 45 m deep, 250 m long and 100 m wide — the 'biggest hole in the world', its designers believed.

The day after Eisenhower announced 'Vanguard', the USSR too announced that it would put up a satellite. A few days later the VIth International Astronautical Federation Congress opened in Copenhagen. Soviet delegates appeared for the first time, led by Leonid Sedov, Chairman of the Academy of Sciences Commission on Interplanetary Communications. He confirmed that a satellite would be launched — and within two years. A large new rocket launcher would be used. Soon after, a colleague, A.G. Karpenko, was reported in Pravda as saying that two satellites would be launched. One would fly between 200 and 1000 km, the other between 1516 and 2000 km.

The final go-ahead was given at a closed meeting held in the Academy of Sciences in Moscow on 30 August 1955. Present were delegates of the Central Committee of the Communist Party of the Soviet Union and, on the science side, Sergei Korolov, Mstislav Keldysh and Valentin Glushko. Korolov promised the new launcher would be ready in one or in one and a half years. 'We must not lose time', he said. His life's dream was nearing fulfillment.

KHRUSHCHEV

The success of the Soviet space programme in its early years was very much due to two very different men with two very different purposes. Korolov was, as has been seen, a designer and visionary committed to the conquest of space [6]. Khrushchev had other purposes. Nikita Khrushchev ruled the USSR from 1957 to 1964, seven brief years which are well-remembered beyond what such a time span might merit. He was also a leading political personality in the years 1954 to 1957. He was Khrushchev of the U-2 incident, of the Cuban missile crisis, and he was John F. Kennedy's opposite number during his presidency. In some ways Khrushchev was the archetypal Russian – big, fat, alternately angry or wearing a giant grin from ear to ear, a man of cunning and short temper. While no liberal, he wanted to take the USSR out of the darkness of the Stalin era, and was both ambitious and adventurous. He believed the USSR could overtake and surpass America's rate of industrial and technological progress. The USSR had to be a superpower visibly equal to the United States. Visibility was all-important to Khrushchev, and if it reflected on him personally, all the better. Hence the ploughing up of the Virgin lands, designed to produce a surge in agricultural production. Hence the Aswan High Dam in Egypt, the missiles in Cuba, and the brinkmanship in Berlin. Hence, too, the space programme. Korolov introduced Khrushchev to the Earth satellite and the giant booster needed to launch it, in 1955. Khrushchev was awed:

> We gawked at what he showed us as if we were a bunch of sheep seeing a gate for the first time. We were like peasants at a market place. We walked round the rocket, touching it, tapping it to see if it was sturdy enough. [7]

A space rocket combined Khrushchev's demand for visible progress and achievement with excitement in its own right. Korolov's rocket, the A-1, would be the first inter-continental ballistic missile (ICBM). This suited Khrushchev's effort to reduce the size of the postwar army and replace it with more modern rocket forces, while sneaking a lead over the United States at the same time.

PREPARING FOR FLIGHT

Work on the A-1 and the two satellites went on, spurred by news of America's steady progress with 'Vanguard'. On 6 March 1957, Radio Moscow confirmed that the first satellite would be small, spherical and weigh about 50 kg.

Even so, there were still hitches. The Central Committee had only authorized building on the A-1 and the satellite – it insisted on final approval before anything actually happened. This nearly did not come: in early June 1957 the first A-1 exploded on its launch pad. Korolov feared severe criticism, and other scientists began to demand his job: 'You think we are building ordinary machines? Or that only American Atlases explode?' he retorted [8].

More dangerous perhaps, was the meeting of the ruling Politburo held on 17 June 1957. Khrushchev – Korolov's last ally at this stage – was ousted from power by six votes to one. The six members feared his growing power and authority. Down but far from out, Khrushchev called a full meeting of the Communist Party Central Committee.

With the help of the Red Army, his supporters were flown in from the remotest corners of the USSR, and his enemies were delayed when their aircraft developed sudden technical problems and so on. Khrushchev won the showdown. The rocket project was given its final go-ahead. For Khrushchev, an early technological triumph would solidify his new position as Premier. Late in June, Soviet magazines announced that the construction of the first orbital satellite was complete. The first launchings would take place in a matter of months, and the satellites would be superior to 'Vanguard'. The first satellite would have two radio transmitters, operating on 20 and 40 megacycles.

Soon after, an American reconnaisance plane, the high altitude U-2, flew over Baikonour and saw that the new launching pads were complete. A huge blast trench beside the launch tower showed that it would be something big.

Finally, on 3 August 1957, Korolov's A-1 was fuelled up. It flew. It went 6500 km and came down in the Pacific Ocean off the Kamchatka peninsular. The USSR had the ICBM, and Korolov had something that could launch his satellite [9].

It is worth saying a little about the A-1, not only because it launched the first satellite, but because it was the main booster in the Soviet rocket programme right into the 1980s, with over 600 successful firings. The A-1 had a central core with four RD-107 engines (designed by Glushko) which burned at liftoff. Korolov's achievement was to add no fewer than four further strap-on units to the side of the rocket, each with four engines. Thus no fewer than 20 engines burned simultaneously at liftoff. At a certain altitude the strap-ons came off and the central unit brought the payload into orbit. Mass production of the rocket was possible once its basic reliability was verified. Total thrust was 398 000 kg, orbital payload 1600 kg. It was delivered to the pad horizontally on a huge railcar. It was then tilted upwards to the vertical at the pad itself and set in the restraining arms of the pad. It was then fuelled up. A minute from launch, the arms would swing back and off it would go.

DESIGNING SPUTNIK

Korolov decided on a simple design for the first satellite, already called 'Sputnik'. It was called P.S. (Preliminary Satellite) though many of the other designers called it S.P. (for Sergei Pavlovich Korolov). In effect it was a radio transmitter in a spherical steel ball. Four whiplash aerials streamed out behind. Senior Engineer for Sputnik 1 was Oleg Ivanovsky.

18 September 1957. Radio Moscow confirmed that the launching was coming soon. It was the centenary of Tsiolkovsky's birth. Perhaps they would have liked to have launched on that date, but it came and went unmarked.

20 September. Korolov left the design bureau in Moscow for Baikonour by aircraft. He lived at the launch site for the next two weeks in a small wooden-frame house in a wood. It was a ten-minute walk to the launch pad in one direction, a ten-minute walk to the assembly building in the other.

Several days later. Work was finally complete. In the huge assembly building, like a giant aircraft hangar, the time had come to fix the Preliminary Satellite into the nosecone of the A-1 booster. The giant rocket, on its side and cradled by the railcar, loomed and filled the room. At the front of the hangar were Korolov, the State Commission for Space Flight, the designers and engineers in their white coats.

Satellite engineer Oleg Ivanovsky was leading deputy designer of the world's first artificial satellite Sputnik 1, launched by the Soviet Union on 4th October 1957. From 1958 to 1961, Ivanovsky was the leading designer at the spacecraft design bureau, under academician Sergei Korolov, and he was one of those who saw off Yuri Gagarin on the world's first manned spaceflight in April 1961.

A crane lifted the Preliminary Satellite in its grappling hook. The small glinting silver sphere was guided into the nosecone. The crane halted in the dim hall. An engineer gave the signal to the transmitter. In the huge echo-filled room the 'beep beep beep' sound boomed off the walls. It would be the last time its signals would be heard on earth. A contact was plugged into the satellite and the beeping ceased abruptly. The contact was designed to be broken again only when the satellite reached orbit.

2 October. The starry darkness of a southern Russian night. The massive steel doors of the assembly building groaned open. The polished nozzles of the rocket were cold grey in the night. The railcar creaked its slow way down to the pad.

3 October. Sputnik was on the pad. One day to go. The sun blazed its autumn sunshine over the bare steppe as the booster was fuelled up. As the day wore on the liquid oxygen began to boil off and cold compressed air had to be doused on the booster to cool it off. Korolov climbed the service tower to inspect his rocket for the last time. He then made a final telephone call to say that it was ready to go.

4 October. Several attempts to count the rocket down failed. There were exasperating delays. The sun had set and it had turned dark when Korolov decided on one last attempt. With a white lab coat covering him he took his place in the underground command bunker 100 m from the rocket itself, protected by steel doors and thick reinforced concrete. He waited, microphone in hand, watching through a submarine-style periscope. Not far from the final minutes of the count, a lone bugler, identity still unknown, ventured onto the concrete apron and blew a long series of trumpet blasts before vanishing. His long tones resounded around the pad and the booster bathed silently in floodlights in the background.

Finally it happened. Blinding flames shot out through the trench. Clouds of vapour surrounded the rocket. Its body quivered and it began to rise. It dazzled and deafened the watchers, and lit up the periscopes and the bunkers and service towers for miles around. Twenty separate engines fired in unison.

Sputnik rose rapidly and ever more rapidly. It headed off into the night sky in the northeast, more and more blurred and hard to follow each second. The strap-on boosters peeled away and dropped silently down to oblivion. Soon it was nothing but a speck in the night sky, just one of a million constellations. It was nearly midnight, or 10.30 p.m. by the Kremlin clock tower. The launch team clapped and cheered wildly. All had gone well, but there was no way of telling for sure. Just 50 km/hr too little energy and the Sputnik would tumble to Earth after a mere half hour's flight.

There was only one way to know, and that involved a wait of 90 minutes. When the Sputnik had completed its first orbit it would be back over its launch site. Its transmitter should then be working with its familiar 'beep beep beep' characteristic. If the sound was heard, success would be total. Silence would mean failure, and the reason would perhaps never be known.

Korolov, the scientists, designers, engineers and launch team gathered inside the assembly hangar. Loudspeakers had been rigged to the satellite receiver. They held their breaths and listened. Against the infinite crackle of radio space it came. An audible, distinct and clear 'beep beep beep' — there was no mistaking it! It must have been an exhilarating moment. Korolov was carried to an improvized speaker's platform. A squat,

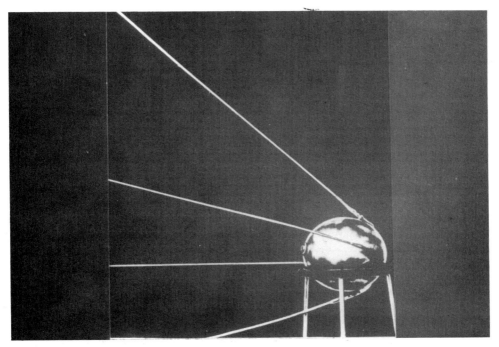

Launched from Tyuratam on 4th October 1957, the world's first artificial Earth satellite, Sputnik 1, shocked the West. For some time attempts persisted to prove that the whole event was a fake, but the launch of Sputnik 2 a month later finally silenced the critics.

firm, square and thick-set figure, his normal sternness broke down. He summoned exhausted energies, and, eyes aflashing, spoke:

> The conquering of space has begun. Today we have witnessed the realization of a dream nurtured by some of the finest minds who ever lived. Our outstanding scientist Tsiolkovsky brilliantly foretold that mankind would not forever remain on the Earth. Sputnik is the first confirmation of his prophecy. We can be proud this was begun by our country. [10]

Sputnik began circling the Earth every 95 mins between 228 and 947 km.

THE REACTION

Khrushchev reacted casually at first. Later he recounted that when Korolov phoned him and told him Sputnik was in orbit, he, Khrushchev, congratulated him and the engineers involved, and calmly went to bed.

That was not the reaction in the West. Sputnik was a story that was reported quietly at first but grew as each day passed and its impact set in. The BBC reported Sputnik's launch with a peculiar mixture of astonishment, bemusement and uncertainty about how to deal with this new event:

> Moscow radio has announced within the past half hour that Russia has successfully launched an earth satellite. It is going round the earth in an elliptical trajectory at a height of about 560 miles. The launching was part of Russia's geophysical year programme. [11]

It was two or three days later that the impact of Sputnik began to be felt. Sputnik had a deep and positive effect on Soviet public opinion. In one area of science, whatever its long-term significance, the USSR had achieved technological superiority. Khrushchev took advantage of this public success to consolidate his power base. He removed wartime hero Georgi Zhukov from his powerful military position, demobilized a million soldiers, and set up a new missile wing on an equal footing to the Red Army, the Red Air Force and the Red Navy.

The effect it produced in the United States varied between shock and panic. Subsequent surveys revealed that within months nearly all Americans had heard of Sputnik and that most people perceived it to confer an advantage on the USSR and a disadvantage on the United States. Press reaction discussed Sputnik in terms of American prestige, and American scientific and military reputation being at stake.

Virtually alone in not being swept along in this atmosphere of shock, fear and humiliation were the senior politicians of the Washington administration. President Eisenhower: 'One small ball in the air does not raise my apprehensions, not one iota. We must. . . find ways of affording perspective to our people and so relieve the current wave of near hysteria' [12].

Lyndon Johnson, the opposition Democratic Party's Congressional leader, did not see things that way at all. He heard the news of Sputnik at his ranch in Texas and he had wires humming to Washington within the hour. Of course there was an element of political opportunism in Johnson: Sputnik was an easy stick with which to beat the administration and a complacent and ever more ineffective Eisenhower presidency. But Johnson was also motivated by what he saw as a threat to America's national security; by a belief in technology; and by a belief that America must always be first in everything. Johnson had nearly always voted for anything the military had wanted and took an equally generous view of the need for military research. He had tried to persuade the Pentagon to set up a space programme as far back as 1949.

Johnson set up a Congressional 'Preparedness Committee'. The title told it all. For the next six months he called a parade of scientists, generals, industrialists, to testify to America's lack of preparedness. The administration was blamed, the schools, higher education. And as if to rub salt into an already gaping wound, the Russians did it again.

SPUTNIK 2

On 9 October Pravda warned that: 'The Soviet Union will launch a sputnik carrying animals as passengers. Detailed observations will be made of their behaviour' [13].

On 3 November 1957, Sputnik 2 was duly launched. It weighed no less than 508 kg, five times more than its predecessor. There were two compartments on Sputnik 2. The principal compartment — similar to Sputnik 1 — had instruments for measuring cosmic rays, temperature and pressure. The real innovation was a special compartment to carry a dog. A mongrel called 'Laika' was chosen. She was a veteran of earlier rocket tests and known for her even-temperedness. She was put in a harness inside a small pressurized cabin covered with soft material. Sputnik 2 took off in the daytime: telemetry from the satellite showed she suffered no ill-effects either from launch or entry into orbit. While weightless she barked, moved about the cabin, and took food from a dispenser. There were widespread protests from dog lovers, and after a week the air gave out and she died.

Sputnik 2 only added to the shock inflicted by Sputnik 1. Its size, the presence of an animal on board, the high altitude of the orbit (225 by 1671 km), the fact that it came only 30 days after the first launch — all these facts underlined the enormousness of the Soviet lead. Although few people said so at the time, the flight of an animal could only mean the serious intention of putting a man into orbit, sooner or later.

Both Sputnik 1 and 2 were observable from the ground as small pinpoints of light crossing the sky just after dusk and just before dawn. Sputnik 1 made more than 1400 revolutions over a period of 90 days before it burned up. Radio experts tuned into its 'beep beep beep'. Much was learnt about air density at Sputnik's altitude and about how soon it would cause a satellite to slow down and burn up.

Sputnik 2 was much easier to spot from the ground, since the rocket remained attached to the satellite. In its final orbits the cylinder turned end over end and flashed as a bright beacon in the night sky until it was incinerated. Sputnik 2 burnt up in April 1958 after 163 days and 2370 revolutions.

Both sputniks had by then long since eclipsed the flagging American space programme. The Johnson hearings — which, as coincidence had it, opened just after Sputnik 2 — gathered momentum and heard warnings that became more and more apocalytical with each passing day, warnings which were exacerbated by the humiliating first American attempt to launch a satellite.

The slow but technically ambitious 'Vanguard' programme eventually found its way to the launch pad at Cape Canaveral, Florida, on 6 December 1957. The countdown reached zero, the pencil-shaped rocket lifted off and for a brief intoxicating second it looked as if America might get a satellite in the same year as its rivals. But the joy lasted only a moment, for two seconds into the flight the thrust collapsed. Vanguard 1 fell back on its pad and disappeared in an enormous cloud of smoke as it exploded like one of the old airship disasters. The tiny capsule was flung free of the holocaust on the pad. Pad personnel found it with its aerials sticking out of the sand in a nearby Florida beach, its radio chirping away, until someone put it out of its misery.

The Kremlin offered its condolences. The London press labelled it alternately Kaputnik, Flopnik and Stayputnik.

This final humiliation galvanized the administration in Washington into action. Von Braun and his army team were given permission to launch their original satellite, for which they had sought approval in 1955 and which they could have put up in 1956. The Redstone–Jupiter C was made ready with a small pencil-shaped satellite on top, 1 m long and weighing 5 kg. The Von Braun rocket rose flawlessly into the night sky on 31 January 1958. Not only that, it was a stunning scientific success: with a single geiger counter on board, it discovered that the Earth has huge radiation belts around it. These were named the van Allen belts after the scientist involved.

SPUTNIK 3

More than this belated success was needed to expunge the memory of Sputnik. The ill-fated 'Vanguard' project experienced further failures and did not know success until on 17 March 1958, Vanguard 1 achieved orbit. It was one of the smallest satellites ever launched − 1 kg. By this stage, the Johnson hearings had nearly run their course. The timing was more than helpful to him: he had begun his own presidential campaign in January 1958. He summed up:

> The Roman Empire controlled the world because it could build roads. Later when men moved to the sea, the British Empire was dominant because it had ships. Now the Communists have established a foothold in space. [14]

Already Johnson was seeing Sputnik in global and historical terms. If the USSR was going to take the high road to space, then so too would the United States, guided of course by the senior senator from Texas.

As if to add a riposte to Johnson's counter-attack, the USSR put up Sputnik 3 on 15 May 1958. It was a prototype scientific laboratory weighing over a tonne and a half, and it contained a computer installation to run its scientific instruments. It was powered by solar cells and batteries, and orbited from 226 to 1880 km, 106 mins. Sputnik 3 had the shape of a silvery shining perfect cone with aerials and proturbances. It returned information on micrometeorites, the Earth's radiation belts, cosmic rays, solar radiation, the density of the upper atmosphere, and the effect of high energy particles. Well might Khrushchev deride Vanguard 1 as a mere 'grapefruit'.

Sputnik 3 found the outer edge of the Van Allen radiation belt. It made 10 037 revolutions of the Earth, eventually burning up in 1960 after 691 days of flight. It had simultaneously demonstrated that Soviet lifting capabilities were matched by scientific expertise.

OFF TO THE MOON!

Khrushchev himself never attended a space launch but he was well able to notice the consternation that the first three Sputniks produced abroad and the public satisfaction evident at home. The impression spread of a thrusting Soviet technology under the progressive and efficient leadership of Nikita Khrushchev. He pressed Korolov to produce more spectacular spaceshots. Korolov in turn was happy to oblige — indeed it enabled him to move faster and further than he could otherwise have imagined.

What was the next step then? As early as 1957 the Soviet space planners had looked at their long-term objectives [15]. Obviously a manned flight was a desirable objective. But a more powerful booster was needed and an entirely new spaceship to carry a space-man. The recovery of a satellite had never been attempted, still less practised to satisfaction. A whole new area of work was needed on how a human could survive in zero gravity. Potential spacemen had still not even been recruited.

So a manned flight was still some distance away, and design work would take at least two years. What the A booster did offer in the meantime was the chance to send payloads beyond the Earth's atmosphere and immediate orbit. By the addition of a small upper stage of 5000 kg thrust it would be possible to send small payloads of about half a tonne to the Moon, Mars or Venus. Accordingly, three Moon shots were prepared for 1959, two Mars shots for 1960 and two Venus shots for 1961.

By mid-1958 the American programme was showing new signs of life. It took some time for the Americans to turn a disorganized space effort into a coherent rational and planned programme. Three things were to happen.

First, the Americans realized in early 1958 that by using their Able booster they too could send very small payloads into space towards the Moon — perhaps before the Russians if they moved fast enough. Second, a space agency was set up to plan ahead — the National Aeronautics and Space Administration (NASA), which was inaugurated on 1 October 1958. Third, within seven days, it in turn announced a man-in-space programme called Project Mercury. Its objectives were: 'to send a man into orbit, investigate his capabilities and reactions in space, and return him safely to the Earth' [16].

Already a subtle form of space leapfrog had begun to dominate planning. It ran on the lines of: what kind of space activity could one side devise that might get that side ahead, albeit temporarily, of the other?

The American Moon shots of 1958, hastily put together, were a disaster. The probes varied in weight between 6 and 39 kg and were designed to pass close to the Moon. The first on (17 August) blew up after 16 km of flight. The next, called Pioneer 1, reached the then-amazing altitude of 113 000 km and fell back to Earth (11 October). Pioneer 2 and 3 never got that far.

Despite these mishaps, the probes had a morale-boosting effect on American public opinion. There was huge press coverage. The Cape Canaveral range (all it had been to date was an air force and coastguard station) became part of the American consciousness. Boosters, rockets, countdowns, the Moon, missions, these words all entered the vocabulary. America was fighting back, and if the missions failed, there were credits for trying.

MECHTA – DREAM

The new year was barely two days old when Korolov's first Moon probe left the pad at Tyuratam and hurtled skywards. With apparently effortless ease it achieved escape velocity (40 234 km/hr) and headed moonwards. Designated Lunik 1 or Mechta (Dream'), the Moon probe was spherical in shape and weighed 361 kg. It carried instruments for measuring radiation, magnetic fields, and meteorites. On 3 January, when 113 000 kmd out from Earth, Lunik 1 released a golden-orange cloud of sodium gas so that astronomers could track it. It was visible in the sky over the Indian Ocean.

By the second day, it was apparent that Lunik 1 would not hit the Moon as had been planned. On 4 January it passed by at a distance of 5955 km. Lunik 1 went on into orbit around the Sun between the Earth and Mars. En route it found that the Moon had no magnetic field and that the Sun emitted strong flows of ionized plasma – the 'solar wind'. Lunik 1 was a dramatic start to Moon exploration: it ventured into areas of space never visited before.

Whatever Lunik 1's intentions, Lunik 2's were abundantly clear. Sent up on 12 September, it was very similar in design to Lunik 1, and at 390 kg carried similar instrumentation. A sodium vapour cloud released on 13 September told ground observers

The first mooncraft, Lunik 1, was launched on 2nd January 1959. This 361-kg probe passed 5955 km from the Moon and continued its journey, sending back signals from up to 800 000 km from Earth, providing information about interplanetary space for the first time.

that its course was dead on target. Korolov and the designers gathered in the control room as Lunik 2 neared the Moon. Signals poured back loud and clear from Lunik 2 against the eternal static of deep space. Then in an instant they were cut short and there was utter silence! Lunik 2 had made it, reached the Moon, and impacted onto it at great speed. Celebration all round.

It was a bull's eye. Lunik 2 hit the Moon just after midnight on 14 September, crashing somewhere between the craters Archimedes, Aristillus and Autolycus. To the Americans this knife like precision only added insult to injury. Not that they were given much time to recover. Three weeks later, and on the second anniversary of Sputnik 1, Lunik 3 lifted off the pad. It weighed 434 kg.

The Lunik 3 mission caused speculation at first. Far from taking a rapid course out to the Moon, Lunik 3 swung lazily round the far side after a longer transit time, and passed under it at a distance of 7890 km. As it pulled round the far side — that side perpetually turned away from Earth — the Sun angle was behind Lunik and shining on the far side. It was then that Lunik 3's unique design came into its own. Cylindrically shaped, Lunik 3 carried solar cells for energy, photoelectric cells to orientate one side to the Sun and the other to the Moon, gas jets for stabilization, and a transmitter. Lunik 3's cameras whirred into action. For a full 40 minutes the two lenses took pictures of no less than 70 per cent of the Moon's far side. They were vistas no human had ever before seen.

Lunik 3 swung around the Moon, taking a figure-of-eight trajectory back towards the Earth. Its return put it high in the northern sky and in an ideal position for Soviet ground tracking stations. Lunik 3 was orientated towards Earth and the film was developed on board. It was developed automatically in a developing unit, dried and wound into a special canister. A television device was brought into play to scan the film, which was then transmitted by radio to the ground. Unfortunately, this process broke down at an altitude of 470 000 km, when image quality was still poor.

Nine frames were transmitted. Within days, the USSR released the historic first photograph of the Moon's far side. It was hazy and fuzzy, but it gave a bird's eye view of the Moon's hidden side. It was the first time the view from space had ever been presented to people on Earth, the first time a space probe had ever obtained data that could never have been obtained any other way. The photographs bore little relationship to the more detailed maps later accumulated during the 1960s, but that did not matter then. Lunik 3 was able to show that the far side was all mountainous, with the exception of two dark mare regions — the Mare Moscovrae and the Mare Desiderii (Moscow Sea, Sea of Dreams).

1959 therefore closed with the Soviet Union having demonstrated not only formidable lifting power in its boosters, but extremely accurate long-distance techniques of space navigation. It was a psychological and technological *tour de force*. The unfortunate Americans lurched from one disaster to another. Pioneer 4 (March 1959), it is true, passed the Moon by 60 000 km, but four Moon probes during 1959—60 failed totally, none even reaching low Earth orbit. If there was indeed a space race, the gap between the two big powers was, if anything, widening.

3

Yuri Alexevich Gagarin

November 1959 was a watershed. The first stage of the Moon programme was over: the Moon had been passed, hit, and circled. Sputnik had been completed. The Luniks and the Sputniks had impressed the public at home and the world at large. The Americans were trailing, but by late 1959 had begun to put their house in order with the formation of NASA and the announcement of the Mercury manned space programme.

Manned flight was the obvious, next, irresistible stage. A decision on this could not be put off much longer. In the A rocket there existed sufficient rocket power, with a third stage, to put a four tonne manned spaceship into orbit. Korolov had been working on possible designs for a manned space capsule since 1958 [1].

In November 1959 there took place a vital meeting of the Academy of Sciences, chaired by its greying President Mstislav Keldysh. Also present were (naturally) Korolov, Valentin Glushko, Academician Vasily Parin, engineer Alexander Mrykin, General Nikolai Kaminin representing the Red Air Force, and Academicians Sisakayan and Stepnov. At least one senior scientist argued long and hard against the idea of manned flight at all. The rockets simply were not reliable enough. Unmanned flights were cheaper, safer, and yielded as good results. Would a man survive the radiation, meteorites, weightlessness? A compromise proposal was put forward for a suborbital flight — up and down ballistically to a height of 200 km. That would really be up in space. There were none of the risks of orbital insertion, losing radio contact, and retrofire. It would be over Soviet territory all the time. The flight would last 15 mins, including 5 mins of weightlessness.

Korolov let the scientists fight it out, but it was Glushko's intervention that was decisive: 'Now that we have the chance to send a man into space, the idea meets with opposition from certain comrades. I do not understand this' [2]. Korolov quickly added. 'A ballistic flight will cost a lot of money and will be risky. The results will be very meagre. Science needs a flight around the Earth. Not a small step forward, but a stride forward that is decisive and daring' [3]. Keldysh, who said little until the end, weighed in behind Korolov. No limit should be placed on man's desire to explore space, he pleaded. They were indeed ready for the next giant step. Sputnik had set going a force of irresistible momentum, and any failure to take the next step – whatever that was – would be tantamount to a loss of nerve.

The Academy's recommendation – to go all out for orbital flight – went straight to the Government. Khrushchev readily agreed. Vice-chairman of the Council of Ministers Konstantin Rudnev was appointed head of the State Commission for Space Flight, thus keeping a direct line to the Kremlin and Khrushchev himself. Sergei Korolov was deputy.

THE SHOOTING DOWN OF GARY POWERS

Korolov's team worked flat out to get the manned spaceship airborne. As of November 1959, a first piloted flight was still a year away. Detailed design work still had to be completed and a team of pilots recruited and trained.

With a large booster Korolov had some latitude with the design of his spacecraft. When the Americans were busily wind-testing bullet-shaped craft with special ablative heat shields, Korolov had a stroke of genius: make the spacecraft absolutely round, a perfect sphere; weigh one end heavily with ablative material and, just like a ball leaded at one end, it would automatically turn that end head first into the searing heat of reentry. By contrast, America's Mercury was cone-shaped and the base had to be carefully pointed in the right direction if the craft was to come back. Korolov's sphere made those problems irrelevant. The A booster was uprated to prepare the way for the new manned spaceship, now to be called 'Vostok' or 'East'. The new upper stage had a thrust of 5600 kg.

The first tests took place in January 1960: a stripped-down Vostok forerunner was hurtled 10 000 km downrange from Baikonour, arcing over 1000 km high in the process, and was lobbed into the Pacific Ocean. Great accuracy was achieved. The Soviet Navy picked up the nosecones from the sea, but not without attracting some attention from the Americans, whose naval bases at Kwajelein Atoll, Hawaii, and Johnston Island were not far away. The American realized that a new generation of rocket was under test, and may have suspected a manned link. As it was, 1960 was the fourth year in which the American U-2 spy plane was operational.

The U-2 had been developed by Lockheed amidst great secrecy in the early 1950s. It was a small black jet plane with enormously long thin wings and gulping air intakes. It looked like a stranded seagull, and could have been mistaken for a glider instead of a self-propelled aircraft. The similarity is not irrelevant, because the U-2 was designed to soar high in the atmosphere at 25 000 m, where the air is thin and the big intakes are essential to extract every molecule of oxygen that can be found. The U-2 was to soar silently, at great height, for enormous distances, over Russia, beyond the reach of the flak guns.

Thus it was that on 1 May 1960, the CIA, learning that the first test of the new rocket was imminent, and picking up increased radio traffic from its listening posts in Turkey, ordered a U-2 into the air that summer's morning. The prize was to photograph the A booster on the pad at Baikonour with the Vostok on top. The pilot was a young Air Force lieutenant called Gary Powers.

His U-2 left the ground from a USAF base in Afghanistan. The ungainly black plane climbed for height. It headed out across the Kazakhstan steppe and passed right over central Baikonour. Cameras clicked and whirred as they caught sight of the A booster sitting on its pad, almost ready for takeoff.

Gary Powers, breathing oxygen and in a heated pressure suit, turned his plane north to Sverdlovsk in a giant loop before he would turn back. That was as far as he got. Without warning, his plane was suddenly buffetted by a thundering explosion in the tail. The plane rocked and shook and began to spin sickeningly to earth. Before it was too late, Gary Powers bailed out, and parachuted into the forests of the Urals. He was captured and put on spying charges: Khrushchev stormed out of the Paris summit conference then under way. Angrily he denounced the Americans for spying and organized a well-publicized trial. It was the last spy flight of the U-2: the Americans never took on Russia's surface to air missiles again [4].

SPUTNIK 4

Whether delayed by the snooping U-2 flight or not, the manned prototype got away two weeks later. Sputnik 4 reached orbit on 15 May 1960, flying from 312 to 368 km, 65 degrees, 91.1 minutes, and weighing 5000 kg — again, another weight record. A sure indication of the designers' intentions was given when it was announced that a dummy cosmonaut was aboard the cabin.

Sputnik 4 was the first of eleven 'Vostok' type spaceships to go into orbit. The capsule itself consisted of a spherical cabin with heavy shielding on the outside. The pilot was to be placed on a large ejector seat fitted to rails: he could eject out during ascent, and eject out by parachute during descent. In the cabin was a simple control panel and porthole, Earth globe to show position, clock, and 'Vzor' orientation device. To the right was a control handle so that a pilot could orientate the spaceship. Clustered around the cabin walls were water and food containers, logs, radio, tape recorder and air purifiers. Parachutes were forward. Behind the cabin was a cylindrical-shaped service module. This contained attitude control thrusters, oxygen and nitrogen storage bottles, aerials and, most importantly, the large retrorocket. Once this was fired to commence the descent, the two modules then separated.

It was a daring and simple design. But it all had to function flawlessly. Each Vostok had 15 000 m of electrical wires in it, 240 valves, 6000 transistors. An unheard-of degree of reliability was being insisted upon in people used to the standards required for jet planes. The chief designers of Vostok were — apart from Korolov himself — Alexei Ivanov, Yevgeni Alexandrov and Norair Sisakayan.

As if to remind the designers of the dangerous waters into which they had now ventured, Sputnik 4 gave its own form of warning, and it was just as well that only a dummy cosmonaut was on board. On 19 May, the retrorocket was turned on. But instead of gently braking Sputnik 4's movement back towards Earth, it fired it into a high elliptical orbit. Sputnik 4 and its dummy cosmonaut circled the Earth for another four years until October 1965 when they burnt up. Still, the programme laboured onwards.

ARRIVAL OF THE COSMONAUTS

Another uncertainty was who would fly the first spaceships. There were no known ground rules, and these simply had to be invented by Korolov and the others. It was decided to recruit an initial group of 20 cosmonauts – a word invented to be different from the existing American term of 'astronaut'. The 20 had to be brave, reliable, physically fit, not prone to panic, capable of mental endurance, and familiar with the notion of 'things up there'. The last of these factors alone suggested that the selectors should look towards the Red Air Force, and so it was that the call went out for trainee cosmonauts in late 1959. Of the 20 selected, nearly all were aged 25 to 35 and Air Force test pilots. They were:

Yuri Gagarin
Gherman Titov
Andrian Nikolayev
Pavel Popovich
Valeri Bykovsky
Vladimir Komarov
Pavel Balyayev
Alexei Leonov
Boris Volynov
Yevgeni Khrunov
Georgi Shonin
Viktor Gorbatko

Group photograph of Soviet pilot-cosmonauts who flew on the missions Vostok 2 to Soyuz 7 inclusive. Vladimir Komarov, who piloted Soyuz 2, was killed on re-entry. Front row (left to right) Anatoli Filipchenko, Valeri Kubasov, Vladimir Shatalov, Valentina Nikolayeva-Terreskhova, Viktor Gorbatko, Vladislav Volkov, Georgi Shonin, Alexei Yeliseyev. Back row (left to right) Pavel Popovich, Boris Yegerov, Pavel Belyayev, Alexei Leonov, Georgi Beregovoi, Gherman Titov, Konstantin Feoktistov, Andrian Nikolayev, Yevgeni Khrunov, Boris Volynov, Valeri Bykovsky.

Valentin Bondarenko
Valentin Varlarmov
Anatoli Kartashov
Grigori Nelyubov
Mars Rafikov
Ivan Anikeyev
Valentin Filateev
Dmitri Zaikin.

Of these first 20, only 12 flew, and the last eight in the list never got into space at all [5]. Hundreds must have applied, but as the Americans found with their first group of Mercury astronauts, some made it to the final selection who would not have done so in later years. Nelyubov, Anikeyev and Filateev were drummed out of the squad in late 1961 after a drunken brawl in a railway station. Nelyubov, brilliant, ambitious but ultimately unstable, later threw himself under a train and was killed. Mars Rafikov suffered from 'burn out', left the squad, continued test flying awhile, and ended up manager of a building cooperative in Alma Ata. 24-year-old Valentin Bondarenko perished tragically. On 23 March 1961, with Gagarin's flight only weeks away, Bondarenko was burnt alive when he caught fire in an oxygen chamber on a training test. Doctors struggled for eight hours to save him, but burn shock overcame the youngest of the team of cosmonauts. Anatoli Kartashov, described by Titov as a 'splendid pilot', injured his spine on a centrifuge run that took him to eight times the force of gravity. The doctors dismissed him from the squad. Valentin Varlarmov dislocated the vertebrae of his back in a swimming accident. He died suddenly of a brain haemorrhage in 1980. Finally, Dmitri Zaikin, backup commander on Voskhod 2, had been waiting eight years for his first flight when in 1968 a medical review board failed him and he had to leave the programme.

The identities of the missing eight cosmonauts was not known until special articles about them were published by *Izvestia* in April 1986. Until then, these men appeared only eerily, from time to time, in photographs and film clips that somehow eluded the censors' scissors and airbrushes. Any of them could have been as famous as Gagarin or Leonov, but fate decided otherwise.

THE BEST AND THE BRIGHTEST

Russia's first twenty cosmonauts represented the cream of the country's test pilot establishment. Yuri Gagarin's story is by no means untypical, even if in the course of the first few months' training he was to emerge as the most determined, energetic and ambitious of all the cosmonauts.

Yuri Gagarin, a short-haired, bright, boyish-looking pilot, was born in 1934 near Smolensk, western Russia. In his youth he learned to be a foundryman and went to several industrial schools. He enlisted in the Saratov flying school in his spare time, went to pilot training school, and joined the Soviet Air Force as a fighter pilot in 1956. Because of his short height he always put a cushion on the seat of his MiG fighter. In 1957 he married a nursing student, Valentina, at his base, and then transferred for arduous service in the Arctic. Their first baby, Lena, was born in 1958.

The school museum keeps with great care this photograph showing Yuri Gagarin (third from the left in the second row) in his school years.

In 1959, on his own initiative, he wrote to his superiors, applying to join a group of cosmonauts 'if such a group exists'. His application was filed. Gagarin was in time called up, put before a medical board, and selected as a cosmonaut on his 26th birthday in March 1960. It is quite possible, granted what we know of him later, that he determined at this stage that he was going to be the first one to fly. But at first he was not permitted to tell anyone about his work, not even his wife Valentina, for it was so secret.

Gagarin's stand-in, Gherman Titov, was a year younger than Gagarin. Curly-haired, Titov was a distinguished cadet from Volgograd Air Force pilots school. Unlike most American astronauts going into training at around the same time, whose spare-time interests tended to be vigorous and virile athletic sports, Gherman Titov was a sophisticated, widely read man with a special interest in poetry.

Andrian Nikolayev was older and known as the 'iron man'. Born in 1929 he was the first non-Russian member of the team (he was Chuvash) and spent his youth as a forester and lumberjack. Unlike the others, he did not start his aviation career as a pilot but as a gunner and then a radio operator. Dark, serious, Andrian Nikolayev once found himself in a flaming crashing jet fighter. Rather than eject he insisted on bringing his plane down to the ground, walking away without a scratch when survival had seemed impossible. He was able to sweat out the isolation chamber longer than anyone else: it was a blacked-out room where cosmonauts were put for days on end without reading matter or clocks, and they were alternately frozen or baked to test their endurance. Hence the epithet, 'the iron man'.

Pavel Popovich was actually the first cosmonaut to arrive at the training centre. A veteran of military aviation school and an Arctic pilot too, he was the most extrovert member of the team. Extremely popular, he had a fine tenor voice and was constantly singing. His own flying record was eclipsed only by that of his wife, Marina, who was a colonel in the Red Air Force and had achieved numerous aviation records flying high-performance jet aircraft.

Valeri Bykovsky was the same age as Gagarin. A quiet and confident man, jet pilot, parachute instructor, he booked his flight by being the first person to test out the isolation chamber over a prolonged period. Over time, he became the man who always tested out training devices before others were let loose on them. Bykovsky was the only one to argue back about safety considerations — and he paid the price.

These were some of the first cosmonauts to get missions. Some of the others had to wait up to ten years — far longer than they or anyone else could have anticipated.

The type of man selected was not so very different from those selected for Project Mercury in the United States at the same time. The NASA people looked to the country's top 500 test pilots. Like their Russian opposite numbers, they had to be in perfect shape physically, have superbly quick reactions, and be graduates of military test school with over 1500 hours flight time. They had to have college degrees in physical sciences or engineering — unlike in the Soviet Union where the less educated ordinary working man was upheld as the model citizen. The 500 were narrowed to 110, then 36, largely by volunteers dropping out or because of small medical flaws. Others were eliminated for suspect motivation like personal glory. Family background had to be impeccable — divorces were out of the question. The final selection down to seven was a hard one for NASA, and by their own admission a somewhat arbitrary one. The NASA seven were several years older than Russia's twenty.

In retrospect, it seems some mistakes were made by both sides in their first crew selections. Both groups contained men who were bigger on bravery, daring and adventure than persistence and theoretical engineering knowledge. Of the second and third selections, the spacemen stayed longer in their respective programmes and commanded more missions. These later selections were older pilots with more of an engineering background, with quieter and more stable personalities. Drop-out rates were also significantly lower.

One thing which neither side seems to have taken into consideration was the media interest which their spacemen excited. NASA's seven heroes were subject to a special and unusual contract with *Life* magazine which got sole publicity rights. Americans added the seven astronauts to their pantheon of film stars, war heroes, sports personalities, dynamic politicians, two years before any of them had even flown! These astronauts embodied the 'Ideal American' — adventurous, mature, family man, straight-talking, patriotic.

It was probably worse on the Soviet side. There was no 'potential' hero in the Russian squad. Once you flew, the world knew about you; until you did, you were quite unknown. Names were not released in advance, and like the Chief Designer, the cosmonauts had the protection of total anonymity. After a flight, however, there was the abrupt transition to life beneath the public gaze in a country where heroes were few and far between. Soviet officialdom tended to be suspicious of heroes, who could too easily become a political threat. Cosmonauts were not perceived as a threat, and, apart from the Secretary General of the Communist party, they became the best-known public Russians both outside and inside their own country. They personified all that was best about the new Soviet state, celebrating its youth and scientific and technical progress.

SPUTNIK 5

The summer of 1960. Training of the twenty cosmonauts got into its stride. General Kaminin was put in charge of the squad and was responsible for progress. Anatoli Karpov was chief trainer. The training itself consisted of flying jet fighters, parachuting, survival experiences, managing the centrifuge, enduring the isolation chamber, physical fitness, and learning how a spacecraft works. Photographs from the period suggest there was a fair amount of survival training. Cosmonauts would be deposited in the middle of nowhere and told to find their own way home, using their own navigation and resources. This was against the day that they might land badly off target.

Despite the failure of Sputnik 4 to return to Earth in May, it was time to proceed to the next stage. The reentry manoeuvre simply had to be got right or otherwise manned flight could not be seriously contemplated. What was required was that the spacecraft be orientated at 45 degrees to its flight path. With the wrong angle it would either shoot up into a higher orbit or descend too fast and be incinerated.

Sputnik 5 was put into orbit on 19 August 1960. There were two differences from Sputnik 4. First, instead of a dummy cosmonaut, there were two dogs on board. Second, only a week earlier, the Americans had recovered one of their own capsules from the Pacific Ocean. It was called Discoverer 13. It was one of the few things the Americans had actually achieved before the USSR. It proved it could be done.

The two dogs were huskies and were called Belka and Strelka. Belka was the Russian word for 'squirrel' and Strelka was 'little arrow'. They were selected from a batch of a hundred dogs at the Pavlov Institute near Leningrad in January 1960. Belka and Strelka went through training not dissimilar from that of the cosmonauts themselves. They were fitted out in bright orange zipper-fastened nylon suits with globe-shaped helmets. They spent several weeks in a model spaceship. They were subjected to vibration, noise, high temperatures and G-loads. Aboard the space ship, the ejector seat for the manned space-ship was converted into a giant ark for the two dogs and other animal cargo. This included two white rats, 28 mice, several hundred insects, plants and seeds from onion, peas, wheat and maize. Television cameras were fitted so that the dogs could be observed in flight.

The second objective of the flight — after recovery of the ark — was to study the ability of organisms to withstand zero gravity and radiation. The latter was the more feared, ever since the discovery of the van Allen radiation belts in 1958. For every organism aboard Sputnik 5 there was a control one on the ground: the two would then be compared.

What was not revealed at the time — not in fact till many years later — was that human specimens were also aboard. Three doctors from the Moscow Institute of Experimental Biology volunteered small flaps of skin from their shoulders and thighs. These were placed in sterilized glass bottles. The question of manned flight was being approached with enormous care, both from an engineering and biological point of view.

DOWN IN THE FIELDS

The noise and vibration was terrible as Sputnik 5 lifted off. The dogs, frightened, shifted restlessly around the cabin. Every movement was relayed back by TV. As it shot towards

The first 'cosmonauts' were the two dogs Belka (pictured here) and Strelka carried aloft by Sputnik 5. They could be observed by television cameras mounted in the spacecraft. After 18 orbits their capsule re-entered the Earth's atmosphere and parachuted to the ground. The dogs survived showing that successful recovery was possible from orbit.

orbit the pressure eased. Strelka and Belka settled down. After eight minutes, Sputnik 5 was in orbit of 339 by 360 km, 65 degrees, 90.7 minutes. News of the launch was immediately relayed to the world and first to the Hall of Columns courtroom in Moscow where Gary Powers was being found guilty of espionage. The judges were at that moment considering sentence.

Ground stations were able to pick up signals from the Sputnik. They were heard in Paris and London and they sounded like dots and dashes. All went well. The environmental system provided air and kept the temperature at an even 18°C, with constant humidity and pressure. Radiation dosage seemed to be within the limits allowed for. The dogs sucked food and water from tubes and taps at intervals. They got used to weightlessness after about five minutes hanging in the cabin apparently lifeless.

August 10. After 18 orbits, just a full day into the mission, it was time to begin the much-feared recovery sequence. The retrorockets blasted. Gravity gradually returned to the cabin. The descent cabin separated. Its skin glowed red hot, then white hot as it headed into the fires of reentry.

Down through the atmosphere. At 8000 m a pressure device in the cabin sensed the return to the atmosphere and parachutes popped out and unfurled. The ejector seat, carrying the ark, fired, and the two cabins descended under parachute, gradually drifting apart. The sphere-shaped cabin was coming down at 10 m/sec, the ark with its precious cargo at a gentler 6 m/sec. It was a classic scene. The two spacecraft were spotted coming down by farm workers, just like in the science fiction stories. Both bumped down, the ark in a meadow. The farm workers gathered round. Silence. No aircraft. No suggestion as to where the strange container had come from. They peered closer and saw a printed metal message: 'Please inform the Soviet space centre immediately on discovery'. Cars were already bouncing over the fields to the spot and to the surprised workers. So accurate was the landing that it came only 9 km from the place planned.

Belka and Strelka had survived. They were alive and well. The flight was a technical triumph. Recovery was possible. Animals could successfully fly in space. Above all, the Vostok spaceship design was known to be sound. A day-long manned flight could not now be far away.

The success of Sputnik 5 was hard on the Americans. Only the previous week they had scored one space success after another. The United States recovered Discoverer 13 from orbit — first. It put up the first communications satellite, Echo 1. The Air Force launched its Atlas missile 8000 km into the south Atlantic. The X-15 rocket aircraft climbed to a new record height of 31 000 m. Were the tables turning? But now this week of triumphs had been completely overshadowed by the flight of the 4½ tonne ark. Sputnik 5 was clearly the manned spaceship in prototype and it was now only a question of time before it had human cargo. This was a point that the USSR made no effort to conceal.

Practical possibilities are now being created for man's flight into outer space. (Radio Moscow, 21.8.1960)

A manned space flight could be made in the near future. Less than three years after the launching of the first spaceship we are on the immediate threshold of manned flight. (The Vice-President of the Academy of Sciences, quoted on Radio Moscow, 21.8.1960) [6]

FROM EISENHOWER TO KENNEDY

The American programme exhibited none of the steadfastness of purpose of the Soviet one. President Eisenhower could only be described as extremely lukewarm, if not downright sceptical, about ventures into space. NASA had yet to find its feet. The Mercury programme lurched along uncertainly. Long-term space planning was subject to intense rivalries between NASA, the US Air Force, the US Army and the US Navy. Although America had its seven astronauts in training, it had never been officially stated that its objective was to beat the Russians into orbit. It was simply assumed. And after Mercury, there were no objectives at all.

Eisenhower was, ever since Sputnik 1, under immense pressure to permit a massive expansion of the space effort. As early as December 1957 the US Air Force came up with a plan to put a man on the Moon by 1965. The army, not to be outdone, promised it for even earlier. Even now, the Moon was being wheeled out as the only objective worth contemplating. Such was the post-Sputnik hysteria.

Eisenhower responded to all the military pressure in the least expected way. he handed space over to a civilian agency. NASA, the space agency he set up in April 1958, was to be a civilian agency whose administrator would be appointed by the President. This decision led to a 20-year-long separation of scientific and military space objectives. The military were free to pursue military space programmes if they wished, but they would be just that – military. They would have to be financed from the military's own budget, and not by NASA. Even so, NASA got off to a shaky start. Mercury was dependant on an Air Force booster, the Atlas. The military kept on presenting one man-on-the-Moon scheme after another, each one madder and more extravagant that its predecessor.

NASA soon realized that in the absence of Presidential directives, indeed in the face of Presidential scepticism, it would have to set its own space objectives. NASA set up a steering committee on manned space flight in May 1959. Within a year it had come to two significant conclusions:

(1)   The only two possible goals for a long-term space programme were a manned Earth orbiting space station or a man-on-the-Moon.
(2)   A Moon flight was the more challenging of the two, and the public would be prepared to pay for it.

Even while NASA was deliberating, the Army and Air Force continued to be at each other's throats. The Army, under von Braun, designed a huge booster-to-end-all-boosters, the Saturn. The Air Force designed something cheaper, the Titan 3, and a manned space-ship to go on top, the Dyna-Soar. Called thus for 'dynamic soaring', it was a winged military reconnaisance plane that would circle the Earth with a single pilot.

By 1960 NASA had produced the notion of a spacecraft called 'Apollo', a project Mercury follow-on, which would lead somehow to a man-on-the-Moon by 1970. Congress criticized this schedule as too leisurely. Eisenhower, not to be hustled into anything, ordered a scientific study of all the manned projects. He was not impressed. In late 1960 he vetoed the Saturn programme, gave a tiny $30m to the post-Mercury missions, and privately stated his intention of scrapping Mercury after its first flight.

COUNTDOWN TO ORBIT

What a contrast this is to the orderly development of the Soviet programme in the same period. The corps of Russian rocketeers that went back to the 1920s and 1930s, having survived the war and the purges, and with a clear vision of the steps forward, had persuaded the politicians in general and Khrushchev in particular to accept a satellite programme in 1955 and a manned programme in 1959. The State Commission linked the Kremlin and the Academy of Sciences to the launch pad, fulfilling the dreams of the designers and the internal and external political needs of their masters. By comparison, the American programme was in turmoil: an unimpressable President, a restless Congress, an hysterical public mood, a gut reaction driving the generals moonwards, and three military services competing with a small civilian operation.

The election of John F. Kennedy as President in November 1960 meant no immediate change. It is true that Kennedy regarded Eisenhower as weak, complacent, and pedestrian; but the Mercury programme was going so painfully slowly that Kennedy did not want any early association with it himself.

Kennedy was inaugurated as President on 21 January 1961. NASA's Mercury programme got off the ground successfully ten days later when Mercury-Redstone 2 carried the chimpanzee 'Ham' 280 km downrange in suborbital flight. The booster over-heated and the capsule overshot its landing point badly. Washington ordered a further delay until 25 April so that the problems could be sorted out. Kennedy was busily occupied with Laos and Cuba and did not want to be beset with space issues just yet. Little did he realise that Soviet scientists were making desperate efforts to get their manned spaceship operational.

DISASTER

The triumph of Sputnik 5 had filled the design team with optimism: a final rerun of the mission over two days would pave the way for a day-long manned flight in early 1961, perhaps as soon as February. The Americans were still some way off a Mercury flight, and there was growing confidence that one of the twenty cosmonauts now in training would be the first into orbit. Unless Khrushchev intervened. Noting the success of the Moon probes in 1959 and noting that opportunities existed to send spacecraft to Mars in October 1960 and Venus in February 1961, Khrushchev ordered Korolov to aim for the planets. With the Americans not even able to put up a Moon probe, a Soviet shot to the planets would demonstrate Soviet prowess even more intolerably.

Korolov would probably have preferred to have waited to see the first manned flight through before contemplating these diversions. But the 'launch window' to Mars — the most favourable opportunity when its orbit was nearest to the Earth — occurred only infrequently. The next opportunity for Mars would be November 1962, and for Venus August 1962. Khrushchev was not prepared to wait. He signed the cheques: two space-ships were built for each window. Each would weigh 500 kg and carry elementary instruments to photograph and study the planets. A backup probe would be built as well. By happy coincidence, all would arrive at their respective targets — Mars and Venus — at the same time, during the third week of May 1961.

The Mars shot was of particular importance. Khrushchev himself would be in New York for the United Nations Autumn Assembly when it was due. What better crowning glory than to be there just as his two spaceships streaked towards Mars? And just so as to ensure that nothing could go wrong, and to override Korolov's natural caution, he appointed Field Marshal Mistrofan Nedelin to be in supreme command of the Mars project. Khrushchev arrived in New York on 19 September 1960.

Mars 1 failed. The pumps in the third stage, hurriedly developed, did not develop enough thrust for ignition to begin. The Mars ship reached 120 km, and then fell back into the atmosphere. Two days later, Mars 2 did likewise. An identical failure.

Khrushchev was furious. The space shots had already been delayed, and he had had to extend his stay in capitalist America several times. He flew home on 13 October, fuming and empty-handed. Diplomatic observers were puzzled as to exactly what was going on, but Khrushchev could be so unpredictable and bad-tempered that they suspected nothing more. Back home, Khrushchev carpeted Nedelin. He would take no further excuses. The backup Mars probe, an engineering model and not designed to fly was ordered out of the hangar. There was to be a third desperate try before the Mars window closed [7].

Nedelin and his team worked round the clock to ready Mars probe 3. Late on 23 October all was set. Nedelin was in charge. Korolov was supervising. He must have had his misgivings about the enterprise. All Russia's top rocket experts were there. Mikhail Yangel, Ivan Gvay, Dmitri Yefremov, Nikolai Pavlovsky. The arms swung back, exposing the rocket bathed in night-time searchlights. The count reached zero. Nothing. Not a sound. Silence throughout the steppe. It just did not light up. Seconds passed. Then minutes. Nedelin knew he could never explain this one away to Krushchev. It was ridiculous. The rocket would just not take off and no one had a clue why! Mistrofan Nedelin ordered an inspection. Loaded with fuel as the rocket was, he ordered his men out of their bunkers. Ladders were put up around the booster. The technicians began a minute inspection. Quite what they expected to find was unclear The proper procedure was to drain the rocket of all fuel and start again. But this would take time – and would have to be explained to Khrushchev. It was a mad venture.

No one knows exactly what happened or what had initially prevented the take off. For, take off it did. Or tried to. But the restraining arms still clapsed the rocket to the ground. It surged against them and then it blew. The whole pad went up in an appalling shattering bang that was heard a hundred miles away. Fires blazed and turned the steppe to daylight. It was an inferno. Nedelin was incinerated. So was anyone within about a mile of the explosion. The bodies were unrecognizable. Korolov and Yangel had wisely stayed in the bunker – shaken and doubtless restraining a burning anger against Khrushchev and his political whims. A story about an air crash was concocted to explain away Marshal Nedelin's untimely death.

SECOND DISASTER

Repair work to the devastated pad proceeded rapidly. By early December, as winter closed in, it was ready again. On 1 December Sputnik 6 climbed into the sky with dogs Pchelka and Mushka aboard. All proceeded perfectly and the flight went into a second day. If it went well, then a day-long manned flight would follow.

Just then, nature reminded the scientists just how fragile their efforts were. The retrorockets fired on 3 December on schedule, but at too high an angle. The capsule plunged steeply into the atmosphere and burned like a fiery meteor. Pchelka and Mushka were no more. It was a sobering moment. All the calculations had to be gone over again and all the systems checked. This was one of the key phases of the flight that simply could not be allowed to go wrong. The designers and Korolov then made two significant decisions. First, in order to reduce guidance risks, the first manned flight would be limited to just one orbit. Second, two dress rehearsals would be required before even that would be tried. Only then would they be sure.

Even so, there was to be a further delay as the two Venus shots ordered by Khrushchev were got out of the way. Only one thing was sure: whether they flew or not, no one was going to countenance the same risks, rush or hurry as had been done in the desperate efforts to reach Mars the previous autumn.

The first mission was only marginally more successful than the October Mars probes: unlike them it actually reached Earth orbit. But when, after the first orbit, the time came to ignite the third stage onwards toward Venus, nothing happened. The problems of pumping propellants around in weightlessness still had not been mastered.

The failed Venus shot was explained away as Sputnik 7, orbiting at 223 by 328 km and weighing a record 6483 kg. It was announced that the mission was over soon after it completed its first orbit. There was much speculation in the West as to what the flight was all about. There were even suggestions that it was a manned flight that went wrong, but the much heavier weight than either Sputnik 4, 5, or 6 should have told these experts that it was different [8].

Venus was then appearing as a brilliant shining star in the cold dawn sky. It was a tempting target. In its orbit inside the Earth's track it came as close as 40 million kilometres to Earth. Transit times for a space probe were only four months, half that of Mars. Virtually the same size as the Earth, it was shrouded in thick cloud. Beneath those steamy clouds there might be life: swamps? vegetation?

'Good morning Venus!' hailed the Western press as Sputnik 8 performed on schedule on 12 February. The fourth stage did everything it should have. From a parking orbit of 227 by 285 km, a small probe called at first an Automatic Interplanetary Station, and later, more poetically, Venera 1, curved away from Earth in a circular orbit set to intercept Venus's path on 19 May.

Venera 1 was an entirely new design. 2 m high, weighing 644 kg, it had a domed top, a cylindrical body, and two solar panels to soak in sunlight and turn it into electricity. A butterfly-net high-gain antenna picked up signals from a new deep space tracking station at Yevpatoria in the Crimea; a long arm antenna sent information back. It had instruments to study cosmic radiation, micrometeorites, and charged particles.

The first probe to the planet Venus, Venera 1, was launched in February 1961. Unfortunately contact with it was lost about two weeks after launch.

The world watched as Venera 1 headed into regions of space never explored before. On 19 February it was nearly 2 million kilometres away from the Earth, travelling at 3.9 km/s. From early on it was known that Venera would come within 100 000 km of Venus — no mean achievement over a journey of 270 million kilometres. A stream of data was sent back over the airwaves. A series of thermal shutters which opened and closed protected the hermetically sealed instruments from the heat and cold of deep space. To mark the historic flight, the spaceship carried a small earth globe and a map of the solar system.

It was a brave attempt; but the planned communications session with the probe on 27 February never materialized. Venera 1 was lost. A team of scientists from the USSR travelled to the British radio observatory, Jodrell Bank, to use its giant dish, but to no avail. Venera 1 kept its secrets. To this day nobody knows why it went silent [9].

Two more Sputniks followed in rapid succession: Sputnik 9 on 9 March and Sputnik 10 on 25 March, a mere two weeks apart. These were indeed dry runs for a manned flight. Sputnik 9 carried the dog Chernushka, made one orbit around the Earth, and came down in the planned landing zone. Sputnik 10 had another husky aboard, Zvedochka. It was a repeat of Sputnik 9's performance in every detail. Korolov had ironed out the bugs at last. The moment of truth, the final test, drew near. The prairie flowers were blooming on the steppe, peeping through the few patches of snow that lay round about. Warmth and life were returning to the spring earth.

'THE SPHERICAL SHAPE OF THE EARTH'

5 April. Final assembly of the manned spaceship in the huge 20 m high hangar at the cosmodrome. Korolov and the State Commission were present and all the cosmonauts were at the launch site. They watched the assembly process from Korolov's glass office on the second floor inside the building. Konstantin Rudnev, the chairman of the State Commission was there; so too was Valentin Glushko.

The manned spaceship was carried by crane across the assembly hangar and placed gingerly on the third stage. Fasteners were tightened and connectors joined. The nosecone was put in position. The long grey, white and silver rocket lay on its railcar in the hangar, shining under the arc lamps, pointing towards the pad.

8 April. The last meeting between the State Commission and the cosmonaut team. Its purpose was formally to select the pilot and the backup. One of the few pieces of documentary film from the time shows the scene. Nearly twenty cosmonauts in green military suits huddled around desks in a crowded room. Up at the front, Korolov and the State Commission.

There had never been much doubt that Yuri Gagarin would be selected. Korolov had long identified him as the brightest and most balanced of the team. Gagarin for his own part had always made his desire to be first abundantly clear. The meeting was a short one: Gagarin thanked the Commission, addressed his colleagues, and it was all over. Gherman Titov was named the backup, and Grigori Nelyubov was put in reserve.

10 April, 4 p.m. Final meeting of the State Commission, this time on its own. Korolov formally requested permission 'to bring the launch vehicle to the launch pad and prepare for blastoff on 12 April'.

Selected by Sergei Korolov (right) as the brightest and most balanced of the team of twenty candidates, Yuri Gagarin was chosen as the first cosmonaut to be launched into Earth orbit; Gherman Titov was named as his back-up.

11 April, 5 a.m. It was still dark when the hangar doors clanked back and the railcar, with the manned spaceship on its back, began the hour-long journey to the pad. The darkness, pierced by the lights of the site and the air of expectation, must have reminded the older hands of the days just before Sputnik 1.

1 p.m. Yuri Gagarin was driven to the pad. The rocket had been erected behind him. The chief of the cosmonaut squad, General Kaminin, presented Yuri Gagarin to the assembled workers on the launch pad. Applause broke out when Kaminin told them Gagarin had been selected. Supervisors from each of the launch teams came forward to offer their good wishes.

Gagarin and Korolov went up the escalator lift to the top of the pad. Together they spent an hour going through the final checks, the problems, the procedures. Bulky, sturdy Korolov going over his creation together with the short, stocky, youthful Gagarin, a man not even half his age, trusted for the ultimate assignment. Parting advice.

For Korolov, the strain was almost too much. His heart, weakened by exhaustion, the frantic preparations and the worry, came close to giving out on this the threshold of his triumph. He made it back to his wooden cottage surrounded by peaceful poplars fifteen minutes away. He took pills and medicine, and collapsed into bed. Sleep overtook him. When he awoke, it was already dark and well into the night. It was 3 a.m. Korolov felt much better now. He would live to see the great day. He opened the window. The cool night air of April caught him in the face. Six hours to go. He phoned Rudnev. He could not sleep either. They arranged to meet at the flower bed outside the cottage before heading off to the pad in Rudnev's car. The only people who did sleep that night were, ironically, Gargarin and Titov. They were in the special 'cosmonauts' cottage', a wooden building right beside Korolov.

12 April, 5.30 a.m. Gagarin and Titov were woken up by Kaminin and trainer Karpov. Up quickly. Sensors were attached to their bodies to record their every moment. Woollen underwear. Layer upon layer. Finally attendants put on the bright orange suit, the gloves and the boots. Then the helmet, the letters 'CCCP' (Russian for USSR) inscribed on top.

Down at the pad, dawn was coming up over the eastern horizon. At 7 a.m. final checks were under way. The rocket was fuelled up and wisps of liquid oxygen burned off from time to time. Cold winds whipped around the cabin of the 30 m high spaceship, now named Vostok 1. Designer Konstantin Feoktistov climbed into test the cabin, switches, lights, radio. It was warm in there. All in order.

By 7.30 a.m. the designers, engineers and pad workers were assembled at the base of the rocket. Korolov, Glushko, and Keldysh stood together chatting. The minibus arrived next from the cosmonauts' cottage, Gagarin and Titov aboard. At this stage any hopes Titov might have had of making the flight were fast evaporating. Gagarin was healthy and ready to go.

Yuri Gagarin stepped out, walked gingerly across the apron and took some steps up the elevator. He turned around, aware that he must address the throng of designers and pad workers. Such a contrast to Cape Canaveral. Any candidate astronaut would have exchanged a few pleasantries, even a joke, and climbed aboard with a merry 'send her up!'. Not so at Baikonour. All were conscious of Russia's historic destiny in space, aware of three unbroken generations of space dreaming, planning and designing. Now history hung heavy in the air. The world would in time come to treasure this moment. Gagarin spoke:

Dear friends, close and unknown, fellow countrymen, people of all countries and continents! In a few minutes this powerful spaceship will carry me to the far-off expanses of the universe. What am I going to say to you in these final minutes? [10]

He paused. His voice trailed away. . . .

Right now, all my life seems to be one wonderful instant. Everything I have ever done, everything I have ever experienced, was for the sake of this minute.

He found it hard to continue. . . .

Am I happy, setting out on this space flight?

He paused again.

Of course I am. In all times and epochs the greatest happiness for man has been to take part in new discoveries.

It was probably his first public speech. As he stood there about to leave this planet with all its security, warmth and life, the full enormity of what he was about to do was slowly sinking in. He was the representative of the human race. He reached out to them:

I say to you, dear friends, goodbye, as people always say to each other when setting out on a distant journey. I would like to embrace you all, friends and strangers, distant and close! Farewell!

It was 90 minutes to blastoff. Yuri Gagarin disappeared into the lift. In minutes he had clambered into the Vostok. The hatch was closed. He was on his own.

Korolov had meanwhile disappeared into his underground concrete bunker. 'Up periscope!' he commanded. He focussed his sights on the rocket. All systems were brought into line: the rocket, the pad, the tracking systems, the computer command centre in Yevpatoria. Telemetry poured in from the booster. Television screens showed Gagarin in the cabin, just waiting.

One hour to go. 'Zarya, how do you read?' called Korolov to Gagarin on the final communications run. Zarya, the Russian for 'dawn' was the code name for earth control. The radio circuit was clear. Music was piped aboard to soothe Gagarin's nerves. The cosmonaut would have little control over the flight himself: if something went wrong he would open an envelope, find the number of the combination to take manual control over the autopilot, and fly Vostok himself. It was an arrangement no NASA pilot would have stood for.

Six minutes. Kaminin and Popovich gathered round Korolov at the periscope. They had gone through so many hours waiting. Now it was really going to happen. The pace quickened. Inevitability set in.

'Key to go position!'

'Air purging!'

'Idle run!'

'Ignition!'

Flames licked around the base. The rocket struggled to be free. A rumbling roar shook the bunker. And away it went!

'Poyekali!' 'Away we go!' triumphed Gagarin.

The booster rose, gathering speed every second. Eyes followed intently upwards. Gradually it bent over in its climbing, heading into the northeast. Four bright light blobs were all that could be seen of the engine chambers as Vostok disappeared from sight.

For Korolov it was nerve-racking, for contact with Gagarin broke down during the ascent. Fears grew. Had the G forces overcome him? But it was only temporary. Off came the engine fairing as Vostok reached the airless zones. Gagarin was on his own now: ejection was no longer possible. Light flooded into his cabin and momentarily blinded his eyes.

Eight minutes. Engine cutoff. The rumble and shaking of the booster subsided abruptly. Silence, total silence, enveloped Vostok. Yuri Gagarin had reached orbit, somewhere over eastern Siberia. They had done it!

Vostok was 181 km high and its orbit was to reach as high as 327 km. As Gagarin gazed through the two portholes of his silent spaceship he began to take in the vastness of the planet. Later, he was to describe it in his own words. They tell it best:

I saw for the first time the spherical shape of the Earth. You can see its curvature when looking to the horizon. It is unique and beautiful.

The day side of the Earth was clearly visible. The coasts of continents, islands, big rivers, the surfaces of water were distinguishable.

It is possible to see the remarkable colourful change from the light surface of the Earth to the completely black sky in which one can see the stars. The dividing line is very thin, just a belt of film surrounding the Earth's sphere.

It is of a delicate blue colour and the transition from the blue to the dark is very gradual and lovely. When I emerged from the shadow of the Earth, the horizon looked different. There was a bright orange strip along it which again passed into a blue hue and once again into a dense black colour. [11]

Vostok was travelling at 8 km/s. It headed across the vast blue of the Pacific. Mariners had taken months and months to cross this great ocean but Gagarin would transit in 20 minutes. Down below, tossed on the waves of the ocean, Soviet tracking ships turned their antennae skywards to hear the signals and telemetry of Vostok and the voice of its occupant.

By now, news of the flight was out. At 9.59 a.m. (6.59 a.m. in Britain and 1.59 a.m. in America) Moscow Radio came on air with the historic announcement. Static crackled as in slow measured tones, straining with excitement, the reader began, conscious of history in the making:

Today, 12 April 1961, the first cosmic ship named Vostok, with a man on board, was orbited around the Earth from the Soviet Union.

He is an airman, Major Yuri Gagarin . . . .

At Cape Canaveral, America's Mercury astronauts were awoken and told. It must have hit them like a cold wet sponge. None of their names would go down in history but instead a diminutive Russian major whom no one had ever heard of.

Gagarin hurtled on. He accustomed himself to weightlessness. He wrote notes on a pad, and when he finished, it floated free and lodged under the seat. An hour into the flight and he was over Cape Horn, South America. Night fell:

I have never forgotten it. The stars were so clearly visible — blindingly bright and full-bodied. The sky was blacker than it ever appears on earth, with the real slate blackness of space. [12]

The automatic guidance system locked on. Gagarin's next task was to test the ability of a man to eat and drink in space. He took away some tubes from their racks, squeezed them and found no difficulty. Little water droplets floated around the cabin.

Vostok flashed into daylight and the Sun marched over the eastern horizon. Gas jets hissed in the vacuum. Vostok turned around to prepare for retrofire. All this time, Gagarin reported back his every move, his every sensation. His voice came through the mushy crackly short wave.

10.25 a.m. Rockets fired briefly over west Africa. They cut 500 km/hr off Vostok's speed. It was just enough to send the spaceship dipping into the atmosphere. Still 6000 km from home, Vostok descended in a giant arc over bodies of land and water towards its motherland. The fires of reentry glowed red around the portholes. Was the trajectory right? Would the heat burst through?

Out of radio contact (the heat was enough to ionize radio waves), Gagarin could only wait and hope. He was pressed into his seat ever harder as the G forces built up. But reentry heat did not break through. The G forces eased off. The worst was over. Outside, the sky was no longer black, but blue. He was back in the atmosphere once more.

At 8000 m the hatch on Vostok blew away. His ejector seat then shot him away in turn. Real air blew in Yuri Gagarin's face once more. With an enormous tug the parachutes jerked him upwards. He was floating under canopy.

Where was he? Down below were ploughed fields, the squares of state farms, the springtime of April. Gagarin floated earthwards, orange-suited under a white parachute. The main Vostok capsule, much heavier, was descending some distance away at a greater speed.

The flier was first noticed by a woman planting potatoes with her six-year-old daughter. Members of a tractor brigade had seen him descending from afar off and they rushed to the spot. They reached the capsule first, blackened and giving off heat and still far too hot to touch.

'Where am I? Where's the nearest town?' Gagarin kept on asking. 'I must report my return to Earth!' he argued as he pulled off his white helmet. But for the 'CCCP' on it, and news of the flight on the radio, they might never have believed him.

The capsule in which Yuri Gagarin was launched into space lies in a field after its successful return to Earth. The outside has been scorched and blackened by the fierce heat of re-entry. Gagarin had ejected from the capsule at 8000 metres altitude.

ALL OVER

Gagarin's flight lasted a mere 108 minutes. It was an epochal flight. No one could ever make that first flight again. Nothing would ever be the same again. Elation swept the USSR. Crowds flocked onto the streets. Millions tuned in their radios to hear more about the flight and about the man who made it. Strangers greeted each other in the street. Choirs sang in his honour. Roads were named after him. Khrushchev was alert to the advantages to himself. He phone the cosmonaut: 'You and I together with all our people shall solemnly celebrate this great exploit. Let the whole world look and see what our great country is capable of. Let the capitalist countries catch up with us' [13].

The Americans fully realized what a blow this was to their own plans. Sputnik took some days, even weeks to sink in. Gagarin's effect was total and immediate. 'Another Pearl Harbour' was a typical American reaction. The Americans had consciously tried to beat the Russians to the goal of a man-in-space: their suborbital flight was set for 28 April. They had been beaten and soundly beaten for Gagarin had gone for a full orbit. The Americans were still at least six months from that. Congressmen fumed. Editors railed. Kennedy called a panic meeting of his senior advisors: 'Just tell me how to catch up. Let's find somebody. Anybody. I don't care if the janitor over there has the answer, if he knows how' [14]. So they recollected afterwards. Kennedy's reaction was quite different from Eisenhower's. He made no attempt to play down Gagarin. It was one in the eye. Kennedy was reeling and there would have to be some kind of response. He was reeling three days later when his Bay of Pigs invasion of Castro's Cuba collapsed. His Presidency seemed near to collapse too.

Gherman Titov was the first to greet Gagarin. He landed at the nearest airfield and rushed to congratulate him on behalf of his colleagues. For the cosmonauts and Korolov, it was their best day ever. They were swept away with unrestrained joy that obliterated all the bitter memories of past failures. It was such a monumental success that no propaganda machine could ever exaggerate. The last big psychological barrier had been smashed and manned space flight was here to stay.

At 9.00 that night they celebrated in a dacha (country cottage) amidst woods on a hill overlooking the river Volga. In speeches, extravagant commitments were made about conquering the cosmos. No one minded.

Gagarin rested the next day. He took Titov for a boat trip and long walks to advise him about his flight while his memory was still fresh. On 14 April he flew to Moscow.

The hero's welcome in Moscow attracted world-wide attention for it was the first time that a transnational telecast had been arranged. The European Broadcasting Union carried the whole show live — to the curious Europeans and the furious Americans. As his Illyushin-18 propellor plane flew in over the spires of the Kremlin, seven jets rose in escort. It landed at Vnukuvo Airport. In military coat, Gagarin marched along a thick orange carpet to the stand. He saluted Nikita Khrushchev, who was bubbling and chuckling away, stood to attention for the Internationale, and they drove into the city.

Moscow had known nothing like it since Victory Day in 1945. Millions turned out, flowers were everywhere, and May Day banners were hastily put up ahead of time. Gagarin's parents turned up in their work clothes, he in his carpenter's cap, she in her old shawl. In a curious way, they symbolized the old Russia and the new.

The crowds were so big that the cosmonaut team could not fight their way through. There was a public meeting in Red Square, a reception in the Kremlin, and speeches

Yuri Gagarin had risen from being virtually unknown to become a world hero. Away from the lime-light he relaxes water-skiing in this photograph.

galore. Khrushchev had a field day. He was radiant throughout. There was tribute to Tsiolkovsky, praise for Soviet scientists, mocking comments for America's puny efforts, and promises of more spectacular flights to come. Gagarin was kept in the limelight. Two reasons explained this. First, until that day he was virtually unknown and now he was a world hero. Second, almost no film of his flight had been released. Gagarin at a reception was about as close as most people would get to his achievement for the time being.

Gagarin was soon thrust into a world tour. He was sent first throughout the Socialist countries, then further abroad. His youthful looks, his broad smile, his quiet manner carried instant appeal. He went to Europe, America and Cuba. He visited Britain in July 1961. An open Rolls Royce, registered YG 1, was provided for him. Thousands lined the route from the airport. He toured London, met the Queen and spent a day in Manchester with the Amalgamated Union of Foundry Workers. By this time the Americans had emerged from their trance and put together a space plan of truly colossal proportions.

4

The first heroes (1961–63)

Gagarin's triumph was barely a week old when President Kennedy sent his Vice-President and Chairman of the Space Council Lyndon Johnson the following memorandum:

(1)   Do we have a chance of beating the Soviets by putting a laboratory in space, or by a trip around the Moon, or by a rocket to land on the Moon and back with a man? Is there any programme which promises dramatic results in which we could win?
(2)   How much additional would it cost?
(3)   Are we working 24 hours a day on existing programmes? If not, why not? If not, will you make recommendations how work can be speeded up?
(4)   Are we making maximum effort? Are we achieving necessary results? [1]

The tone of this directive was unmistakeable. The race was on, and there was no question about it and it was a race. 'Dramatic results' was what was sought after. Scientific considerations did not figure in the directive at all.

All this suited Johnson of course. He had long argued for greater space involvement and had taken the view that superiority to the Russians was not just desirable, but imperative. Being a politician, he could add the growing space industry to his burgeoning empire of influence. He consulted NASA, von Braun and the Pentagon. NASA argued for a Moon landing. A crash programme could achieve that by 1967 for $34bn. It would cost $22bn for a 1969 landing date. Von Braun concurred, pointing out that in order to reach these targets nearly all other programmes would have to be left aside. Even the Pentagon agreed to help: this was no time for interservice rivalry.

This process of consultation took a week. In the middle of it, on 25 April, America tried again. NASA planned a full-scale demonstration of the man-in-orbit flight. The larger Atlas booster would put up a Mercury capsule which would orbit the Earth twice and be recovered in the ocean. It would put the United States on a par with Sputnik 5 and would mean an American in orbit in the autumn.

40 seconds into the flight at 5000 m, the Atlas booster exploded sky high. Debris rained down on frightened journalists who dived under their cars to avoid injury. The escape system did work though. Alan Shepard was due to fly 150 km high a few days later: it gave his suborbital mission an added sense of desperation.

On 1 May Johnson assembled his documentation and recommendations. It was his response to Kennedy's letter of a few weeks earlier. Johnson never had any real doubt that a man-on-the-Moon was the only worthwhile goal. It fitted in well with his own boundless ambition. It was highly visible. Either you did it or you didn't. It had none of the ambiguities of orbital stations, whatever they were.

The pace quickened. On 5 May the Americans at last put up their own spaceman. Alan Shepard, a tall rugged test pilot, took his Mercury capsule up 180 km over the Florida coast, turned it round in the vacuum, and brought it back into the Atlantic Ocean. Millions listened with bated breath to his crisp reports. They gasped when he read out his altitude figures, and they were mightily relieved when the helicopter fished him out of the sea. Reporters babbled away in excitement: it was Buck Rogers come true. 15-minute flight or not, America felt a thrill of excitement. National honour was at least partly restored. Shepard was greeted as a hero. The nation was jubilant.

On 7 May, riding high on the wave of elation, Johnson presented his Moon plans to the President. They were countersigned by NASA administrator James Webb and Defence Secretary Robert MacNamara. They recommended a man-on-the-Moon programme as the principal American space objective. 'National prestige' was cited as the main reason. There was little or no mention of science. There was reference instead to Soviet success. It was admitted that the programme was unjustified by scientific, commercial or military criteria. It is worth noting that no attempt was made to assess Soviet objectives in space. They were automatically and uncritically assumed to be a man-on-the-Moon as soon as possible, perhaps in 1967, the 50th anniversary of the Bolshevik Revolution.

John F. Kennedy took little time to think over the Johnson report. He summoned the Congress into special session, and told them: 'I believe that this nation should commit itself to achieving the goal, before the decade is out, of landing a man on the moon and returning him safely to the Earth' [2]. Costings put the price of the venture as $20bn. The Senate approved the proposal after a debate of only one hour. Only five out of 95 Senators spoke. The initial response to the idea was slightly less than enthusiastic: perhaps the implications had not sunk in. But Kennedy had, perhaps even inadvertently, captured something in the American psyche. That autumn he addressed a gathering of college graduates, and his speech was repeatedly interrupted by applause:

We choose to go to the moon. . . (applause) . . . .
We choose to go to the moon. . . (more applause). . . in this decade not because it is easy but because it is hard. That goal will serve to organize and measure the best of our energies and skills. That challenge is one we are willing to accept, one we are unwilling to postpone and one we intend to win. . . (more applause). . . . [3]

The contrast with the Soviet programme is startling. The USSR had a tradition of rocketry, a general series of goals, a vision of the future that dated from the 1920s and before. Helped on by Khrushchev, it is true, but there was continuity. The Americans, on the other hand, had embarked on a man-on-the-Moon programme that was conceived, planned, announced and set in train in a period of only five weeks, motivated largely by a desire not to be beaten to technical supremacy, and originating from a new President desirous to achieve something, anything. Not content with the more realistic objective of going around the Moon first, the Americans were starting a lap behind the USSR and set themselves an extra lap to run. It was by all accounts a panic decision, a gut reaction. Few people were consulted. Hardly any other options were considered. In another age, it would have been a recipe for national disaster. But any critics (if there had been any) reckoned without NASA's organizational capabilities and American industry booming in top gear.

GOOD MORNING EARTH!

The haste with which the American programme was put together was soon forgotten. As if to underline the wisdom of the new venture, NASA prepared a second mission to follow Alan Shepard. The pilot was Virgil Grissom.

Once again the scene shifted to Cape Canaveral. The excited crowds, the shimmering heat, the exasperating countdown delays. Grissom lifted off on 21 July. Up he went, 190 km high and back down into the ocean. Then suddenly all the radio commentaries were interrupted and suspended. Music played. The worst was suspected.

As his capsule bobbed in the ocean, Grissom's hatch blew off. The cabin filled rapidly with water. The astronaut scrambled out, swallowing water, and was rescued by helicopter. His helmet was being investigated by a 3 m long shark when it was found. His capsule sunk to the bottom. Could America now get a man in orbit, a proper space flight, before the Russians repeated Gagarin's flight?

The cosmonaut team — all twenty of them — had spent most of May vacationing near the Black Sea at Sochi. They were joined by Korolov, his wife and daughter, and some senior trainers. It was their first rest since they were recruited. Gherman Titov was appointed backup, though it was agreed that Grigori Nelyubov would fly the third mission.

The aim of the second flight was to do what the first flight was originally to have accomplished: a full day in space. Gagarin would have flown a day but for the accident which befell Sputnik 6. Actually there was little choice about the duration of the mission. Vostok could not come down on Soviet territory once it had gone three orbits for its flight path moved far to the west. And it would not be near the landing site again till orbit 16.

Gherman Titov remembered going asleep in the cosmonauts' cottage the night before the mission. It was hot and stuffy so he had to open the windows and run fans. He fell asleep listening to the metallic sounds that came from the assembly workshop. But at night-time, as in any desert, the temperature fell, waking him. He turned off the fans. He must have contemplated the fact that he would be the first man to sleep in space. The following day was Sunday 6 August, and two men, Titov and Nikolayev, left for the pad

Four early Soviet cosmonauts (left to right) Gherman Titov, Pavel Popovich, Alexei Leonov and Andrian Nikolayev.

in the transfer van. There was none of the tension of 12 April. The two men joked and sang.

Vostok 2 lifted off at 9 a.m. The rocket sped away rapidly from the scorched summer steppe and headed into the Sun. At one stage anyone looking upwards might have imagined there were two bright suns close together in the sky, so brilliantly did the rocket flames shine.

Vostok 2 (mass 4731 kg) went into an orbit of 178 by 257 km, 64.56 degrees, 88.6 minutes. As weightlessness descended on the cosmonaut, Gherman Titov floated free, upside down, and headed for the first of seventeen sunrises and sunsets that he was going to experience over the next day. Titov scheduled an activity for each orbit. Throughout, he was observed on TV at 10 frames/s. Ground observes noted him eating the first space lunch on orbit 3. It consisted of purée, meat and liver pâtés and black currant juice. Some of the juice escaped and floated off round the cabin. On orbit 4 to 5 Titov manoeuvred his spaceship manually, something Gagarin had not done. Gas jets moved it around its centre of mass. At the same time Titov took movie pictures of the Earth out of the window, using a 'Konvass' camera. Primitive and of poor quality, these pictures nevertheless conveyed something of the speed of orbital travel, as Vostok 2 soared over mountains, clouds, seas, and oceans.

It was on orbit 6 that Titov came across one of the first major problems of space travel: nausea. Of all the terrible afflictions that orbital travel was predicted to bring — from madness to genetic mutation — nausea was subsequently to prove both the most mundane and most intractable. Over the next twenty years nausea was to afflict 50 per cent of all travellers in space, Russian and American alike. All that Titov was trying to do was go to sleep. Yet as he did so he got more and more disorientated and sicker and saw his control panel floating away above him. By lying perfectly still he overcame his vertigo and got to sleep.

The reason for space sickness, it was subsequently determined, was loss of balance from a disorder in the inner ear. Otoliths — tiny stones in the liquid-filled inner ear — normally signal a change of balance or position to the brain. In weightlessness the otoliths lose their reference point.

Despite the nausea, Titov eventually slept soundly — indeed he overslept the 7½ hours planned by 35 mins. 'Good morning, Earth!' hailed one British daily, celebrating the fact of Titov's being the first man to awake to the world from orbit. The effortless smoothness of the second Vostok flight was one of the main features to strike Western observers. As night fell that summer evening, Vostok 2 could be seen as a bright light crossing the sky from the southwest to the northeast over a period of three or four minutes. It crossed the United States too.

The nausea passed. The cosmonaut was bright and alert come early 7 August. He wrote up his logbook and prepared for the return to Earth. The retrorockets fired on orbit 17. Titov blazed through the upper atmosphere. Outside the cabin, flames turned from pink to scarlet to purple and crimson. Titov ejected from the cabin and came down by parachute. He landed only 200 m from a railway line. He had been up for 25 hr 18 min, and had covered 703 143 km.

Soon after landing, he was met by Andrian Nikolayev and Yuri Gagarin, the latter just back from a triumphant tour of the United States. There was a debriefing the next day at the Zhiguli Hills overlooking the Volga. A parade through Moscow followed. There was then another reception at the rocket assembly plant when a beaming, proud Titov presented Sergei Korolov with his flight log book.

The pilots of Vostoks 1 and 3 in relaxed mood; Andrian Nikolayev (left) and Yuri Gagarin.

For observers, Titov had confirmed Soviet space supremacy. Gagarin was not just a 'lucky first'. A full day in space was, coincidentally, the objective of the last Mercury mission — and the Americans had yet to make even one flight into orbit! What would the Russians do next?

THE SOYUZ COMPLEX

Only in retrospect is it possible now to see the period of autumn 1961 as the critical time for the long-term future of the Soviet space programme, just as indeed it was for the Americans. By September 1961, two facts were clear:

(1) The USSR had, through Vostok 1 and 2, shown that a man could fly in space for at least a day in a reliable spaceship.
(2) Although the American programme was both late in time and inferior in size and design, the Americans had set themselves the target of a man on the Moon by 1970. No one doubted the seriousness of American intent, and the memory of the effort American industry made to overwhelm Japan's economic performance within months of the Pearl Harbour attack of 1941 was not lost.

The decisions which faced the USSR in the autumn of 1961 were:

(1) Should the USSR go full ahead with a man-on-the-Moon programme like the Americans? Or set a different objective?
(2) If the former, what method of reaching the Moon should be chosen?
(3) What type of spaceship should follow Vostok?

These would have been the choices faced by Khrushchev, Korolov and the Academy of Sciences. The first decision was largely a political one, the others were technical.

Something is known of how the Americans came to be involved in a man on-the-Moon race: nothing is known of how the equivalent Soviet decisions came to be taken. But piecing together the events afterwards, it seems that a decision was taken around this time to agree on a Russian on the Moon sometime around 1970 or perhaps 1971. Judging from subsequent events, it seems that the Kremlin's analysis that it was unlikely the Americans could reach their target before 1970 was a key factor in the Soviet decision. This underestimation of American abilities was a serious misjudgement.

A whole new series of boosters, machines and spaceships were commissioned and designed. Automatic moonships were to pave their way. The next series of Luna (formerly Lunik) mooncraft would soft-land on the Moon in 1963 to find out the strength of the surface. Lunar orbiters would follow, to map landing sites and investigate near-Moon space.

A man-on-the-Moon programme was logical for both Khrushchev and Korolov. For the Communist leader, there was no choice about it. Having built up a substantial lead over the United States, it was inconceivable for him to give that up voluntarily. Since the Americans had shown their hand, the Russians could not do less. Khrushchev had always bragged quite openly about Soviet space achievements, and whatever one could say about the Soviet economy or foreign policy, space technology was the one area of world affairs where they were indisputedly way out front.

The method by which the USSR would go to the Moon presented a challenging engineering problem, to say the least. There were basically three possible approaches:

(1)   direct ascent
(2)   Earth orbit rendezvous
(3)   lunar orbit rendezvous.

Direct ascent was the most popular method in the science fiction literature of the time. The 'Stories of Tintin' cartoon shows the type of method. A huge rocket – it really would have to be utterly enormous – would put up a moonship which would fly direct to the Moon, slow down coming in to land, touch down, and deposit two or three astronauts directly on the surface. There would be no orbiting around either the Earth or the Moon or any diversions like that. After a period of exploration, the cosmonauts would climb back into their mother ship and fire direct back to Earth. It was a simple method, a crude method, and involved the minimum of new techniques. On the debit side, the landing part was hazardous, involving braking from several thousand kilometres per hour in a few minutes and finding a good touchdown spot at the same time. It left little margin for error or for engines failing. Last, it would need a massive booster of at least 7 million tonnes thrust, or fourteen times more than Vostok's 408 000 kg.

Earth orbit rendezvous (EOR) was to the Russians a more natural proposition particularly to anyone bred on the theories of Tsiolkovsky. A command ship, a lunar ship and a rocket block would link up in Earth orbit and set out for the Moon. The complex would go into lunar orbit, whence the lunar cabin would descend to the surface. After the period of exploration it would take off and link up with the command ship still orbiting above. The latter would then blast out of Moon orbit and head home. The model had two advantages: it needed less powerful boosters; and it could be aborted at an early stage before leaving the relative safety of Earth orbit. On the other hand, rendezvous had never been tried before, either in Earth orbit, or more significantly, in lunar orbit a quarter of a million miles away.

The third method, a variation on this, was lunar orbit rendezvous (LOR). A much larger booster would place both command ship and lunar cabin direct in moon orbit, cutting out the Earth orbit stage. The rest of the mission then proceeded like the Earth orbit rendezvous method. It was a simpler method, but depended on a big and reliable booster, though nothing as big as needed for direct ascent.

Korolov opted for the second method: Earth orbit rendezvous. It was based on a design called the Soyuz Orbital Complex, the design of which only reached the West in June 1983 when a book was released in Moscow called *The creative legacy of Sergei Korolov*. It was edited by Mstislav Keldysh. It went out of print within hours and one reason was that it included the design of the Russian moonlanding plans. Whether these designs were supposed to be released (it could have been an accident) is not known, but space-watchers realized their significance within minutes. Only 600 copies were printed [4].

The design of the Soyuz complex was completed late in 1961 and shown to the cosmonaut squad early in 1962. The Soyuz complex consisted of three components:

(1)   A rocket block, which was launched 'dry' (not fuelled up) and which was the largest single unit. It contained automatic rendezvous and docking equipment and was labelled the 'Soyuz B' by Korolov.
(2)   A space tanker, containing liquid fuel, called the Soyuz V.
(3)   A new manned spacecraft, called the Soyuz A.

The Korolov blueprints which found their way to the West show only how the Soyuz complex could have been used for a round-the-Moon flight, not a Moon landing itself, so we must speculate a little about the details of the latter mission.

The Soyuz complex was a more imaginative and complicated design than anything ever proposed before or since, and was eminently feasible. The word 'Soyuz' in Russian means 'union' and central to the design was the idea of joining together a number of spacecraft in earth orbit. Although the three units were all given the Soyuz title (A, B and V, the first three letters in the Russian alphabet), the three spacecraft were entirely different from each other. Only Soyuz A was ultimately known to the West and it became the principal Soviet manned spacecraft for 20 years.

Soyuz A
Soyuz A was a new generation spaceship, 7.7 m long, 2.3 m diameter, and with a mass of 5800 kg. The design was radical, to say the least. At the bottom was an equipment section with fuel, radar and rocket motor. On top of this was a cone-shaped cabin for a three-man crew. Orthodox enough so far; but on top of that was a large cylinder-shaped orbital module. This provided extra cabin space (the cabin on its own would be cramped) and room for experiments and research.

The Soyuz A actually bore more than a superficial resemblance to a moonship designed by the General Electric Company in the United States in 1960. NASA was at the time tendering for a design for its own moonship, and General Electric's tender was one of 14. Its design was for a three-module craft of 7400 kg, with what General Electric called a propulsion module, a reentry module and a mission module. These corresponded exactly to the three sections of Soyuz A. So did the Russians steal the American Moon plans? Not quite. Korolov would have had access to these designs, which were public. It is possible he saw them and was inspired by them. It could have been a coincidence, but the resemblance between the two designs is uncanny.

NASA rated the General Electric design high on human factors, but low on escape methods, instrumentation and communications, and chose another instead.

Soyuz B
Soyuz B, or the rocket block, was a strange part of the jigsaw. It was the main booster rocket that would take the Soyuz complex out of Earth orbit and put it en route for the Moon. It was to be launched with tanks empty, but with enough fuel of its own to manoeuvre for orbital rendezvous. It was 5700 kg on entry to Earth orbit, including 1490 kg fuel of its own, and had a capacity of 2400 kg more. It was 7.8 m long.

Soyuz V
This was the tanker and it would carry little but fuel. Its own mass was 1455 kg but it would carry 4155 kg fuel to be transferred to the rocket block. Three tanker loads were

needed to fill up the rocket block with enough fuel for a lunar journey. The total fuel of three Soyuz Vs, just over 12 tonnes, would give a speed of 3061 m/s. It is no coincidence that when Apollo 11 burned out of Earth orbit for the Moon in July 1969 its thrust was 3039 m/s.

The planned sequence of events for a Moon flight was as follows. On day one, the rocket block would be launched into an orbit of 226 km, 65 degrees. It would be tested out to see that its guidance and manoeuvering units were functioning. On day two, the first of three tankers would be launched. Because the fuel was volatile it would have to be transferred quickly. The rocket block would be the 'active' spacecraft and would carry out the rendezvous and docking manoeuvres normally on the first orbit. Fuel would then be transferred in pipes from the tanker to the rocket block. After three tanker linkups, a Soyuz A manned spaceship would be launched. It would be met by the rocket block, which, using its newly transferred fuel, would then blast moonwards.

One of the attractive features of the Soyuz complex design was that it used the existing A booster. No new rocket would be required. Admittedly it would take five such launchers to send one Soyuz complex moonbound, but there was nothing impossible about it. The major obstacles to be overcome were orbital rendezvous and in-flight refuelling, but even the Vostok programme could do some work on the former. But assuming all went well, and a first Soyuz flight took place in 1964 or so, a manned flight around the Moon might be only a year and a half further on.

For a landing mission, a lunar lander would be needed, and correspondingly more fuel to get out of Earth orbit. But if the Soyuz complex worked, where was the problem? Add a lunar module and two more tanker missions to the rocket block, and it was done. And was not this how Tsiolkovsky said it would be done?

THE TESTS THAT WERE NEEDED

Accordingly, work began at once on the whole question of manned rendezvous and docking, long before the Soyuz A was to be ready. A tracking fleet was needed to keep in contact with the spaceships when they were outside the radio range of the USSR, which they would be during much of a lunar mission, and shipyards were ordered to build three large tracking ships. Spacesuits too would have to be tested, but that would have to wait until Soyuz itself entered service.

It was Korolov's intention to bring all these elements together sometime around 1965. By then, the Luna probes would have soft-landed and circled the Moon. Come 1966, a man-around-the-Moon flight could be made, with a landing to follow in 1970 once the lunar hardware had been tested. Korolov nearly pulled it off, and if Khrushchev had not interfered, he probably would have.

The obvious follow-on to Gherman Titov's flight was simply a longer mission — perhaps three days. Sergei Korolov, however, thought ahead just one stage further. Since orbital rendezvous — and first orbit rendezvous indeed — was so critical to the Soyuz complex, could not some early work be done on this problem? Even though Vostok was not manoeuvreable, could they not test launching accuracy by launching one Vostok into close orbit with another, seeing how close they could come?

Thus was conceived a daring and frightening plan. Daring, because when even getting one man into orbit was cause enough for jubilation, two in orbit simultaneously would astonish the world. Frightening, because it would frighten the Americans into believing that the Russians had mastered the techniques of orbital rendezvous at a time when it was only slide-rule theory at Cape Canaveral.

Vostok 3 would be launched, to be followed by Vostok 4 one day later. The pilots in line were Grigori Nelyubov, Andrian Nikolayev and Pavel Popovich. Because it would take some time to prepare the mission, a launch date was set for August 1962, still some way off. Meanwhile, throughout the land, design institutes hummed as the Moon designs were honed from theory to hardware.

AMERICA'S ROUTE TO THE MOON

Even as the Korolov design bureau struggled to produce the design later known as the Soyuz complex, so too were America's engineers labouring to put out a plan with a similar purpose in mind. Owing to the relatively uncentralized nature of the American programme at the time of 1960–62, the American project emerged in a manner that would have struck both Korolov and Khrushchev as disorganized and haphazard.

First off the drawing board — and designed some time even before Kennedy's announcement — was the manned spacecraft. The Space Task Group at Langley, Virginia, came up with a prototype mooncraft as early as July 1960. The group was led by Maxime Faget, the designer of the Mercury capsule. They called it Apollo. It would carry three astronauts in shirtsleeve environment, would employ a powerful manoeuvring engine, and would have the ability to navigate independently of the ground in flights lasting up to ten days. Apollo would have the ability to fly in and out of lunar orbit, and would consist of a cone-shaped command module atop a service module which held the rocket engine and nozzle.

But which method would the Americans use? The von Braun team favoured Earth orbit rendezvous, but they were in a minority. Virtually everyone else favoured direct ascent using a massive rocket which in time came to be called Nova. This would be a giant rocket-to-end-all-rockets, with a thrust of 6 million kilograms and able to put up 180 tonnes. It would be 7 m higher than a football field was long. This leviathan would be in keeping with the nation that built the Empire State Building and the Hoover Dam. Suggestions that it could not or should not be done would be un-American.

Even though Nova was NASA's favourite throughout 1961, the von Braun team at Huntsville Alabama continued to sow doubts in peoples' minds. Instead, they put forward a booster called Super-Saturn. Two of these, each half the size of Nova, could do the same job using Earth orbit rendezvous. The Nova people replied by pointing out that Earth orbit rendezvous had never been tried before, that orbital refuelling was an unknown quantity and potentially dangerous, and the two Super-Saturns would have to be launched with enormous accuracy. Long countdown delays were the norm in 1961. Direct ascent was a no-nonsense, straight, it'll-get-us-there approach.

Yet, on closer examination, direct ascent could be seen to have its own drawbacks, quite apart from the size of Nova. The main one was: just how do you land on the Moon? The moonlander would have to be streamlined and pencil-shaped, by virtue of its position on the top of the Nova. So how do you land a pencil-shaped object on the moon, steering from the top? How do you look down from the top? Or could you land on the side? Or would it then turn over?

With both these proposals under fire, a third emerged. Lunar orbit rendezvous was the campaign of a Langley engineer called John Houbolt. He borrowed the idea from a paper from Yuri Kondratyuk of 1930. Houbolt's proposal was first made in December 1960.

LOR had two advantages: it cut out the Earth orbit rendezvous stage; and the thrust required to put two spacecraft in lunar orbit was actually not that much more proportionately than that needed for EOR. The lunar cabin could be entirely purpose-built, since it did not need to return to Earth through a reentry; and any problems about viewing the landing site could be forgotten.

All three methods were in the melting pot at NASA during the springtime of 1962, with EOR a firm favourite, having ousted direct ascent. NASA chiefs then asked the questions:

Which was the most likely to succeed?

Which was the safest?

Which was soonest?

Direct ascent failed all three criteria, so it boiled down to a choice of EOR or LOR. What clinched it was that on 7 June 1962 von Braun changed his mind. He now backed LOR. It was simpler than EOR, as safe, and in his reckoning could be accomplished six months sooner. NASA announced on 11 July 1962 that LOR would be the method. Later that summer, President Kennedy toured all of NASA's growing empire and in October the contracts were set up.

Apollo would now compete with the Soyuz complex, LOR with EOR. Both countries had to build new rockets and hardware. Saturn V would compare with an uprated A-1, now called the A-2. Apollo and Soyuz had a similar function and performance. The lunar cabins were not that dissimilar either. The method of going there was in fact the chief distinguishing factor. For the Russians, EOR was the only outcome for a generation brought up on Tsiolkovsky. It was more logical, and it may have been marginally safer. It could also be tested out soonest, as the Americans were soon to find out to their cost.

THE SPACE TWINS

As 1962 came in, America still had not put a man into orbit. This was rectified when after months of exasperating delays John Glenn rocketed into orbit on 20 February. John Glenn seized the imagination of the American people. There was live minute-by-minute coverage from the scorching launch at Cape Canaveral to splashdown in the Atlantic five hours later. His reports by radio were heard sharp and crisp as he passed over the Indian Ocean. . . then Australia. . . then California. They heard John Glenn describe the sunrises, the sunsets, his old booster tumbling below; fireflies (small particles) outside the cabin; and the oceans and landmasses below.

Crisis struck on the third and last orbit when telemetry indicated that the heat shield had come loose. The whole nation prayed as he came through reentry and the shield stayed in place. John Glenn was welcomed home as a hero no less so than Gagarin or Titov in their countries. He was feted everywhere — there were ticker-tape parades, and schools were named after him. He came to embody all the best American virtues: military career, family man, smart-looking, gentle in his manner, a patriot. American honour was indeed restored.

NASA ran a repeat mission in May. Aurora 7 went aloft on the 24th, carrying Malcolm Scott Carpenter. His flight was at least as nerve-wracking as John Glenn's. By the third orbit he had run out of fuel — partly because some thrusters had been used inadvertently, partly because he had used excessive fuel and time in orbit getting pictures of the sunsets. He had to align Aurora 7 for reentry himself.

His tiny Mercury capsule was yawing 27° out of alignment by the time of retrofire. The rockets did not fire and by the time he pressed the button himself, four seconds later, Aurora 7 was way off course. He was not heard from again, and radio commentators concluded that he was lost. In sepulchral terms, they prepared the nation for the worst. Two hours after the estimated splashdown time, a rescue plane spotted Carpenter in a dinghy. He had come down 330 km off course and not far from Puerto Rico. But NASA's confidence, if anything, improved.

It was now a full year since Kennedy had laid down the great challenge.

THE IRON MAN

In the USSR the next Vostok pilots were entering the most intensive phase of training. The 'Iron Man', Andrian Nikolayev, took his place in Vostok 3 and Pavel Popovich was appointed to Vostok 4.

The upcoming double flight was the best-kept secret the Russians ever had. Normally, leaks about new missions reach the West beforehand, and on some occasions the names of the crew get out. But on this double flight, not a hint escaped. 4 August was the last night the cosmonauts had in Moscow before the flight. Andrian Nikolayev held a party in his spacious bachelor apartment accompanied by fruit and wine. In the same building Pavel Popovich celebrated with Marina and daughter Natasha. At 11 p.m. the party was over. A final planning session was held in Star Town, and the next morning the space squad and their backups took an Ilyushin 18 propeller plane for the lengthy journey across Russia down to Kazakhstan.

On 6 August Gherman Titov held a celebration to mark his own flight a year earlier. Sergei Korolov came as well. His eyes were bloodshot: the strain of preparing the new flight and designing the Soyuz complex had taken their toll.

Vostok 3 headed off at 11.30 a.m., 11 August, a Saturday. In eight minutes Andrian Nikolayev was in orbit, silent and free, and settled down for a marathon four-day journey, quadrupling the existing day-long record. His orbit was 183 by 251 km.

Nikolayev, known as the 'Iron Man' on account of his extraordinary fortitude in the isolation chamber, became the first man to float free in his cabin out of the restraining straps. An encouraging sign was that when he tried to go to sleep some orbits later he felt none of the nausea that had afflicted Gherman Titov.

'Long trip likely by Soviet spaceman' was a typical Western press headline [5]. Andrian Nikolayev was expected to fly several days. A number of radio stations on the ground in the West picked up his voice as he reported back. Moscow television showed him smiling and waving and spinning his log book and pencil around the cabin. The best-known of the tracking stations was the huge 80 m dish operated by Sir Bernard Lovell from Jodrell Bank in Cheshire in England. He had become something of an expert on 'what the Russians were up to'. Any reporter wanting to get a line on the latest Vostok or Luna probe put a call through to Jodrell Bank.

At 11.30 p.m. on Sunday morning, 12 August he heard his radio technicians were tuning in to pick up Vostok 3 as it flew overhead. He got the shock of his life. Instead of picking up the sole voice of Andrian Nikolayev talking calmly to ground control, he got the bubbling voice of an excited new cosmonaut reporting from Vostok 4. Two cosmonauts were now circling the Earth!

As Vostok 3 passed over Baikonour on its 16th orbit it was most precisely tracked by ground radar. Vostok 4 counted down amazingly smoothly and without a hitch. Right down to liftoff, new data was fed into Vostok's computer, giving exact altitude, azimuth and orbital inclination.

And accurate it was! As Pavel Popovich soared into orbit aboard Vostok 4 his entry point in orbit closed to a mere 6500 m from Vostok 3. It was a moment of triumph. Just a year and a half after Gagarin, the USSR had two cosmonauts flying in orbit within sight of each other, or, put mathematically, a mere 1/2000th of an orbital radius. Andrian Nikolayev, alone for the previous day, could see Vostok 4 gleaming in the sunlight through the porthole as it rose to meet him. The two of them and Yuri Gagarin, the capsule communicator, were wild with delight.

Vostok 4's orbit measured 180 by 254 km. Lacking a manoeuvring engine, the two cosmonauts drifted gradually apart, but retained continuous radio contact. Pavel Popovich was an enthusiastic flyer and kept up endless chatter with the ground. As he swept across the Pacific Ocean, he recorded:

> The spacecraft is flying at an incredible speed so the view keeps changing. Now I can see a starry sky through the right view port. It is inky black. The big bright stars are visible as from Earth but they don't twinkle. The little ones look like bright pin points.
>
> The space craft is coming out of shadow. What a view! A person on Earth will never see anything like it. This is the cosmic dawn. Just look! The Earth's horizon is a vivid wine colour. Then a dark blue band appears. Next comes a bright blue band, shading off into the blue sky. It keeps widening, glowing, spreading out, and the Sun appears. The horizon turns orange and a more delicate lighter blue. Beautiful! [6]

The launching of Vostok 4 threw the West into frenzy. For sheer nerve, daring and imagination, the double flight was overwhelming. The significance of the close approach on the first orbit was lost on no one. The Press Association science correspondent, in a wire dispatch that was used throughout the world, was one of many to be entranced in a report that appeared in many newspapers on the morning of 13 August, 1962. Although he was far from accurate in his assessment of what Vostok could actually do, the same could not be said for his assessment of the implications of the close flight. One would almost think he had seen the design of the Soyuz complex:

> At about 8.30 a.m. this morning the Russians may decide to make an attempt to send the two cosmonauts now in space on a flight to the moon in one of two spaceships describing almost identical orbits around the Earth.

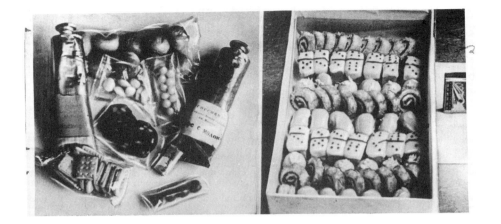

Examples of the food that Vostok 3 and 4 cosmonauts Nikolayev and Popovich ate in outer space. A handful of small bread pieces eaten by cosmonauts; available to suit any taste.

They are travelling at 18 000 mph only a few miles apart. When the two astronauts are near their control base, an attempt may be made to bring them together. This would be the most critical time in the history of space exploration. [7]

Sir Bernard Lovell, elder statesman of the Soviet space watchers, volunteered that the flight was 'the most remarkable development man has ever seen'. President Kennedy, holidaying in Boot Harbour, Maine, was reported to be 'severely jolted'. Nikita Khrushchev was of course having a ball and spoke repeatedly to the men by phone.

Once the first shock had passed, there was little to do but watch as the flight went into a third and then a fourth and finally a fifth day, with no signs of any difficulty. The next American flight, it was pointed out contemptuously, was to be a long one of nine hours. No linkup was of course forthcoming – a first orbit approach was all that had been contemplated. By the 33rd orbit, the 'space twins' were 850 km apart and by the 64th, 2850 km.

Because of the length of the flight, a huge range of experiments could be conducted. Medical instruments kept a continuous watch on the cosmonauts' pulse, breathing, strain, sleep, eyes and nervous system. The two men tested how water bubbles formed in a flask in zero gravity. As they observed the Earth by night they could make out the lights of cities.

The marathon came to an end on Wednesday morning, 15 August. As if to flaunt their precision, the reentries were timed to take place together. Andrian Nikolayev came down by parachute at 9.52 a.m. after 64 orbits, Pavel Popovich at 9.57 a.m. after 48 orbits (four and three days respectively). The next Saturday, Moscow gave the two heroes the welcome they deserved.

For Korolov's design of the Soyuz complex, now maturing, the flights of Vostok 3 and 4 were immensely encouraging. The first orbit approach of 6.5 km was better than what had been hoped and took much of the fear out of the notion of orbital rendezvous. The length of the flight, the effortless precision of launch and landing, the reliability of Vostok – these things were icing on the cake. But by the time Vostok 5 left the ground, disappointments in the unmanned programme had been encountered.

VENUS MARS AND THE MOON

The promising start made by Venera 1 on its flight to Venus in early 1962 encouraged Soviet scientists to try a major assault on Venus in the late summer of 1962. The Venera 1 experience indicated that real discoveries could be made once problems with long-distance communication were sorted out. Three probes were built. None of them in fact ever even got away from Earth, still less to Venus. At this stage some major flaws in the escape stage of the new A-2e booster began to emerge, flaws which were to frustrate one deep space probe after another for a full two years.

What was to be the second probe to Venus took off on 25 August, 1962. The escape stage failed to restart and the probe decayed on 28 August. A second launching met the same fate on 1 September, decaying after five days. On 12 September, the third escape stage exploded into seven large pieces. All these launches were monitored by American radars in Turkey, although details were not released by the Pentagon until 1965 [8].

What was basically affecting the upper stage was the difficulty in igniting propellants in zero gravity. During the boost phase, propellants are forced by gravity into the pumps. Once in $0G$, these conditions no longer hold true, and propellants begin to behave in peculiar ways.

American space probes during the same period were not much more successful either. Of the three American space probes to the Moon in 1962, Ranger 3 missed the moon by 37 000 km and Ranger 5 by 700 km. Ranger 4 crashed on the far side, its radio dead. Of its Venus probes, Mariner 1 crashed into the South Atlantic Ocean, though Mariner 2 was more successful, flying by Venus in December 1962 and returning a stream of valuable data.

Similar problems plagued Soviet attempts to reach Mars in 1962. Again, three probes were prepared. The first launch was on 24 October. The probe broke up trying to struggle free of Earth's atmosphere. It broke into so many pieces that it nearly persuaded American radars that the United States was under missile attack. The Cuban missile crisis was then at its height. Another Mars probe on 4 November failed to leave orbit and decayed two months later. The only bright spot in the five out of six failure rate was when on 1 November the Mars 1 probe successfully got away. Within days it was clear that it was working well and on an accurate path to the Red Planet.

Mars 1 was much more sophisticated than its Venus predecessor. It weighed more, at 894 kg, and was larger: a cylinder 3.3 m long, with solar panels giving it a wing span of 4 m, and it had a huge umbrella-shaped high-gain antenna. It carried a midcourse correction engine, and thermal radiators. It was an ambitious experiment for its day, carrying, as well, television cameras, meteoroid detectors, and instruments for reporting on the atmosphere radiation fields and the surface of Mars. The information being collected was telemetred to Earth every five days.

At the time, Mars held out major hopes for astronomers and science fiction addicts, not to mention scientists themselves. Smaller than Earth but larger than the Moon, cooler because it was further away from the Sun, there were indications that it had an atmosphere. Its red colour was visible by telescope; the more discerning could make out polar caps and possible waves of vegetation. Perhaps there was life.

Mars 1 headed out into the raw cold of deep space. It picked up and measured the solar wind. Meteoroid matter declined the further it moved away from the Earth's orbit. Sometime in the new year the ground control centre in Yevpatoria adjusted its course so that it would pass 6000 km from Mars come 19 June 1963.

Sadly, it was not to be. On 21 March 1963, the orientation system broke down, and as a result the transmitters no longer pointed towards Earth. Maybe photographs were indeed taken as Mars 1 approached the planet in June but they were transmitted somewhere else. Mars 1 was 106 million kilometres away at the time of the breakdown, which was a new record for long-distance communication.

Observers, therefore, were nonetheless impressed. Despite America's triumph with Mariner 2 Mars 1 was seen to be more ambitious. They would have been less impressed, perhaps, if they had known of the five failures that lay behind Mars 1.

BACK TO THE MOON

That these problems were still not ironed out became obvious once more with the premature resumption of the Moon programme in early 1963. The objective of the three 1963 Moon probes was nothing less than a soft-landing of the Moon. A soft-landing was absolutely essential to landing cosmonauts on the Moon. Not until a probe soft-landed would it be possible to know the exact nature of the lunar soil, the dangers of rocks and craters, and the amount of radiation on the surface. These measurements were essential because they would determine, in the first two instances, the strength and size of the lunar module's landing legs.

The Moon probe designed to soft-land bore all the hallmarks of Korolov's design influence. There were two modules. The instrument compartment, cylinder-shaped, carried a combined manoeuvring engine and retrorocket, orientation devices, transmitters and fuel. The lander, in a sphere attached on the top, was quite small, only 100 kg. It was ball-shaped, and on landing would shoot out, and once it settled on the surface, a camera would peep up to take pictures. It followed very closely the popular image of what an alien probe landing on Earth would look like.

The final approach to landing would be the most difficult phase. The rocket on the 1500 kg vehicle had to fire at the correct angle about 46 seconds before the predicted landing. Too early, and it would run out of fuel before reaching the surface, pick up speed again, and crash to pieces. Too late, and it would impact too fast. Thanks to more problems with the upper stage, these issues were to remain academic throughout 1963.

The first Moon probe went up on 4 January, and the second on 2 February. The first failed to eject from Earth orbit, the second broke up and crashed into the Pacific near Midway Island. Again, these launches were not announced at the time [9].

Luna 4, launched on 2 April 1963, got off to a more promising start, and first reports indicated how satisfied the controllers were with the accuracy of the flight. Tass added:

Scientists have to clarify the physical conditons cosmonauts will meet, how they are to overcome landing difficulties and how they should prepare for a prolonged stay on the moon. The human epoch in the moon's history is beginning. There will be laboratories, sanatoria and observatories on the moon. [10]

This heady enthusiasm soon evaporated. On 4 April the USSR announced that Luna 4, of weight 1422 kg, would fly past the Moon at 9301 km. Contact was lost two days later as it entered solar orbit. The Russians claimed — quite unconvincingly — that a lunar flyby was all that had been intended. But they shut up about health resorts on the Moon for the time being.

Korolov ordered a complete redesign of the A-2e upper stage. Seven failures out of nine attempts was a rate of attrition no programme could sustain. An unmanned probe, Cosmos 21, was sent up in November 1963 to test the improved upper stage, but it may not have been successful.

SCHIRRA AND COOPER

America's Mercury project recovered its nerve after the near-disaster on the Carpenter flight and after the double shot of the Vostok 3 and 4 joint flight. The decision was made by NASA to double the existing flight time by a six-orbit mission. Cdr. Walter Schirra was put into space on 3 October 1962. His six-orbit flight went perfectly and he rode his Mercury capsule down into the Pacific Ocean right beside a waiting carrier.

On 15 May 1963 Major L. Gordon Cooper took the last Mercury capsule aloft on a day-and-a-half mission. It was much the most successful venture by NASA to date. He overcame one problem after another in his tiny capsule and flew it back through a hair-raising manual reentry after the automatic electrical system failed. The flight also entered the history books because of the extraordinary way in which it was possible to observe objects from orbit was first noticed. Cooper reported seeing planes, boats, trains, roads, cars and houses from orbit. No one believed him at first — indeed they began to be con-cerned for his sanity — until he flew with colleague Charles Conrad again two years later and Conrad vouched for him.

NASA at one stage considered firing aloft a seventh Mercury capsule late in 1963 for a three-day mission but decided otherwise. Mercury was officially closed in August 1963. The extra mission would have held things up for at least six months, achieve little more than what Gordon Cooper had done, and, as NASA was learning very fast, would have cost time. And times was what it was all about now.

NASA's Moon programme was now in full swing, even if it had not produced any hardware as yet. Originally Mercury was to lead to the three-man Apollo in 1965. But the large new ship could not possibly be ready by then. An intermediate spacecraft called Gemini was commissioned. Although similar in shape to Mercury, it was significantly different in concept and performance. Gemini would carry two men and would be fully manoeuvrable. Its task would be to test the vital technique of orbital rendezvous until NASA felt it could do it in its sleep. Gemini would test the techniques of Apollo before Apollo. It would fill a two-year gap. A new team of astronauts was recruited to fly Gemini in September 1962.

Despite these uncertain and pragmatic origins, Gemini was destined to be brilliantly successful. The first flight was set for late 1964. NASA chose veteran Virgil Grisson and novice John Young to fly the first Gemini and they began training at once.

SPACEWOMAN

Similar considerations probably inspired Sergei Korolov to wish to repeat the Vostok 3/4 flight in the summer of 1963. The Soyuz, like Apollo, would not be ready for manned tests until 1965 at the earliest. A repeat of the double flight would provide more experience of orbital rendezvous and extend the duration record to five days.

But then political considerations intervened. Khrushchev, it appears, had the brain-wave of putting a woman into the last Vostok. This decision had political overtones. Not only could the USSR demonstrate its technological superiority to the world, but also its social advantages. The USSR made much of its claims to female social equality at the time, and even more so after June 1963. There is some evidence to suggest that female participation rates in some professions — like science, engineering and medicine — were much higher in the USSR than in the USA at the same time, even if the role of the Russian woman in the home remained traditional. But Khrushchev had a point. What was unthinkable in America provoked a Soviet response of 'well, why not?'. And since Vostok required much less 'flying' than Mercury, it could easily be handled by someone other than a jet fighter ace. Not that Russia's spacewoman, Valentina Terreskhova as she became known to the world, was taken off the streets to fly into space: she was an aviator in her own right.

Five woman astronauts were selected on 16 February 1962 – Valentina Terreskhova, Irina Solovyeva, Valentina Ponomareva, Tatania Kuznetzova and Zhanna Yorkina. [11]

Valentina Terreskhova was a slim small girl with black hair and a quiet manner who came from the ancient Russian city of Yaroslavl. Her father had died fighting the Germans during the war and her youth was not easy. She left school and found work in a textile combine as a loom operator. There she might have spent her life had she not applied to join the local flying club. She took up parachuting as her speciality and made her first jump in May 1959 when she was 22. On one jump she came down in the Volga and almost drowned, but undeterred, she went on to make 126 jumps. If fearlessness and determination were qualities required for flying into orbit she had plenty of both.

At the time of Gagarin's flight, Valentina wrote to the Space Commission expressing her wish to fly in space – as did hundreds of other women and thousands of men. The letters were filed, and in the case of the women's applications, the files were reopened the following year. Valentina probably forgot all about her flush of space enthusiasm of April 1961 until she was called up for interview.

The male cosmonauts seem to have regarded the arrival of the five women with surprise and amusement. Yuri Gagarin found it necessary to warn his male colleagues against teasing them. Terreskhova in particular was supervised by Yuri Gagarin and Andrian Nikolayev and she became very friendly with Nikolayev. This actually served as a useful cover, for otherwise the appearance of women in Star Town would filter out to the West and the plan would be blown. Instead, Valentina was explained away as Nikolayev's girlfriend, who was taking a close interest in his professional career.

Preparations for the new double flight went ahead, and in May 1963 the State Commission confirmed the appointment of Valeri Bykovsky as Vostok 5 commander and Valentina Terreskhova as pilot for Vostok 6. Her flight was to last just one day.

The June heat was soaking the summer cosmodrome when on 14 June 1963, Valeri Bykovsky soared into space. His orbit measured 179 by 234 km, 65°, 88.4 min. His mission got off to a low-key start and observers expected a flight running to about a week.

Soon, however, rumours began to leak out of the impending flight of a woman cosmonaut [12]. No attempt was made to refute them and it might not have mattered had Vostok 6 taken off on schedule the following day. But technical problems forced a hold, and the second mission was put off for 24 hours.

In the meantime, viewers had to concentrate on Valeri Bykovsky. TV pictures showed him passing floating objects around the cabin and writing the log. Tass regaled listeners with details of his diet: sausage pie, roast beef, and chicken filet. From orbit, Bykovsky reported seeing rivers, lakes and seas. Roads and towns were visible and their lights stood out clearly by night.

Whatever had been rumoured about the launch planned for 15 June, what happened the next day left no one in any doubt. Soon after midday, Vostok 6 soared aloft carrying white-helmeted, orange-suited Valentina Terreskhova. The USSR exulted. Excitement in the cities reached a peak unknown since the flight of Yuri Gagarin. The Russians made no effort to conceal their glee, and the effect of a female cosmonaut was felt in the West even by those who would find difficulty in appreciating the technical significance of

Colonel Valeri Bykovsky first flew as the pilot of Vostok 5 in June 1963. He was due to be commander of the cancelled Soyuz 2 mission but later flew as commander of Soyuz 22 and Soyuz 31.

particular scientific achievements or aspects of orbital rendezvous. Telecasts were made from orbit showing a smiling, cheerful Valentina in obvious good health and in full control of her situation.

Vostok 6 entered orbit within sight of Valeri Bykovsky — a mere 5000 m away — an achievement of even greater accuracy than with Nikolayev and Popovich the previous year. They quickly established good shortwave radio communication with each other, though they soon began to drift apart. Vostok 6's orbit was 182 by 232 km, 88.3 min. Valentina Terreskhova was originally scheduled to land on orbit 17. What may have influenced the designers to keep her up longer was the fact that on the first day she overslept so long that ground control began to wonder if she was still alive. If she was able to sleep that well, so the thinking went, she would be well able to stay up there.

The rest of the flight was, after the early excitement, a comparative anticlimax. By 18 June, Terreskhova had flown in space for longer than all of America's astronauts put together. The two cosmonauts continued their observations of the Earth and the stars.

The order to land came on the 19th. The simultaneous reentry of the last flight was not repeated — Valentina Terreskhova came down at 11.20 a.m. and Valeri Bykovsky at 2.06 p.m. He had been up for a record five days and 81 orbits and she for three days, 48 orbits. She herself came down by the method she knew best — parachute. Her landing provided a contrast of the old and the new. She came down on barren steppe on the site of the old caravan routes to the East. She was spotted coming down by herdsmen on horseback minding their sheep. They galloped to her spaceship and peered in to gasp at the modern creation. She was welcomed as a hero and given the traditional meal of

Valentina Vladimirovna Terreshkova rose from being a cotton mill worker and amateur parachutist to become the first woman cosmonaut in June 1963 aboard Vostok 6. She later married fellow-cosmonaut Andrian Nikolayev amid much publicity, and the couple had two children before their marriage ended in divorce.

cheese, flatcakes and fermented mares' milk. She was still devouring it when the rescuing helicopters arrived.

Valentina Terreskhova and Valeri Bykovsky got a festive reception in Moscow the following Saturday. On 3 November 1963, she and Andrian Nikolayev were married. It was the romantic conclusion to the double flight and the nearest the Russians ever came to Hollywood. Valeri Bykovsky and Yuri Gagarin were the witnesses. There were endless toasts. The celebrations went on all night. Nikita Khrushchev was in his element and sang repeatedly. Russia had a leading role in space, he said, and the capitalist countries would never catch up.

Khrushchev allowed a rare concession at the wedding. Cosmonauts awaiting their first flight, and the Chief Designer, were permitted to appear in public. Photographs taken at the ceremonies reveal both Korolov and Valentin Glushko. It was a rare and happy privilege for them.

The Nikolayev–Terreskhova marriage was, so far as could be seen, not so enduring, although a baby was born in June 1964. Valentina took the name of 'Nikolayeva-Terreskhova' but the former part was used less and less in the 1970s and eventually disappeared altogether. The two were rarely seen together after the first two years [13]. It is probably not fair to suggest, as some people have, that their marriage was ordered by Khrushchev. No evidence supports this, and the Soviet separation and divorce rate is a high one. Valentina Terreskhova went on to a political career in womens' and peace organizations and by 1983 reached Government rank during the brief Andropov era. She made many visits abroad but was considered a lacklustre and humourless performer. She remained the only spacewoman for 19 years.

The six Vostok cosmonauts are pictured here together (left to right) Gherman Titov, Yuri Gagarin, Valentina Terreshkova, Valeri Bykovsky, Andrian Nikolayev and Pavel Popovich.

KHRUSHCHEV'S INTERVENTION — AUTUMN 1963

By this stage both the Vostok and Mercury programmes had reached the end of their useful lives. In fact, they terminated only a month apart. The Soviet programme was faced with a gap of at least two years, perhaps three, before the new Soyuz was ready. During this time the Americans would be able to move ahead with Gemini, due as it was to start in late 1964. It seems that Khrushchev could not bear the thought of this and ordered a programme together to frustrate such an eventuality. The autumn of 1963 also saw some other strange happenings in the Soviet space world as the man-on-the-Moon debate spilled out into the open, but that was later [14].

To what extent Korolov accepted, condoned or approved Khrushchev's intervention one can only speculate. The Mars disaster of 1960 can only have made him hostile. But Khrushchev either had a short memory or was unable to learn from mistakes, for he ordered a special programme whose sole purpose was to beat America's Gemini to each of the four areas where Gemini was likely to score an advantage: multimanned flight, spacewalk, duration flight, and orbital locking.

Korolov may have conceded the undesirability of a two-year gap and may even have seen advantages in an interim set of missions. But he also saw that by trying to beat Gemini, his own outstanding Soyuz design would be held up — and it could eclipse Gemini in a single mission. It would put back the first Moon flight. There would be unacceptable risks too, for the only way that Khrushchev's demands could be met would be by modifying Vostok — ripping out the ejector seat to provide the extra space for the larger crew. This meant doing without an escape method during launch and landing.

Korolov put forward a compromise: the idea of a seven-day mission by a doctor on a solo Vostok 7. A young Moscow doctor, Boris Yegorov, was nominated. This would achieve a long flight, take a minimum of risks, and impose the least delay. But Khrushchev was adamant.

So the dust was taken off some designs Korolov had prepared when putting together the Soyuz complex plan [15]. The designs were for an uprated, manoeuvrable Vostok able to rendezvous with a series of payload modules and rocket modules. The revised Vostok was a four-mission programme: a multimanned flight, a spacewalk, a duration flight, and a docking. It would be called Voskhod, or Sunrise. It would beat Gemini point by point over 1964–65.

It was a foolish intervention by Khrushchev. The abandonment of safety considerations was due to him alone, and the time lost may have cost the Russians the Moon race.

POLYOT – NOVEMBER 1963

Despite this, work proceeded apace with the Soyuz complex. One of its essential components was the manoeuvrable rocket block, Soyuz B. This was the unit which would go up first, dock with the tanker craft, take on fuel, and await the manned Soyuz A for the lunar flight. As it was unmanned, an early test was possible [16].

Two such tests took place. At the time, little was said about them, and Soviet histories since 1969 have virtually omitted them altogether. Little wonder, for they form part of a programme best forgotten. They received a separate designation — Polyot, meaning 'flight' — and they are the only non-Cosmos design whose configuration has never been published.

The data released about Polyot 1 (1 November 1963) and Polyot 2 (12 April 1964) was minimal. The launch statement simply said that Polyot was highly manoeuvrable and performed several changes in flight path soon after reaching altitude. These were as follows:

Name	Period	Initial orbit			Period	Final orbit		
		Perigee	Apogee	Incl.		Perigee	Apogee	Incl.
Polyot 1	94.0	339	592	59.92	102.46	343	1437	58.92
Polyot 2	91.86	242	485	59.92	92.31	303	479	58.06

In addition, Polyot 2 used its manoeuvring engine to get into orbit in the first place.

These manoeuvres demonstrated — in those days — a formidable amount of rocket power, accuracy and manoeuvrability. Polyot 1 demonstrated a thrust that had been estimated at 383 m/s (Polyot 1) and 480 m/s (Polyot 2), based on a dry mass of 1950 kg, and such figures can be calculated from the data about the orbit changes. We now know that the mass of Soyuz B was to be 1800 kg and the extra 150 kg can be accounted for by the need to take on board additional instrumentation to monitor the rocket's behaviour.

About 1000 kg of fuel was carried by each Polyot – enough to give a thorough test of the Soyuz B system. By all accounts these secretive Polyot manoeuvres were highly successful. But even as they were flying, the Soviet space programme was convulsed by a crisis that went much deeper than Khrushchev's problem of how to beat Gemini. And, uncharacteristically, the crisis split the West.

THE DAY THE RUSSIANS PULLED OUT OF THE MOON RACE – OR DID THEY? (AUTUMN 1963)

In the summer of 1963 Professor Sir Bernard Lovell of Jodrell Bank spent three weeks in the USSR. He toured radio and optical telescopes and spoke to senior academicians in Moscow and Leningrad – a privilege available to few Westerners at the time. On his return he dropped a bombshell:

> A few weeks ago I was under the impression that the landing of a human being on the moon was the centrepiece of the Soviet space programme. But this is not the case. They have withdrawn from the moon race... because they found it too costly to protect a man from solar radiation and there may be no solution to getting a man back safely. Instead they will soft-land automatic probes on the moon and launch a large optical telescope within five years. The telescope will be 1 m in diameter and weigh several tonnes and the platform would be crewed by an engineer and an astronomer who could orbit for five or six days at a time. [17]

However his remarks were swiftly repudiated by one of the people he had met earlier – Mstislav Keldysh, President of the Academy of Sciences. On Radio Prague he said: 'If Lovell thinks this, he came to the conclusion by himself' [18]. By September, Sir Bernard Lovell had swallowed his words. In Washington he affirmed, complaining that he had been misquoted: 'I have every reason to believe that the Russians are trying to get to the moon every bit as fast as the Americans' [19].

One thing that would have made life awkward for NASA at the time was a Soviet withdrawal from the Moon race. While at first sight it would appear to give them, the Americans, a clear run to their target, it would also take away the principal reason for the race in the first place. NASA's funding was based on this competition with a mighty rival and it might well freeze up if the race appeared no longer to exist.

Perhaps it was all a big misunderstanding. At the September 1963 conference of the International Astronautical Federation in Paris, Yuri Gagarin told the assembled delegates:

> A flight to the moon requires a space vehicle of tens of tonnes and it is no secret that such large rockets are not yet available.
>
> One technique is the assembly of parts of spaceships in near-Earth orbit. Once in orbit the components could be collected together, joined up, and supplied with propellant. The flight could then begin. [20]

It was clear from these remarks that the Moon race was on and that Earth orbit rendezvous was the USSR's chosen method of getting there.

Then the whole issue blew up again in new form. On 26 October no less a person than Nikita Khrushchev formally announced Russia's withdrawal from the Moon race:

The Soviet Union is not at present planning flights of cosmonauts to the moon. Soviet scientists are studying it as a scientific problem.

The Americans want to land a man on the moon by 1970. We wish them luck and we will watch to see how they fly there and how they will return. I wish them success. Competition would not bring any good but might to the contrary cause harm because it might lead to the death of people. [21]

There was some surprise at Khrushchev's remarks and quite a lot of scepticism. NASA neither believed him nor wanted to believe him and claimed their intelligence showed the USSR had a big new booster on the way. 'Russia delaying American flight to the Moon?' was a typical Western newspaper headline. Khrushchev was not trusted and there was immediate suspicion that he was undermining the American effort by appealing to public opinion by casting doubts on the project.

Khrushchev's remarks were not reported in the domestic Soviet press (neither were Sir Bernard Lovell's), which may be significant. There the matter rested. Kennedy was dead three weeks later and his successor, Lyndon B. Johnson, never entertained any doubts about America's role in space and the desirability about getting there as fast as possible One of the first things Johnson did was to move all future spaceflight training planning and mission control to Houston in his own home state of Texas – a full 3000 km from the launch site in Cape Canaveral.

So where does that leave the peculiar happenings of the autumn of 1963? At first sight, Lovell appears to have made a mistake and Khrushchev was being his usual devious political self. But was there more to it than that? Did the Russians think seriously of pulling out of the Moon race in 1963 and were kites being flown? Did Lovell become embroiled in an internal battle between the anti-Moon members of the Academy of Sciences and the pro-Moon faction?

When asked about the controversy years later, Sir Bernard Lovell did feel that the period had been the occasion of such a battle:

I am sure there was an acute division of opinion about the relative importance to be attached to space-based research and earth-based science. In the space programme emphasis would be placed on the space platform concept and a man would be sent to the moon when his safe return could be guaranteed. The time scale for the USSR was much longer than the USA and depended on the operation of a space platform in the first instance.

These circumstances no doubt gave a great impetus to the faction who maintained that the scientific results could be achieved by unmanned flights to the moon.

Of course a similar divergence of opinion occurred in the USA but the manned faction won in this case.

I do not think there was a conscious decision to withdraw from the moon race in the early 1960s. [22]

So what did happen? All we have on the record is the Lovell visit and the Khrushchev speech. We have good reasons to project the intervention of the Voskhod missions and we can see how that was holding up the oncoming Soyuz programme. Was that all? It seems unlikely. The Soyuz B design finished its lifetime with Polyot 2 in April 1964 and never flew again. The Soyuz V never flew, although it must have been ready for its first mission around this time. And Soyuz A, whose orbital module was to be altered significantly compared to the published 1961 design, did not emerge till 1966–67. Clearly, there was a change of course during this period. Some fairly devastating decisions must have been taken that effectively scuppered Korolov's old Soyuz complex design and the evidence suggests this happened around 1963–64.

We can now try to piece the jigsaw together. 1965 saw the emergence of a large new booster, the D booster or Proton. It was capable of putting at least 12 tonnes into Earth orbit — or sending 4 or 5 tonnes to the Moon. More important still, the concept originated in a rival design institute, the Chalomei Institute [23]. The Proton booster had never been part of Korolov's original plan for going to the Moon, yet suddenly in 1965, it was. Only one conclusion is possible: that in this period the Russians abruptly changed their approach to going to the Moon. This intervention — perhaps by Khrushchev again and competing design institutes — was even more serious in its repercussions than the Voskhod programme.

Of the old Soyuz complex design of 1961, the Soyuz B and V were scrapped. Soyuz A alone survived. It would now be developed in three versions:

(1) An earth-orbiting engineering model, 6500 kg, with three men, close to the old Soyuz A design (this subsequently flew as Soyuz 1 to 11).
(2) A lunar flyby spacecraft, 5300 kg, without the orbital module, able to fly one man around the moon (this subsequently flew as Zond 4 to 8).
(3) A three-man uprated Soyuz, called Heavy Zond, 10 500 kg, designed to have a central place in the lunar landing (this flew eventually as Cosmos 379).

These changes meant that the methods Korolov had designed for the lunar flight were abandoned and the Soyuz B tests went to waste. The man-around-the-Moon would be achieved by a Zond on the new Proton booster. It was a simpler cruder method, with a direct flight there and back, and no rendezvous was involved. Although a man-around-the-Moon flight would now be achieved sooner than expected as a result, there was no equivalent short-cut for the landing project. For this, yet another booster would be needed. This new rocket would have to be the largest ever built and in the Saturn V class. Called the G booster, it would be a true behemoth, 94 m tall and with a thrust of 5.4 million kilograms [24].

The G booster would be able to put a fantastic 140 tonnes into orbit — rocket booster and lunar module together. On day 2 of the Moon-landing mission a Proton would launch a Heavy Zond with three men aboard. They would then rendezvous with the rocket and lunar module in Earth orbit using its thrust. It was Earth orbit rendezvous as before, but the pattern, the structures and the hardware had changed out of all recognition from the 1961 plan. One can only imagine how Korolov felt.

These changes committed the USSR to developing a new range of hardware not envisaged when the Soyuz complex began. The Soyuz complex had originally put the

USSR a full year ahead of Apollo but by going back to the drawing board again in 1963–64 the USSR put itself back behind. The redesigned Moon programme may have had positive features and may have been more sensible if there had been time to play around with – but there was not.

Two other types of hardware should also be mentioned. First, the lunar module. Although it was not to fly until 1970 (as Cosmos 382), detailed design study must have begun during this period. Second, an unmanned series of automatic Moon probes was also ordered. Three types were planned – an orbiter, a roving vehicle and a Moon scooper – all to fly on the new Proton booster. They were approved for a number of reasons. First, to prepare the way for manned landings. Second, as a concession to those who argued for unmanned exploration should manned flights turn out to be too expensive. And the most unsaid reason, in case the manned programme failed and a credible alternative programme had to appear in its stead.

These developments were perhaps the real significance of the Lovell and Khrushchev controversies. The Russians probably never came close to pulling out of the Moon race. But there was a very real debate going on inside the Government and Academy of Sciences as to how to get to the Moon, with the original plans being put under very strong pressure from the advocates of unmanned flights, the advocates of different time scales, and the advocates of different methods of getting there.

And the critics won. Korolov's plan was altered in mid-stream. Soyuz B and V were dropped. The Proton booster, with its deceptive promise of an early direct around-the-Moon flight, Zond, Heavy Zond and the monstrous G project were added. An unmanned contingency programme was added too.

Much time was lost.

5

The race to the Moon:
the target draws near (1964–66)

Despite the upcoming plans for new manned flights and new lunar flights in 1964–65, the USSR's planetary programme continued apace. There was a determination to reverse the earlier humiliations. Free from the need to put together planetary missions at very short notice, as he had been in 1960, Korolov was able to put the planetary exploration programme on a systematic basis. No fewer than six separate planetary designs are to be found dated 1964 in Mstislav Keldysh's book *The creative legacy of Sergei Korolov*. These designs formed the basis for the Mars and Venus probes of the years from 1964.

Korolov designed three subsets to his Venus and Mars designs. For each, he designed two heavier probes (Mars A, Mars B, Venera A, Venera B): one was a lander and the other was a photoreconnaissance flyby mission. He also designed a smaller subset with an entirely new designation, Zond, or 'probe' or 'sounder'. Quite what Korolov had in mind with the 'Zond' title no one knows, because over the next number of years the Russians were to use the 'Zond' title to cover Venus probes, Mars probes, Moon-to-Mars probes, engineering tests, and their man-around-the-Moon programme. The designation caused untold confusion. Probably Korolov had in mind an engineering development spacecraft that would also be used for interplanetary flights.

The spacecraft designs of 1964 were as follows, and the figures are quoted from *The creative legacy*:

	Venus			Mars		
Designation	Venera A	Venera B	Zond A	Mars A	Mars B	Zond B
Purpose	Lander	Flyby	Flyby	Lander	Flyby	Flyby
Mass (kg)	948	935	800	1042	1037	996
Impulse (kg/s)	10 600	10 600	800	NA	NA	NA
Example	Venera 3, 4,5,6,7,8	Venera 2	Zond 1	Zond 2, 3		

Despite this elaborate planning, the outcome was disappointing. The first probe of the 1964 window to Venus was launched on 27 March 1964, but failed to leave Earth orbit and was named Cosmos 27. More successful was the second attempt on 2 April. It was the first probe to carry the Zond designation and was described by the Russians as a 'deep space engineering test'. Zond 1, at 825 kg, was very much a Venus mission, though the Russians persisted merely in describing its positions in the sky, without mentioning the word Venus. It successfully altered its course twice, once at 563 780 km, and then again later. Its purpose was to take photographs of Venus, and it managed to place itself onto an encounter course of 99 780 km for 19 July 1964. But the radio was long since dead by that date.

Two probes were also prepared for the next Mars window, which opened in November 1964. Only one was launched, and it was a very low-key affair. The reasons for this became apparent when the Russians admitted that the probe had lost one of its solar panels. As a result, it had to manage on only 50 per cent of its expected power supply. After a mid-course correction, its signals failed.

Zond 2 (in reality the design belonged to the Mars A category on Korolov's table) weighed in at 1145 kg and was a sophisticated probe. It carried a descent craft and was remarkable as the first craft actually designed to land on another planet, presumably using large parachutes. This was long before the Americans had even thought of planning landing missions.

Western observers noted Zond 2's phenomenally accurate course to the Red Planet, and put it down to good tracking and navigation devices. Zond 2 shot past Mars on 6 August 1965 at a mere 1500 km. But had its radio worked it could have headed straight into the planet's atmosphere and might even have landed its descent craft, thereby achieving an astonishing and early breakthough.

Zond 2 was also worth remarking on insofar as it tested low-thrust ion plasma engines [1]. Six such thrusters were carried and they were fired during the period 8–18 December. But the admitted loss of the solar panel caused the launching of an accompanying craft, Zond 3, to be postponed to iron out the problems that had caused the panel loss. Zond 3 was launched the following summer, with Moon photography an added objective.

Perhaps encouraged by this, three probes were once more prepared for Venus in 1965. The last of the series failed to get through on 23 November and became known as Cosmos 96. Of the two that did, one was a flyby probe, Venera 2, and the other represented an adventurous new departure and was a lander. Venera 2, 963 kg, of 12 November, was not that dissimilar to Mars 1 and it carried similar equipment. An accurate launch put it on flyby course of 24 000 km with an arrival due in February 1966. A television system was set up to broadcast the flyby. To everyone's enormous frustration, communications failed at the moment of flyby. Nobody has ever known why, for everything had worked perfectly till then, including 26 communications sessions.

Venera 3 was to try something never before attempted: landing on the planet. Wasp-shaped with solar panels, umbrella antenna, cylinder and motor, one end held a bucket-shaped descent capsule, 90 cm across. It was to be released as Venera 3 approached Venus: parachutes would open and it would descend into the raging hot atmosphere.

Originally, Venera 3 would have missed Venus by 60 550 km, but in the first month after its 15 November launch no fewer than 13 300 measurements were taken of its course before a correction on 26 December. It was aimed dead centre at Venus.

Again, silence! Contact ceased abruptly as Venera 3 arrived. Nothing was heard, no signals received. Soviet scientists could only listen to the unceasing crackle of the space ether as their two probes fell into the mysterious void.

By 1 March 1966, when Venera 1 crashed into Venus — it was the first probe to reach another world — Russia had made 17 Mars and Venus shots and none had carried out their full and intended mission. The Americans had made four similar attempts, and two, Mariner 2 and 4, had been spectacular successes. Mariner 4 flew past Mars in July 1965 and sent back, laboriously slowly, 22 pictures. There were no canals, but craters galore.

Upper-stage failures were to plague the deep space programme right up to 1973 and long-range guidance failures were to wreck a four-strong Mars fleet two years later still. Long before this, the Americans had reached a launch record close to 100 per cent. By 1965 there was a serious reliability problem in Soviet technology which boded ill for more important ventures nearer to home.

SUNRISE

Reluctantly, perhaps, Korolov prepared the first of four 'beat-Gemini' Voskhod missions. The word Voskhod means 'sunrise'. Korolov's morale cannot have been too high. Voskhod was delaying his long-cherished Soyuz programme and he had just seen his Moon plans turned inside out by politicians and colleagues alike. With mixed feelings then an uprated A booster was prepared, enough to enable a payload of 5320 kg to be put into low Earth orbit.

There were several new design features. First, a spare retrorocket was fitted on the nose as a safety measure. A long Voskhod flight would need a high orbit, but it would be one which would not decay naturally before the air ran out. So a spare retrorocket would ensure that no one got stranded in orbit.

Second, the removal of the ejector seat of the Vostok meant that a crew of three, rather than two, could be carried. Since the pressurization system had, to date, proved very reliable, there was no reason for not going ahead with three men without suits. To upstage the two-man Gemini with a three-man Voskhod would add to the achievement.

Third, as Voskhod would need only one pilot, this allowed two of the crew to be scientists (or anything else for that matter) — again here there was potential for further advantage.

Finally, the lack of ejectors held consequences for the landing. A landing in seats would make for quite a jolt, even broken bones being a possibility. Accordingly a retrorocket was fitted to the base of the capsule below the (now detachable) heat shield to cushion the impact. It would fire 1½ seconds before the moment of touchdown.

The choice of a mission commander was not a hard one and it fell naturally to the most unflown backup — Vladimir Komarov. Born in 1927, he was older than the others — square-jawed, solid, firm and reliable. He had impressed all when, grounded after Popovich's flight owing to irregular heartbeat, he had toured all the leading heart specialists in Moscow collecting endorsements verifying that it would not impede a space flight. He was returned to flight status in 1963, just in time.

The two non-pilot spare seats meant the recruitment of the third group of cosmonauts — Feoktistov, Yegorov, Markarov, and Lazarev. Komarov's backup, also from the 1960 class, was Boris Volynov.

Konstantin Feoktistov was to play a fundamental role in spacecraft design in the post-Korolov era, eventually taking his place. Tall, white-haired, most distinguished-looking, he was and is quite unmistakeable. He can be seen in all the later Soyuz mission films at mission control, quietly supervising. He was to typify the blurring of distinctions between fliers, designers, theoreticians that is one of the programme's greatest strengths.

Konstantin Feoktistov, born in 1926 in Voronezh, was a child prodigy. He mastered maths and physics at the age of ten in order to learn Tsiolkovsky's formulae. A scout during the war, the Germans captured him, shot him in the head and left him for dead. He recovered, entered the Bauman Technical College in Moscow in 1943, and got a degree in engineering in 1949. He was a theoretical lecturer to the cosmonaut team in 1960. After his flight he wrote up his doctorate, and, never associated with the Moon programmed, reemerged to head up the space station programme in 1970.

Boris Yegorov was also intimately involved in the space programme. A youngish, short, slim, dark-haired doctor, he was one of the leading space doctors and had a key role examining cosmonauts both before and after their flight. How he secured this position we do not know, but his father was Moscow's leading brain surgeon. He had specialized in both aviation medicine and the inner ear (the location of the nausea problem), which could not have been more relevant. He had been put forward for a postulated Vostok 7 flight in 1963.

Training for the mission appears to have been minimal. Some reports say that only six months' training was given to both Feoktistov and Yegorov. The doctor was required to make eleven parachute jumps which, as an experienced engineer, he cannot have found too taxing. Strangely, for a person of his standing, he was to disappear from the programme after his flight and was rarely quoted or heard of again.

Oleg Markarov, a tall thin engineer not given to exuberance, was a more recent Bauman graduate (1957) who had been involved in spacecraft design ever since his graduation. He stood in for Feoktistov, left the group of four when it was disbanded, and was reselected for the 1966 cosmonaut group.

Vasily Lazarev, the last member of the team, was a square-faced, resourceful-looking man of firm build from southern Siberia. He enrolled at military medical school, and got an aviation medicine degree in 1952. He kept this up while learning how to fly and test Soviet Air Force jets for the next few years. He applied for the 1960 class, was rejected for less than perfect physical health, was admitted for the Voskhod flight, and again in 1966. In some ways he was better equipped than Boris Yegorov who lacked his aviation experience.

Preparations went ahead. A one-day test run was carried out on 7 October with Cosmos 47. It appears to have gone faultlessly. Cosmos 47 orbited at 177 by 413 km, 90 minutes, and was recovered after 16 orbits.

BLUE JACKETS

The way was clear for Voskhod 1. The crew of three, all smiling broadly, Komarov, Feoktistov, Yegorov, stepped out of the transfer van at the pad. They may even have felt ill at ease that they were not wearing space suits. Instead, they had silver-grey woollen suits with blue jackets. Up they went in the lift, and the three swung into their spacious cabin, which was heavily padded with soft foam and embellished with light blue instrumentation panels. All they needed to do was don small white helmet headphones and they were ready to fly.

Voskhod 1 blasted into the autumn sky and settled into a safe orbit of 160 by 408 km, 64.54 degrees, 90 minutes, the longest period ever. Boris Yegorov, peering out of the right porthole, at once spotted the Siberian forests and tundra. One striking impression followed another. The lights of the settlements and cities of Australia, the white icecap of Antarctica, the shimmering lights of the southern Australia aurorae.

Compared to Vostok, this was real passenger service. The three men ate on Caspian roach, caviare sandwiches and vacuum-packed roast beef slices. They talked to Mr Khrushchev by radio link. They sent greetings to the hotting-up scenes of battle in North Vietnam. Vladimir Komarov guided the ship around. High quality pictures of 25 frames/s were sent back. Boris Yegorov took blood samples. Konstantin Feoktistov photographed the stars.

In terms of the international reaction, Voskhod 1 had exactly the desired effect. 'Three men in space!' the headlines screamed, when everyone would have considered two a huge advance. American Malcom Scott Carpenter: 'I wouldn't have been surprised if two had been sent up. But three — the Russians seem to do this, just what you don't expect them to' [2]. The *New York Times* spoke of Russia widening its space lead and of 'an air of resignation among US officials'. It was another humiliation, for the three-man Apollo would not be ready until 1966 at the earliest and the Americans had not even thought of flying doctors or scientists, let alone in shirt sleeves.

How long would this flying circus go on? The launch announcement stated the objective. 'The purpose of the flight is. . . to carry out extended medical and biological research in conditions of prolonged flight' [3].

Yet out of the blue the announcement came on the afternoon of 13 October that the crew were down. They had been up 24 h 17 min. They had flown 16 orbits. The Voskhod came down 2000 km southeast of Moscow. The parachute came out at 5300 m at a speed of 240 m/s. Just as it touched down, the new soft-landing rockets blasted to ease the jolt. It was as gentle as promised! The three cosmonauts opened the hatch and clambered out onto the flat steppe land. A helicopter crew was soon to hand.

Speculation at once broke out that there had been a premature return to Earth. However, Voskhod was swiftly eclipsed on the front pages by new startling news from Moscow. After speaking to the cosmonauts from his holiday dacha on the Black Sea, Nikita Khrushchev resumed his autumn holiday. Even as he did, in Moscow the plotters moved. At a special meeting of the Central Committee of the Soviet Communist Party, the members, tired of Khrushchev's adventurism, voted him out of office. Late that night the CPSU was able to announce a triumvirate to take his place:

President. Nikolai Podgorny
Chairman of the Council of Ministers: Alexei Kosygin
First Secretary: Leonid Brezhnev.

The new men were younger, more pragmatic, less prone to foreign adventures; and of the three, Alexei Kosygin was considered to be *primus inter pares*. At the time, such an interpretation of the palace coup was reasonable, but within a number of years it was clear that the jowly, bear-like, bushy-eyebrowed Brezhnev was really out in front. By 1977 he was able to edge out Podgorny from the Presidency and take it for himself. Kosygin's health declined and when this pale-looking quiet man lost his health in the late 1970s he was replaced by the even quieter and more unobtrusive Nikolai Tikhonov. Leonid Brezhnev's health began to decline at about the same time and he eventually died in November 1982.

It was fitting in some ways, ironic in others, that Nikita Khrushchev, the man who had both given the space programme the decisive political impetus it needed and at the same time interfered with it intolerably, should speak to the three spacemen in orbit as his last public function. He 'retired' immediately, was occasionally seen out walking in the park, and died in 1971. It was, at least, a more civilized way to run politics than in Stalin's time.

And when the three heroes of Voskhod 1 returned to Moscow on the 15th for a triumphant reception, if they had any opinions on going up during one man's premiership and coming down during another's, they kept their thoughts to themselves.

Where however does this leave the question about the duration of the Voskhod 1 flight? There is an inconsistency between the launch announcement of a 'prolonged flight' and the return to Earth 24 hours later. As if to confuse matters still further, we now know that Komarov asked for a 24 hour extension to the flight, and Korolov refused, saying enigmatically, 'there are more things in heaven and earth than are dreamt of in your philosophy' (quoting Hamlet) [4]. Was this a coded reference to the palace coup in the Kremlin? Did the new rulers order Voskhod down to indicate their displeasure with Khrushchev's space spectaculars? No one knows. A political intervention to bring Voskhod down seems most unlikely – to plotters trying to bring down their chief at enormous personal and political risk, a spaceship's orbital duration was probably the last thing on their minds. The hardware evidence – Cosmos 47 – unambiguously favours the notion of a one-day mission only. All this leaves us with the unsatisfactory explanation that the launch announcement was in error.

OUT INTO THE ENDLESS VOID

No sooner had the Voskhod trio returned than preparations began for the second stage of the Voskhod programme. As the winter snows and winds closed in on Baikonour, the earliest a new mission could go was mid-March. Which, by happy coincidence, was the date set for the much-delayed Gemini programme. In Florida there was no real seasonal problem about when to launch, but the inland Baikonour winter introduced new and serious operational risks.

'The first spacewalk' was set, early on, as the objective for the second Voskhod mission. Even though the mission had been ordered up to compete with Gemini, a spacewalk test was in any case essential for a manned lunar landing. No ordinary spacesuit would do: the life-support system had to be a backpack (as would be needed on the Moon), not simply a connecting air hose (which could not be trailed around on the Moon's surface).

The problems of a moonsuit or spacesuit were not to be glossed over. Any cosmonaut venturing outside his cabin would need a huge amount of protection – from the vacuum, meteorites and the intense heat and cold. It would have to keep him at a comfortable temperature and ensure he did not overheat. The suit would have to not 'balloon out' and prevent him from returning. If different atmospheres and pressures were being experienced, measures would have to be taken to prevent the 'bends' that afflicted deep sea divers. Altogether it was a risky undertaking. Voskhod itself presented an additional problem. Because not enough air could be carried to repressurize it after depressurization, a separate airlock had to be carried. Once again, Korolov's genius came to the rescue.

Space limitations did not give him much to play around with, so he designed an inflatable airlock which could be cast away after use. It would inflate once Voskhod got into orbit. The two-man crew, both wearing suits, would let air gush into the airlock. The one spacewalker would then climb into the airlock, a tunnel-like cylindrical tube, and close the door behind him. He would then exit from the airlock, which would be gradually depressurized. He would use the same method, in reverse, to return.

INAUSPICIOUS START

It was to be a mission fraught with danger, and there were three nasty shocks ahead. First was the dry-run advance mission. Cosmos 57 was put up on 23 February into a 195 by 512 km, 90 minute orbit. Although the hatch was deployed on schedule at the point of entry into orbit, Cosmos 57 then broke up into 180 fragments. No one knows why. It did not hold up the planned mission, then three weeks away, but it cannot have inspired much confidence.

The crew continued their preparations. The prime crew came from the 1960 class. They were Pavel Belyayev and Alexei Leonov. Pavel Belyayev was the commander. He was a World War 2 fighter pilot and had fought the Japanese. He had fallen out of the 1960 class a year after joining when he smashed an ankle during a bad parachute landing. He exercised relentlessly till it healed, and it was on Yuri Gagarin's insistence that he was reselected in 1963.

Alexei Leonov was to appear again, and to the West he became one of Russia's best-known and most personable cosmonauts. He had a colourful personality that was to shine through the more staid biographies of his colleagues. His ambition in life was to be the first man on the Moon. He might well have been so. When selected in 1960 he was known for his enormous determination, athleticism and courage. When a boy of 15, he made himself a bicycle from spare parts and cycled endlessly each day. He went to Air Force school and was later a parachute instructor. A chatty, cheerful man, fair-haired, a smile never far away, he had two brushes with death in his early years in training. One night

Pavel Belyayev (left), Vladimir Komarov and Alexei Leonov appear in high spirits on the bus *en route* to the launch pad for the lift off of the space craft Voskhod 2 in March 1965.

his car left the road when returning home and plunged through ice into a pond. He struggled out, also rescuing his wife and the driver. Soon after, when bailing out of an aircraft, his ejector seat jammed and he escaped only by bending the metal strap restrainers with his bare hands. He got free and came down safely.

When awaiting his flight he cycled 1000 km, ran 500 km, and skied 300 km, all within a year. He combined his athletic passions with art. Alexei Leonov was an enthusiastic painter and by all accounts a good one. He focussed on space themes – his own impressions from orbit, sunsets and sunrises, and futuristic drawings of spaceships landing on other worlds. He was a notorious cartoonist and sketch-maker and for many years edited the cosmonauts' own newsletter called *Neptune*.

Such all-round achievements were rarely matched in the NASA camp. Backup pilot to Belyayev was Dmitri Zaikin, the anxious-looking, mysterious, hatted figure who appears in some inadvertently-released photographs of Voskhod 2. Alexei Leonov had two back-ups: Yevgeni Khrunov and Viktor Gorbatko. Both were pilots from the 1960 group. Viktor Gorbatko was a solid military man, experienced professional flier, a man of few words. In appearance and disposition he was not unlike America's Neil Armstrong. Both Khrunov and Gorbatko were to fly in the Soyuz programme.

SNOW FLURRIES

Snow lay on the ground and there were white flurries in the air as Pavel Belyayev and Alexei Leonov, both spacesuited, took the lift to the top of Voskhod 2 on the wintry morning of 18 March 1965. In America, the first Gemini launch was still five days away as Virgil Grissom and John Young went methodically through their countdown drills.

Voskhod 2 reached orbit safely — it was in fact the highest orbit ever at 173.5 by
497.7 km, 90 minutes.

Then, on the second orbit, as Voskhod 2 swung over the Caspian Sea for the first
time, Alexei Leonov struggled in the small cabin to put on his full spacesuit and the
backpack he would need for his protection. To his suit he attached a lifeline to keep him
connected to his spaceship. The line also carried voice communications. The backpack
provided air and devices to regulate the temperature inside the suit.

With a 'good luck' from Pavel Balyayev he pushed his way into the airlock and sealed
the door behind him. He would be on his own now. He was breathing pure oxygen and
was able to reduce the pressure of his suit to 0.27 atmospheres. This was necessary to
prevent his suit ballooning and impeding his exit from the narrow tunnel-like airlock.

Finally came the moment of truth, the opening of the airlock. Scorching bright sunlight flooded in, the blinding brightness of the direct rays of the Sun. Alexei Leonov felt
as if he was at the bottom of a well and peering out from deep in the Earth for the first
time. Looking up he could see the inky blackness of space and the unblinking light of the
stars.

He pulled himself gingerly out of the airlock. Television pictures captured his diver-
like figure as he emerged. He gasped, contemplating the 500 km that separated him

Cosmonaut Alexei Leonov was the first deputy commander of the cosmonaut training centre. He
became a cosmonaut in March 1960 and piloted Voskhod 2, on which mission he completed the first
EVA. He was later assigned to Soyuz 19, the Russian part of the Apollo—Soyuz Test Project.

from the ground. Down below was the lure of the Black Sea and the snow-capped peaks of the Caucasus Mountains.

Alexei Leonov got his breath back and finally cast himself free into the abyss of space. He soared, he swam, he turned end over end, exuberant at the new freedom conferred on him. The whole universe was before him and below him stretched the still-frozen expanses of the Volga basin and, further to the north, the Ural mountains.

He disappeared from the sight of the eye of the camera. Then, eerily, loops of line appeared, followed by Alexei Leonov's white suit. Marked sharply on the top of his helmet were the initials 'CCCP'. He grew in confidence, felt the lightness of the sensation of zero gravity and moved a full 5 m away from his ship to admire it.

Voskhod was now at the northernmost point of its orbit and about to track southwards again, heading for the Pacific. It was time to climb back in. This was where the trouble started.

First of all, the movie camera which had been recording all his movements snagged. It would not go back in the airlock and instead got wedged in the entrance. By the time he had forced it in, Alexei Leonov was sweating profusely and producing more perspiration than the suit could absorb. Then, much worse, he could not get back in himself. His suit ballooned to the point where he just would not fit. He pushed and pushed, all to no avail. Sweat had covered his eyes and in a helmet he could not clear it. He was using up air fast. His heart was pounding madly.

He reduced his suit pressure from 0.4 atmospheres to 0.3. No good. Down to 0.27, the permissible limit. Still would not fit. He faced disaster. But this was the kind of thing he had trained for five years for. He eased the suit pressure down still further, to 0.25 atmospheres. With a heave of desperation as much as of personal strength, he finally went through. Alive!

He clambered back in, to be greeted by Pavel Balyayev who was just as relieved himself. The airlock was then cast free. Leonov had been 10 minutes in open space and 12 minutes struggling to get back in. Not that this was known at the time – such difficulties were glossed over. As a result, the Americans underestimated the problems of spacewalking and, in orbit a year later, Gemini 9's Eugene Cernan nearly came to grief when he overheated and his helmet fogged up from overexertion.

The next orbits were mundane by comparison. The two men rested, ate, and talked to the ground. They passed outside the range of ground stations from orbits 8 to 13 so they slept. At 5.12 a.m. the following day they actually passed quite close to another orbiting Sputnik, circling the Earth about a kilometre away, though they could not identify it. The world below applauded their feat. Even *The Times* of London described it as 'fantastic history' in its opening account. The London *Evening Standard* showed American astronauts about to follow in pursuit, captioned 'Follow that cab!'. Virgil Grissom and John Young went glumly through their tasks. They had been left at the starting post – again.

At least so it seemed until the very next day, 19 March. Most people expected the Voskhod to return on its 16th orbit. There was silence. There were no reports all morning. None in the afternoon either. Then, late on, a report that the crew were down and were being picked up. In fact nothing of the sort was happening. They were down, and alive, but in a north Russian forest, surrounded by a pack of hungry wolves.

As Voskhod 2 reached retrofire point on orbit 16, the rocket should have fired for

56 seconds to brake it out of orbit. Nothing happened at all. Belyayev would have then pressed the manual button himself, but he held off. Wisely, in the event. Voskhod 2 had strayed out of attitude and this had alerted the computer, automatically preventing a retrofire. Balyayev and ground control argued over what to do next and a manual return was agreed, to take place on orbit 17.

Alexei Leonov had been put to the test the previous day and now it was his commander's turn. Pavel Balyayev had to get the orientation right manually or they'd never return. At 11.30 a.m. he pressed the switch and wham! off it went.

It was accurate enough to get them home — but only just. It was a hot and scary reentry, so hot that the capsule was enveloped in flames and all the communications aerials were burned off. As a result, they had no means of telling anyone where they were. They were, in fact, over a thousand miles off course by now. As they drifted in to land, they were not greeted by the flat steppe that they had hoped for, but mountains and forests, clad in winter snow. Voskhod 2 crashed into big fir trees and the parachutes snarled high up in the trees.

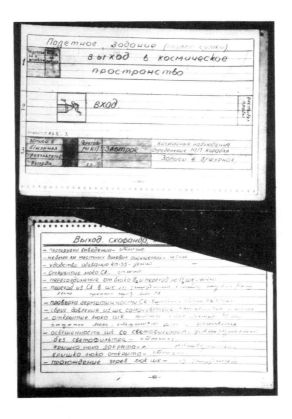

Two pages from the log book of the spacecraft Voskhod 2. It was on this flight that Alexei Leonov took his 'walk in space' which was televised, and pictures of him were splashed over the front pages of the world's newspapers. Voskhod 2 made an emergency landing in a forest and the crew had to fight off wolves before they were rescued.

The two men were out in five minutes and it was bitterly cold. It was well over half way through the day and darkness was only four hours away. There was silence all about. They realized no one would know where to look for them. They did not know themselves where they were, though they surmised (correctly) that they were down in the Ural mountains. The rescue and welcome team were a full 1300 km away and the pressmen with them realized something was wrong when they were sent home empty-handed. Ground control at once summoned aircraft to search for the missing cosmonauts. The worst was feared. But Leonov and Belyayev had been trained for this kind of situation. They set up a radio beacon and collected wood to start a fire. And waited.

Three hours later the drone of a searching plane could be heard in the distance. It came closer, flew overhead and circled — and flew away again. Help was coming. Not long after, a helicopter arrived, but the ground was too rough to land and after dropping supplies it too flew away. They had come down near the city of Perm, capital of the Urals.

By now darkness was falling, and the cosmonauts faced a night in the snow and the forest. The cold was bitter indeed and they huddled around their fire for warmth. The baying of wolves could be heard. The baying grew closer, and frosty breath from lurking shadowy forms could be made out between the pine trees.

More rescuers arrived at daybreak and the crew were airlifted out to safety. The account of the full extent of their campfire ordeal did not come out for many years.

2000 correspondents gathered at the post-flight press conference on 26 March. Mstislav Keldysh proclaimed:

Voskhod 2 opens up prospects for the establishment of orbital stations, the linkup of spaceships in orbit, and the carrying out of astronomical and geophysical explorations. It would be possible in the near future to place in Earth orbit a space research institute in which scientists specializing in the most diverse fields would work. The results of Voskhod are extremely important for flights to the Moon. [5]

The significance of Leonov's suit was at last apparent. His autonomous backpack unit, quite unnecessary for Earth orbit, but essential for the Moon, was given a heavy emphasis. Konstantin Feoktistov elaborated:

Voskhod 2 brings the moon flights much closer. [6]

Leonov himself was less bashful:

What we must do is work towards the goal of the moon calmly and thoroughly and without any rush. I think that those who work that way will be first on the moon. I dream of this being accomplished by men of our detachment. Well if I am lucky I will get this assignment. [7]

Soon after, two books were released. One showed 20 sketches by Leonov himself of spaceships landing on the Moon and men exploring it. The second was called *Men and the moon*, introduced by Gherman Titov.

As for the Voskhod programme, Belyayev revealed at the press conference that a two-man Voskhod could orbit the Earth for a month. It could also manoeuvre in space and change orbit like the Polyot craft [8]. Although this was not realized at the time, Belyayev was in fact describing the next two Voskhod missions.

PROTON

Gradually the pieces of the Moon programme were coming together. The autonomous moonsuit had been tested. For the long-distance tracking of manned Moon missions, six large freighters were converted into tracking ships in 1965–66. And the D booster, essential for launching the new Zond to fly around the Moon, was ready.

The D booster, later called Proton, was designed by Valentin Glushko, and was the most advanced rocket in the world for 20 years. Its RD 253 engines recycled the exhaust gases to create a closed circuit turbine system. Pressures of hundreds of atmospheres were obtained on delivery. Each engine weighed a modest 1280 kg. The turbines went round at a fantastic 14 000 revolutions a minute. Temperatures reached 3127°C in the engine chambers and its walls were plated with zirconium. It could put 12 tonnes into orbit, and later models could launch 21 tonnes [9].

The first mission of the D booster was a splendid success. On 16 July 1965, it climbed into space and injected into low orbit a 12.2 tonne space observatory called 'Proton 1'. It unfurled gigantic solar panels, and at once set to work observing gamma rays, cosmic rays and electrons.

The real significance of the 16 July launch was not the Proton 1 satellite, but the booster. To NASA chiefs, it proved that the USSR was back in the big booster business and competing for the Moon [10]. Ever since the rumoured 1963 'withdrawal' of the Russians from the Moon race, the Americans had worried that they were in a one-horse race, and Congress was getting uneasy about spending so much money on a race that might not exist.

For the Russians, it meant that a major hurdle had been passed. Leonid Sedov, of the Soviet Academy of Sciences, went as far as to say in August 1965: 'It (the Proton launching) opens the way to the moon' [11]. So much so, that it provoked yet another change in the schedule of manned flights.

Voskhod 3, it will be recalled, was planned as a month-long, two-man flight during the late summer of 1965. A crew was even trained to fly it. They were Boris Volynov and Georgi Shonin, with, as backups, two new cosmonauts recruited in 1963 – Vladimir Shatalov and Georgi Beregovoi. The Voskhod 4 mission, in which the spare retrorocket would have been replaced by a rocket designed for space rendezvous, would have linked up with another unmanned spaceship [12]. No crew had been chosen and the mission was still some time away – the spring of 1966.

But the success of Proton and the rapid progress of Gemini in America affected Soviet thinking. Gemini 3 made a short three-orbit test in March 1965. Gemini 4 made a four-day flight which included Ed White's outstanding spacewalk. Gemini 5 orbited the earth eight days in August 1965. Gemini, despite its long delays, was shooting ahead at a rapid pace. Far from paralysing America as Khrushchev had intended, the Voskhod programme was stirring the sleeping giant into action. Apollo was not far behind, and the American determination to beat their own self-imposed 1969 deadline grew cockier every day.

Speed was of the essence. To save time, Voskhod 3 was scrapped. A biological satellite was put in to replace it. The same fate befell Voskhod 4. It was decided to put Soyuz into top gear, since it could do a rendezvous on its first mission and a long flight on its second. Korolov would have found this ironic. Voskhod was invented because Soyuz was too far away on the time scale. Now Voskhod was being cancelled to bring Soyuz forwards. The cancellations were most unpopular among the cosmonauts. In July 1965 two journalists were also selected for cosmonaut training: they were Yaroslav Golvanov and Yuri Letunov. But likewise, plans to fly them were dropped.

The success of Proton meant that the around-the-Moon Zond flight was now much nearer. Perhaps it could be got ready for a flight around the Moon by November 1967, just in time for the 50th Anniversary of the Bolshevik Revolution of 1917. Such a flight would wipe out any advantage that the Americans might derive from Gemini in the meantime.

The psychological effects of an around-the-Moon flight on the Proton booster would be devastating. A solo Soviet cosmonaut, bravely making the lonely voyage out to the Moon, whipping around the far side a mere 1000 km above the surface, filming and reporting on sites never before seen by the human eye, and then zooming back to a hero's welcome: this would even out-class Gagarin. The Russians would go down in history as the first to reach the Moon. The humiliated Americans might well withdraw and leave the matter of the landing to the Russians as well.

So, some time around midsummer 1965, Soviet space planners reached a number of important decisions. These were: to abandon the Voskhod programme; to proceed immediately to Soyuz and fly it manned in 1966 if possible; to ready the Proton booster for a manned around-the-Moon flight for November 1967; and, using the G booster and related equipment, to plan a Moon landing for around 1969–71.

There is a footnote to this period, and that is the flight of the astrodogs of 1966. Voskhod 3 was replaced by a less expensive unmanned duration mission. Two dogs, called Veterok and Ugolyok, each in separate containers, took the place of cosmonauts. The mission was called Cosmos 110 and took the two dogs right into the van Allen radiation belt. It flew at 51.85 degrees and out as far as 900 km. The launch date was 22 February 1966. There was a thorough test of the circulatory system in the space environment. Both dogs were clad in spacesuits. Full data on how they reacted was telemetred back each day. Eventually their capsule came down intact and was recovered on 16 March after 21.75 days. The dogs survived and were in good condition. Dr Boris Yegorov was the medical expert in charge.

THE MOON BECKONS

Korolov's design team proceeded all out with the Moon exploration programme which dominated the Moon race. Some of the excitement leaked out, and in 1965 there was published in Moscow a book called *Na Zhdiot Luna* (*The Moon awaits us*). In it Gherman Titov wrote:

> I myself dream of flying around the moon. Practical considerations dictate that a flight to the moon be preceded by a flight around it. Today's cosmonauts have a good chance of getting a close look at the moon. [13]

As the cosmonauts waited for Soyuz to be made ready, all attention focussed on the vital unmanned missions scheduled for 1965–66.

Ever since the failure of Luna 4 and similar probes launched in 1963, the Korolov design bureau was determined to eliminate the types of faults that had arisen. The new soft-landing probes had designs very similar to Luna 4. But the elimination of faults was easier said than done, and when the first of the new probes took to the skies in 1965, it too became stranded in Earth orbit. The 1470 kg probe, called Cosmos 60, was put up on 12 March 1965.

The next spacecraft did improve on Luna 4's record. Luna 5 got away on 9 May 1965, and set off in good working order. It carried out a mid-course manoeuvre and headed straight for the Sea of Clouds. But when the time came to fire the retrorockets for touchdown, nothing happened! The rockets just did not come on and Soviet scientists in the control room listened helplessly to Luna 5's signals as it crashed into the Moon at great speed. Its equipment exploded and set up a cloud of dust measuring 80 km wide and 225 km long.

Luna 6 was a disaster more in the style of America's Vanguard programme. Put up flawlessly on 8 June 1965, the time came on 10 June to make a mid-course manoeuvre. However although the rocket switched on correctly, it would not turn off! The engine continued to blast away remorselessly, sending Luna 6 off in the opposite direction. It missed the Moon by no less than 161 000 km, a record.

Coinciding with the redesign which followed, an entirely new probe was prepared with an entirely different purpose in mind. Taking off on 18 July 1965, it was announced as Zond 3. Little information was given and it was listed as a Mars probe. It carried a lander, like Zond 2. In fact, nothing further was heard of it until 15 August, when a new space success was revealed. Zond 3, everyone was told, had followed the Luna 3 flight path and had taken detailed pictures of the Moon's far side en route to Mars. Zond 3, a 950 kg probe, had shot past the Moon at a distance of 10 000 km some 33 hours after launch en route to a deep space trajectory. Its ƒ8 camera blinked away for 68 minutes at 1/100th and 1/300th of a second. The details shown were excellent and were on 1100 lines (the American Ranger cameras of the same time were half that). Soviet scientists waited till Zond 3 was 1.25 million kilometres away before commanding signals to be transmitted by remote control. They were rebroadcast several times and Zond 3 was still functioning on 16 September.

There was grandeur in the photographs as Zond swung around the Moon's leading edge – whole new mountain ranges, continents and hundreds of craters swept into view. It was exactly how a cosmonaut might see it, and Soviet astronomer Max Rebrov reminded people that Russian spacemen planned a trip around the Moon before alighting there.

A series of Moon maps were compiled on the strength of Zond 3's pictures. These maps would make a manned flyby of the Moon a much more meaningful operation and the cosmonauts would know what to look for.

Zond 3 also had much to do with the Mars and the Venus programme. Like Zond 2 it carried plasma engines, but the main task was long-range photographic relaying, a test which it passed with flying colours. (Its ultimate fate as a Mars probe is not clear). Zond 3 may have encouraged the designers to believe that in their next soft-landing mission, Luna 7, they would at last meet with success. The 1506 kg space probe, launched on the

A photograph of the Moon obtained by the television camera of the Soviet automatic interplanetary probe Zond 3 on 20 July 1965. The picture was taken from a distance of about 10 000 km above the lunar surface and showed for the first time a region of the Moon situated between its visible part and the lunar far side first photographed by Lunik 3 on 7 October 1959. This made it possible to tie in some of the far-side features with those already known.

Sputnik anniversary of 4 October 1965, went through all stages flawlessly right up to retrofire. After the predicted touchdown, scientists tried to contact the capsule which should have been deployed. Hours passed: silence. Luna 7 was down in the Ocean of Storms near the crater Kepler. But no response.

Eventually they gave up. 13 hours after touchdown they admitted that Luna 7 had failed. 'Most operations necessary for a soft-landing were carried out', the statement said [14]. Their conclusion: the retrorockets had fired too early, had slowed the capsule down to zero, but with fuel exhausted, it fell the rest of the way unaided and was irreparably damaged. But they had nearly done it.

Two months later, Luna 8 followed the same path, lifting off on 3 December. 83 hours into the mission the rockets switched on. Too late, it transpired, and the probe was destroyed. A soft-landing was proving an elusive target — more so than any previously attempted. Yet another probe was prepared. But tragedy lay ahead.

DEATH OF A DREAMER

Luna 8 was the last probe that Sergei Korolov was to witness. He was dead a month later. He was admitted to hospital on 13 January 1966, for the removal of colon tumours. No less a person than the Minister of Health, Dr Boris Petrovsky carried out the operation. Midway through, he discovered a more serious tumour. He continued the operation far beyond the safe limits of anaesthesia, doubly foolish because of his own lack of recent practice. A large blood vessel burst; haemorrhaging began; and Sergei Korolov's heart — weakened as it had been by the toil of the labour camps — simply collapsed. Frantic efforts were made to revive him, but on 14 January 1966 he was pronounced dead. Had a better — or just a different surgeon operated he might have lived for years longer. His death was quite avoidable [15]. It was the last act of political interference in his life.

Once dead, his identity and importance could safely be revealed, and indeed it was, following burial in the wall of the Kremlin on 16 January 1966. A flood of Korolov literature followed which was still going strong and revealing new information about his life and times nearly twenty years later. No efforts were spared in the telling of his boundless energy, iron will, limitless imagination and engineering genius.

This could have been mistaken for nostalgia, but it was not. With Korolov's death the Soviet space programme was never the same again. The driving force went out of it and with it that unique ability to command, inspire, bargain, lead, design and attend to detail. After 1966 the programme had many excellent designers, planners, politicians, administrators and prophets, but never all together in one person. Not that this was immediately obvious. The programme continued on much as before. Design and testing of the upcoming Soyuz proceeded apace — indeed it was a tribute to Korolov that twenty years later it was still carrying cosmonauts into space. But the sense of direction slackened. Indeed the absence of Korolov may have made the critical difference to the climax of the Moon race in 1968—69, as we shall see.

'AHEAD AGAIN'

Luna 9, 1583 kg, got away on 31 January 1966. It may actually have been the last one manufactured in this phase of soft-landing spacecraft. It did not disappoint its planners. 46 seconds before impact, the retrorocket fired, exactly on schedule. It halted Luna 9 dead in its tracks. The little 99.8 kg capsule separated and bounced along the rocky, dusty, lunar surface like a heavy-bottomed toy. It settled. On the top part, four petal-like wings unfolded. Four minutes later, four 75 cm aerials poked their way out of the dome, slowly extending.

Luna 9 was down in the Ocean of Storms between the craters of Reiner and Maria. On Earth, ground controllers gathered that winter night, in tense expectation. The descent module's signals had died as it crashed. They had to wait 4 minutes to know if the capsule had survived, if its instruments were still functioning, and whether they would get usable information. Or would they be robbed of victory yet again?

They were not. It was an agonizing wait. Then exactly on schedule, from the walls of the control room where loudspeakers had been installed, flooded in the beeps, pips and humming squeal of the signals of Luna 9, direct from the surface of the moon! It was a sweet moment. For the first time a spacecraft was transmitting directly to Earth from another world! It was a historic moment and Radio Moscow at once attempted to assess its significance:

A softlanding was one of the most difficult scientific and technical problems in space research. It s a major step towards a manned landing on the moon and other planets. [16]

Its importance was not lost on the West. 'New space lead for Russia' and 'Russians move ahead again' were typical headlines. Once again, America's equivalent project called Surveyor had managed to get itself a year or two behind schedule. American engineers were quick to point out that their craft was much more sophisticated than Luna 9. Surveyor planned a real parachutist-type landing, with no rough-landing capsules, and would do a more detailed job. But, so what? people asked. It was still in the shed.

For the next few days the eyes of the world focussed on the Moon. At 4.50 a.m. on 4 February Luna 9's television camera was switched on. It was a tiny thing weighing only 159 g. It was a mere 60 cm above the surface. It began to scan the lunar surface, turning through the full 360 degrees, a process which took 100 minutes. The camera was in fact the main instrument on board; the other was a radiation recorder.

A series of communication sessions was held between Earth and Moon over the next three days, which was as long as the batteries permitted. Some sessions lasted over an hour. The principal one was held on 4 February from 6.30 p.m. to 7.55 p.m. (Moscow time) and it sparked off a diplomatic incident. This relay was the big one – the one with the pictures.

The ever vigilant British radio dish at Jodrell Bank had been listening in to the Luna 9 signals all during the flight. Sir Bernard Lovell and his team had got into the habit of listening in ever since Sputnik. Whilst this was not important compared to the general radio astronomy programme, it meant that they knew of upcoming space developments long before they were officially announced.

That evening, as the communications session began, it was realized that what was coming in was a broadcast of television pictures and that they were not in code. On an inspiration and a hunch, a car was speedily dispatched to Manchester to pick up the *Daily Express* TV facsimile machine. The car collected it, dashed back, and the facsimile machine was at once linked up to the radio receiver. The staff were breathless with excitement as the facsimile at once began converting the signals into standard newspaper photographs. They were rapidly developed in the darkroom and two minutes later an operator emerged with dripping prints exclaiming, 'It's a beauty!'

The print was passed round to Sir Bernard Lovell and the animated reporters. They could only gasp. The tall, authoritative Sir Bernard drew a deep breath and could only utter, 'Amazing!' There it was – the face of the Moon. The camera's eye stretched to a sloping horizon and there loomed rocks, pebbles, stones and boulders, scattered randomly across a porous rocky surface. In the far distance was a crater dipping down. Long shadows accentuated the contrasts of the other-worldly glimpses of the Moon's stark surfaces.

In minutes, the world had seen the photographs. The Russians were furious at the thought of the West scooping 'their' pictures. Sir Bernard was accused of sensationalism and irresponsibility. In fact he had his scales slightly wrong and the real pictures were flatter. But from then on, picture transmissions from Russian space probes were always coded, and the Russians became much smarter off the mark in releasing data anyway.

Transmissions were to continue for several days. More photographs were picked up – eight in all – showing the lunar horizon stretching to the far distance and Luna 9 obviously settled into a boulder field. It was eerie, but reassuring. If Luna 9 could soft-land, then so too could a manned spacecraft: it would not suffocate in a field of dust, as some had feared.

Its battery exhausted, Luna 9 finally went off the air for ever on 6 February after transmitting 8 hr 5 min of data over seven communication sessions. The Ocean of Storms returned to its customary silence and desolation. Luna 9 had done all that was asked of it: it had survived, transmitted, and photographed, and its timer had ensured regular broadcasts from the Moon to the earth. Another barrier was down and the Americans had been beaten once again.

LUNAR 'INTERNATIONALE'

Booster problems returned to haunt the onward Moon effort. In March 1966 the third Proton booster (Proton 2 had gone aloft in November 1965) crashed in flames. On 1 March 1966, Cosmos 111 failed to leave Earth orbit for the Moon.

Luna 10 eventually got away on 31 March 1966. No sooner was it streaking towards the Moon than it was announced that it was directed towards an entirely new objective – Moon orbit. Again, this was essential for manned lunar flight. Again, the American equivalent lunar programme called 'Lunar Orbiter' was still months away.

8000 km from the Moon, Luna 10 was turned around in its path and its rockets blazed briefly but effectively. They knocked 0.64 km/s off its speed, just enough to let the Moon's gravity field to capture it. Luna 10 was pulled into an orbit of 349 by 1017 km, 71.9 degrees, 178.3 minutes. Luna 10 had the same base as Luna 9 but with a

The Russians were responsible for placing the first satellite in orbit around the Moon. This was Luna 10 (shown here) in April 1967. The spacecraft provided the first detailed information on the nature of the lunar surface.

scientific orbiting capsule on top. It was shaped like an immersion tank with aerials sticking out and it was designed to answer the key question: would cosmonauts survive the radiation levels of near-Moon space?

But first things first. Luna 10 celebrated the latest Russian first in fine style. Celestial mechanics meant that Luna 10 would enter the first of its lunar orbits just as the Communist party was assembling in Moscow for its Congress – the first Congress of Brezhnev and Kosygin. As it rounded the eastern edge of the Moon, Luna 10's transmitter went full on and relayed the bars of the 'Internationale' – in turn broadcast over loud-speakers direct to the Party Congress over the static of deep space. It was a triumphant moment and the 5000 delegates had good reason to stand and cheer wildly.

Luna 9 may have surprised people by its early closedown, but Luna 10 lasted much longer. Its mission lasted way into the summer and did not end till 30 May after 460 lunar revolutions and 219 communication sessions. A stream of data was sent back by its magnetometer, gamma ray detector, infrared radiometer, cosmic ray detector and meteoroid counter. Cosmonauts would be able to survive in near-Moon space.

One by one the last impediments to a manned lunar landing were being ticked off [17]. The Moon was safe to land on. The radiation levels were acceptable. The far side was mapped. Now a detailed photoreconnaissance of sites was needed.

Luna 11 was fitted out for this purpose. It was a heavier probe at 1640 kg, and part of the research equipment was attached to the basic module. It left Earth on 24 August and entered Moon orbit of 159 by 1200 km, 27 degrees, 178 minutes. However it seems to have been only partially successful. No TV pictures were returned and the mission ended on 1 October.

No such difficulties attended Luna 12 (22 October). It entered orbit of 100 by 1737 km, 15 degrees, 205 minutes, and carried a full-scale television observation unit. A series of 1100-line pictures were taken, scanning the surface in blocks of 52 km^2 from a height of 100 km (in fact the same height as America's later Apollo). The mission lasted three months and ended on 19 January 1967 after 602 orbits. A Soviet photograph released late in 1966 showed cosmonauts Yuri Gagarin, Alexei Leonov, Vladimir Komarov and Yevgeni Khrunov pouring excitedly over its pictures – looking for landing sites?

One surprise arising out of Luna 12 was the discovery of unexpected orbital perturbations. As Luna 12 orbited, its orbit became progressively more irregular and twisted out of shape. This was due, it was later found out, to heavy concentrations of mass underneath the lunar surface that distorted orbits, as magnetic anomalies did on Earth. They became known as 'mascons', named by the Americans from 'mass-concentrations'. They were an unwelcome development because complete precision was required if an accurate lunar landing was to be achieved. Errors of only 3, 4 or 5 km in orbit could bring a landing spaceship down in crater fields instead of a flat patch by mistake.

The decision was taken – it is surmised, because almost no data about this particular mission was released – to fly Luna 12's backup to identify these mascons and try to map them. Luna 14 was flown out to the Moon on 7 April 1968 and it entered lunar orbit of 160 by 769 km, 42 degrees, 160 minutes.

The last scheduled flight in the series was Luna 13. It went aloft on 21 December 1966, and made two course corrections en route to the Moon. Retrorockets fired at a distance of 69 km and Luna 13 bumped down onto the surface of the Moon in the Ocean of Storms between the craters Craft and Selenus.

True to earlier traditions of economy and not repeating its predecessor, Luna 13 was more advanced than its soft-landing precursor Luna 9. It had an upgraded TV camera. For six days, till 30 December, it sent back a series of panoramic sweeps of surrounding craters, stones and rocks. Sun angles were low and the shadows of Luna 13's antennae stood out against the ghostly lunarscape.

Luna 13 represented a significant advance in that it carried two extensible arms which folded down like ladders onto the lunar surface. At the end of one was a mechanical soil meter with a thumper which tested the density of the soil. At the end of the other was a radiation density meter. Their conclusion was that moonrock was similar to medium density earth soil.

So, by New Year's Day, 1967, the USSR's unmanned lunar reconnaissance programme was nearly complete. The automatic spacecraft had done about all they could do. The time had come to move decisively towards the manned lunar flyby of November 1967. The Zond spacecraft and its manned equivalent, Soyuz, were just about ready.

POLITICAL CALCULATIONS

Much of this scheduling depended on Soviet perceptions of American progress. Undoubtedly many KGB papers found their way to Leonid Brezhnev's office during this period, variously estimating American aspirations and capabilities. America's response to Gagarin had so surprised Soviet planners that an early around-the-Moon shot was, as time went on, a more and more important objective.

But were the Americans likely to be intimidated by an early Soviet around-the-Moon flight? There is no absolute answer to this question, for one set of events did follow and not another, and so the hypothetical question cannot be answered one way or the other. However such assumptions were a key part of Soviet political estimates and calculations. Here, once again, the interplay of political analysts and space planners may once again have cost the Russians dearly, for by early 1967 it was clear that American progress had been more rapid than had been anticipated.

American resilience became more and more obvious throughout 1965 and 1966 in three areas: the manned programme, the lunar programme and the Apollo/Saturn programme.

The manned programme, Gemini, with dubious origins as an intermediate spacecraft in between Mercury and Apollo, turned out to be a spectacular success. Gemini 4 was America's first spacewalk. Gemini 5 was an eight-day endurance test. Gemini 6 and 7 rendezvoused in space in a marvellous aerial ballet high over the blue of the Pacific Ocean. Gemini 7 pushed the endurance record to 14 days, and Gemini 8 achieved the first space docking in March 1966. The last four Geminis were put up only two months apart. Gemini 9 refined spacewalking. Gemini 10 docked with no fewer than two targets. It then used the Agena target to boost the combined assembly to 800 km over Arabia. Gemini 11 achieved first orbit docking. Gemini 12 went through all the manoeuvres again. During this period, not a single cosmonaut left the ground.

Not that Gemini did not encounter problems: it did, and the crew of Gemini 8 were nearly lost. But Gemini proved that rendezvous and docking could be done again and again. The ten missions gave the better part of twenty astronauts vital experience. The old days of frustration were left behind.

The unmanned lunar programme had two elements: a soft-lander, called Surveyor, of which seven were built; and a lunar orbiter, of which five were built, and called simply enough 'Lunar Orbiter'. Both were preceded by Luna 9 and 10 respectively, but between them they represented what were in effect engineering advances.

Of the seven Surveyors, all but two succeeded. They soft-landed very gently and had proper landing legs. Several survived into the lunar night and Surveyor 1 returned no fewer than 11 000 pictures over six weeks. Surveyor 7 returned 21 000 pictures from the crater Tycho. One Surveyor relighted its engine and took off, albeit briefly, from the lunar surface. The last three analysed the soil and had mechanical shovels. Surveyor ended in early 1968.

The Lunar Orbiter series ran from August 1966 to August 1967. All went correctly into lunar orbit. Each returned about 200 pictures and, by late 1967, 99 per cent of the lunar surface had been mapped, in some places better than some regions of Earth.

The third component, Saturn/Apollo was proceeding quietly but relentlessly. The first Apollo capsule arrived at the Cape in August 1966 and Virgil Grissom, Edward White and Roger Chaffee were nominated to take it through its paces in early 1967. The lunar module — perhaps the most troublesome part of the lunar machinery — would be ready in mid-1968. Von Braun's giant Saturn V would be available in August 1967. The pieces were all coming together.

Von Braun's Saturn V was like the Pyramids of Egypt in terms of its scale. It was higher than a cathedral, 110 m high. The bottom stage was so huge it had to come by barge to the launch site as no other earthly means of communication could carry it. A tall man could be swallowed up in just one of its nozzles. It would gulp fuel at 15 tonnes/s. The Saturn V was then put together in a slab-like vehicle assembly building (VAB), a structure so enormous that special air-conditioning had to be designed to prevent thunderclouds from forming near the roof.

One of the strengths of the NASA programme was that once the 1961 objective of man-on-the-Moon-by-1970 had been set, NASA had a fairly free hand to pursue it as it saw fit. This it did with single-mindedness. NASA was never phased by Soviet success. Throughout Gemini, both NASA and President Johnson repeatedly affirmed that America would get to the Moon first. In the public mind the Russians were generally considered to be ahead, even right through the Gemini missions when they clearly were not. Johnson was thought to be boosting morale by encouraging NASA, but in fact Johnson really believed what he was saying and NASA, for its part, grew more and more self-confident.

The Soviet programme, whilst it started from a similar base (Apollo compared to the Soyuz complex), was interfered with: first by the Voskhod enterprise, second by the replacement of the Soyuz complex by an alternate Moon landing plan involving the D booster and G booster, third by the scrapping of the Voskhod 3 and 4, and finally by the addition of a contingency unmanned programme.

Because of these interventions, the Soyuz programme had slipped badly: originally it had been planned for late 1964. It suffered a programme failure of its own too. In February 1966 it was ready for its first unmanned test, using a Cosmos designation. The countdown went to zero — and nothing happened. The new escape tower system should have fired the Soyuz free from the about-to-erupt rocket: but it too stayed silent. In the event the rocket did not blow up, but it meant taking the escape tower back to the drawing board.

However, not to worry. By the time of the Madrid Conference of the International Astronautical Federation in the autumn of 1966, Soviet scientists and cosmonauts promised the Americans a series of spaceflights that would eclipse the Gemini programme in just a single shot. It would put the USSR where it rightly belong: out in front.

6

So near but yet so far: the Moon race, the final stages (1967–74)

As the Moon race geared up for its climactic final stage, a whole new generation of cosmonauts was ready to take on new assignments, adding to the strength of the original 1960 group of 20, at this stage down to about 14 in size. There were some changes.

The third group of cosmonauts (after the original 20 and the women's group) was selected in January 1963, although some additional members came in as late as 1964. About 12 men were chosen. They differed from the 1960 group in terms of age and experience. It was felt that young fighter pilots were less essential than before. In the upcoming Earth orbit flights and tests, complex manoeuvres would be required: experienced senior pilots were thought to fit the bill better, and the age of this third group varied from 35 to 43. They were:

Georgi Beregovoi
Vladimir Shatalov
Anatoli Filipchenko
Georgi Dobrovolski
Alexei Gubarev
Vitally Zholobov
Yuri Artyukhin
Lev Demin.

The first five in the list were pilots, the last three engineers.

Georgi Beregovoi was at 43 the oldest, born in 1921, and a veteran of 185 combat missions in World War 2. He was a favourite with Western correspondents after his flight:

a big, tall, expressive man with huge eyebrows, he was prone to talking volubly and excitedly. Western correspondents always tried to corner him away from official supervision as he often gave away information that was supposed to stay secret.

His close associate, Vladimir Shatalov, from Leningrad, was more cautious. Typical of the new group, he was a flight instructor, then a regimental commander, and then an Air Force inspector. The same was true of the severe-faced Anatoli Filipchenko, a man of similar background and with a bent for underwater spear fishing.

Georgi Dobrovolski had the distinction of failure — he had tried hard to get into the Soviet naval service but had been turned away and had reluctantly entered the Air Force as a second option. Alexei Gubarev had actually seen combat, as a pilot with the Koreans and Chinese against the Americans in the Korean War in 1952.

Of the subgroup of engineers, Vitally Zholobov was an oil engineer — and the only Soviet cosmonaut with a moustache. In fact he looked like the hero of *Dr Zhivago*. Yuri Artyukin was a worker in the research laboratories of the Zhukovsky Academy. And Lev Demin, also a research worker, had been forced out of flying because of poor eyesight. So already the standards were in some ways less severe, and the criteria broadening.

The 1963 group introduced a new practice in cosmonaut selection — the division of groups into pilots and engineers. The former were nearly always military men, the latter civilians with good research qualifications. It was a policy that was more advanced than NASA, who did not so divide their crews until the Shuttle programme in the 1980s.

Two years later it was decided to expand the cosmonauts corps still further. The new group of pilots and engineers would be required in the post-Moon-landing era, and as a result they were very young as they would not expect to fly for five years or so. In fact the group became subsequently known as the 'Young Guard'. 20 such cosmonauts were selected in October 1965, all aged 23. Because of their youth, and the likelihood of their not flying for some time, a high rate of attrition was built in to the recruitment, so about three times the number required were selected. This was a wise policy because only six from this group ever flew;

Pyotr Klimuk	
Gennadiy Sarafanov	pilots
Vyacheslav Zudov	
Leonid Kizim	
Yuri Glazhkov	engineers
Vitally Rozhdezhvensky.	

The attrition rate was predictably high and over the years 1966–67 at least five cosmonauts were drafted in to fill the places of those who for various reasons dropped out. They were:

Yuri Malashev
Valeri Lazarev (reselection)
Vladimir Lyakhov
Vladimir Kovalyonok
Ivan Korniev.

In 1966 the State Commission recruited one of its most significant and important groups — a squad of twelve senior engineers, and their appointments were confirmed on 5 September 1966. These engineers were much more experienced than any recruited to date and most were intimately involved in spaceship design. They were brought in to fill the engineer's seat on the Moon landings and they would play a major role in designing the moonships of the post-Moon-landing era. These twelve included:

Alexei Yeliseyev
Vladislav Volkov
Valeri Kubasov
Vitali Savastianov
Nikolai Rukhavishnikov
Viktor Patsayev
Oleg Markarov (reselection)
Georgi Grechko.

These men were aged 30–35 and all were civilians. They were to play a key role in the Soviet space programme in the 1970s. Alexei Yeliseyev was typical. He was an expert in maths and physics and got a MSc in Space Engineering at the prestigious Bauman Technical School in Moscow in 1967. He was Eastern-looking, youthful, balding, always smartly turned out, often, like Feoktistov, seen in the control room during the missions.

Vladislav Volkov was a designer from the Moscow Aviation Institute. Valeri Kubasov worked in the Korolov design bureau and got onto the cosmonaut team after representations from Korolov following a paper he wrote called impressively 'The correction of interplanetary trajectory using radial impulses of heliocentric velocity'.

Vitali Sevastianov was a popular, cheerful and lively lecturer to the Young Guard cosmonauts when he applied for the position of cosmonaut himself. A versatile man, he was also television anchor-man on a Moscow television Science Series called 'Man, the Earth, and the Universe'.

Nikolai Rukhavishnikov had been with the Korolov design bureau since 1957 and was an expert in solar physics. Viktor Patsayev was an expert in radio research.

A final group was selected around this period. Twelve scientists were recruited in the Voskhod tradition, people who had little aeronautical or design experience but a specialization in science, and who were fit enough to fly in space. They would take the third seat in Soyuz or Heavy Zond in the flights planned for 1970–73, whether to the Moon or Earth orbit. They were specialists in physiology like Rostislav Bogdashevsky, or in astronomy, medicine, biology, or zoology.

So, by early 1967, the USSR had recruited no fewer than eight cosmonaut groups and had on its active list 14 pilots from the 1960 group, 6 pilots and 6 engineers from 1963, 20 Young Guards, 12 design engineers and 12 scientists — about 50 or 60 cosmonauts in all.

At this stage, the senior cosmonauts were divided into three training groups. This was the first significant use of the training group concept — groups of teams and their backups assigned to cover specific missions or groups of missions. Some were in both, and they were assigned as follows:

Early Soyuz tests in Earth orbit
Vladimir Komarov
Valeri Bykovsky
Alexei Yeliseyev
Yevgeni Khrunov
Yuri Gagarin
Georgi Beregovoi

Zond around the Moon flight
Pavel Belyayev
Alexei Yeliseyev
Vladimir Shatalov
Valeri Kubasov

Lunar landing group
Alexei Leonov
Valery Bykovsky
Yuri Gagarin
Pavel Popovich
Vitally Sevastianov
Georgi Dobrovolski
Pyotr Klimuk
Yuri Artyukin
Georgi Grechko
Oleg Markarov
Nikolai Rukhavishnikov

There is some overlapping here, for some would gain their experience on one flight to use on the next. The lunar landing group was dispatched off to the Black Sea in 1967–68 to practise water landings and flying helicopters. There is only one purpose for which it has ever been desirable to train cosmonauts to fly helicopters and that is lunar landing. At the same time the American Apollo astronauts were training on helicopters and a 'flying testbed'. Neil Armstrong in fact nearly died on one.

Of the Zond group, Pavel Belyayev was later appointed to the first around-the-Moon shot. The other three were spotted in photographs of Soyuz-type capsules but with one peculiar difference. The instrument panel did not have an Earth globe. *Ergo*, the spaceship they were training in was not designed to fly in Earth orbit.

In the first group, all three were identified in photographs of the period associated with the upcoming flight of Soyuz 1, now drawing near.

SOYUZ

Soyuz is worth detailed examination: its successors were still flying twenty years later, a lasting tribute to the designing achievement of Sergei Korolov.

Leaving aside the lunar versions (Zond and Heavy Zond) and the Earth orbit successors (Soyuz ferry, Soyuz T and Progress) the basic Earth orbit engineering model, flown on

Soyuz 1–9, was about 8 m long, 2.75 m wide, with an internal volume of 3.8 m³, a launch weight of 6575 kg and a descent capsule weight of 2800 kg, and a thrust of 417 ΔV.

Soyuz consists of three modules: equipment, descent and orbital. The equipment module contains retrorockets and manoeuvring engines, fuel, solar wings and supplies. The acorn-shaped descent module is the home of the cosmonauts during ascent and descent, with a side hatch and an end hatch. There are portholes, a parachute section, and three contour seats. The orbital module, attached on the front, is circular, with spacewalk hatch, lockers for food, equipment and experiments. As it is more spacious, the cosmonauts live there rather than in the cramped descent module.

From Soyuz protrude a periscope for dockings, two seagull-like solar panels, aerials, docking probe on the front, and flashing lights and beacons. The periscope can be swivelled both ways.

Before its first piloted test, two models of Soyuz were flown. These were:

Cosmos 133	Nov 28 1966	181 by 232 km	51.9 degrees	88.4 minutes
Cosmos 140	Feb 7 1967	170 by 241 km	51.7 degrees	88.5 minutes

'FIRE IN THE SPACECRAFT'

Even as these two Cosmos missions were taking place, the American space programme was paralysed and going through the most traumatic period since its establishment. On a windy day at Cape Canaveral NASA lost three of its best astronauts in a ground test in horrific circumstances.

Soyuz's competitor, Apollo, had arrived at the Cape on 19 August 1966, and on 6 January 1967 had been placed atop the Saturn IB rocket that was to take it into orbit for three weeks of tests after a launching due on 21 February. It would put America into the final stretch of the Moon race.

A last countdown test had been scheduled for 27 January and at 1 p.m. Virgil Grissom, Edward White and Roger Chaffee boarded Apollo 1 for its last on-the-pad check-out. It was a long procedure which had got to T − 10 minutes at 6.31 p.m. when a voice was heard to shout over the intercom: 'Fire in the spacecraft!' Chaffee could then be heard calling, 'We've got a bad fire! Get us out!' He went on: 'Open up here!' There was a last scream. Outside Apollo 1, the leader of the pad team ordered his pad technicians to get them out, but was only able to watch helplessly as the spacecraft burst into flames. A wave of heat blew him in the face and thick smoke gushed out.

Grissom, White and Chaffee died nearly at once. The fire was both lethal and rapid and thrived on the high-pressure oxygen pumped in at 16.7 psi instead of the normal 14.7 psi (pounds per square inch). All that was left of Apollo 1 was a blackened shell.

NASA and America were shocked. Nothing had ever prepared the American people for this kind of disaster, and least of all were they able to accept it after the effortless performances of the last of the Gemini series. People might have been psychologically more accepting of a disaster on a mission, at a moment of exposure to greatest danger. But completely unexpected and on the ground, and in a fire, of all things! It was not long before questions were being asked.

NASA set up a Review Board within hours. It had reported by the end of April. What it came up with was a mixture of the honest, the reassuring and the disconcerting. Honest, because it revealed serious flaws in Apollo's design; reassuring, because of the refusal to cover up a story of multiple negligence; disconcerting, because some of the mistakes made should not have been made by a competent household electrician. The Review Board listed pages and pages of wrong-doing. These included flammable fire-hazardous material in the cabin; a hatch that took at least 90 seconds to open; lack of firefighting equipment; poorly insulated wires which could easily fray and set off a spark that could begin a fire, which was probably what had happened.

But the Review Board dealt only with the more immediate aspects of the cause of the fire. It did not ask the more basic question of whether safety corners were being cut in order to win the space race. It did not suggest that complacency might have set in after six accident-free years. And a whole angle to the fire — the running battle between NASA and the prime contractor, North American Rockwell, about schedules, standards, costs and safety — did not come out at all. NASA was subsequently criticized for, and Congress taken to task for condoning, a report which found out only the immediate shortcomings in an effort to get NASA airborne as soon as possible. It avoided asking the deeper questions.

THE FIRST FLIGHT OF SOYUZ

As April drew near, so too did rumours of an impending space flight. 18 March marked the second anniversary of the last Russian manned flight — that of Voskhod 2. General Kaminin, head of cosmonaut training, announced that a new flight was coming up soon. By 15 April, no Western correspondent in Moscow could be unaware of a big mission in the offing. By 22 April, rumours were flying thick and fast. At 11.45 p.m. that evening RTE Radio News (Dublin) was able to announce that a single-man flight was on the pad and ready to go. The next day was the anniversary of Lenin's birth.

The rumours were accurate. A big shot was planned. Soyuz 1 would go first, with a single cosmonaut on board. Vladimir Komarov, 40, Voskhod 1 veteran, was the appropriate choice for this first and most challenging mission. 24 hours into the flight, Soyuz 2 would follow, commanded by Vostok 5 veteran Valeri Bykovsky. Two new-comers, Yevgeni Khrunov (1960 group) and Alexei Yeliseyev (only a year in training) would fly with him.

The rendezvous would simulate the Moon linkup. Soyuz 1 would be the active craft and would rendezvous on orbit 1. Then the show would really begin. Khrunov and Yeliseyev would don suits, leave Soyuz 2 and transfer into Soyuz 1 to join Komarov. The two ships would then separate after about four hours. Komarov, now accompanied by Khurnov and Yeliseyev, would be back on the ground by the end of day 2, Bykovsky following on the 26th.

So in 72 breathtaking hours the Soyuz craft would demonstrate Earth orbit rendezvous on the first orbit, transfer, spacewalking and a primitive space station, and put the USSR back out in front. The usually accurate UPI correspondent predicted:

The unamimous feeling here in Moscow is that Russia will try a series of manoeuvres in earth orbit never tried before and then venture out within the next year or eighteen months for a manned flight around the moon. [1]

Meanwhile, at the cosmodrome, what was actually happening? Vladimir Komarov had arrived there several days earlier and at midnight Moscow time reached the pad in his transfer van. On his own this time, but wearing clothes similar to the overalls of Voskhod 1, he strode across the apron and with a final wave gestured goodbye to the launch crew. Round about were his backup (Yuri Gagarin), the Soyuz 2 crew and the mission director Andrian Nikolayev.

At 3.35 a.m. Moscow time (not quite sunrise local time) the A2 rocket, with its revolutionary cargo aboard, lit the sky up all about and headed off in the direction of the onrushing dawn. Eight minutes later Vladimir Komarov was again in orbit, testing out the most sophisticated spacecraft ever launched.

The orbit of Soyuz 1 measured 201 by 224 km, 51.7 degrees, 88.6 minutes. News of the launch was announced to the world. These were about the last facts that were ever known officially about Vladimire Komarov. We know that he tested the spaceship from 1.30 p.m. to 9.20 p.m. that day, reported back at 10.30 p.m. that evening and again at 4.50 a.m. the next morning, and that by 6.30 a.m. he was dead. Officially the story was that he died on reentry when the parachutes snarled. So what went wrong?

It is clear from examining the Soyuz 1 mission, and many studies have been made of it, that at least two things went wrong on Soyuz 1. First, there was the immediate cause of the disaster, which made Komarov the first man ever to die on an actual spaceflight. Second, there is the need to answer the question: why was Soyuz 2 not launched, which it should have been around 24 hours into the mission? Several explanations are possible:

(1)   There was a major countdown failure on Soyuz 2, so serious as to make Komarov's continued flight unnecessary, so he was ordered down.
(2)   Soyuz 1 hit trouble from early on. Soyuz 2 was put off and all efforts were concentrated (unsuccessfully in the event) on getting Komarov back alive.
(3)   All Soyuz 1 was, was a 24 hour test of a brand new capsule, a test which went suddenly wrong at the last minute.

The last explanation was accepted for many years, right down to 1977 when the Russian censors released photographs of an unsuited Komarov with a suited Yeliseyev and suited Khrunov; with an unsuited Gagarin and Bykovsky — exactly the configuration of the long-rumoured crews. Soon after came another picture, showing Komarov at the pad, surrounded by the other crews and backups, with flowers in his hand, the flowers with which a cosmonaut is always presented just before flying.

Such photographs of cosmonauts or groups of cosmonauts are never taken accidentally and they were entirely consistent with all the pre-flight rumours about the mission. Another factor which cast doubt on the official explanation of the mission was the nature of Soviet statements made before the flight, both official and unofficial. They were worded in such a way that a one-day test flight could only be seen as an anti-climax. Yuri Gagarin had only just written in a magazine article: 'It is not sensible to put a spacecraft into orbit for a short time. For that reason the transfer of crews and delivery of supplies

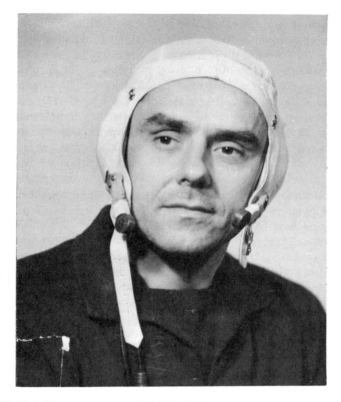

Cosmonaut Vladimir Komarov, veteran of the Voskhod 1 flight, who died when his Soyuz 1 capsule crashed near Orsk in the western USSR. There were a number of problems encountered on the re-entry, and officially the parachute lines of the spacecraft snarled causing the crash landing; however, a number of more colourful explanations have been advanced.

to orbiting craft is being studied' [2]. The long delay of 12 hours in announcing Komarov's death also needs an explanation if a parachute failure was all that was involved.

The first theory is more plausible. A countdown problem is an occupational hazard for any space launch, and it could well have happened this time. But of itself it does not explain why Komarov had to come down immediately. He would surely have flown the originally planned 48-hour profile. Instead he landed on orbit 18, coming down in western Russia, like no other spacecraft before or since. Why the hurry?

Soyuz crashed near the Urals by a town called Orsk. There is a small memorial there to Vladimir Komarov now. It is a simple shining slab with a symbolic rocket on top, and his medals and a stern picture of the lonely man on the side. It is covered in flowers and there is a little wooden fence round about.

But Orsk is way off the beaten track. It is nowhere near a normal landing line. So could it have been some kind of emergency landing? Could Soyuz 1 have gone wrong from early on? It is possible. There were very few flight reports from Soyuz 1, no telecasts and only one radio broadcast. There were no launch pictures, not even any of Komarov at the pad. This was low-key, even by the then camera-shy standards of the

Soviet press agencies. It was suspiciously low-key. Was something amiss even by the time the launch was being announced to the world, something that ground controllers were straining every nerve to resolve [3]?

It is possible. Observers have offered many explanations. These include: the solar panels did not deploy, thus starving Soyuz of electrical power. There was a breakdown in the electronics. The stabilization system went wrong. There were wilder ones too, such as that Komarov s old heart trouble suddenly reasserted itself and he collapsed in orbit. The one which best fits the known facts suggests that there was an electronic guidance failure. Komarov tried twice to reenter, succeeded on the third attempt, but that in spinning the spacecraft through reentry to even out the G forces he overspun the spacecraft to the extent that it was still spinning at parachute deployment so that the lines snarled.

A further variation on this is that Soyuz 1 never made it through reentry. After all, no body was ever produced and the 12 hour delay could explain the fabrication of a coverup story. A parachute failure is a 'bad luck' explanation — more acceptable to the public than news of major technical shortcomings.

The Russians always stood by the parachute failure story and issued many a statement to try to scotch the post-flight rumours, some extremely colourful versions of which emerged over time. These included detailed exchanges between a dying Komarov and a sobbing Kosygin in ground control telling him he'd always be remembered. One British writer, Chapman Pincher, was probably nearer the truth when he wrote the next day:

> As with the Apollo catastrophe, when a frayed electrical wire may have been the cause, the really difficult problems in Soyuz may have been brilliantly solved and the easy ones skimped. [4]

Regardless of the cause or the nature of Komarov's death, all sides were agreed on its implications: the Soyuz 1 disaster would halt the Soviet programme in its tracks just as effectively as the Apollo fire did the American one only four months earlier. Both disasters raised the same question of each side cutting corners or just being plain careless in its desire to win the Moon race [5]. These were questions both sides were eager to avoid in their mutual desire to get flying again.

Such were the feelings of Vladimir Komarov's loyal comrades as they laid his remains to rest in the Kremlin wall two days later. It was a sombre and chilling occasion, an unwelcome reminder of the real costs of the Moon race. As the bands played the haunting Chopin funeral march, the grim-faced and tight-lipped cosmonaut corps, now diminished to nine men and one woman, swore that the programme must go on relentlessly. There could be no turning back.

LAST LAP IN THE RACE: ZOND

The Soyuz disaster forced a reappraisal in the USSR similar to that under way in NASA under the aegis of the Review Board. And by late summer, the planners had decided on a new sequence of events to take account of the delays imposed by the Komarov disaster.

The Soyuz 1/2 mission would be now flown unmanned twice, once as soon as possible and then again in early 1968. The first manned Soyuz would not attempt to repeat Soyuz 1/2 but would instead involve one manned Soyuz and one unmanned. Yuri Gagarin was at once appointed to fly this testing mission, scheduled for mid-1968. The original Soyuz 1/2 profile would then fly straight after. It was better to err on the side of caution. And in parallel with the design review of Soyuz, work would go flat-out on the stripped-down Soyuz which would fly around the Moon with the Zond designation.

And so the years 1967–68 were to witness frantic attempts by both sides to get men to the Moon, initiating a relentless game of leap-frog between the two superpowers.

Three initial Zond tests were carried out around the time of the Soyuz 1 disaster. These were Cosmos 146 (March 1967), Cosmos 154 (April 1967) and Cosmos 159 (May 1967). All flew on the Proton D booster and none was satifactorily explained at the time [6].

Some clues emerged many years later in 1981 when the Masyonstroenye Press published a book by Valentin Glushko called *The history of rocketry and spaceflight in the Soviet Union*. He let out two facts: Cosmos 146 weighed 5017 kg and reached the escape velocity of 11.2 km/s. Now 5017 kg is nearly the exact known weight of Zond, and Cosmos 146 did not escape into the solar system. The only possible explanation is that it was driven backwards into the atmosphere at escape speed, thus testing reentry from the Moon. The Americans did such tests twice – on Apollo 4 and Apollo 6 [7].

The second was Cosmos 154, which went into an orbit of 185 by 215 km, 51.3 degrees, on 8 April 1967, and flew for ten days. It is possible the capsule was recovered from the Atlantic. And a third test was done not long after. Cosmos 159 was, according to the best evidence available, the first test of the instrument module of the lunar orbiting 'Heavy Zond'.

These three missions were at the time thought to be associated with the Soyuz 1 mission because of the similar orbits and inclinations: but the fact that the timing of the tests seems to have been quite independent of Soyuz 1 (and unaffected by the disaster) indicates a parallel programme of a different time scale. Which was what Zond was.

THE ANNIVERSARY OF THE BOLSHEVIK REVOLUTION

25 October to 7 November 1967, marked the anniversary of the period in 1917 when Vladimir Lenin, Leon Trotsky and a handful of their disciplined supporters seized state power in chaotic war-torn Petrograd. It was, particularly since it was the 50th anniversary, too important to go unmarked by some kind of space achievement. The real question was not if it would be marked, but how.

The Soyuz disaster meant that the chances of flying a man around the Moon for the anniversary were nil. Zond and Soyuz were too closely related, and there was no way that Soyuz could be brought up to standard in time, regardless of how well Zond went. So the best that could be hoped for was an unmanned flyby, paving the way for a manned one in 1968.

Working overtime, the designers and launch teams got the first unmanned round-the-Moon Zond out to the pad by mid-September 1967 [8]. The countdown began for a launch on 28 September. It was the most impressive sight ever seen at Baikonour. The huge red-and-white D-1e booster, 82 m high, weighing 1 028 500 kg, Soyuz cabin atop, tipped by a pencil-spear of an escape tower, was taking with it Russia's Moon hopes. It sat squat on its giant pad, shrouded by its gantry, as engineers fussed with one technical problem after another.

The controllers missed their launch window on 28 September and they missed a second one on 26 October. Time was running out, but by this time the Soyuz programme was back in gear again. Cosmos 186 was first to appear, beginning a series of flights that would requalify Soyuz for manned flight once more. It went up on 27 October 1967 and was followed three days later on 30 October by Cosmos 188.

Cosmos 186   208 by 234 km   51.7 degrees   88.7 minutes

Cosmos 188   200 by 276 km   51.7 degrees   89.0 minutes

Using totally automatic radar, direction-finding and sounding devices, Cosmos 186 at once closed in on Cosmos 188 in the manoeuvre Komarov was to have carried out in April. Whatever past difficulties there had been, the manoeuvres that followed went with astonishing accuracy and precision. At orbital insertion, 188 was only 24 km away. 186 closed rapidly, within two-thirds of an orbit. One hour later over the South Pacific, they clunked together to form an automatic orbiting complex. 3.5 hours later – or at the equivalent moment of lunar injection – they separated. 186 was down the next day, 188 two days later. It was a flawless display of advanced robotics. It proved the feasibility of first-orbit rendezvous and the viability of Soyuz-style docking, and it took some of the fears out of lunar orbit rendezvous when all this would have to be done a quarter of a million miles away.

However, the elation surrounding the Cosmis 186–188 mission was followed by a disheartening experience three weeks later. Zond, which had missed two launch windows, took off at last on 22 November, but got no further than low Earth orbit.

Rather than run the embarrassment of trying to reach a real Moon the next time and fail again, it was decided that the next Zond would aim towards a simulated Moon the next spring. It would involve the same type of return trajectory as a real Moon flight. But time was pressing even more now, for the Americans were nearly back on their feet again.

Virtually unaffected by the Apollo fire, the enormous Saturn V booster was nearing completion under the direction of Peenemünde veteran Wernher von Braun. It was this German's last and most brilliant achievement, the climax of his engineering career. Von Braun had been working on Saturn V since 1962 and his ultimate project was now reaching the moment of truth. It is a tribute to his genius that this giant creation, five times larger than anything ever before flown, was to take to the skies eleven times and complete every assignment.

In the still relatively young von Braun the Russian rocket engineers at last met their match. His Saturn V was not merely giant with its height of 110.6 m, launch weight 27.7 million kilograms, thrust 3.4 million kilograms – it was a miracle of efficiency and precision. It used – for the first time – the supercold, ultrapowerful and extremely difficult fuel of liquid hydrogen. And after the fire, ground testing ensured that the words 'frantically thorough' were an understatement of the engineers' approach. The Saturn V arrived at the pad in late August 1967 for its first, unmanned test.

After three days' counting down, the first Saturn V at last reached the magical moment of zero, during the winter darkness of 9 November 1967. The five monstrous engines belched and roared for nine full seconds before generating enough thrust for liftoff. Night turned to day. Pillars of smoke billowed into the night sky. In the midst, the Saturn V rose. The roar of the engines knocked people over three miles away as Saturn bent over towards the Atlantic Ocean. At 58 km, travelling at 9658 km/h, the main engines cut off, the bottom stage separated and there was a sharp flash as the second stage lit up. Its blue flames pushed Saturn out of sight into the night sky and it was lost to view.

Saturn V put an unmanned capsule, Apollo 4, into orbit atop its third stage. After two revolutions, that third stage was restarted. Then Apollo fired its own motor to push its orbit out to 40 000 km, before blasting it back into the atmosphere to simulate a lunar return at high speed. After an eight hour flight the blackened and charred capsule was fished out of the sea.

This morale boosting success was underscored when on 22 January 1968, NASA got its lunar module aloft for the first time. It was designated Apollo 5. The bug-shaped, spidery lunar module was put through its paces in six revolutions during which all its major stages were tested. The flight went so well that a second orbital test planned for June 1968 was cancelled.

AMERICA MOVES AHEAD

With the successful missions of Apollo 4 and 5, NASA was now moving well ahead. The USSR had failed to produce its three equivalent pieces of hardware — its own lunar module or large booster, or to demonstrate high speed lunar reentry return. In fact it was nowhere near doing so.

What was the public perception of the Moon race at this stage? Coverage of space events was at this particular period less than it had been for ten years, largely because no manned flights had taken place since April 1967 and none now looked likely until the autumn of 1968. Public interest tended to revolve around manned flights, and as a result the significance of all these unmanned events was not properly appreciated. Indeed, the Cosmos docking and the Apollo 4 and 5 flights were perceived as peripheral.

The existence of a space race now seemed to some to be debateable. What if there was none? The USSR showed little evidence of having hardware comparable to the United States with its Saturn V and lunar module. The Cosmos docking — and the method of docking was odd but that could just be the Russian way of doing things — could equally point in the direction of Earth-orbiting space stations. If anything, the Soviet challenge was fading.

FADING CHALLENGE?

This was not how NASA saw it. CIA and other intelligence briefings throughout 1967 and 1968 insisted the race was for real and that a large booster would be on the pad before very long. Congress briefings always contained a warning that although America was confident of being on the Moon first, no one should be too surprised if the Russians got round it first. And the CIA also warned that, regarding the hardware, absence of evidence was not evidence of absence.

As if stung by the successes of Apollo 4 and 5 — and being in the unusual position of having to play catch-up rather than the other way round — the Soviet literature reinforced the notion of a continuing Soviet challenge in early 1968. A series of rumours in February and April 1968 repeated the suggestion of a Soviet manned flight later in the year. Valeri Bykovsky in Hungary predicted animals would soon precede man around the Moon [9].

So seriously did NASA take the Soviet challenge that in the spring of 1968 it was decided to fly men aboard the next lunar module and to manrate the third Saturn V assuming the second test was successful. Originally ten unmanned Saturn V tests had been planned. The long-term NASA plans had suggested a manned Moon-landing on the seventh Apollo flight but these plans were being rapidly telescoped.

So NASA was, for the first time in its history, upping the ante, and advancing its schedules to beat anticipated Soviet targets. It had never done this before. NASA was never criticized for doing so: had the USSR manrated its lunar module or its G booster on its second test it would have certainly been criticized for recklessness.

The next Zond got away successfully on 2 March 1968, aimed at a hypothetical Moon. However, what happened after its first few hours of flight remains to this day a mystery. Of the tens of thousands of spacecraft and bits of spacecraft and debris and junk tracked by Western radars, Zond 4 alone bears the cryptic obituary 'elements no longer maintained'. Some people believe it crashed back into the atmosphere, others believe it ended up in orbit around the Sun. No one — not even the Russians — seems to know. Zond 4 may have been crippled by a communications failure. Certainly the mission was not completed successfully. An attempt to repeat it on 20 April failed too. So far, of three Zond attempts, two had failed completely and one was more a failure than a success.

Nothing seemed to be going right. The Soviet Union was slipping. NASA was on the march again and on 4 April 1968, Apollo 6 went up on the second Saturn V. It was intended that it would repeat the dazzling success of Apollo 4. But now it was NASA's turn to gasp as one thing went wrong after another. Two minutes into the mission the red lights flashed as the whole Saturn V structure went into a wild 'pogo' effect — shaking up and down violently. Soon after, some parts of the lunar module adapter section shook free. This was the least the pogo effect would do. Worse vibration, and the astronauts would not be able to read their instruments. Worse again, and it would break up.

That stopped, and more trouble started. On the second stage, two engines shut down for no reason. Apollo 6 went into an orbit of 172 by 395 km, instead of one circular at 175 km. Then the third stage refused to ignite. Apollo 6's motor had to do its reentry manoeuvres itself instead of the Saturn third stage. This it did, and the capsule was recovered after a reentry at a much lower speed than planned.

Undaunted by this flirtation with disaster four times over, NASA then announced that its Saturn V was 'manrated' as from 29 April and they were now happy to fly astronauts on top of it. The faults had been ironed out, NASA assured everyone. It revealed its new plan: a three-man Apollo in the autumn in Earth orbit; then an Earth orbit test out to 6000 km before the new year; and a lunar module test in the spring; a lunar orbit next, a final test, and then a landing.

The investigators of the Apollo 6 difficulties were indeed thorough and exhaustive. Still, the NASA decision so soon afterwards was open to the accusation of haste. It is unlikely if such swift man-rating standards would ever have been used before or since. James Webb's decision must have shocked and exasperated the Soviet space planners: the two goals of Moon landing and around-the-Moon flight were now slipping from their grasp.

Some consolation could be drawn from a repeat of the Cosmos linkup of the previous winter. On 15 April, Cosmos 212 (the active ship) linked to Cosmos 213, this time in a record 47 minutes, beating America's Gemini 11 (94 minutes). Television showed the last 400 m of the docking manoeuvre as the spacecraft aligned their wing-like panels one to another. Millions saw the separation 3 hr 50 min later over the blue vastness of the Pacific. The way was now clear for the first Soviet manned mission for a year.

FAREWELL TO GAGARIN

Sadly, the pilot, who had been assigned the mission was now dead. Early on the morning of 27 March 1968, and not long after his 34th birthday. Yuri Gagarin had taken off with flying instructor Vladimir Seryogin on a routine flight test aboard a MiG-15Uti aircraft from a flying field northeast of Moscow. It was part of his regular flight training to keep him in trim for flying the next Soyuz.

Not long after takeoff the MiG stalled. Rather than eject, Gagarin and Seryogin tried to restart the engine. They failed. The MiG crashed into a forest near the airfield and burned [10].

Gagarin's wife Valentina was in hospital at the time having an operation for a stomach ulcer. She was able to get up and walk on the 26th and the following evening phoned home to check whether Yuri had returned from his day's flying. She called for an hour and a half and was eventually told the line was out of order. Something began to nag at her that things were wrong.

Then, the following morning, quite unexpectedly (she said later), Valentina Terreskhova, Pavel Popovich and Andrian Nikolayev appeard. She recalled:

As soon as I saw them, my heart was gripped with fear.
'Has anything happened?' I asked them.
'Yes', they said, `yesterday morning. . .'. [11]

It could not have come at a worse time. Always popular, accepted as a leader, Gagarin had taken upon himself the task of solving the problems that had killed his friend Vladimir Komarov. Now he too was gone. His nine comrades bore his body through the streets of Moscow two days later amidst black scenes of great grief. It was a further blow the great adventure could ill afford.

Almost as if to take advantage of the USSR's sagging position in the space stakes, NASA Apollo programme manager George Low began to advance the notion of an early Apollo flight to the Moon. As of the summer of 1968, NASA planned three Earth orbital flights before going anywhere near the Moon.

Sorting out the problems in the lunar module, was, despite the success of the January flight, taking longer than expected and the next LM might not be ready to fly until some time into 1969. Why not, argued Low, do a lunar flight first, using the Apollo command cabin only, and then test out the LM later? He put forward an ambitious — or looked at another way, reckless — plan: if the Apollo 7 Earth orbital flight were successful in October, Apollo 8 could go around the Moon two or three months later. Apollo 9 could do the LM tests in Earth orbit and Apollo 10 could do the LM tests in lunar orbit.

Low's scheme was logical enough — testing what was available when it was available rather than waiting. As for the gamble of the first Moon flight, it had to be done sooner or later, so why not sooner? It would be just as dangerous one flight later, just as psychologically challenging. But there were some negative sides to the plan. Apollo 8 would be only the second Apollo to fly. And it would be only the third flight of the Saturn V. Unlike their rivals, NASA had absolutely no means of testing out Apollo on a round-the-Moon trip, unmanned and automatically, before putting humans on board. So the proposal was not without risks.

George Low's proposal was quickly accepted at senior management level within NASA, including von Braun. Administrator Webb and President Johnson took several weeks to agree. They must have been sceptical about flying around the Moon a spacecraft that had not yet flown and which had already incinerated its first crew. But agree they did — on the strict condition that Apollo 7 was entirely successful. And Apollo 6-style faults would not qualify.

So it was that on 19 August 1968, NASA announced a revised Apollo schedule. Apollo 7, crewed by astronauts Schirra, Eisele and Cunningham would test out Apollo in a ten-day Earth orbit shake-down cruise starting on 11 October. Apollo 8 (Borman, Lovell, Anders) would go to the Moon (lunar orbit or figure-of-eight flyby) in late December; and Apollo 9 (McDivitt, Scott, Schweickart) would test out the LM, back in Earth orbit when it was ready. That was expected to be March 1969.

Surprisingly little public notice was taken of this announcement in the West. Partly this was because it was during the summer break, partly it was because of the disbelief that the USSR was still racing. Another factor was that Apollo 7 had yet to fly, and even thinking of doing anything beyond that could be written off as either day-dreaming or wishful thinking.

THE RIPOSTE

But the announcement must have put the wind up the planners in Moscow and Baikonour! They almost certainly considered the Americans out of their minds to man-rate a spacecraft for Moon flight on only its second mission and before the first flight had even taken off. Based on the more conservative safety considerations in Soviet thinking, such a proposal in the USSR would have always been a non-starter. The step-by-step Soviet plan of the time called for two Zonds around the Moon, with a simultaneous Soyuz requalification. Only if this went properly would they contemplate a manned Zond-around-the-Moon, probably in January 1969 at the earliest. So the NASA announcement hurried this up out of all proportion. The manned Zond — it would be Zond 7 — would now have to be ready at least a month earlier to beat Apollo 8. The heat was on.

As luck would have it, the launch window that might take Apollo 8 to the Moon opened for Apollo on 21 December but opened much earlier in the USSR — in fact from 7—9 December. This was entirely due to the celestial mechanics of the optimum launching and landing opportunities. So training for Zond 7 was speeded up, and, there is now good reason to believe, Pavel Balyayev was selected as pilot, and either Valeri Kubasov, Vladimir Shatalov or Alexei Yeliseyev as backup. Could they still do it?

Autumn was in the air and the night-time temperatures were cool once more when at midnight on 15 September 1968, Zond 5 rose off the pad at Baikonour and the glare from its Proton launch vehicle silhouetted the gantries, huts and assembly buildings for miles around. It all went effortlessly well. 67 minutes later, Zond 5 was moonbound, right on course. Its cabin contained turtles, fruit flies and other living organisms, and the spacecraft weighed 5500 kg.

On 17 September at 6.11 a.m. Moscow time, Zond 5 successfully corrected its course. Only then did Moscow reveal the craft's existence. This semi-secret approach excited the interest of Jodrell Bank Observatory where Sir Bernard Lovell quickly switched on his radio dish to track the enigmatic Zond 5. He picked up strong signals at once.

On 19 September he was able to reveal that he thought the spacecraft had been around the Moon at a distance of around 1950 km and was on its way back. This information was based on the signals he had received. But nobody really knew. Moscow categorically denied that Zond 5 had been anywhere near the Moon.

If the mission planners had been as inept as the Soviet news service, the flight would have failed at this stage. As it was, Zond 5 had seen the Earth diminish to the size of a small blue ball in the distance. Any cosmonaut then on board would have been treated to the fantastic spectable of the Moon's craters, deserts and rugged highlands sweeping below him in stark profusion. Zond soared around the Moon's far side, and then, as it neared its eastern limit, the full earth rose gently over the horizon, a welcoming beacon to guide the three-day flight home. Would a cosmonaut soon see this breathtaking vista?

20 September. A belated Russian admission that Zond 5 had indeed been 'in the vicinity of the Moon' (as if any spacecraft happens to find itself in the 'vicinity' of the Moon) was eclipsed by new, even more startling news from Jodrell Bank. A human voice had been picked up from Zond 5! Was this a secret breakthrough? Had a man been aboard all along, and would the Russians then announce an historic first?

Not likely, said Sir Bernard Lovell. It was a tape-recorded voice, designed to test voice transmissions across deep space. He expected the next flight would have a cosmonaut aboard. Jodrell Bank continued to track the probe till it was 80 000 km from the Earth and picking up speed rapidly.

Zond 5 was indeed returning to the Earth. At 5.30 p.m. Moscow time, 21 September, it reached the limit of the Earth's atmosphere over springtime Antarctica, met its 10 by 13 km reentry frame dead on, slammed into the atmosphere at 11 km/s and burned red hot to a temperature of $13\,000°C$. G forces built up to 16G. Soon the ordeal was over. A double sonic boom, audible over the Indian Ocean, signified survival. Parachutes lowered the simmering, still glowing Zond 5 into the Indian Ocean at 7.08 p.m. Beacons popped out to beep the location of the bobbing capsule.

A ship from the Soviet Navy moved in, took Zond out of the water, and hoisted it aboard; in no time it was transferred to a cargo ship en route to Bombay where it was transferred into a large Antonov air transport and flown back to the USSR.

Success at last! The capsule was intact, the turtles had survived, and the guidance had been perfect. In one sweet week, all the reverses of the past 18 months had been wiped out. Two tests — a repeat mission and a Soyuz test — and the Moon could be Terra Sovietica. The first glimpse out of the porthole, the historic descriptions, the joy of rounding the corner of the Moon — these could yet be Soviet achievements.

All NASA could do now was cross its fingers and hope against hope that the Russians would not somehow do it first. They now knew they could. Before long the Russians released information which confirmed NASA's worst fears. They announced that Zond was identical to Soyuz, but without the orbital compartment. It had air for one man for six days. It carried an escape tower. The *Soviet encyclopedia of spaceflight* (1968) rubbed it in: 'Zond flights are launched for testing and development of an automatic version of a manned lunar spaceship' [12].

No sooner had Zond and its precious cargo reached Baikonour at the end of September than the three-week countdown began for the next Soyuz, designed to put right the faults that had plagued Soyuz 1 and 2 in 1967. There would be no ambitious crew transfer this time, just a four-day solo test of rendezvous performances. There would be a one-man crew, to simulate the Zond flight. He would be Georgi Beregovoi, 47, then the oldest man to fly in space, and he was standing in for the late Yuri Gagarin. His wartime experience, his age, his courage, equipped him superbly to fly such a dangerous mission. Everything depended on him. The test was critical. And the portents were not good. Georgi Beregovoi had already tried to fly the mission before, that August. Soyuz 2 had gone into orbit, and he was all ready to fly Soyuz 3 up to it the next morning. But Soyuz 2 developed trouble and was hastily renamed Cosmos 238 before people could suspect something was amiss. His own flight had been stood down [13].

SOYUZ VINDICATED

Evaluating the performance of Zond 5 in preparation for Soyuz took several weeks and Soyuz was not ready to go until 25 October. So close were the American and Soviet programmes to each other at this stage that Soyuz 2 flew only three days after the first test of America's new Apollo. It was uncanny. It needed such close parallels to persuade many Western observers that there was indeed a race at all.

11 October. Four years less one day after Russia's three-man spaceship, the Americans were airborne with Apollo. A bright start, with the red, orange and yellow flame of the Saturn IB propelling Apollo 7 into a safe orbit, set the tone for the rest of the mission. Twice veteran Walter Schirra, with novices Walter Cunningham and Don F. Eisele, put Apollo through its paces. The main service engine fired exactly as the engineers wanted, a full eight times.

The three astronauts sent back repeated telecasts from their roomy cabin with its rows of switches and nooks and crannies. They were clearly delighted, confident and fully at ease. The astronauts caught colds and had a few rows with ground control, but that was all that could be reported on since the flight was otherwise going so well. No one remembered the fire any more and it almost seemed that it was because they had nothing left to test out that Schirra, Eisele and Cunningham dropped out of Earth orbit on 22 October and splashed down in the Atlantic.

Nothing now stood in the way of an Apollo 8 Moon flight in December. On 11 November 1968, NASA's new Administrator Thomas O. Paine confirmed that Apollo 8 would fly to the Moon and make ten lunar orbits, and he gave the date for the launch as 21 December. He may well have doubted whether his team of Frank Borman, Jim Lovell and Bill Anders would be the first to report back from deep space, for by 11 November there were two good reasons to think they would not be.

Even as Apollo 7 floated in the Carribean swell, Soyuz 2 and 3 were trundling down to their pads, flat on the backs of their railway launchers. On the 25th, Soyuz 2 went aloft into an orbit of 185 by 224 km, 51.7 degrees. A new procedure was followed for this mission. Rather than launch the active craft first, and risk the non-launch of a passive craft second, leaving Beregovoi in orbit with only half a mission to perform and some explaining to be done, they would put up the passive craft first and fly the normal profile from the moment of insertion. As for the problem of a Soyuz 2 announcement provoking speculation of an imminent Soyuz 3 launch (and suggestions of failure if none took place) the Soyuz 2 launching was simply not announced for 24 hours!

At 12.34 p.m. on 26 October, the swing arms fell back and Soyuz 3 roared off the pad at Baikonour into the misty drizzling midday sky. A smiling Georgi Beregovoi (backup Vladimir Shatalov), wearing blue overalls and new Soyuz soft hat, had boarded his craft only an hour before. Eight minutes later he was in orbit and the mission began immediately.

He turned his spacecraft around and orientated it towards Soyuz 2. Radars began their search. Direction-finders 'pinged' their target. Figures flowed into the computers. Within a revolution, automatic systems had brought Soyuz 3 to within 200 m of Soyuz 2. Beregovoi resumed manual control and kept station with it for some time.

Then he pulled away to a distance of 565 km. 'This is Argon. . . this is Argon. . ,' his voice and his call-sign could be heard repeatedly in ground control in Yevpatoria. He rested and transmitted an orbital telecast from his spacecraft, showing viewers around his spacious home and pointing the camera out the window for a view of the Arctic.

Then a second rendezvous. Soyuz 3 began the chase once more, closing in on 2 from a distance of half a thousand kilometres. Once more at 200 m, Beregovoi took up manual control. No docking was made and we do not know if one was planned. On 28 October 1968, Soyuz 2 returned to Earth and was recovered in Kazakhstan.

The main part of his mission over, Georgi Beregovoi spent 29 October observing the Earth and its weather, typhoons and forest fires, and the stars, the Moon and the planets.

The next day, 30 October, was the moment of truth. On his 61st orbit, Soyuz 3 fired its retrorocket for 145 seconds over Africa. At mission control, memories of the last flight were uppermost in peoples' minds, but they need not have worried. At 9000 m the parachute blossomed out.

Thick early snow lay on the ground and the temperature was 12°C below zero. Helicopters were in the air looking for Beregovoi and villagers were outside their houses on the lookout too. Strong winds blew the capsule sideways into a snowdrift and the impact was so gentle that Georgi Beregovoi barely noticed it. Villagers waded through the snowdrifts, and amidst flecks of snow the grinning flier had his picture taken before being whisked away for debriefing.

TOLD TO SIT DOWN

Georgi Beregovoi's brave flight instilled new confidence in the programme. At his press conference in Moscow on 5 November, the ever-voluble Beregovoi was promoted to Major-General. New crews were ready for fresh journeys, he promised. Soyuz could dock in either direction, he disclosed in passing. When newsmen tried to follow up this tantalizing revelation, Mstislav Keldysh told Beregovoi to sit down: 'You are tired now,

Colonel'. Senior officials hinted at orbital space stations as the next step, with Moon flights later, but they were giving nothing away [14].

Whatever the next step was to be, it happened sooner than expected. Less than a week later, Zond 6 headed away from Earth onto a Moon trajectory (10 November). Two days later it adjusted its path and on 14 November rounded the Moon at a close point of 2418 km, with its automatic camera clicking away, taking metres and metres of photographs of the Moon's surface.

Zond 6 was returning to Earth. Its jets fired briefly on 15 November, 251 900 km out and again a day later. It was on pinpoint-accurate course for home. NASA was in a dry sweat. If this worked, only a cosmonaut could take the place of cameras and the test animals. It was not the kind of mission that needed a third rehearsal. On 18 November a British newspaper reported: 'The spherical cabin of Zond 6 splashed down south-east of Madagascar. Then the capsule was bobbing in the ocean for about eight hours before Russian ships recovered it' [15].

But this report could not have been more wrong. Zond 6 was nowhere near the Indian Ocean. It was back at Baikonour cosmodrome being excitedly examined by Soviet scientists. Zond 6 had reentered over the Indian Ocean at 45 km altitude, but had pointed its heat shield at 90 degrees to the flight path. This generated a cushion of lift underneath the Zond, pushing it back into space. It was skipping across the atmosphere like a stone skipping across water, its speed now down from 11 km/s to 7.6 km/s. Zond 6 soared back into space in an arc, and several minutes later began its second reentry, this time coming down vertically. The atmosphere halted it in its tracks, and at 19.6 km above the land, travelling at 200 m/s, parachutes bloomed open. . . to lower Zond 6 gently into the hands of waiting recovery terms in Kazakhstan [16].

It was a perfect technical achievement. The Russians had now gone round the Moon twice, and Zond 6 had cut out the ocean splashdown in favour of the much safer standard recovery zone. Any cosmonaut on Zond 6 would have survived and told a marvellous tale. Zond 6's reentry pattern was in fact much more sophisticated than that of Apollo, requiring extraordinary precision, accuracy and timing. G forces may have been as little as $3G$.

So, on 17 November, final preparations began for launching Pavel Belyayev to the Moon on 8 December at 2 p.m. aboard Zond 7. He would be back on 14 December, a full week before Apollo 8. Apollo 8 could do what it wanted: for it would be runner up.

WAITING. . . WAITING. . . WAITING. . .

With the flight of Zond 6, the Western press rediscovered the Moon race. *Time* magazine ran a cover of an American and a Russian in spacesuits elbowing each other out of the way as they both raced moonwards. Newspapers printed cutaway drawings of 'The Zond plan' and 'The Apollo plan'.

Pavel Belyayev and his backup Valeri Kubasov flew in from Moscow on 6 December. At the cosmodrome, snow blanketed the ground in pure whiteness, a contrast with the brooding grey gantries.

NASA was keeping its fingers crossed. The Apollo 8 plan now included ten lunar orbits, which they knew was more than Zond was capable of doing. Astronauts Borman, Lovell and Anders were right in the middle of their pre-flight checks. Their Saturn V was already on the pad. Space chief Leonid Sedov was predicting a Soviet man-on-the-Moon within the year. In London, Independent Television prepared to go on air with special news features the moment Zond went up. Models and spacesuits decorated the studio. The whole world was waiting. . . .

DECEMBER 8 PASSED AND WENT. . . [17]

Two weeks later Frank Borman, James Lovell and William Anders burned their Apollo motor for four minutes on the far side of the Moon and slid into Moon orbit. 'The Moon is essentially grey. . . no colour. . . looks like plaster of Paris. . .' echoed Jim Lovell's prosaic voice as he described in a telecast what he saw. With the picture quality of an early black-and-white movie, crater after crater rolled by, then lunar sea, then upland, then more craters. Never mind the quality, it was the Moon and there were three Americans circling it. On Christmas morning they fired their motor again and blasted back to the little ball of Earth they had proudly displayed on their cameras. And on 27 December they were fished out of the Pacific Ocean, tired, unshaven, but alive.

It was an epic flight. There could never be anything like it again. The sheer bravery of the adventure, voyaging out a quarter of a million miles from the refuge of our planet to the harshness of the tempting Moon; the grandeur of the lunar craters; three days' travel away; the Earth, a small blue jewel in the black sky; the five or six danger points where a wrong fraction in the computer could bring instant (or, worse, slow) death – all these things impressed people deeply. Suddenly the spectacle of men walking on the Moon within the year became something real, and John Kennedy's historic challenge something feasible after all. The psychological barriers that stood in the way of the Moon landing were coming down.

SO WHAT HAPPENED TO ZOND 7? WHAT OF THE SOVIET CHALLENGE?

We do not know. It remains the best-kept secret of the Soviet space programme. The facts are these: no launch was made on or around 8 December; an attempt was made to launch Zond 7 on 4 January but without a man on board, and it failed; and the establishment of Earth-orbiting space stations, refuelled by Soyuz ferrycraft, was declared to be the main objective of the Soviet space programme following a Soviet Government meeting on 1 January 1969.

No such public announcement was made at the time, but this date crept into a publication many years later. It was such an important decision it could only have been a Government one. And after Apollo 8's success the Soviet Government had good reasons to meet to discuss its space policy.

Unmanned testing of Zond, the G booster, the lunar cabin, and the automatic lunar probe backup programme continued. So far as can be seen, the man-on-the-Moon programme was finally abandoned in 1971.

Taking each one of these events in turn, the reason for the non-launch on 8 December has never leaked out, unlike many other stories. Pavel Belyayev himself died of acute peritonitis a year later and after December 1968 the Russians largely stopped talking about man-on-the-Moon. Indeed they made a great virtue of saying they had never been so foolish as to have been in the Moon race at all. Automatic craft were a cheaper way of doing it. And manned orbiting stations were the thing of the future.

We can presume – and it is only a presumption – that a significant section of the Soviet space community did want the 8 December launch to go ahead. Two Zond tests had been enough, they would have argued, and if Apollo 8 succeeded, all the investment would have been for nothing. But a majority may well have argued that two tests were not enough, that the Proton D booster was simply not yet adequately reliable, and perhaps Apollo 8 would be delayed and not yet fly for another few months or so. The majority viewpoint had its way, a compromise decision being taken in its favour. There would be just one more unmanned test in January and then a cosmonaut would fly. The decision could be called one of caution, or loss of nerve, depending on which side one took.

Indications of this change of policy came as soon as 10 December when Academician Blagonravov announced that 'additional tests would be necessary before sending cosmonauts to the Moon'

The failure to fly to the Moon on 8–14 December had major implications for the long-term space programme, and the Soviet Government intervened to try to reestablish some more rational priorities. The deliberating process concluded on 1 January 1969, and it must have been a painful experience trying to accept the nature of the defeat at the hands of Apollo 8.

At first sight, it appears that the USSR withdrew from the Moon race, pretended it had never been in it in the first place, and began work on a space station project instead. In fact, that would be only a superficial analysis of the decision that was reached. It certainly was decided to adopt a space station as the principal space objective. Unlike the Moon race, space stations could not be side-stepped. They were central to any programme to explore space. Even if America never existed they were still the logical thing to do. It was better to start sooner rather than later.

It was decided to fly just one more around-the-Moon unmanned test before manrating the Zond/Proton combination. If it succeeded, then the option of flying around the Moon remained and could be exercised if the political climate was right and coming in second seemed better than not at all.

So Zond 7 was launched on 4 January 1969. It crashed in flames. A cosmonaut would have survived on the escape tower, but the mission was lost. Those who had urged caution on 8 December were vindicated. Proton was not yet ready.

And so the Moon programme moved into second place in the order of priorities. The literature talked more of space stations and less of flying to the Moon. The switch of emphasis was not as dramatic and sudden as was later supposed, but was decisive nonetheless. A space station was already part of the American programme. In 1972 a Saturn upper stage was to be converted into an orbital workshop called Skylab. Three astronauts, delivered to it by Apollo, would work aboard it for up to two months.

A Soviet station – it was soon codenamed Salyut – would not be as demanding as the Moon programme. The Proton booster could launch it, and 'it' could therefore have a payload of 19 tonnes. Soyuz – as Beregovoi had just shown – was well able to carry out rendezvous and docking manoeuvres. It could be the ferry. There was little danger involved in using the Proton booster since Salyut's crew would be sent up only after it was sent into orbit first, unmanned. And the whole project could be ready in two years.

The political explanation could be made to fit: orbital stations were cheaper and of direct economic benefit compared to the propaganda stunt of Apollo.

There was a rider on the Government decision of 1 January. Although the man-round-the-Moon programme was kept in abeyance, the man-on-the-Moon programme was kept alive. Hardware flown around the period 1969–71 had no other use than that of flying men onto the lunar surface. Why was this? Having just put Zond into cold storage, the Russians would have been absurdly inconsistent to simply test out designs of lunar hardware just to see if they worked, with no intentions of using them.

So there has to be another explanation. Did the intelligence reports from the United States suggest that Apollo was still some way off from a lunar landing? Did they suggest that newly elected President Nixon hankered after cancelling Apollo, the brainchild of his political rival, John Kennedy? Could Congress pull the rug out from NASA if there was an Apollo failure? Might American will — now severely tested by Vietnam, student protests and race riots — falter, and then see the Moon as a low social priority that could be dropped? And would it be that difficult to withdraw, now that the Soviet challenge had been seen to be unable to maintain the pace? And after ten lunar orbits, had not John Kennedy's memory been sufficiently honoured?

All it needed was some mishap, bad luck, major technical failure or political misfortune and NASA might be cheated of its goal by its political masters. For if that were to happen, the USSR could then move in with its own lunar programme to put men on the Moon and sweep the board. On such hopes — slender in retrospect but not necessarily so at the time — the Moon programme was kept alive.

DESPERATE VENTURES

So although the man-round-the-Moon programme had been put in suspension, and a manned space station adopted as the main objective of the programme, the remainder of the Moon programme still had several stages to run. These included: tests of the lunar cabin, the G booster, the contingency unmanned programme, and also some Zond capsules which could be flown either manned or unmanned as circumstances dictated.

The contingency unmanned lunar programme had been drawn up to support the man-on-the-Moon effort in the period immediately after the conclusion of the Luna soft-landing missions. Its three models — a moonscooper, a lunar orbiter and a roving vehicle — would test equipment and techniques that would assist in the actual manned flight itself. But the Russians must have all along seen it as a counterbalance to Apollo should Apollo move ahead of their own programme, which it now very definitely had done.

The moonscooper was taken most seriously in the West. While only a minority in the West still believed the Russians were running any kind of Moon programme that involved getting cosmonauts to the Moon, all commentators were prepared to believe in a programme that would attempt to get moonrock back before Apollo. Such a flight would take at least some wind out of Apollo's sails. Early in 1969, rumours reached the West that such a moonscooper was in existence. These rumours were well founded, and the moonscooper was ready for launch on 15 April 1969, just one month after America's Apollo 9 had tested out the lunar module in the relative safety of earth orbit.

The moonscooper was technically very complex. The base was a set of landing engines, fuel tanks and instrumentation — the same base as the manned lunar cabin then being designed: 3.96 m. On top sat the cylindrical instrumentation unit, the spherical return capsule atop it in turn, and underneath the ascent stage. A long robot arm, not unlike a dentist's drill, swung out from the descent stage and swivelled round into a small hatch in the descent cabin. Its height was 3.96 m, weight 1880 kg. The plan was for a four-day coast to the Moon, with the upper stage lifting off from the Moon for the return flight to Earth. Such a mission required extreme accuracy. If Russia could get moonrocks back before Apollo by automatic spacecraft and without risking human life, it was at least a respectable second best.

The first such moonscooper prepared for launch failed. The second, on 14 June 1969, did not do any better. Both coincided with the worst phase in the development of the Proton booster. At the time of the second attempt, there were floods of rumours of a planned Moon attempt. The previous month, May 1969, had seen the triumph of Apollo 10: Tom Stafford, Eugene Cernan and John Young had flown out to the Moon, and Cernan and Stafford had brought the LM down to less than 14 400 m over the lunar surface in a dress rehearsal for the Moon landing itself. Apollo 11 had been set for 16 July, and the Americans had tested about all they reasonably could before actually touching down.

LAST DESPERATE THROW

Time was running out for the Soviet challenge — whatever that was. Everyone realized there would be some challenge, though no one seemed sure exactly what.

Hence the rumours of early June 1969. The venue was the Paris Air Show — an event held every two years, which is not only the showpiece of the European airspace industry but is also used by the two superpowers to promote their wares. On 2 June, United Press reported:

> The Soviet Union plans a major spaceshot in the next few days, a United States official said.
>
> A moon shot might be involved. He could not say whether it would be manned. [18]

In Paris itself there were friendly encounters between cosmonauts Vladimir Shatalov and Alexei Yeliseyev on the one hand and the Apollo 9 trio of McDivitt, Scott and Schweickart on the other. 'Space rivals link up on Earth' was the type of caption the papers loved. Smiles concealed the grim seriousness of the struggle between them.

Then the second rumour. Russia was still in the Moon race and planned a landing in 1970. Few really believed this one, but at least a minority of reporters stood by it and quoted Alexei Leonov as source. The story, as elaborated, was that the man-on-the-Moon programme had been speeded up on the insistence of the Soviet defence ministry, which did not want the Americans to have a free run on the Moon. Leonov, speaking to Japanese reporters was quoted as saying: 'The Soviet lunar probe would be launched from a space station assembled in orbit around the Earth' [19].

The third rumour was more credible. It quoted an unnamed cosmonaut as saying that a moonscooper was ready to fly and samples of lunar rock would be on display to the world next month. Some press writers even hastened to label the proposed contraption

'Scoopy', perhaps reminiscent of the 'Snoopy' that Apollo 10's lunar module had been called.

But June came and went and nothing whatever happened. Or so it was thought. As July opened, the eyes of the world began to turn to Cape Canaveral and focussed on the personalities of the three courageous Americans selected for the historic journey of Apollo 11 — Neil Armstrong, Michael Collins and Edwin Aldrin. The Soviets just weren't up to it.

In fact, there was truth enough in the rumours. The man-on-the-Moon programme was still very much alive. 'Scoopy' had flown — and failed — on 14 June. More important perhaps was an event which had taken place just two days before that: the G booster was at last ready. But on 12 June it had suffered a horrific pad disaster. The rumours, were as usual, rooted in truth [20].

The G booster, as tall as its rival the Saturn V, was carried out on a railway flatcar — astride two railtracks it was so wide — from its 250 m long assembly building. It lumbered down painfully slowly to the pad which was located a full 5 km from the Soyuz pad. It was a pad totally different from that of the Saturn V and was like a train turntable at a railway terminus, for it was built on similar principles.

Dwarfing all else beside it, the behemoth reached its turntable destination. It was raised slowly by its 140 m high turning tower and cradled by it. Such a turntable enabled accurate launch angles to be prepared for the linkup manoeuvre required for Earth orbit rendezvous, and the high turning tower with crane atop was employed for lifting the third stage into place.

Near the pad too were a 100 m tall umbilical tower and towers with floodlights and cameras. It was a worthy birthplace for such a space monster, the focus of Russia's Moon landing dreams. It must have stood out on the steppes for miles around as engineers scurried around preparing it for its first test flight.

But it was not to be. As propellants were being loaded aboard for a static fuelling test on that 12 June 1969, a leak sprung in the third stage. In seconds flames spread and engulfed the whole magnificent vehicle, turning tower, pad and rocket into a blazing inferno. It was wrecked from end to end. All that was left was a blackened smouldering ruin. No one died or was injured: the 1960 disaster meant that there were no longer any short cuts taken on safety. But with it died Russia's last hope of landing on the Moon anytime around the time of Apollo 11, or near enough in the popular mind not to matter.

On 14 June the rumour trail went cold, abruptly and finally. But just imagine if on the 12th the G booster had succeeded and if on the 14th the Scoopy also had done its work! The Americans would have been cheated of their moonrocks, and the success of the G booster could have cleared the way for a Soviet Moon landing the following year, within a year of the Americans. The United States, knowing Russia was really in the Moon business (and the G booster had no other use at this stage) might have been tempted to cut some corners in the ensuing panic and could even have lost a mission.

GAME UP?

To Soviet space planners it was clear that the game was nearly up. Foiled by the Apollo 8 success, worried by booster unreliability, frustrated by one pad failure after another, the past two years had been marked by misfortune after misfortune. Nothing seemed to go right. It was a dramatic contrast to the early days when they could do no wrong and the Americans could do no right. It was the other way round now, and Apollo steamed on from one brilliant achievement to another, dazzling the world like an acrobat who has practised a million times; except that, as everyone knew, NASA had not.

One last desperate throw of the dice remained. A third moonscooper — it was probably a backup model — was prepared and hustled to the pad in early July. The scientists expected that the Proton booster would let them down again. It was probably to their surprise that it did not. As if to scorn the earlier run of failures, it hurtled Luna 15 moonwards on 13 July 1969. If all went well, its tiny recovery capsule would be back on Earth on the morning of 24 July. The Apollo 11 capsule was not expected back until later in the same day. The Americans could still be beaten, by just a few hours. It was like Scott and Amundsen racing to the South Pole in 1912.

Luna 15 produced the expected level of consternation in the West. The press, perhaps bored with the ability of Apollo to do everything, however difficult, exactly on schedule, thrived on this competition. Most observers thought Luna 15 could be a scooper, but doubted whether the USSR had the technological ability to pull it off. A typical view was the following in the British *Daily Telegraph*:

> While the moonshot is regarded as a last-minute attempt to detract from the American effort, it is not thought the Russians can land and bring back samples. The technical complexities are thought to be too great. [21]

But as the Apollo 11 launching drew near — it was now only three days away — one absurd idea rivalled another. Luna 15 would jam Apollo 11's frequencies. It was there to 'spy' on Apollo 11 — like the Russian trawlers during NATO naval exercises, presumably. It was there to report back on how the Americans did it. It was a rescue craft to bring back Armstrong and Aldrin if they got stranded.

15 July. Luna 15 is exactly half way to the Moon. Jodrell Bank — invariably tracking it — said it was on a slow course to save fuel. It was right. So there was more speculation as to the ulterior motives of choosing a slow course to the Moon to save fuel. Sinister implications were read into the tiniest details.

16 July. At 2.32 p.m. Apollo 11 blasts skywards from Cape Canaveral. It is a beautiful launch, and soon the astronauts are gazing out at the blue globe of our planet as they shoot away from it at 36 000 km/hr. They send back pictures showing their own relaxed humour. The hours of danger lie ahead.

17 July. Luna 15 breaks into lunar orbit. It exact path is closely watched. Its path measures 133 by 286 km, 45 degrees, 2 h 30 min. Scientists, experts, engineers, everyone short of a clairvoyant is called in to the television studios to comment on every change of path or signal. Jodrell Bank reports back that its signals are of an entirely new type never heard before. Georgi Beregovoi, who could always be counted on to be indiscreet, lets it be known that: 'Luna 15 may try to take samples of lunar soil or it may try to solve the problem of a return from the moon's surface' [22].

18 July. Jodrell Bank expects a soft-landing by Luna 15. But it does not materialize. The bets are still that it is a moonscooper. But instead of landing, the probe changes orbit. Each revolution now lasts 2 h 35 min, 94 by 220 km, 126 degrees, bringing it closer to the Moon.

19 July. The cool-as-cucumber crew of Apollo 11 slips silently into lunar orbit after three days of flight. They go through the final checks of the lunar module 'Eagle'. They are in the Moon's shadow: back on earth, excitement and apprehension mount as the full significance of the undertaking begins to sink in. Tomorrow, after two million years on the planet Earth, *Homo sapiens* prepares to set foot on another world. Luna 15 continues to circle, descending on its 25th orbit to 85 km. It does not appear to be in any hurry to land. One source from Moscow says it is selecting landing sites.

20 July. The big day. Neil Armstrong and Edwin Aldrin move into the LM 'Eagle'. Late that afternoon, they cast their spider-like cabin free from Michael Collins, orbiting solo in the command and service module (CSM), called 'Columbia'. 'The Eagle has wings!' the excited astronauts exult. For a full orbit they fly side-by-side. Back at mission control the visitors gallery is filling with administrators, politicians, astronauts. The voices are hushed, the tension mounting. The night will end either in miraculous triumph or terrible disaster.

Flash from Jodrell Bank. On orbit 29, Luna 15 fires its motor behind the Moon on the instructions of ground control. Its new orbit brings it still closer to the surface. The perigee dips to 16 km, with an apogee of 109 km, 127 degrees, period 114 minutes. The perigee is just over the Apollo landing site in the Sea of Tranquility. The plot thickens.

Soon after 9 p.m., 'Eagle' starts its powered descent. It is the point of no return. Down and down and down descends the LM. The craters and rock fields are coming closer every minute. Five minutes into the descent the alarms flash: the computer is overloaded! Hasty advice from ground control: press on! Ten minutes into the descent and the 'Eagle' should be just over the right landing spot on the lunar surface. Instead, Neil Armstrong, peering through the window sees a crater the size of a football field and filled with rocks the size of cars. He's way off course. He takes over manual control and flies the LM like a helicopter to find the right place. Eleven minutes into the descent. Skimming over crater fields, Armstrong rejects one site after another as too rough. The fuel warning light comes on. He's 25 m high above the surface and out of fuel.

21 July. Armstrong landed with just 20 seconds of fuel to spare and on the only flat site in the area. The 'Eagle' was down and they had done it! It was a brilliant piece of flying. Six hours later Neil Armstrong was down on the lunar surface and soon Edwin Aldrin was down there with him. They walked, jumped and hopped across the surface, took pictures, picked up moonrocks, unfolded experiments, and laid out a scientific station. In the Western world, 600 million people stayed up through the long summer night and celebrated with them, watching the ghostly and jerky TV images, the first ever of men on another world.

To such glassy-eyed and jaded watchers, Luna 15 became an irrelevance. Machines meant nothing compared to brave men actually out there and as recognizable as you or me. Late on the 20th, Jodrell Bank reported that Luna 15 was still in low lunar orbit, so low down that if it did not soon alter its path it would crash into a lunar peak. It is doubtful if many people cared, so overwhelming was the Apollo experience. Luna 15 was nearly an annoyance.

22 hours after landing, Neil Armstrong and Edwin Aldrin were standing in their LM counting down for liftoff from the lunar surface. It was another critical phase. If the motor, which was no larger than an automatic dishwasher, did not fire, then they would be there for all eternity. The air in the LM might last another day, but Michael Collins

would have to return home on his own.

Just as they went through this last phase came a final newsflash from Jodrell Bank. It was to serve as Luna 15's epitaph:

> Signals ceased at 4.50 p.m. this evening. They have not yet returned. The retrorockets were fired at 4.46 on the 52nd orbit and after burning for 4 minutes the craft was on or near the lunar surface. The approach velocity was 480 km/hr and it is unlikely if anything could have survived. [23]

The crash site was the Sea of Crises and it marked the graveyard of the Russian ambitions to somehow beat the Americans to the Moon. Luna 15 smashed to tiny pieces.

It is worth making a passing mention of how the American triumph was explained by the Russians to their own people. Prior to the Apollo landing, reports of the mission had been meagre, but once Armstrong and Aldrin were on the Moon, news coverage was more generous. At the main 5 p.m. evening news on the 21st, half an hour was devoted to the landing, most of it showing pictures of the moonwalk. The commentator described the landing as the 'realization of a dream'. Georgi Petrov, then Director of the Soviet Institute of Space Research, made no effort to conceal his admiration, nor even to trot out the new official line that 'automatic probes were better'. Wistfully he remarked:

> Maybe for the same expense automatic stations might have done more. But the fact of a man being on the moon is great in itself and this represents the self-assertion of mankind. [24]

EPILOGUE TO THE JULY MOON

The luck of Neil Armstrong, Edwin Aldrin and Michael Collins held and they were back on Earth on 24 July. For Russian space planners it marked — or so it seemed at the time — the ultimate humiliation. Beaten in the round-the-Moon race, beaten in the on-the-Moon race, and beaten decisively too: even the moonscooper, which could have saved at least some honour, had flopped. Defeat had been snatched from the jaws of victory.

Some strangely unconvincing reasons were advanced to explain away Luna 15. The Soviet press even had the nerve to claim that: 'If it hadn't happened to coincide with the dramatic Apollo lunar flight, it would hardly have received a mention at all' [25]. So what was Luna 15 then? Just a new Moon probe. A survey ship that was highly manoeuvrable. Indeed, it had a flexibility that the American moonship did not have because it could manoeuvre freely, unlike Apollo which was stuck in narrow equatorial orbit. One wonders if the author — one Pyotr Petrov — even believed this himself.

RETROSPECTIVE

History is no respector of failures. Looking at it back over the years, the failure of Zond, then the G booster and then the moonscooper, all look so inevitable, the products of poor planning and hasty execution. By contrast, the nearly effortless triumph of Apollo looks so easy, the inevitable outcome of superior planning and brilliant design. That is not how it looked at the time. There was a real battle of the giants for the Moon prize — and it could have gone the other way. Imagine if Belyayev had been allowed to fly round the Moon on 8 December, as he nearly had been? And when Sir Bernard Lovell in 1983 reflected on the events of the summer of 1969, he speculated: 'It is not hard to imagine the effect on world opinion if in July 1969 the Americans had a disaster and the Russian automatic recovery had been successful' [26].

However, no one was about to dismantle Baikonour or disband the cosmonaut squad. This appalling defeat — or so it seemed at the time — was not reason enough to abandon the space programme altogether. Over 1969 the planners thought through their mistakes and errors, and rational planning began to reassert itself once more — perhaps for the first time since the Kennedy challenge. With other peoples' targets and schedules no longer uppermost in their minds, they could now concentrate on their own; and they did.

The manned programme had, ever since January 1969 been turned around in the direction of Earth-orbiting stations — the emerging Salyut programme. This work would continue. The man-on-the-Moon programme would continue too: not with a view to landing on the Moon but with a view to verifying the hardware that had been developed, like the G booster and the lunar cabin. So much investment had gone into these programmes that it was better to test out the technical concepts involved than write them off altogether and deny oneself the benefits of the design work.

If these tests went well, and if by some chance Apollo faltered, a manned Moon landing could still be kept open as an option. The moonscooper flights would be followed through, along with their subsidiary programmes (the rover and orbiter) and presented to the public as an 'alternative' to Apollo. The Zond series would be flown to conclusion to iron out the problems that had frustrated the December 1968 planned mission. Such equipment testing would take place at a planned pace. It would not be leisurely, but not hasty and corners would not be cut. Sir Bernard Lovell again: 'The Soviets continued to believe that the Americans were taking unjustifiable risks' [27].

All this kept several divisions of the Soviet space programme occupied till 1976 when the Moon was abandoned indefinitely. The success of the post-Apollo Soviet Moon programme showed what could have been achieved had it been allowed to develop at a more rational pace, free of the hectic rush of the pre-1969 days.

The last two flights of the Zond series were accomplished with an *élan* which put the previous year's failures firmly in the shade. Zond 7 left Baikonour on 8 August 1969, only two weeks after Luna 15's demise and at about the same time as the Apollo 11 astronauts were emerging from their biological isolation after their Moon flight, isolation designed to prevent them bringing back evil bugs. It was then a new Moon and a full Earth, and striking and beautiful pictures were taken of the Earth's full globe over the Moon's surface en route to and from the Moon. Movie cameras whirred as Zond skimmed round the lunar far side at 2000 km.

Zond 7 swung round and headed back to the Earth, skipped like a pebble across the atmosphere to soft-land in the summer fields of Kustanai in Kazakhstan. How easy it all seemed.

Zond 8 (20—7 October 1970) carried tortoises, flies, onions, wheat, barley and microbes, and was the subject of new navigation tests. Astronomical telescopes photographed the Zond as far as 300 000 km out from Earth to check its trajectory. Zond 8 came as close as 1120 km to the lunar surface.

Zond 8 took an entirely new return trajectory. It slammed into the Earth's atmosphere over the North Pole and it carried out a series of aerodynamic skip-and-lift manoeuvres right down to parachute deployment. Its path took it over the pole, Russia and India and eventually into the Indian Ocean where it was found by the oceanographic vessel *Taman*.

These two tests – and they represented the last of the Zond series – were the ultimate expression of deep space high speed return engineering skill. No cosmonaut boarding the next Zond would have felt ill at ease in the course of such complex and dangerous engineering manoeuvres. The fact that the Russians never flew a man around the Moon was taken subsequently as an indication of the lack of the necessary skill: but the Zond reentry manoeuvres belie such a thesis.

GRAVEYARD OF THE GIANT

If the last two Zonds were engineering triumphs, the sad saga of the G booster reached a less happy ending. It actually became the most unsuccessful rocket in the history of astronautics.

Unlike the Saturn V, with which it was comparable, the G booster did not use liquid hydrogen but conventional fuels and these should not have presented insurmountable problems, even after the catastrophic fire of 12 June 1969. But was not until two years later that static testing of a second model was complete. The countdown then began for another launch in June 1971. American observers in Turkey spotted it heading for orbit only to see the radar traces of what must have been a spectacular explosion at 12 000 m altitude.

There was another casualty of this failure: Korolov's successor in the rocketry section, Mikhail Yangel. He died the following 25 October of overwork resulting from the G booster programme. He was 65 and had been close to Korolov since 1937.

Whatever the problems were, they were never properly ironed out. The third G booster rose from the pad 18 months later, in November 1972, and also suffered a first stage failure.

By this time it was clear that the G booster would never support a man-on-the-Moon programme. Its role gradually shifted in the planner's eyes towards being a rocket that would put a large space station into low Earth orbit. Work did not cease in November 1972, though for many years this was given as the termination date for the G programme. One pad was mothballed, it is true, but a new structure was built on the other G pad for the static testing of a fourth prototype. This new structure was 122 m tall and tests were carried out there in the spring of 1974.

These proved unsatisfactory and the project was then finally abandoned. The designers admitted defeat, and these pads saw no life again for nearly a decade. The G booster thus became the only instance in which a team of rocket designers adopted a certain objective and totally failed to meet it. The exact reason for this is unclear. Soviet rocket engineering, so long the most advanced in the world, slipped indisputably into second place behind the United States with the excellence that was represented by NASA, von Braun, and the teams that built Saturn V and, later, Shuttle. Was this decline caused by the absence of Korolov? Were there failures in other branches of engineering that left the rocketeers with insoluble problems? We shall never know.

THE SECRET MOON CABIN

1974 therefore marks the end of the Soviet man-on-the-Moon programme due to final design inability to build one of the most crucial components, a failure just as decisive in its own way as Neil Armstrong's achievement in getting their first in 1969. It was all the more ironic in view of the successful – and extremely secret – moonship tests of 1970–71 [28]. These tests took place as part of the Cosmos programme and carried the following designations:

Cosmos 379   24 November 1970
Cosmos 382   2 December 1970
Cosmos 398   26 February 1971
Cosmos 434   12 August 1971.

These four flights, it must be said, did arouse controversy at the time. All used the inclination of 51.6 degrees which has been characteristic of all manned and lunar flights since 1967. They were all highly manoeuvrable. But these facts were only enough to cause suspicion. Observers felt they had something to do with the manned programme or Salyut or Soyuz, but no one could figure out exactly what.

There it might have rested and been logged as just another mystery but for two things. In 1978, a nuclear-powered Soviet spy satellite, Cosmos 954, went out of control and eventually crashed on Canada. Not long after, another Cosmos, Cosmos 434, began to spiral down to Earth. One Soviet spokesperson insisted there was no need to worry since, because it was in their words 'a prototype lunar cabin' it had no nuclear fuel and therefore posed no danger.

Second, several Western experts, including an IBM computer specialist, set to work doing calculations on the four flights, based on their known manoeuvres and compared to the thrust and propellant that would be needed to move a Soyuz and a Soviet lunar module into and out of lunar orbit. The work was an engineer's nightmare, but the hypothesis did hold up. It was a typical demonstration of how Soviet space activities could be reconstructed based on a fairly small amount of actual hard fact.

To do this, it is necessary first to look at the actual manoeuvres performed. They were quite substantial:

		Period (min)	Perigee (km)	Apogee (km)
Cosmos 379	Orbital insertion	89	192	232
	Manoeuvre 1	99	190	1 210
	Manoeuvre 2	259	175	14 035
Cosmos 382	Orbital insertion	143	305	5 045
	Manoeuvre 1	159	1615	5 072
	Manoeuvre 2	171	2577	5 082
Cosmos 398	Orbital insertion	88	189	252
	Manoeuvre 1	98	186	1 188
	Manoeuvre 2	216	203	10 903

		Period (min)	Perigee (km)	Apogee (km)
Cosmos 434	Orbital insertion	89	188	267
	Manoeuvre 1	100	189	1 328
	Manoeuvre 2	228	186	11 804

All but Cosmos 382 were put into low orbits by the A booster; of these three, all carried out their first manoeuvre within 3.5 days of launch and the second manoeuvre between 4 and 10 days. Again, the similarity of the final orbits can be noted. Cosmos 382 is different from this pattern and, significantly, used a Proton D booster.

Second, and here we go into the realms of speculation, Cosmos 379, 398 and 434 had weights of between 7080 kg and 7500 kg which squares well with the known maximum capacity of the A booster (7600 kg) and the weight of the Earth orbit Soyuz (6800 kg). Their weight does not square with the known weight of heavy Zond (10 500 kg) but this is explicable if some module parts not necessary for engine testing were left out of these missions.

So the conclusion may be reached that tests of the lunar-orbiting Zond were carried out, the first of the manoeuvres having a thrust identical with that required for lunar orbit insertion (265 m/s) and the second having a thrust identical with the speed required for exit from lunar orbit and trans-Earth injection (1531 m/s).

Cosmos 382 fits in better with the description of a lunar module like the American LM. The Soviet lander has been estimated to weigh about 18 900 kg (about the lifting capacity of the D booster), consisting of a descent stage of about 13 200 kg and an ascent stage of 5700 kg. The American LM weight is about the same at 16 000 kg. The two manoeuvres of Cosmos 382 were similar to the thrust required for the firing of a descent stage for a landing on the Moon; and then the ascent stage for getting off the Moon again.

Other explanations have been advanced for these four spaceshots. Some hold them all to be based on the lunar-orbiting Zond; others think them all to be part of a lunar module. It may not really matter: what is fair to conclude is that these tests are explicable in terms of the manned Moon programme and are not explicable in terms of any other programme known to be under way at the time, including the Salyut programme.

As was seen from the earlier analysis of Soviet space planning in 1969, these flights in 1970—71 were designed to prepare the way for a Soviet man-on-the-Moon, assuming that the G booster also became available and that the political circumstances were such as would make a Soviet man-on-the-Moon second publicly acceptable. At one stage that second eventuality nearly took place.

In April 1970, American astronauts Jim Lovell, Fred Haise and Jack Swigert were en route to the Moon for the third lunar landing and were two days out from Earth when their spaceship Apollo 13 was blown apart by an explosion. By the skin of their teeth they got back to Earth by using their lunar module as a lifeboat, but for a while there was a real chance that Apollo would falter and fail. NASA's critics moved in for the kill, pointing out the risks involved and the low scientific returns, the high investment at the expense of neglecting pressing domestic problems. Apollo 14 was postponed. NASA was forced to cancel Apollos 18, 19 and 20. Skylab was delayed to 1973. Perhaps the Kremlin figured that with Apollo in the doldrums and possibly even in danger of elimination, a

Soviet lunar landing and a followup programme to really explore the Moon might be credible. It is interesting to note that the Cosmos tests did take place during this period of doubt.

But NASA was back on its feet sooner than anyone expected. Apollo 14, after a shaky start, carried out Apollo 13's mission in January 1971; Apollo 15, in July 1971, was more impressive still. It spent three days on the Moon, the LM coming down at the foot of the 5000 m high peak of Mount Hadley. Against this spectacular alpine backdrop two astronauts roamed the surface at will in a lunar rover, venturing far from their safe refuge. NASA could not be beaten, still less emulated, at this stage.

In December 1972 (Apollo 17) the Americans left the Moon, for at least a generation. Twelve of their astronauts had landed there and explored its desolate wastelands. It was a superb achievement, the greatest in history. The book closed. The Americans could look back in pride.

For the Russians, it had been a time of anguish and frustration. They had designed, built, and tested moonships. They had trained cosmonauts to fly there. They had spent nearly as much energy in the venture as their rivals, only to have nothing to show for it at the end. So the Russians shut up about the Moon. They pretended they had never been in the race at all. They regrouped, rethought and redesigned: for there was work to do.

7

The space centres

BAIKONOUR

Late on the evening of 27 April 1975, a group of American astronauts left Moscow airport. Their Aeroflot plane headed east, into the darkness. After a while it passed over the mighty river Volga and its wide flood plain. Two hours into the flight and the land below them rose as they skirted over the southern Urals. Then the astronauts were over scrubby desert. Down the plane came after a three-hour flight and taxied in to its parking place at the airport.

Out jumped the three Americans — Apollo veteran Tom Stafford, Mercury trainee Donald Slayton and newcomer Vance Brand. A minibus promptly collected them. It was still dark, but they could make out a large signpost announcing that they were entering a place called Leninsk. The road to their hotel took them past endless avenues laid out at right angles like their own American cities, and flanked by 15-floor blocks.

As dawn broke they realized they were in a large city of at least 10 000 inhabitants. It took another half hour to drive to the engineering base and the nearest rocket pad was 3 km further on. In the far distance stretched more pads, tracking towers, silos, fuel depots, static test towers. Railway lines weaved their way around all the facilities.

The astronauts gradually began to appreciate the sheer size of Leninsk. It was up to five times the size of their own Cape Canaveral. It had schools, cinemas, palaces of culture, restaurants, hotels, cafes, even its own stadium and local TV and radio station. Leafy trees lined the main streets.

Leninsk is not remarkable in two senses: it is an average modern Soviet city with fairly typical layout and the normal type of facilities one might expect. It has the support services that one would reasonably expect of a place devoted to hurtling rockets into deep space.

What *is* remarkable is that 'Leninsk' does not officially exist. It will not be found on any Soviet map, despite its 50 000 inhabitants. The nearest place marked is Baikonour, which is the old railhead 250 km to the northeast. Nevertheless the Russians call it — and have always called the whole outfit — 'Baikonour Cosmodrome'. Tom Stafford and his crew were the first Westerners to see it and report back on it, even though they were flown in by night to ensure that they would see as little of it as possible. They were about to take part in the only joint Soviet—American spaceflight and Tom Stafford had made a visit to Baikonour a condition of his taking part [1].

The cosmodrome is in fact not hard to locate on the map. It is in the railway line between Moscow and historic city of Tashkent. Head northwest out of Tashkent, and the train crosses the Kyzylumkum desert. It is endless, flat and arid. For most of the journey, the train runs parallel to the river Syr Darya. After 600 km the train reaches the town of Dzhusaly, a mining town, and after that there is a bend in the river. The train enters a much larger built-up area: it is Tyuratam old town, and the cosmodrome has been growing up around it ever since. If our train traveller carried on, he would skirt around the north of the Aral Sea and eventually reach Kyubyshev on the Volga before pulling in to Moscow a day later.

Of all the many secrets in the Soviet space programme, the nature of Baikonour (or Leninsk or Tyuratam, depending on the name of choice, — or even Zvezgorod, 'Star City' as it has been called by one recent official publication) is one of the best-kept and has always been shrouded in mystery. Our present knowledge of it is based almost entirely on Tom Stafford's visit and photographs from American Earth resources satellites like Landsat. The Landsat pictures, taken at the best time — in early March each year, are most informative because the snow is melting and the buildings and railway lines stand out clearly against the white snowy background [2].

Work on the cosmodrome began in 1955. The first engineers to arrive lived out in shacks and tents and caravans, and started work with picks, shovels and their bare hands. In the summer it is roasting hot, and they must have lain out at night alongside the old caravan routes to the East, gazing upwards to the stars that their descendants might one day reach from the launch sites they were building.

The first thing they did was to run a spur off the old Tyuratam railway in a triangular shape 19 km north into the wasteland. It was flat, scrubby land with occasional bushes and grasses. It is often windy. The first snow falls in October. From December to February the snow is relentless and deep. In March it eases. In April the flowers blossom and flourish for two or three moist weeks. They die down before the heat of the desert sun in May.

The location — and the deception of 'Baikonour' — had much to do with the politics of the Cold War. The cosmodrome was to be the launch pad for Russia's new military missile, the A booster. The old test site at Kapustin Yar was simply too close to the American radars in Turkey. Tyuratam was more remote, and less inhabited: rockets that failed would crash in desert and not be noticed [3].

As for the title 'Baikonour' — well and good if the Americans believed the rocket site was there (and they had no reason to disbelieve it). If war broke out and the American missiles rained down on Baikonour they would be annihilating territory far from the real rocket base. As a deceit it succeeded for a good ten years before the Americans realized the cosmodrome was far away to the south. All this time, Baikonour was, and remained what it is today, a sleepy little village railhead.

By mid-1957, two years after they started, the first stage was completed. An airport had been laid out; a large and long hangar-like assembly bay had been constructed; and a launch pad for the A booster was put up. So too were a tracking centre and a fuel storage area.

The whole network was linked by railway. Baikonour differs in two major respects from Cape Canaveral. The first is that rail is the mode of transport, not road. Rockets are carried flat on their back on railcars from the assembly hangars to the pad. It is a crude system made easier by the fact that the gauge of the Russian railways is the widest in the world. When the Americans built their Saturn V, they had to build vast road crawlers.

The second difference is that most rocket equipment is assembled and put together at Baikonour itself in cargo bays and hangars. In America, most assembly work is contracted out all over the country and the parts are then put together at a central point. The final testing out at Cape Canaveral is done out of doors on the pad: in Baikonour it is done in the hangars because of the bad weather.

The A pad completed in mid-1957 is Baikonour's most famous pad. From it, rose Sputnik, the first Lunas, Vostok, Voskhod, Soyuz 1—8, Soyuz 19 and 25.

Any spaceship about to depart is first of all tested out rigorously in the Space Vehicle Assembly Building or the MIKKO. All the telemetry is checked through, and the satellite is immersed in a vacuum chamber. It is then moved along rails for mating with the upper and lower stages of the booster. This process is completed a day before launching.

On the big day, the entire structure, 50 m long, trundles down to the pad at a cautious 3 km/hr. The transporter reaches the pad, which is a concrete platform on heavy cement legs. Around it is a giant flame trench, looking like a reservoir empty of water. Once at

A Soviet A-2 launch vehicle carrying a Soyuz spacecraft makes its way by rail to the launch pad on a giant transporter 50 metres long.

One of the major strengths of the Soviet space programme from its earliest days has been its fleet of expendable booster rockets. Developed as variants of Soviet Intercontinental Ballistic Missiles (ICBMs), the basic design of each launch vehicle is modified several times to produce boosters tailored to specific missions. The best example of this design approach is the A-type launch vehicle used for the first Sputnik in 1957, and variants of which have continued to be utilized ever since.

These two views show an A-2 launch vehicle being prepared on launch pad B of the 'Baikonour' Cosmodrome at Tyuratam, complete with its Soyuz spacecraft. The A-2 upper-stage on the A vehicle (developed from the SS-6 ICBM) is 8 metres long and 2.58 metres wide, and generates 30 tonnes of thrust. The A-2 is by far the most used launch vehicle in the Soviet programme.

the pad the transporter arm lifts the rocket up to the vertical. It is a delicate operation requiring extreme care. The booster is held up to the vertical while clamps rise up like a bear trap to grasp it at all levels so that engineers can inspect it at all levels.

Once on the pad turntable, the A booster is fuelled up, starting at about five hours before liftoff. This takes two hours and nearly 300 tonnes of liquid oxygen and fuel are pumped in through snaking hoses sucking the fuel from underground storage depots.

An hour before liftoff the high gantries are lowered. Any cosmonaut on board will now feel the Soyuz gently rocking in the wind. New fuel still has to be pumped on board till the very end. Liquid oxygen boils at −190°C and wisps of it always surround a rocket's stages.

The fuel hoses are pulled away at 60 seconds before liftoff. 20 seconds to go and the electrical lines are removed. The rocket's electrical systems must use their own batteries now. The ignition command is sent and flames roar out into the trenches. When the thrust exceeds the rocket's own weight, the four lower arms still restraining it fall back like petals on a flower and let the rocket free.

The way all this is done has much to do with the military requirements of the late 1950s. The USSR needed a versatile rocket force − hence one based on railways. The rockets could be moved around everywhere and hidden in sidings off lines in Siberia.

They were not tied to fixed pads and silos where they could be knocked out at will. The USSR needed a system where the rocket could be erected quickly and fired. The A booster could be got out from assembly to pad and fired in about an hour. The A booster was designed for simplicity and mass production — in fact, over 600 have been launched. Keeping it going has been nothing short of an industry: the factory producing it has produced a nozzle every 12 hours since the space age started!

So busy was the first historic pad that a second one was constructed to share some of the launch load. Pad B as it has been called was built 30 km away to the northeast. It is basically the same although there are differences in detail in the position of local buildings, railway tracks and lightning towers [4].

Work on pad B began in 1964 and it was completed in 1966. The first launch from there took place in October 1966 and Soyuz 9 was the first manned craft to use it. Most Soyuz and the later Progress craft have gone from there, though not Soyuz 11, 16, 19, and 25. Pad A was overhauled and modernized as soon as pad B was available. Interpreters of space photographs claim there are two additional A pads which were used for the Luna soft-landers, Venera 1 to 8 and which are now used for unmanned Cosmos satellites.

Sometime in 1965 work began on a new series of pads to the northwest near some salt lakes. About twenty — perhaps as many as thirty — were constructed, and they were military in nature. It is thought they were for a new type of military rocket, the F booster. They were completed in 1967 and for a while they were the basis for the USSR's satellite-killer programme. They do not seem to have been in use since the Strategic Arms Limitations Treaty (SALT) between General Secretary Leonid Brezhnev and President Richard Nixon.

More significant were, in the long term, the developments in the east — about 35 km east of the original Sputnik pad. Here the designers chose to locate two pads to support the Proton D booster which was to fly first in 1965. En route, and beside the railway tracks, lay an assembly area laid out like an industrial estate. Not much is known of the Proton pads, and no complete film of a Proton launch was released until 1984. Each pad is flanked by two 88 m-high towers which combine the functions of lightning conductor, TV camera point and floodlamp location.

Finally there are the two G pads, set up to support the man-on-the-Moon effort. Although Proton was sited a long way off from the original Sputnik pad, the two G pads were placed a mere 3.5 km distant. Work began in 1963 and was completed in 1968. The completed G pads must have been impressive: two enormous pads, matched by 183 m tall towers, feeding from an assembly hangar of a length of 250 m, about the same size as the old Zeppelin airship sheds.

And, as we know, the G booster met a fate similar to the airships. After the 1972 launch failure, static tests were run briefly in 1974 until the pads were abandoned. They were mothballed, and it was their deserted shell that Tom Stafford and his team spotted during his visit a year later.

So they remained until in 1981 engineers began reconstructing their rusty structures into a pad for the G booster's replacement — the sleek, ultramodern Energia booster, a heavy-lift rocket that would take up 150 tonnes into low Earth orbit and, as such, a worthy successor to the G. And in October 1982 it saw life again when a prototype Energia booster was assembled on the pad for a full-scale fuelling test.

VOLGOGRAD STATION – KAPUSTIN YAR

The Volga river is the longest and best-known waterway in all of Russia. It has a place deep in Russian history. It was on the banks of the Volga in 1942 that Hitler's invasion was stopped at Volgograd and turned back. All the more ironic, for in 1947 many Germans found themselves back on the Volga building rockets for their former foes. Somewhere between Volgograd and where the Volga flows into the Caspian Sea was designated as the site for testing the old German A-4 rocket.

This became Russia's first rocket base. Like Baikonour, it was constructed beside a river and built around two towns – Kapustin Yar (by which name the base is known) and Akhubinsk. The towns lay on the main railway line between Astrakhan and what was then known as Stalingrad, now Volgograd. Both towns had an airport. The land was dead flat. Just like at Baikonour, the rocket pads were built upon a triangular rail network which had Kapustin Yar to Akhubinsk as it base and the pads as the apex.

Kapustin Yar – its name means 'little cabbage patch' – was used extensively for A-4 tests in 1947–49 and for its more advanced successors over 1949–52. The first space rabbits and dogs flew on their suborbital hops from Kapustin Yar. It was abandoned in 1953 when the decision was taken to relocate all future rocket activity on Baikonour. Kapustin Yar retreated into silence and the winds, the desert and the weeds began to claim it back.

There the story might have ended but for the start of the Moon programme in 1961. The space planners realized that Baikonour would be working flat out for many years – the D, F and G pads were all built over 1963–68 – and that at least some diversification was needed to prevent the overloading of the Baikonour launch and tracking teams.

Another consideration was the start of a new space programme in 1962, the Cosmos programme. The 'Cosmos' designation was to become the most over-used classification in the history of classifications. When Cosmos 1 went up on 16 March 1962, it was announced as a new series of satellites for the scientific exploration of outer space. 100 had flown by December 1965. The 1000 mark was passed in 1978, by which time a Cosmos launch was a weekly event. The 1500 mark came in 1983.

Such a launch rate would suggest an obsession with scientific data verging on the fanatical. Of course it was not; and by the 1970s a close examination revealed that the programme was at least three-quarters military. The start of the programme was innocent enough. After Gagarin's flight, the Sputnik programme had outlived its usefulness, since its purpose had been to pave the way for manned flight. Granted that the long-term manned occupancy of space was still some way away, there was a need for a series of small satellites that would report on the ionosphere, radiation, solar wind, meteorites and all the other million features of near-Earth space.

For this, the Cosmos series was designed, and a new booster with it. It has been labelled the B booster and NATO gave it the codename of 'Sandal'. The B booster, designed by Mikhail Yangel, was in service from 1962 to 1977, and was long, thin, and pencil-shaped. It was the smallest of all the Soviet boosters, 30 m tall, weighing 43 000 kg, and had a first stage thrust of 7200 kg. It had enough thrust to put a mass of 500 kg into an orbit of 300 km.

Cosmos 1 was the first of many such small scientific payloads. But before long the 'Cosmos' designation was being used to cover anything and everything. Cosmos designations have already been encountered as failed moonshots, manned precursors and rendezvous tests, and in the course of time they were to be used to cover major space station components (1267, 1443). The vast majority were, however, flags of convenience for military missions of many types, from photoreconnaissance to satellite killers.

One of the ways in which the Cosmos programme is intelligible is its classification system. Satellites are never — deliberately that is — fired into random orbits. 51.6 degrees, for example is always used for manned flights. The 'degree' is the angle at which the satellite crosses the equator and 51 degrees also means that the satellite will orbit between 51°N latitude and 51°S latitude. Cosmos satellites have always fitted into patterns according to launch site, inclination, altitude, and time till recovery. Once you have this data, interpretation becomes possible.

Just as Baikonour concentrated on the technology-proving missions, so Kapustin Yar was specialized in small scientific payloads. (The third cosmodrome, Plesetsk, has been almost entirely military.)

Over the period 1962—73 the B-1 booster put up 60 small payloads from Kapustin Yar, averaging about seven a year. 18 of these may have been military. The civilian ones orbited every 93 minutes or so at an altitude of 250 km, reporting back on conditions in near-Eath space. It was a modest and successful venture.

The B booster was to serve as the basis of the first Soviet—international space venture, called perhaps unimaginatively, Intercosmos. It was the brainchild of Boris Petrov, a well-built, dark, most imaginative scientist. In the mid-1960s he put together something called the Intercosmos Council, which included representatives of the USSR, the East European Socialist countries, and later, Cuba and Vietnam. Its purpose was two-fold: to give Soviet allies a chance to participate in the Soviet space programme and to enable the USSR to benefit from the special scientific disciplines developed in other countries. It was formally set up in the Academy of Sciences on 31 May 1966.

The first of the Intercosmos satellites sponsored by this Council took off from Kapustin Yar on 14 October 1969 on a B-1, and it was the first of nine such missions. All were in the 300—400 kg class. Each of the small satellites had a specialized task. For Intercosmos 1, built by scientists from Czechoslovakia and the German Democratic Republic (GDR), it was to study solar radiation. Intercosmos 2 investigated the iono-sphere; 5 and 8 the geomagnetic field, and so on. Intercosmos 9 — the last of this series out of Kapustin Yar on a B-1 — was called Copernicus 500 in honour of the great Polish scientist's 500th anniversary. Built in Poland, it was concerned with solar radiation and the ionosphere, and orbited on 19 April 1973.

When the B rocket was operational, Kapustin Yar became the site for seven or eight small satellite launches a year. In addition, some pads were build in the late 1960s for a new series of sounding rockets — the original function of Kapustin Yar. Called 'Vertikal', they brought small scientific packages to altitudes of about 1200 km before they parachuted back for recovery. Occasional such launches were made throughout the 1970s and they filled a gap by flying short-duration missions for which a satellite would be too expensive.

The B-1 rocket, associated mainly with Kapustin Yar, was retired in 1977 after 144 launches. By this time it had long since been eclipsed by a new launch site to the far north. Kapustin Yar continued its minor role with occasional spaceshots of small scientific payloads. Then in 1982 it became the base for the first orbital tests of the Soviet space shuttle, the Kosmolyot.

THE NORTHERN COSMODROME

The town of Kettering in the north of England is a very ordinary one, and like many towns of its size in the 1960s it had a grammar school. Like many grammar schools it emphasized science in its upper classes, with a strong practical bent. The science teacher, Mr Perry, was keenly interested in electronics, radios and space research: he involved his class in the building of radio tracking devices. Whether by accident or design — history does not record — he and his students found that their radio trackers could be tuned in to Soviet Cosmos and other transmitters. It was a good combination of practical electronics, learning and current affairs.

It was not long before Kettering Grammar School (or the Kettering group as they came to be called) began to build up expertise in following the Soviet space programme. They were soon able to classify all the different programmes by their signals and find out when satellites were recovered. At one stage they were picking up manned spacecraft telemetry long before the launches were officially announced. The teacher and his students built up a world-wide reputation and the American media began to depend on Kettering for interpreting obscurer missions.

Cosmos 112 on 17 March 1966 seemed at first sight just another Cosmos mission until Kettering took a look at its orbital path, high point and low point, and tracked it back to somewhere northeast of Leningrad, just inside the Arctic circle! It could not be! Check again. Sure enough: check after check brought the launch point back to the same place. Cosmos 114 on 6 April 1966, repeated the pattern. They had discovered a secret and hitherto unknown cosmodrome!

Until 1987 there was no official reference to the northern cosmodrome, called Plesetsk, in the West [5]. It is located around the towns of Plesetsk and Kochmas on the Emtsa river. The nearest big city is Archangel. Plesetsk is basically a military launch centre but also carries scientific satellites requiring Polar orbits. Plesetsk is at 63°N, near the Arctic circle. The summer nights are long and it never really gets dark. In winter there are only a few hours greyness at midday amidst remorseless night. It is near enough to Sweden for an observer there to see the occasional launch in the far eastern sky arcing into the distance.

Plesetsk is much more compact than either Baikonour or Kapustin Yar, and because it is military it is heavily protected by surface-to-air missiles. The launch pads are clustered around the Kochmas industrial area. There are up to four A pads, and several F and C pads. The B rocket also used Plesetsk until 1977.

Why choose such a site — so near to Sweden — where it was bound to be found out sooner or later? Russian geography and orbital mechanics provide the answer. A northerly launch site was needed to get satellites into Polar orbit. Such orbits are perfect for ground surveillance because a Polar-orbiting satellite covers the planet every 24 hours. It is also suitable for weather satellites, which must cover the same ground path. Also, the north-western USSR was the part best-developed in terms of communications. Building it further east, say in Siberia, would have been madness for it would not have been possible to reach the site easily.

In the mid-1980s then, there were three operational cosmodromes. Baikonour (the equivalent of Cape Canaveral) used for manned, deep space and technology satellites; Plesetsk (the equivalent of the US Air Force base at Vandenberg California) for military payloads; and Kapustin Yar (the American equivalent would be Wallops Island Virginia) for small scientific payloads.

In 1982, for example, the payloads broke down as follows:

Baikonour: Manned related   8
              Deep space   2
              Applications   7
              Military   23

Kapustin Yar: Manned related   1
                 Military   3

Plesetsk: Scientific   1
             Applications   6
             Military   50

As can be seen, Kapustin Yar launches are infrequent. Plesetsk is the most frequently used base (more than one launch a week) and its military orientation clear [6].

GETTING THERE: THE BOOSTERS

For the period 1957–84 the USSR flew only six rocket boosters to support its entire space effort, and that includes the failed colossus known as the G booster. One of the problems of the Soviet programme in this period is the failure of the Soviet literature to make much, if any, reference to its rocket boosters. Some are still, officially, secret. The situation is also complicated by the fact that Western sources use different classifications for these rockets [7]. Thus the Sputnik booster is alternatively known as the Sputnik rocket, the A booster, the SL-6, or the Sapwood (NATO name). The boosters are listed as follows:

Name	Years of service	Length (m)	1st stage thrust
A (A-2 dimensions)	1957–	49.3	408 000
B-1	1962–77	30	72 000
C-1	1964–	31.4	176 000
D (D-le dimensions)	1965–	59.5	1 442 000
F (F-2 dimensions)	1967–	44.9	226 000
G	1969–72	93.7	5 400 000

The A booster, as we have already seen, played a key role in the Soviet space programme from the moment of Sputnik onwards. With its core and four strap-ons and twenty nozzles roaring at liftoff, it is unique in the rocket world. As the years went by, the engineers simply added more and more to the top, till the rocket reached to nearly 50 m with the Soyuz escape tower, compared to the more modest 29 m it started at as Russia's first ICBM.

The A became the most-used booster in history. From two launches in 1957, it progressed to 34 by 1967, 47 in 1972 and 63 in 1980, or more than one a week. The rate showed no signs of slackening.

Naturally the A has been through many versions. The basic one launched the first three Sputniks. It was modified as early as 1959 when a small first stage was added, enough to get Luna 1–3 off to the Moon and the first Vostoks into orbit. The A-1, as it has been called, could send 1550 kg to the Moon or 4730 kg into Earth orbit. After Vostok, it was used for the early military reconnaissance and meteorological satellites and was retired in 1971.

The next modification was the fitting of a large second stage, 9.4 m long and 2.6 m in diameter. This was the A-2 and it first appeared in 1964 with the Voskhod. This model turned out to be highly reliable and was used for the Soyuz and Progress missions, carrying up to 7500 kg.

The other variant was the A-2e, the 'e' meaning escape. This first appeared in 1960 with the first attempted Mars launch. After that, it was used for all the early deep space missions: Venera 1–8, Mars 1, Zond 1–3, Luna 4–14. Its capability was to accelerate 1665 kg to escape velocity.

On a typical mission – let us take Venera 8 – the A-2e would rise on its twenty nozzles. The strap-ons would burn out and blast free after 2 minutes. The rocket would now be 50 km up and well above the thick layers of the atmosphere. The core would fire a further 3 minutes. The payload would then orbit our planet for one revolution – possibly two – and it would be aimed at the right keyhole in the sky. The escape stage would light up and fire a full 243 seconds – just over 4 minutes. The long struggle against gravity would be over, Earth vanquished.

The B-1 has already been examined in the context of its base, Kapustin Yar. The B-1 had a shortcoming: the size of its payload, which was less than 500 kg. The next available booster was the A-2 with a payload of up to 7500 kg. This was a big gap – and there were a variety of satellite needs in between. To meet these needs, the C-1 was developed. NATO codenamed it 'Skean'. As for the B-1, the designer was Mikhail Yangel.

The C-1 looked like the B-1 but was fatter – perhaps biro-shaped if the B-1 is called pencil-shaped. Both were nearly the same height. It was 30 m tall, two stages, and could orbit payloads of 500 to 1000 kg.

C-1 first appeared in 1964 with the treble launching of Cosmos 38–40. At the time the USSR admitted that a 'carrier rocket of a new type' had been launched. After nine test flights from Baikonour, virtually all subsequent missions have been shifted to Plesetsk, about 30 a year. A few have gone from Kapustin Yar, but it is unusual. With the retirement of the B-1 in 1977, the C-1 took over its old functions. The C-1 will probably surrender in turn to a derivative of the SS-11 military missile.

The D booster, with its origins deep in the Soviet man-to-the-Moon effort, became, in the course of time, the workhorse of the deep space programme and the orbiter of heavy payloads into Earth orbit. Despite its unreliability in its early years – and problems which cost the Russians the Moon race – it became very solid and reliable, rarely malfunctioning after 1970.

The D-1, like other boosters, has been constantly uprated. In its original form, in 1965, it put the 12 tonne Proton satellites into orbit. The heavier versions from 1977 on were able to launch the second-generation Salyuts (19 tonnes) and the Star module (20 tonnes). The most commonly used version, the D-1e, was used for geosynchronous and deep space missions. Its capability was 6000 kg to the Moon, 5000 kg to the near planets, or 2500 kg to geosynchronous orbit. The last one is actually a special sub-version called the D-1Ee, incorporating a final adjusting booster, thus making the Proton a 5-stage rocket! The D-1Ee could also manage a small probe to Jupiter or Saturn, weighing up to 930 kg, but unlike the Americans, this was an avenue the Russians chose to defer.

Use of the D-1 built up slowly but surely: it had been used 27 times by 1977, including all the Salyuts, Moon probes from 1969 on, Mars 2–7, and Venus probes from Venera 9. Increasingly it became used for satellites heading for stationary orbit at 36 000 km. So reliable did Proton become that in 1983 the USSR offered it to Western commerical companies on an economic basis. The offer was $24m per flight to stationary orbit, compared to the then going rates of the Space Shuttle ($17m to low Earth orbit) or Europe's Ariane ($22.30m).

In 1982, for example, Proton left its Baikonour pad ten times. The missions included Salyut 7, two Venus probes, five communication satellites (comsats) and two Cosmos missions. It is unlikely to be retired for some time.

HUNTER-KILLERS

Of all the Soviet boosters, the F is the most sinister: over the years 1967–68 it introduced weapons of destruction to near-Earth space [8]. These were SIS (Satellite Interception System) and FOBS (Fractional Orbital Bombardment System). In shorthand these can be called the hunter-killer satellites and the single orbit bomb.

On 19 October 1968, Cosmos 248 rose from Baikonour and entered orbit of 475 by 543 km, 62.2 degrees. Nothing unusual, until a second flight left Baikonour the next day, labelled Cosmos 249. It manoeuvred rapidly and then shot past 248 on a rapid intercept trajectory. It manoeuvred further, headed up into a high orbit of 493 by 2157 km, and then blew apart into hundreds of fragments. Cosmos 252 then did exactly the same thing on 1 November.

To observers, two things were clear. First, that a new and versatile rocket was in operation; and second, that the USSR had developed a means of knocking unfriendly satellites out of orbit. With a fleet of these rockets, all America's satellites — be they spying or on more innocent errands — could be knocked out within two or three hours. In the event of a nuclear confrontation, America's eyes and ears would be put out of action.

It was a system the USSR perfected quickly, and in 1970 it was put through its second full test. Cosmos 373 was the target of a fast interception by Cosmos 374, and a week later, 375. Clearly, the system worked.

What was the new rocket that had given the Soviet military forces such a clear edge? Mathematical and computer interpretation of the interceptor flights linked it to a rocket that had appeared in Red Square in November 1967. That had been an important occasion. On 7 November, the USSR celebrated the 50th anniversary of the Revolution — a full half century since Trotsky and Lenin had stormed the Winter Palace. So for hours, Moscovites were treated to a spectacle of Soviet military might — tanks, MiG jets, soldiers, troop carriers belching their diesel smoke; and then the long, slim rockets on their mobile transporters.

One booster excited immediate attention. Dark, long, grey and slim, it trundled past the reviewing stand. Diplomats and the Western military attachés soon thought they had not seen this one before. NATO quickly labelled it the SS-9 or 'Scarp'. The Sheldon classification gives it the F booster codename. Yangel designed it.

The F-1, it emerged, had a thrust of 155 000 kg, in the class of the American Deltas. 45 m high (much the same as Soyuz), it had three stages, the separation point of the first two being unclear. Its payload capacity was 4000 kg in low Earth orbit, or 3000 kg for an orbit of 1000 km.

The F-1 was developed in three categories. The F-1r was used for the FOBS and had a small retrorocket. The F-1m had a highly manoeuvrable third stage, used in the interceptor flights. And an updated version, known as the F-2, began flying from Plesetsk on 24 June 1977 and was called 'Cyclon' [9].

Once the basic interceptor system had been tested, the USSR moved on to fly it in more demanding combinations. Three tests were carried out in 1971. There were differences. Cosmos 397, launched from Baikonour, intercepted 394, which had been launched from Plesetsk. From now on, the targets were launched by C-1 rockets. Cosmos 397's interception path was a slow one – suggesting the possibility of 'sleeper' interceptors whose hostile intentions might not be immediately apparent.

By contrast, Cosmos 404 was a fast intercept, but instead of exploding and showering its target with debris, it reentered the atmosphere, demonstrating the possibility of photographic inspection followed by recovery. After one launch failure in 1972, the series was discontinued. Western watchers simply assumed the series was now operational and required no further testing. It was presumed that a series of F pads had been installed at Baikonour and Plesetsk, and that these long, sleek missiles would be ready to be released should the unthinkable happen.

Then suddenly in 1976 the interceptor tests were resumed with manoeuvres of new complexity. The target was Cosmos 803 (Plesetsk, 12 February). On the 16th, 804 made a slow intercept and then returned to Earth after close scrutiny and inspection of the target. On 13 April, 814 intercepted 803, closed in for investigation, and returned to Earth – all within one orbit. In December, 886 closed in on 880, and exploded. These flights continued in 1977 with five tests. In some cases the interceptions were far from close, suggesting that long-distance lasers were being tested. Earlier, in 1975, so the CIA claimed, the USSR had used lasers to temporarily blind American early-warning satellites.

It turned out that the gap in tests over 1972–76 had never been intended as permanent and that the Satellite Interception System simply required regular testing. 21 tests had been made by 1983.

A typical test was Cosmos 1375 (6 June 1982), which flew into the standard target orbit (979 by 1012 km, 65.8 degrees, 105 minutes). Twelve days later, 1379 went up from Baikonour at 11.08 a.m. Its first orbit was 140 by 542 km, 65.1 degrees, 91.4 minutes. Using its powerful third stage, it manoeuvred rapidly to an orbit of 537 by 1019 km. Repeatedly burning its boosters, and guided by ultra-rapid computers, the separate manoeuvres were made as little as four minutes apart. At 2.30 p.m. 1379 made a fast intercept of its target at 400 m/s. At 2.50 p.m. it reentered over the Pacific Ocean. Flight time was 3 h 42 min.

The FOBS system was in the long-run less important than the interception system. 15 tests were carried out over 1967–71 and it may have become obsolete not long afterwards. But they highlighted the militarization of space generated by the Cold War. Again, the F booster was used.

Suspicion that something new was afoot began in 1966 with the launch of two unannounced Cosmos flights — now called the U1 and the U2. Then came the orbiting of Cosmos 139 in 1967, orbit 135 by 215 km, 49.6 degrees. The odd thing about 139 was that it made just less than one orbit — although there was no sign that anything had gone wrong.

American defence experts soon grasped what was going on. Their whole defence strategy was based on a Soviet missile attack over the North Pole, with the missiles coming from Siberia. Hence the radar warning lines stretching across Alaska and Canada. FOBS undid all that. Cosmos 139 orbited directly south, over the southern hemisphere, came round from behind, and approached America from the Gulf of Mexico. It was also a 'fractional' bombardment system — meaning that the warhead split into several parts. It had the Pentagon worried: even one Cosmos, coming in from the 'wrong' direction, could do untold damage.

The last test was on 9 August 1971. For several years, FOBS had given the USSR the edge in the nuclear weapons stakes. But by the time the SALT talks were under way following the Nixon *détente* initiatives, the Baikonour FOBS pads were abandoned. At best the system had been barely legal, for the 1963 Test Ban Treaty had forbidden the flying of weapons into space. The Russians had argued that FOBS was not 'orbiting' since it did not quite complete a full orbit.

The F booster's uses were in time extended well beyond FOBS and SIS. From 1967 it was used to put up a series of nuclear-powered ocean surveillance satellites, some of which met dangerous ends. Starting in 1974, F was used to launch ocean ferrets — military jargon for satellites which track, catalogue and keep watch on the other side's naval radio and radar stations. On the happier side, 1979 saw the use of the F-1 for the first time in civilian Earth resources missions.

In 1982 the F rocket flew 12 times. Four were ocean surveillance missions (Baikonour); three were ocean ferrets (Baikonour); one was a geodetic satellite (Cosmos 1410 from Plesetsk); one was a Meteor weather satellite from Plesetsk; and two were electronic intelligence missions from Plesetsk.

'FINDING GOLFBALLS FROM ORBIT'

Mission control at Cape Canaveral simply could not believe it. Trains? Aircraft? But that's what the man said. Was he still sane?

But he insisted. Mission control was listening as astronaut Gordon Cooper reported back on the phenomenal sights from orbit. As he flew his 22 orbits around the Earth, he claimed to see the tracks of boats in the Gulf of Mexico, a plane flying in to land on the east coast, and a steam train in northern India. Then to cap it all, he saw cars on a highway in Texas.

No one really believed him. Astronaut doctors did recall that Cooper's eyesight was unusually good. But it was not until Cooper flew aloft with Charles Conrad in 1965 and confirmed his findings that the truth sank in: the atmosphere was no obstacle, and indeed a help, to observations from space. It seemed to have some kind of magnifying effect that was not visible to high flying aircraft. Cameras were tested to see just how well this process worked, and by 1969 the Americans claimed they could see the shoulder badges and ranks on the uniforms of Soviet soldiers and officers from orbit; and the next year they claimed that they could find golf balls. For the military it was a godsend. Space was an environment from which they could spy at liberty, since the normal rules of not overflying the other's country simply did not apply that high up.

Considering the military and political origins of the space race in the first place it is perhaps not surprising that it became militarized. Of the USSR's 101 launches in 1982, 75 were military. These 75 are in turn divisible into several categories:

Photoreconnaissance
Ocean surveillance
Early warning
Ferret or ELINT (Electronic INTelligence)
Navigation
Communications for the military.

The first one, military photoreconnaissance, was by far the largest single element. Indeed, for the period 1975–83 this accounted for over 30 per cent of all launches of spacecraft from the USSR. And the first of these was Cosmos 4 on 26 April 1962. Its predecessors were small scientific satellites at 49 degrees out of Kapustin Yar on the B-1. But Cosmos 4 went from Baikonour at the then typical manned inclination of 65 degrees. Three days later it was recovered.

Ground tracking of Cosmos 4 suggested that it was similar in shape and size to the Vostok manned craft. It was. Using the same A booster it was simply adapted to carry large cameras where the cosmonaut usually sat. Once it had circled the Earth for the desired period it was recovered in the usual way.

This, the first series of photoreconnaissance satellites, operated from 1962 to 1967. Cosmos 153 was the last. On average, the payload flew for eight days, and all but one flight was in summertime. In mid-1964 the 65 degrees orbit was replaced by one of 51.2 degrees; in 1966 the missions also flew out of Plesetsk at 64.6 degrees.

The second generation of photoreconnaissance satellites was introduced in 1963 and ran to 1978. It took advantage of the uprated Voskhod booster, and indeed the satellite itself cannot have been that much different from the manned craft. It probably weighed up to 6000 kg, compared to 4500 for the first generation.

The second generation flew out of Baikonour at 51.8 degrees and Plesetsk at 65.4 degrees and 72.9 degrees. This type came in three versions: a low-resolution model; a high-resolution one (also recoverable after eight days); and an extended duration model which stayed aloft 12 days. The latter also had a stubby cylinder attached to the front. It was a standard small scientific payload which was normally left behind in orbit when the military film cannisters were returned.

Barely had Georgi Beregovoi stepped out of the returning Soyuz 3 in October 1968 than Cosmos 251 went aloft — the first of the third generation of spy satellites, based on that very Soyuz. This model was still operating in the eighties. Just as with Vostok, the USSR had simply adapted Soyuz to carry recoverable film and canisters.

Cosmos 251 was called a morse code satellite — for some reason it transmitted all its data in morse code. Not that it did not require decoding — it did — but the use of morse was unexpected. The morse code series ended in 1974.

Of the rest of the third generation, there were three categories: low, medium, and high resolution. The low-resolution satellites operated at 212–245 km, skipping the outer edges of the Earth's atmosphere. They flew at 82.3 degrees, and about two went up each year. Filming was in black-and-white, like the rest of the series. Medium-resolution satellites went into low orbit and then manoeuvred up to 400 km. Orbits were 62.8 degrees, 70.4 degrees and 82.3 degrees. High-resolution ones used low orbits at 70.4 degrees, 72.9 degrees and 82.3 degrees. All came back after about two weeks and most used Plesetsk.

The fourth generation of spy satellites appeared in 1976 with Cosmos 949, and went operational in 1980. Orbits at 62.8 degrees, 64.9 degrees, 67.1 degrees, and 70.4 degrees were used. They were based on Soyuz with solar panels, and they were sophisticated. They skimmed just over the atmosphere and each week they used their motor to keep just high enough from burning up. Missions lasted about 44 days. Small capsules were ejected for reentry. Pictures could then be analysed when the satellite was still up there, and the satellite ordered to concentrate on new areas.

A fifth generation was introduced with Cosmos 1643 in March 1985. The series did not send down a recoverable capsule. Instead, images were transmitted directly to the ground.

Between the five types of spy satellites the USSR had developed a comprehensive system of orbital photoreconnaissance based on specialized versions of their manned spacecraft. The Americans, by contrast, developed purpose-built spy satellites. They flew many fewer actual missions — about 3 or 4 a year compared to the USSR's 30 or so. American systems were generally regarded as much more sophisticated.

America's fourth generation appeared as far back as 1970 and was called 'Big Bird'. Big Bird was big — 13 tonnes — and was a converted Agena rocket atop a Titan 3 booster. It had a huge camera of 30 m resolution. About one or two were launched each year throughout the 1970s: each would last about 180 days and eject six small capsules.

America's fifth generation of spy satellites appeared in 1976: the KH-11, or the key-hole 11, its CIA designation. It was similar to the Big Bird but incorporated a giant breakthrough: the replacement of ejected film capsules by direct TV digital transmission — thereby saving on recovery forces and time, not to mention preventing the film falling into the wrong hands. Data could thus be radioed straight down.

Some of the advantage of the KH-11 was blunted when in 1978 the Russians persuaded a CIA clerk, William Campiles, to part with the KH-11 manual for what seems to be a very modest amount: $3000. He was caught and got a 40-year jail term; but the Russians had the manual.

The manned space stations, Salyut 3 (1974–75) and Salyut 5 (1976–77) represented an attempt by the USSR to develop a manned military photoreconnaissance programme, perhaps equivalent to Big Bird in terms of technology, but it may not have been as productive as hoped, because the military space station with large cameras aboard was dropped after Salyut 5.

DID THE RUSSIANS SINK *HMS SHEFFIELD*?

On 2 April 1982, the Argentine navy and marine forces seized the Falkland Islands in the southern Atlantic. It was British territory, though in the nineteenth century it had changed hands many times over. The Argentine military Government seem to have under-estimated the British response, for Prime Minister Margaret Thatcher at once dispatched a heavily armed task force to retake the islands. Bloody engagements ensued, and by July the islands were back in British hands.

The British victory was not bought lightly. The Royal Navy lost several major ships — destroyers, frigates and landing vessels — from missile and bombing attacks from the Argentine Air Force. The first ship to be lost was the guided missile destroyer, *HMS Sheffield*, on 4 May. Early that morning, two Etendard aircraft left their bases on the east coast of Argentina, flew high, and took *Sheffield* into view at the extreme edge of the horizon. Their missile radars took a fix on *Sheffield*. The Etendards dived and dropped swiftly, lest they be caught in turn by the British radars. They primed their under-wing Exocet missiles, fed in the computer data, fired them, and headed for home.

The Exocets sped at wave height across the wintry south Atlantic. Minutes later, one slammed into the side of *Sheffield*. It turned into an inferno and sunk in hours. Most of the crew were saved.

A superb piece of military detection and flying by the Argentian Air Force? Not so, said the American press. Only four hours before the Exocet was fired, a Soviet spy satellite, Cosmos 1355, had passed directly overhead. It had located *HMS Sheffield*, radioed the information to its masters, who had tipped off the Argentinians. So the Kremlin had done it! Or so the story went.

There was nothing new in the superpowers spying on each other's wars, of course. It was a good field test of how other countries fight wars and a good test of how to locate military manoeuvres 'for real'. Ever since photographic reconnaissance started from orbit, there had been a flurry of military satellites from each side whenever a conflict blew up, and each country normally kept some spy satellites in reserve for this purpose.

The first war to get such attention was the Middle East war of 1967, though it was short enough at only six days. Cosmos 463 and 464 were sent up specially to cover the India–Pakistan war of 1971. The Middle East war of 1973 was the first to receive detailed treatment from spy satellites [10]. When the Egyptians attacked on 6 October, the USSR had only the low-resolution Cosmos 596 in orbit. Within hours of the 'Yom Kippur' assault, Cosmos 597 was off from Plesetsk. It was manoeuvrable, and on 6 October so positioned itself that every 16th orbit it was at its perigee point over the battlefield of Syria, Golan Heights, and the Great Salt Lakes. By 10 October, its orbit had drifted westwards to the extent that it no longer covered the battlefield. It was recovered.

The next day, Cosmos 598 went aloft from Plesetsk into 72.9 degree orbit — an improvement on the 65.4 degrees of its predecessors because it got an immediate pass over Syria and needed no further manoeuvres. 598 was a 'morse code' spy satellite. Not only that, but it overflew its tracking station in Yevpatoria in the Crimea a mere 10 minutes after overflying the warring tanks and planes. Thus were the Russians able to get real time coverage over the battlefield. Cosmos 598 came down on the 16th October, by which time 599 was aloft.

Cosmos 600 was more versatile still (16–23 October). It changed orbits so that its path drifted first eastwards, then westwards, over the Middle East. It flew in tandem with 599, 70 minutes apart. Cosmos 603, 607, 609, 612, 616, and 625 all monitored the final stages of fighting and the cease-fire and redeployment which followed.

When General Galtieri's forces landed in the Falklands on 2 April they caught the

Soviet intelligence forces on the hop as much as the British. The USSR had only one reconnaissance satellite in orbit, the fourth-generation Cosmos 1347. Its mission was prolonged to last 50 days, a week longer than any previous fourth-generation model. By the 15th, the USSR was sufficiently organized to get aloft a second fourth-generation model, 1350, from Plesetsk to cover the South Atlantic.

More missions followed in rapid succession: 1352 (medium resolution, 21 April to 5 May); 1353 (high resolution, 23 April to 6 May); and eight more in the period from 21 April to 31 July. At one stage three fourth-generation satellites were orbiting. In addition to the photoreconnaissance satellites, ocean surveillance and ferret missions were flown.

It was Cosmos 1355 that was blamed for the attack on *Sheffield*. Cosmos 1355 was not actually a photographic reconnaissance satellite at all, but an electronic ocean reconnaissance satellite, or ocean ferret in military parlance. It did not carry cameras but electronic equipment — which could indeed have picked up *Sheffield*. It did pass over the ship four hours before it was sunk and it could have located its exact position. Could the information have been relayed to Buenos Aires in time?

It probably could have been, but it probably was not. It would have been at least 20 minutes before any data could have been relayed to the ground. Even assuming this happened, and the USSR appreciated the significance of *Sheffield's* manoeuvres, a political decision would have to be taken to pass that information on to Buenos Aires. That would have taken time, and knowing the pace of decision-making in the Kremlin, a long time. Even then, time was needed to get the Etendards airborne. On balance, the likelihood of all these factors coming together in four hours is slim.

RORSATS — FLIRTING WITH NUCLEAR DANGER

Northern Canada. January 1978. Ice and snow covered the endless wilderness. One silent starry evening, the few Eskimos and Canadians who lived there looked up, and saw a fireball plunging to the northeast. It burned in an arc and disappeared, breaking up in red hot fragments high in the upper atmosphere. Twenty minutes later, the metallic remains of the fireball crashed into the ice and snow near the small settlement of Yellowknife.

The Canadians who saw the fireball probably knew by this stage that they were being visited by something different from the normal run of astronomical phenomena like aurora borealis or a meteor. It was a satellite. And not just a satellite, but one that had gone out of control. And not only that, but one with a nuclear reactor on board.

The Canadian Government, with United States help, lost no time in trying to locate the wayward satellite, now identified as Cosmos 954, origin USSR. 'Operation Morninglight' was mounted. It was an eerie title. The cynic would say that they were more interested in finding and analysing Soviet space debris than making the area safe for the few people who lived there. The Americans may well have called the shots anyway because Canadian search gear could be charitably described as primitive: they had nothing better than hand-held geiger counters.

Hercules aircraft fanned out in grid patterns across the desolate landscape. Occasionally they passed settlements with names like Snowdrift, Great Salt Lake or Fort

Reliance. It could not have been colder and the temperature was −40°C. And as their luck would have it, the area was full of underground minerals and ores, including uranium, that gave false readings which confused the instruments.

It was four days before anything was found. Some resident meteorologists − not, ironically, the search teams at all − came across a patch of melting snow. Presumably some parts of Cosmos 954 had crashed there, melted through the ice, and sunk below it.

The search was abandoned in March 1978. Only 10 per cent of the reactor was found, and a total of 50 kg of debris. Even fewer bits were exhibited to the public, and no one knows quite what happened to the rest, though it is known that it was analysed and buried later in the United States. Eskimos living in the area were told not to eat hunted animals for fear of nuclear poisoning.

So ended 'Morninglight'. There were two sequels. One was a prolonged legal wrangle between Canada and the USSR, the former billing the latter $12m to clear up the mess. The second was a less dangerous repeat of the incident by another Cosmos five years later. But what was Cosmos 954 up to in the first place? And why the nuclear intrigue?

The story goes back to the mid-1960s, or perhaps even earlier when American (and later Soviet) scientists found that a submarine was an ideal place to locate long-range nuclear missiles. Being mobile, it would strike from anywhere. Being invisible, it could hide anywhere.

Earth orbit offered the only possibility of locating enemy submarines, not to mention surface ships as well. For the Americans − with overseas aircraft bases scattered throughout the world − this was no great problem, but for the Russians it was more difficult. And a further difficulty was that Earth-orbiting radars sent up to locate surface or submarine vessels had to be quite large, and they gulped up electrical power. They were energy intensive. They required so much energy as to be well beyond the range of existing solar panels and solar cells. The only alternative was to use nuclear power. As of 1964, the most advanced reactor was 'Ramoshka', exhibited that year at a show in Geneva. 'Romashka' produced 800 watts, and with no coolant system it acted as a long-life and highly efficient battery. It was small but had two disadvantages: it did not produce enough power, and at 500 kg it was far too heavy.

So when the programme of ocean surveillance was approved in the years 1964−65, orders went out to produce a new reactor. It emerged in due course as 'Topaz' and worked on the same principle of converting heat to electricity, except that in this case the conversion was carried out by conductors and diodes.

'Topaz' was infinitely more sophisticated than 'Ramoshka'. Weighing only 105 kg, it had 50 kg fuel (93 per cent enriched uranium-235); it produced 5−10 kW; and had a design lifetime of 300 days. But 'Topaz' had its drawbacks. It was liable to meltdown; and the only way radiation protection could be provided was to surround the reactor with heavy metallic shielding, thus increasing the payload weight. Finally, the reactor had to be brought to power before launch, which meant that for safety's sake, the launching always took place from a silo. Evidence of pre-launch power-up came when a launching failed some minutes into flight on 25 April 1973: zeon traces were found in the crash path.

The F-1 booster, true to its general military useage, was employed for this series of satellites, which have in time become known as RORSATS or Radar Ocean Reconnaissance SATellites. The first flight was Cosmos 198, late in 1967, after the F-1 had been tested out in FOBS tests. Cosmos 954, ten years later, was the 16th such mission.

As missions, RORSATs have remarkably consistent characteristics. All use Baikonour, all enter orbits of 250 by 265 km (±2 km) at 65 degrees. At the end of the operational phase, the reactor is separated from the instrument compartment and its huge radar, and is boosted out of harm's way into an orbit of 900 km, which should last nearly 600 years.

One flight a year was made until 1974 when RORSAT went operational. With the launch of Cosmos 651 and then 654 two days later, the USSR began to operate a system of two-satellite reconnaissance. They were spaced in the same plane of orbit, normally 25 minutes apart.

Cosmos 954 was the first to suffer a major public failure. What happened was simple enough, but lethal: the rocket failed to fire the reactor into high orbit. Surrounded by its heavy metallic casing, it simply decayed after a normal lifetime, crashed, and spread debris over a wide area. Flights were then suspended for two years.

Cosmos 954's public failure concealed the fact that the rest of the RORSAT series was in many other ways disappointing. Despite a design life of 75 days before 1980 and 135 days after 1980, few RORSATs ever achieved that: in fact Cosmos 1176 in 1980 was the first to reach an operational lifetime. Many failed after a few days, owing to poor electronics.

After Cosmos 954, new safety procedures were developed, and with 1240 and 1266 in 1981 the system returned to operational status. Even so, questions could still be asked of the RORSATs' nuclear energy supply. The American sea resources satellite of the same year, SEASAT, could also generate 1 kW (but from two small solar panels) and pick out submarines 100 m below the ocean.

Four RORSATs were put up in 1982. The first of these, Cosmos 1365 (10 May) was implicated in the Soviet tracking of the Falklands war, and the other three covered American naval ships around the world in succession. Then a fresh controversy blew up over another in the series, Cosmos 1402. When its turn came to rise to higher orbit on 28 December 1982, once again the third stage F-1 motor failed to fire. It was at this stage that safety procedures developed since the 954 incident came into play. The reactor separated from its casing, and without the heavy metallic casing, the reactor did not make it to the ground but instead scattered its radioactivity around the upper atmosphere — not ideal, but preferable.

By 1983 the USSR has resolved the worst difficulties associated with the RORSATs. With their large dish radars and their ability to track NATO ships and submarines any where in the world, they gave the Soviet naval command a definite edge should conflict break out and control of the sea lanes become a crucial issue, as it probably would.

ELINTS AND FERRETS: THE LANGUAGE OF STAR WARS

RORSATs were only part of a rapidly developing programme of military surveillance by the superpowers. One key area was 'ferreting' — locating the other side's military radio and radar stations. Not only would these be early targets in the event of war, but monitoring them was an essential part in estimating the strength of the enemy's surveillance methods.

The first ferrets flew in the years 1967–70, and the USSR chose to develop two types of ferret – a large model and a small one. The smaller used the C-1 booster and began with Cosmos 189 in 1967; the larger went up on the A-2 booster in December 1970 with Cosmos 389. A variation – ocean ferrets – appeared in 1974, using the F-1.

These satellites were normally identified by their patterns of orbital inclination and period. The first of these has been called the 'Cosmos at 74 degrees' series. Each satellite orbited at 74 degrees, 95 minutes, and when this was part of a series of four satellites, the system as a whole gave global coverage. Each group of four was replaced every 200 days. Thus, Cosmos 960, 1008, 1062 and 1114 replaced 870, 845, 899, and 924. Other groups operated at 100 minutes and 109 minutes. In fact, the USSR used the 74 degree inclination to pioneer a whole series of military satellites whose exact function it took Western experts many years to figure out [11].

By 1982 for example, the USSR was operating three ferret systems. Three small ferrets in the 500–760 kg class went up from Kapustin Yar at 65.8 degrees on C-1. Three more flew from Plesetsk on C-1 at the old 74 degrees. Four large ferrets on the A-2 from Plesetsk were thought to actually eavesdrop on conversations and reports emanating from radar stations. Inclination was 81.2 degrees.

Ocean ferrets were designed to track naval radars aboard ships at sea, and were dubbed with the clumsy title of EORSATs or Electronic intelligence Ocean Reconnaissance SATellites. Three flew in 1982 – all from Baikonour at 65 degrees on the powerful F-1. Normally two operated together, one in conjunction with the other. It was one of these – Cosmos 1355 – that was blamed for relaying information on the position of the *Sheffield* to Buenos Aires during the Falklands conflict.

THE TROOPS IN THE FIELD

Just as ferrets enabled the USSR to spy on American radars and intelligence gathering, so too were the Russians vulnerable to having their own communications snooped on by the United States. Nevertheless, the Russians badly needed a world-wide military communications system, linking together troops in the field, airborne forces and the Red Fleet at sea. An entirely new approach was used.

The development of the new system began early. In the summer of 1964 (18 August) the USSR announced that it had put three satellites into orbit on one rocket – Cosmos 38, 39 and 40. This coincidentally heralded the arrival of the C-1 booster. Why three though? The answer was simple enough. The top stage of the C-1 went up into its final orbit and a spring was fired from time to time, pushing each of the three satellites into the required orbit in turn. As a result, they become evenly spaced out. A ground radio could use one, then another, then another satellite to communicate as it came over the horizon. Cosmos 38–40 were followed by two more three-in-ones and three five-in-ones. By the end of this series, the Russians had not only tested the viability of the spring-launching device but the military communications system itself.

The system finally went operational in 1970 as part of an eight-in-one mission, and the complete system involved three eight-in-ones, or 24 satellites all told. Cosmos 336–343 orbited at 74 degrees, 1450 km altitude, from Plesetsk, an orbital slot followed faithfully ever since. This first launch took place the day after China's first satellite, China 1, and as a result secured a quite undeserved blaze of publicity. 'Russians steel Mao's thunder' was a typical Western headline, as if the Russians could suddenly order missions up at a day's notice.

By the early 1980s, octuple launches — as they became known — for field communications, were taking place twice a year. On a typical mission, the C-1 from Plesetsk lifted the payload to 245 km by which time it was heading southbound over Kamchatka peninsular. The upper stage then fired into an elliptical transfer orbit of 1800 km apogee, falling to 1500 km northbound off the west coast of Africa. The orbit was then circularized and the eight spherical satellites popped out, one by one, for the correct spacing.

MILITARY COSMOS: OTHER USES

Of the 1500 or so Cosmos launches put up by 1984, the vast majority were military. Of these, the main category was military photoreconnaissance, and the others were hunter-killers, RORSATs, FOBS ferrets and military field communications. Further operational systems developed in the 1970s included the following:

Type	Booster	Site	Inclination (degrees)	Period (minutes)
Military metsat	A-2	Plesetsk	81	104
Early warning	A-2e	Plesetsk	62.9	710
Navigation satellite	C-1	Plesetsk	74, 83	105
Store-dump	C-1	Plesetsk	74	100

In addition, a new system for military aircraft navigation was introduced in 1982, using the old three-in-one approach, but this time on a Proton booster for the first time. They were Cosmos 1413–1415 and each weighed about 4100 kg, orbiting at the unusual altitude of 19 000 km.

Early-warning satellites were modelled on Moloynia communications satellites. They were designed to alert the USSR to a sudden missile attack by picking up the red-hot exhaust fumes of suspect missiles. Up to nine satellites formed a complete network.

The store-dump system was one which enabled military information to be transmitted from the ground (normally far from the receiving base), stored, and then retransmitted to the ground at convenience. In 1982 there was an operational system of three such satellites at 74 degrees, each 120 degrees apart. Store-dump was thought to be linked to the work of KGB agents in the field. Using tiny wrist transmitters an agent was supposed to be able to send a message up to a Cosmos travelling overhead. Once over a ground station some time later in the orbit, the vital intelligence was beamed down.

It is worth looking at one single year to get a good picture of the balance of Soviet military space activity. Between them all, the launches cover virtually every possible legal military application to which space could be put in terms of surveillance. It showed how far the state of the art had come since the days at the turn of the century when a begoggled aviator was sent aloft in a fragile balloon with a set of binoculars. 1982 is the year cited:

Photoreconnaissance	35	missions
Ferret	12	
Ocean ferret	3	
Navigation satellite	8	
Early warning	5	
RORSAT	4	
Hunter-killer	2	
Store-dump	4	
Octuple ($\times$ 8)	2	

Added up, it amounted to a significant investment in hardware, tracking, and rocket and satellite-building. In practical terms, it meant a launch every three days. And because of the sheer variety of the orbits used, inclinations and periods, it also made their replacement by unified multiple space platforms more difficult. For economic reasons, not to mention economies of scale, such a rationalization could not be put off indefinitely.

APPLICATIONS: VOICES FROM THE SKY

The visitor to Moscow needs only take the metro line to Kaluzhko-Rizhkaya from Oktyabraskaya on the south side of the river. The palatial metro will then hurtle north through the city, deep in the bowels of the Earth and passing through the classically sculpted stations going by the names of Paveletskaya and Turgenevskaya. Eventually the visitor emerges at a place called the VDNK — abbreviation for the Exhibition of Economic and Scientific Achievements. VDNK started as a country fair in the 1930s, but no visitor would be under any such misapprehension now. He would at once be confronted by a 30-storey high titanium obelisk symbolizing a spaceship soaring skyward. On entering the exhibition area he would find it is a hangarful of spaceships and rockets of every type imaginable. Displays, models, diagrams, photographs assault the eye: it is a superlative of Soviet space achievement. And in one corner is a relatively unexciting-looking satellite.

Called 'Moloynia', the Russian for 'lightning', it is a cone shape. Eyes and antennas and shiny metallic shapes glisten. At the base are six vane-like panels spread out like a sunflower or a windmill about to turn. It may not look so very unusual, but Moloynia has done more to transform the average life of the typical Soviet citizen than most other spaceship programmes.

Moloynia was the USSR's first communication satellite, or comsat. Russia was a poor second into the comsat race after the United States, and its comsat technology always tended to lag about five years or so behind the United States. But then it has to be said that American comsat development was determined by urgent commercial imperatives absent in the USSR.

Ironically, it was General Eisenhower — the man who was not interested in space — who was the first to use a comsat. It was Christmas 1958 and the President had a tape-recorded message broadcast to the world from an orbiting Atlas Score booster. Come

1960 and NASA was experimenting with beaming signals off a huge orbiting balloon called Echo.

The real breakthrough came in July 1962 when American Telephone and Telegraph paid for NASA to put up a commercial communications satellite called Telstar. It was the first fare-paying satellite for any purpose. Within two weeks, AT&T had linked Telstar up with a set of ground receiving stations in Maine, Britain and France and set up the first live broadcast. In one blow, the cables that had linked the world for a century over land and under seabed were redundant.

People waited up all night for Telstar. Telstar came into position. The lines on the TV sets flickered, straightened out, and the image of a man could be made out sitting at a desk. Soon a live conversation developed between the American and another man in Britain. The old world and the new were linked forever in a new way.

It was not long before the enormous significance of Telstar sank in − helped along a little by a pop song called 'Telstar' which stayed at the top of the pop charts for months. In July 1964 NASA put up Syncom 3 into a 24 hour orbit − an orbit that in effect appeared to hover and stay over the same place all the time. Later that year 'Intelsat' was formed, a multinational user corporation. By 1980 it had 105 member states. That was to come. Intelsat quickly showed its worth. Its first satellite, 'Early Bird', began operations in May 1965. It demonstrated its potential by an 80-minute world-wide *tour de force* in a global hook-up, with scenes from Hong Kong, India, America, and everywhere else. The pictures were sharper than if they had been taken next door.

A Soviet comsat could not be long in coming, and it duly appeared on 23 April 1965 as Moloynia-1. Moloynia became the base of the Soviet comsat system. It used a system of orbits not used by any other type of satellite system − one explicable in terms of the geography of Siberia.

In designing a comsat system, the USSR could not easily use the 24 hour orbit. A stable 24 hour orbit can only be located on the equator, and a transmitter from equatorial orbit would simply not be strong enough to reach the far northern Arctic latitudes of Siberia for which comsat technology would be most useful. But a conventional orbiting satellite in a low orbit covering Siberia would present major tracking problems because it would be overhead for periods of only ten or fifteen minutes at a time.

Hence the compromise 12 hour orbit stretching up to the 24 hour altitude of 40 000 km, but with a perigee of 600 km. Apogee was nearly always over Siberia so that it crossed that part of the sky slowly over a period of eight hours. Three satellites were needed for an operational system. A series of 12 m receiver dishes called 'Orbita' were built throughout the USSR to pick up the Moloynia signals.

By 1987 no fewer than 70 Moloynia-1s had been launched − about three a year. Each weighed about 816 kg, was 3.4 m long, and provided telephone and TV links. In effect, Moloynia made it possible for the remote areas of the USSR like Siberia, the far north, the southern republics and the east towards the Bering Sea, to receive central television. For them, 'today' suddenly arrived.

An improved version, Moloynia-2, appeared in 1971. Heavier, at 1250 kg, it had greater capacity than Moloynia-1, and was used internationally with Orbita ground stations in the east European Socialist countries and with Ulan Bator in Mongolia and with Havana, Cuba. This development coincided with the establishment of a Soviet version of Intelsat, called, not very imaginatively, 'Intersputnik'. As well as the Socialist countries, it included the Soviet-leaning states of Vietnam, Laos, Afghanistan, Algeria, Syria and Yemen.

The Russians have given the name of Molniya to their communications satellites, an example of which is shown here. They are launched regularly into space at a rate of about two or three a year in highly elliptical orbits having their apogee points (greatest distance from the Earth) above the northern hemisphere, to increase the communication time available between various places on Soviet territory.

The Moloynia-2 series was phased out in 1981, to be replaced by Moloynia-3 which first appeared in 1974. 31 had been flown by 1987, all by A-2 out of Plesetsk. Moloynia-3 was able to use much smaller ground stations and, by the early 1970s, terminals were as small as dishes of 7 m. The whole system was air transportable and made outside broadcasts possible. At a general level, Moloynia-1 concentrated on domestic communications links, and Moloynia-3 on the international.

By this time, the trend was well established of using smaller and smaller ground dishes and progressively more and more powerful satellite transmitters. It soon became more economical to have one small dish to each home – or factory or industrial plant – than to have large ground dishes, which only then required further retransmission to the home.

DIRECT TO THE HOME

Despite the success of Syncom in 1964, and Early Bird the following year, and a whole series of Intelsat communications satellites after that, the USSR was very slow to develop 24 hour satellites. The first operational one did not appear until 1975 and two types emerged: standard TV and communications satellites (called Gorizont or Horizon, and Raduga or Rainbow); and direct broadcast (called Ekran or Screen). Another type, called Louch (meaning 'light'), was in the pipeline.

The first 24 hour satellite flew in 1974 and it was an experimental prototype. It was a once-off mission called Moloynia-1S and it went up on 30 July. The tests were evidently successful, for Raduga, Gorizont and Ekran followed not long after.

Keeping track of the new stable of 24 hour satellites became unnecessarily difficult because the Russians decided not to give numbered designations to these satellites, simply their station point over the equator as allocated by the International Telecommunications Union. These stations were called Stationar 1, 2, 3 and so on.

From 1975 to autumn 1987 there were 20 Raduga and 14 Gorizont launches, and, spaced out over the Atlantic, Pacific and Indian Oceans, they were able to provide world-wide TV coverage. Each satellite carried one TV channel and 10 000 telephone lines. The system was used extensively during 1980 to retransmit the Moscow Olympics that summer. They were seen by 2500 million people. The world was shrinking fast.

Raduga and Gorizont moved rapidly into new areas of technology. Raduga-1's channels were used from the beginning to transmit facsimiles of newspapers from Moscow to Irkutsk in the central USSR to Kharbarovsk on the Pacific coast. Thus was *Pravda* available in the Far East within minutes of leaving the printers' works in Moscow.

The quality of Gorizont was superb. In 1983, scientists from University College, Cork, Ireland, built a 1.2 m dish and displayed it throughout Ireland to demonstrate the feasibility of direct television transmissions. In Galway, the quality of picture of Central Channel Moscow was actually better than the country's own RTE, coming from only 200 km away.

Gorizont looked like an automaton out of science fiction. Arrays of shutters, engines, tanks and instruments sat atop a cylinder base. On top of the structure was a huge dish, pointing earthwards.

'Ekran', introduced in October 1976, was more advanced still. Unlike Gorizont and Raduga which carried cable, telephone, facsimile and TV, Ekran carried television only. But Ekran was one of the first national television systems designed to broadcast direct to the homes of isolated communities. The target area was 'footprint' covering Novosibirsk, Irkutsk, and northwest Mongolia. All the people needed on the ground was a small dish rooftop aerial.

By the time Ekran 16 flew in September 1987 the system was well established. Ekran continued the tradition of putting more and more power on the satellite and less and less receiving power on the ground. Ekran had a broadcasting power of 200 watts, compared to a mere 8 to 10 watts on the Raduga. The service as a whole covered 40 per cent of the USSR, or 9m km^2, with Ekran hovering over Sumatra, Indonesia, at 99°E longitude. This precision delivery to scattered communities was made possible by the unusual design of the Ekran: a cylinder pointing earthwards. On top were two solar panels stretching from a long beam. Underneath was a flat electrical board, and, spread out on it, 200 pencil-shaped antennas, pinging downwards.

By 1988 the USSR had done much to close the gap created by Telstar and Early Bird and Intelsat, by its use of the direct-broadcast Ekran, the 24 hour general communications Gorizont and Raduga, and the ageing but functional Moloynias. Whether the 24 hour satellites will be able to provide an adequate service to the Soviet Far East is not known, but if they do, the Moloynias could well be phased out then. Nor was it clear if it would be possible to develop the rapidly expanding technology of informatics and computer communication, then developing at a furious rate in the United States and Europe.

WATCHING THE EARTH

Just as scientists were quick to grasp the opportunities presented by communications satellites, so too did they realize the opportunities presented for weather forecasting. At its crudest, all that was required was a television camera and a means of transmitting its image directly to the ground. Once this was done, it was then up to meteorologists to interpret the images and make sense of the swirling patterns of clouds, fronts and cyclones.

As with the communications satellites, the Americans were first in the field and have maintained a lead ever since, except that in this case the lead was much wider. America's first meteorological satellite, Tiros, which was short for Television and InfraRed Observation Satellite, flew in April 1960 and at once transmitted very useable weather pictures. Within several years the United States had developed a system of Automatic Picture Transmission, APT, using store-dump techniques.

From 1966 the Americans started to use weather satellites from 24 hour orbit, from which position the entire Earth could be scanned at a glance and continuous observation provided. This became operational in 1974 with the Synchronous Meteorological Satellite, SMS-1.

Whether because of the Moon effort or for other reasons we do not know, a Soviet meteorological system from space was slow to develop. A number of experiments were made first — with Cosmos 44, 58, 100, 118, 122 and 144 over 1964–66. Cosmos 122 was the key model and featured a cylindrical body with TV cameras and two solar panels. It was important for another reason: the launch was watched by General Charles de Gaulle, President of France, the first Western head of state to witness a Soviet blast-off. At the time, France was anxious to assert its political independence from the United States and NATO, and the Russians were only too happy to encourage them.

The first operational launch was on 26 March 1969 and it was called Meteor-1. It went up from Plesetsk and it adopted an orbit — which all Meteors followed — of 644 by 713 km, 81 degrees, 100 minutes, though some later Meteors flew up to 900 km.

A second-generation series began in 1975, called Meteor-2, but both series continued in tandem as Moloynia did. By 1987 there had been over thirty Meteor-1s and 16 Meteor-2s. The first Meteor 3 was launched on 24 October 1985.

Meteor was a cylinder. Cameras eyes peered out the bottom, along with antennae and beetle-like sensing devices. Two large solar wings extended from each side. The system hardly changed in appearance from 1969. Its length was about 5 m and Meteor used either the A-2 or the F-2 rocket. It transmitted to 50 ground stations in the USSR, using Automatic Picture Transmission — which means that foreign stations can and do use its data. Information on water moisture in the atmosphere and temperature is transmitted daily down to Moscow and Leningrad. And the Hydrological Service, with its centres in Moscow, Novosibirsk and Kharbarovsk, needs its pictures so as to predict rainfall and snow run-off. Further information is passed on to planes, ships and agricultural institutes.

The USSR claims that the ongoing use of the Meteor data — three are normally operational at any one time — has saved the economy millions of roubles. Advance weather warning has, it is said, saved hundreds of lives. There is no reason to dispute this. It is an example of space applications at their most useful, even if it lacks the glamour of other enterprises.

The series of Russian meteorological satellites began with Cosmos 122, whose launch was watched by Charles de Gaulle. The first launch in the Meteor series of satellites (an example of which is shown here) took place in 1969, and later, more sophisticated versions of these satellites have been launched at regular intervals ever since.

Starting in 1974, Meteor satellites began to take on an Earth resources monitoring role. Cameras were fitted with multi-spectral cameras, enabling photographs of the ground to be taken in infrared and other colours. Such missions received the sub-designation of Meteor-Priroda (Nature) [12].

A more advanced Meteor-Priroda appeared in 1980 with a 10-band scanner with a resolution of 30 m. Using the many colours, different categories of objects appeared in the different scans. Thus it was possible to detect healthy crops from diseased crops, identify oil and gas deposits, follow the progress of sowing and harvesting, identify soils and so on.

Despite the fact that America experimented with a 24 hour weather satellite as far back as 1966, a Soviet version was remarkably slow to appear. In 1975 the USSR announced that it would participate in the 1978–79 Global Weather Watch programme. Its contribution would be a 24 hour weather satellite called GOMS. Eventually in 1980, no GOMS having emerged, the USSR announced that the project had been deferred: it still had not appeared by 1988. While it is not a critical area in space development — and much less important than comsats — Soviet delay here clearly indicated either technical problems, financial shortages, or both.

GOMS was not the only programme deferred. In 1977 the USSR announced a plan to fly seven 'Volna' satellites for maritime and aeronautical communications. They would fly in 1980 and provide rapid links for ship-to-shore and plane-to-shore, using small dish antennae on ships and rabbit-ear antennae, less than 70 cm across, on planes. Another project called 'Gals' was announced at the same time: it was to fly in 1979 and involved four military geostationary comsats. Yet by 1988, neither programme had surfaced. No explanation was forthcoming. NASA's twin plagues of changing priorities and budget cuts seemed to be afflicting its competitor at least as much.

SPACE SCIENCE

Because of the heavy military emphasis of the Cosmos programme, and the slow development of the USSR of space applications, it would be natural to assume that space science was given a very low priority in the overall programme. This was not in fact the case, for since 1962 there has been a continuing scientific programme of observations. Most took place under the Cosmos programme, but some were specific programmes in their own right, like Elektron, Proton, Prognoz, Intercosmos, Astron, and so on. Most were concentrated on the environment of space and the never-ending particles and radiation that stream through it; some have probed deeper still. To list some of the Cosmos probes would give an idea of the range of studies carried out:

Cosmos 1	March 1962	The ionosphere
Cosmos 3	April 1962	Solar and cosmic radiation
Cosmos 8	August 1962	Micrometeoroids
Cosmos 26	March 1964	Geomagnetic field
Cosmos 51	December 1964	Ultraviolet and gamma radiation
Cosmos 97	November 1965	Theory of relativity
Cosmos 215	April 1968	Radiation of hot stars, using eight mirror telescopes and one X-ray telescope
Cosmos 230	July 1968	Solar observatory
Cosmos 243	September 1968	Antarctic icefield mapping
Cosmos 262	December 1968	Ultraviolet stellar radiation
Cosmos 426	June 1971	High energy electrons
Cosmos 470	January 1972	Micrometeorites
Cosmos 481	March 1972	Geomagnetic field
Cosmos 650	April 1974	Solar protons
Cosmos 669	July 1974	Liquid helium radiometer
Cosmos 721	March 1975	Aurora borealis
Cosmos 731	May 1975	Astronomical gamma-ray telescope
Cosmos 906	April 1977	Charged particles
Cosmos 936	August 1977	International biology satellite — landed in Siberia after 19 days
Cosmos 1076	February 1979	Two telescopes to study ocean temperatures
Cosmos 1129	September 1979	Soviet–American biology satellite with 38 rats and 60 quail eggs

Cosmos 1383	June 1982	Rescue for ships in distress
Cosmos 1410	September 1982	Geodesy and mapping
Cosmos 1514	December 1983	Two rhesus monkeys

In addition to this, scientific equipment regularly hitched a lift on board Moloynia and Meteor satellites. By the early 1980s there was a tendency for fewer and fewer Cosmos missions to be used for scientific purposes: such work was diverted into specialist programmes with their own designations, or put aboard other satellites, or put aboard the manned Salyut station. A 1977 Raduga carried a proton detector.

This list is only a sample of announced missions. The USSR generally does not announce the missions of Cosmos satellites — for obvious reasons in the case of military missions; and for fear of embarrassment if on civilian missions results are not forthcoming. As it is, the results are often published long after missions have taken place. Thus, the scientific nature of Cosmos 426 (1971) was not known until the results were published in a journal in 1976.

Throughout this period — and for the forseeable future — the potential of Earth-orbiting satellites remained and remains enormous. Pointing towards Earth, satellites can map the oceans, identify the Earth's resources, find fish, predict crop yields, watch forest fires. Indeed, in 1983 the USSR announced that it would soon launch a new series of Earth resources satellites and agricultural satellites, each with its own designation.

Pointing towards the Sun, satellites can observe its explosive processes which give us heat and light, and explain the mysteries of sunspots and solar flares. Looking further afield, satellites and telescopes aboard them can map the galaxy, find comets, and pick up the mysterious signals from quasars, pulsars and black holes.

Finally, by simply being in space, satellite instruments can measure and analyse the peculiar environment of near-Earth space: a near-vacuum, subjected to streams of particles, rays, electrons, protons, quarks, and all the strange processes of atomic physics. Each day a veritable parade of Cosmos and other satellites chatter back to Earth a stream of electronic blips and bleeps that try to explain the nature of our little-understood environment.

MONKEY BUSINESS

Only occasionally would a Cosmos flight attract much public attention. Cosmos 1887 was one that did: carrying two monkeys, it was a 30-experiment Soviet—American biological satellite with a veritable zoo of insects, rats and fish aboard. It was put aloft on 29 September 1987.

All started well with the two monkeys, Yerosha ('little troublemaker') and Dryoma ('the slow one') Dryoma of course behaved himself, but Yerosha tore off his electrodes, freed his arm, and began pressing buttons at will. The press was thrilled: 'Monkey to ground control: I've taken over!' was a typical headline.

Doctors, biologists and engineers let the mission run its full course of 13 days, taking the view that Yerosha's explorations of the cabin could do no serious harm. But Cosmos 1887 was not out of danger: the return went awry and the cabin came down 3000 km from target, in Mirny, Yakutia, deep in Siberia, in temperatures of −13°C. Rescuers put a tent around the cabin to keep the zoo's crew warm before specialists could arrive to dismantle the craft.

Yerosha and Dryoma were retired to Sykhumi monkey nursery in Georgia. Subsequent investigations blamed the mutiny on a faulty feeder and Yerosha was cleared of allegations that he was not the right stuff for space travel.

FROM ELEKTRON TO ASTRON

One of the consequences of particular Cosmos missions was that they inspired particular types of programmes that might be entitled to their own designation in their own right. Hence the early weather experiments that led to Meteor and so on. An earlier example was 'Elektron', which originated in the early Cosmos radiation studies.

Elektron was a short series – there were only two launches – but they were important nonetheless. They employed the idea of the double study: two satellites were launched simultaneously into widely differing orbits. Overlapping at times they relayed back real-time information as they passed through the radiation belts.

Elektron 1–2 went up on 30 January 1964, and Elektron 3–4 on 11 July 1964. Between them they investigated and mapped the doughnut-shaped radiation belts surrounding Earth. They used irregular orbits:

Elektron 1   394 by 7 126 km
Elektron 2   441 by 67 998 km

Between them – the first in the series being a cylinder with paddle wings, and second a cylinder glistening with solar cells – they returned a deluge of data on the radiation belts, and made it safer for cosmonauts to follow in their tracks. As a bonus, they found the presence of hydrogen and helium high in the atmosphere.

The gangly Proton series was also short, and terminated after four launches over 1965–68. Proton was kettle-shaped with four paddle wings. The first weighed 12.2 tonnes and the last 17 tonnes. Proton originated in the tests of the D booster and would probably not have existed but for these tests which were designed to prepare the way for cosmonauts circling the Moon.

Nevertheless, Proton was no empty shell. Proton 1 (July 1965) and 2 (November 1965) studied cosmic ray and gamma radiation. Proton 3 (July 1966) attempted to locate the smallest cosmic particles known to exist – the quark. And Proton 4 (November 1968) researched high energy cosmic rays.

A new series, 'Prognoz', meaning forecast, took up where Proton left off. Prognoz was much smaller at 860 kg, and used the A-2e from Baikonour. It had a square base, a dome-shaped top from which an array of instruments emerged, and four stretched-out solar sails.

Prognoz – the first flew in 1972 – took a highly eccentric orbit of 560 by 200 000 km, 65 degrees. A second launch took place in the same year, and there was one each in 1973, 1975, 1976, 1977, 1978, 1980 and 1983. Its four-day slow curving orbit, taking it out in an ellipse nearly to the distance of the Moon, gave it a good vantage point for studying conditions on the Sun. Prognoz's main task was to monitor solar radiation, solar flares, and dangerous emissions that might disrupt Earth's weather and cause radio interference. A second but unstated objective might have been early warning for manned Salyut flights and there does seem to be some relationship between a Prognoz launch and an upcoming manned mission to Salyut. Prognoz would be in a position to give advance warning of a solar flare, so that cosmonauts could be called down if need be.

In addition to its main target, the Sun, Prognoz carried instruments for observing gamma and X-ray radiation. Prognoz 2 carried French instruments to study neutrons. After near-annual launches in the 1970s, the rate slowed to one every three years until in 1983 Prognoz 9 went into an extreme orbit of 380 by 720 000 km. Prognoz 10 flew in 1985.

One spacecraft which appeared in a similar orbit to Prognoz, eleven years after that series started, and with a different purpose altogether, was what was ambitiously described as the 'world's first orbiting astronomical space station'. Called 'Astron-1', it went up on 23 March 1983, on a D-le into a highly eccentric orbit of 2 000 by 200 000 km, 51.5 degrees, 98 hours. It was modelled on the Venera 15 and 16 probes which were then on their way to carry out radar observations of Venus.

Astron carried two powerful telescopes — one ultraviolet and the other infrared. The former was 80 cm diameter and built in Armenia, and the other was built in France. The Astron weighed 3.5 tonnes and the ultraviolet telescope was 3.5 m long.

Astron-1 was an ambitious attempt to look deep into the universe: pulsars, quasars, and the constellation of Taurus and the Crab were listed as specific objectives, notably their temperatures and chemical composition. By midsummer 1983, Tass could report that it had obtained the spectograms of distant galaxies. The quality of its images was not then made public and would probably be well short of that from America's giant telescope in space, the 11 tonne Hubble Space Telescope planned for Shuttle launch in 1989.

The USSR's only other national space programmes were fairly minor — 'Radio' and 'Iskra' (the latter word means 'spark'). Iskra-2, a modest 28 kg, achieved space history when on 25 May 1982 it became the first spacecraft to be launched from a space station, the Salyut 7. The two cosmonauts on board at the time simply pushed it through the airlock hatch. It was built by the students of the Moscow Aviation Institute, and was a radio amateurs' target for use by amateur radio societies in the USSR, Cuba and Laos. Iskra-3 was also pushed out of Salyut 7, in November 1982. It had been brought up there by the space freighter, Progress 16.

Iskra-2 followed a tradition of amateur radio satellites. Radio 3—8 were part of a six-in-one shot in December 1981 and followed from Radio 1 and 2, which hitched a lift with Cosmos 1045 on 27 October 1978. To judge how well equipment would work in the vacuum, one was hermetically sealed, and the other was not. They provided a relay station for the USSR's 26 000 amateur radio users.

COURTING IN COMECON

If in the early days of space travel the Americans were quick to share their findings and technology with the Western nations and the USSR was slow, this changed after 1966. Senior space planner and designer Boris Petrov persuaded the Soviet Government that an international council of Socialist and other nations should be established to share space technology and experience and a system would be devised so that the USSR itself would benefit from its allies' specialized institutes.

By the mid-1970s this concept had reached maturity with regular — normally annual — launchings of Intercosmos satellites. As well as the Socialist countries, France and Sweden were regular contributors, with the Americans joining in on biosatellite tests.

France was the most regular contributor to Intercosmos and bilateral space contacts. In January 1972 the USSR put up a French satellite, Aureole, purpose-built to study the strange phenomenon of the polar lights and the way in which electrical fields could light up the northern summer skies. Aureole 2 followed in December 1974 and Aureole 3, a 1000 kg powerful atmospheric probe, in 1981 [13].

Two other French satellites were flown around the same time. Signe 3, a 102 kg satellite for X-rays and gamma rays, left Kapustin Yar in June 1977. Arcad-3 (September 1981) was much heavier at 1100 kg, and spent six months studying the magnetosphere at high latitudes.

Intercosmos 11 to 19, which flew in the period 1973—79, studied such diverse areas as radiation, geomagnetic fields, the ionosphere and charged particles. From Intercosmos 15 on, a standard base spacecraft for station-keeping in orbit, orientation, power and transmission, called a 'bus', was introduced. It could thus be mass produced, and different instruments added on top as specialized equipment. This simplified design.

Not that the contributing countries ever saw much of the mission: their equipment was manufactured, say, in Prague, transshipped to the USSR, and that was the last they saw of it until it flew into orbit months later.

Intercosmos 20 (1 November 1979) used the F-1 for the first time. The satellite itself Czechoslovakia, it was a mere 15 kg. It drifted away from its parent, to see how much atmospheric drag affected a satellite orbit.

Intercosmos 20 (1 November 1979— used the F-1 for the first time. The satellite itself belonged to a new long-life design, and it was the first Earth applications satellite in the series. Similar to Cosmos 1076 and 1151, it carried equipment designed to measure the exact temperature of the sea to within $1°C$, important for fishing, forecasting and ice warnings. Intercosmos 21, two years later, was similar.

There was also a one-off Soviet—Bulgarian flight in August 1981. Called 'Intercosmos-Bulgaria 1300' it used a Meteor design and carried 12 experiments built by the Bulgarian School of Space Research to investigate the Earth's magnetic field.

Intercosmos had by the mid-1980s come a long way from its inception in 1966, and from 1978 onwards had included cosmonauts selected by member countries and flown on the orbital stations Salyut 6 and 7. There was no common fund in the programme: each country prepared its own experiments, the USSR supplied the 'bus' and carrier rocket. In 1975, Earth resources was added to the Intercosmos brief, alongside space physics, meteorology, communication, biology and medicine. And Intercosmos was not limited to Earth orbit only: at the June 1980 meeting of the Space Physics Committee of the Intercosmos Council, member countries were invited to prepare experiments for use on the planet Mars.

By the mid-1980s too, the comsat version of Intercosmos, called Intersputnik, was beginning to rival Intelsat in terms of resources, though not size. In addition to the Intercosmos countries, Yemen had joined, and Nicaragua, and Mozambique and

Afghanistan were contemplating doing so. An Intersputnik ground station was under construction in Algeria.

With the introduction of the Louch system in the late 1980s, the Intersputnik system would be able to offer communications links on the world market at rates comparable to Intelsat. Such a plan had obvious advantages in terms of hard currency and as an export earner. So too did the offer of the Proton booster in June 1983 to Western satellite manufacturers at rates competitive to the Shuttle and the European Ariane.

So although the political world was still divided into the two great superpowers, the space technology world between the two was fluid. Europe had its own booster rocket and space programme, with a Western and commercial orientation. But several countries, like France and India, cheerfully made use of both superpowers to fly their hardware. In addition, Japan, China and India ran their own national space programmes with their own launchers.

KEEPING THE SHOW ON THE ROAD

The organization of the Soviet space programme required a massive managerial effort. A study of how the Soviet space programme is run suggests that it is organizationally more complex than its American equivalent.

Under the American system, NASA is responsible for all new space developments and programmes. The Administrator of NASA is appointed by the President and reports to him. NASA presents its budget to both the President and Congress, and Congress normally argues over the details, adding some programmes and striking some out. NASA is subdivided into sections, like for example, Manned Space Flight. It is NASA's job to coordinate all the different space research institutes, like for example, the Jet Propulsion Laboratory in California, which has special expertise in planetary exploration.

The Soviet system appears to be more complex and in some ways more decentralized. The State Commission for Space Flight is responsible jointly to the Communist Party Central Committee and to the Council of Ministers, but does not appear to have the same status as NASA. Its role appears to be supervisory rather than directive. Few members of the SCSF have ever been identified, though during the late 1950s Korolov had to report to it. The name of the chairman of the Commission, Kerim Kerimov, was finally revealed in 1987 [14]. Yet we know that the Korolov–Khrushchev relationship was a very direct one that does not seem to have been unduly complicated by intermediate bodies. The State Commission's main role appears to be in the area of cosmonaut selection approval and safety. No spaceship can fly unless it is given a clean bill of health by the Commission.

Underneath the Commission are four principal organizations: Technical and Training; Launch Control; Flight Control; and the Academy of Sciences.

Technical and Training is responsible for spacecraft construction and assembly, or the hardware. Its headquarters is 'Star Town', the suburb of Moscow where the cosmonauts and designers live and which is full of training equipment and design offices.

Star Town is worthy of mention in its own right. It is off-limits to non-Russians, so not a lot is known about it. Star Town goes back to 1964 or thereabouts, when it was decided that it was unreasonable for all the growing cosmonaut team to be located in Baikonour/Leninsk. Many of the newer cosmonauts were themselves designers and if they were to play a meaningful part in space design it made sense that they should stay in Moscow where the senior design institutes were located. Hence Star Town, a leafy complex of new estates. Full of apartments, offices and training centres, it became what Houston was to NASA. In 1976 a huge water tank was set up. A prototype Salyut space station was submerged in it so cosmonauts could practise spacewalking like deep sea divers. It all meant of course that most cosmonauts only went to Baikonour to take part in or watch spaceflights. Still, they probably did not mind, for the Moscow climate is gentler than Baikonour's.

The launch control organizations are responsible for the three cosmodromes of Baikonour, Kapustin Yar and Plesetsk. Flight Control operates from the flight control centre in Kalinin and supervises the nationwide tracking net and up to five ships at sea. It is also responsible for recovery and has a fleet of Mil helicopters on call.

Lacking a worldwide ground tracking net, unlike the United States which was able to set up tracking dishes in allied countries like Australia, the USSR was compelled to put its global tracking network aboard ship. As part of the Moon effort, large tracking ships were constructed. The first, the *Cosmonaut Vladimir Komarov* appeared in the English Channel late in 1967. Four more followed.

A unique view of the Soviet flight control centre on 7 April 1986 during the Soyuz T15 mission to the Mir space station. Cosmonauts Leonid Kizim and Vladimir Solovyev can be seen top right with a simulation of the Mir/Soyuz complex below. The current orbital path of the complex relative to the Earth's surface is being watched closely by the seated mission controllers as they study orbital and spacecraft data presented on their screens.

They are large streamlined white ships and with their giant aerials and huge telescope-like domes they look futuristic too. There are several such ships and they commemorate fallen cosmonauts and designers — hence the *Cosmonaut Yuri Gagarin*, the *Academician Sergei Korolov* and, later, the *Cosmonaut Georgi Dobrovolski*. Whenever these big ships sail from their home ports in the Black Sea or the Baltic, it is a sure sign of a major manned mission coming up. Once the fleet is under way, the ships can then be found taking up position in three or four standard locations, which include the North Pacific, the Caribbean, and off Guinea, West Africa.

The real powerhouse in the Soviet space programme may in fact be the Academy of Sciences. It has three space-related sections — the Orbit Calculation Institute, the Design and Flight section, and the Commission for the Exploration and Utilization of Outer Space — the descendent of Keldysh's old Commission on Interplanetary Communication of 1955.

The Commission for the Exploration and Utilization of Space is probably the policy-making unit. It is not under direct Governmental control, for the Academy is a self-perpetuating body of learned men and women of science that predates the Revolution of 1917. It is thought to have about a hundred members and about three hundred corresponding members. To belong is the greatest honour a Soviet scientist can receive.

Proposals for space missions probably originate there and then embark on a process of modification by the Government, the finance departments and the military. Once approved, their execution is supervized by the State Commission for Space Flight, which contracts out the work to design institutes throughout the USSR. These are spread out all over the country. Despite the image of being a highly centralized system — in most ways it is — there are many design institutes competing for the same work. Thus, when a programme is announced, different institutes will bid for it. The one considered the most suitable will be assigned the work.

After 1969, when the pressure of the man-on-the-Moon first programme was lifted, the Commission for the Exploration and Utilization of Space probably became more and more independent. Prestige projects and missions virtually left the space calendar and a shift to space applications became more evident.

Simply because the debate on space spending which is so very open in the United States is not visible in the USSR does not mean that it does not happen. It does, albeit normally behind closed doors. Arguments about the balance of civilian and military flights, about how much to devote to applications and how much to planetary research are just as rampant in the USSR. The abandonment of Mars flights in 1974 (they were not to resume until 1988) and Moon probes in 1976, and the failure to fly deep space probes to Jupiter and Saturn like the American Pioneer and Voyager does not signify that no one in the USSR wanted such missions. Rather it signifies that the scientists who put forward such missions lost the battle for funds, and that other projects where chosen instead.

Just as a host of American programmes were cancelled in the 1970s by budget cuts, so too were Soviet plans, long after missions had been approved and hardware built. These cancellations were different from missions that had been cut out in the 1960s so as to speed up the Moon race. The programmes sacrificed in the 1970s were those that lost out in the decisions as to how to spend scarcer resources. During 1977 and 1978 for instance, the USSR talked repeatedly about a lunar soil recovery mission from the far side and launch dates were even hinted. But in 1980 the talk stopped and the mission never flew. Other, less prestigious missions, with weather satellites like GOMS, and some astronomy missions, were either delayed for long periods or disappeared from the agenda altogether.

ORGANIZATION

Significant organization changes took place after the death of Korolov in 1966 [15]. A number of new design institutes came to the fore, as did designers hitherto eclipsed by the preeminence of Korolov. Vasili Mishin held the title of chief designer from 1966 to 1974. Korolov's rival, Vladimir Chalomei, took on the leading role in the design of manned spacecraft. Mikhail Yangel emerged as a key influence, and his deputy, Vladimir Utkin, was put in charge of shuttle designs in the 1970s.

In 1974, Vladimir Chalomei became the undisputed senior designer. He had been appointed by Stalin as far back as 1944 to investigate and report on the German V-2. Since then, Chalomei had become General Designer of the Aero-Industry (1959) and his bureau had designed the Proton booster, Polyot 1 and 2, and the satellite hunter-killers. In 1969 he was put in charge of the Salyut space station project, and he later became head of the Bauman Institute. His deputies were Konstantin Bushuyev (Director of the Apollo–Soyuz test project) and Yuri Semeonov. Chalomei died in December 1984, and his position as designer of manned spacecraft was passed on to Yuri Semeonov. Cosmonaut Alexei Yeliseyev became director of the Bauman Institute. Semeonov and Viktor Legostayev were thought to be designers of the Mir space station (1986–) [16].

The Soviet space programme was run by the innocuous-sounding Department of Medium Machine-building, a department which had government status and responsibility for both the nuclear and space programmes. In 1986, this fiction was done away with by the reforming General Secretary Mikhail Gorbachev, who established a national space organization in its own right, called Glavcosmos, under Alexander Dunayev.

In the mid-1960s the different design bureaux were decentralized, both organizationally and geographically. The unmanned lunar programme was first to be hived off, in 1965. Georgi Babakin was chief designer there from 1965 to 1971, to be succeeded by Kryukov (1971–78) and since then Vyacheslav Kovturenko. The Electromechanics Scientific Research Institute was charged with the design and production of Meteor and Gorizont satellites, under the leadership of Josefyan and, later, Chekanokevsky.

Navigation satellites, geodetic satellites and the Ekran and Raduga series were built by the Rechetnev bureau in Kharbarovsk; the Kosberg bureau in Voronezh took charge of the Proton upper stage; and the Kozlov bureau in Kharkhov organized military and Earth resources missions.

By the late 1980s, two spokespersons came to the fore. One was Konstantin Feoktistov, cosmonaut from 1964, who was 61 years old in 1987. He was quoted as the expert on manned flight developments, and clearly filled a leading design role. The other was Roald Sagdeev, 62, Director of the Institute for Space Research in Moscow. The Moscow institute came to be seen more and more as the originator of new space missions to the planets, and from 1983 on, Sagdeev gave interviews to a growing number of Western journalists about Soviet space intentions. Informal, suede-jacketed and forthcoming, he showed how a less aged generation was coming to the fore.

Perhaps one day the full history of these remarkable people and their colleagues will be written and they can emerge from the shadows and take their rightful place in the light of day, and be exposed to the credit they deserve. Their achievements surely merit it.

SOVIET SPACE SCIENCE: LOOKING AHEAD

The heavy investment in manned spaceflight and space stations in the late 1970s to mid-1980s meant the neglect of unmanned scientific missions. The Intercosmos missions became, to a large degree, the main Soviet scientific programme, and most of its equipment was provided outside the USSR.

By the mid-1980s there were signs that the USSR was anxious to bridge this gap and in 1983 it announced an across-the-board series of scientific missions to catch up for lost time and investigate a series of space-related disciplines. The programme included two biological satellites, each carrying a rhesus monkey, the first time the USSR had decided to use America's favourite space test animal. The first flew in December 1983; the second in 1987 (Cosmos 1887).

More significant still were the programmes 'Astron' (also began in 1983), 'Relict', 'Gamma', 'SAGA' and 'Interball'. Some of the names may sound the creation of Ian Fleming of James Bond fame, but they give away some of their purpose. Relict is to orbit to 700 000 km and map the entire sky in the 8 mm waveband. Gamma, which has a 1988 launch date, is a 1500 kg vehicle based on the Progress cargo freighter. It is to detect gamma rays and has ten times the sensitivity of anything the West has produced to date.

Gamma's replacement is SAGA, which stands for 'Satellite d'astronomie Gamma' and is due to fly in 1989. As its name suggests, it is a Soviet–French project, to carry a 700 kg telescope called 'Taiga'. Interball, due in 1992, involves two Prognoz satellites at 200 000 km and two sub-satellites of 50 kg in Polar orbits to study the ionosphere.

The French involvement in these projects is no accident. Of all the Western nations, France has the best standing in terms of cryogenics and detection equipment. Cryogenics – the science of keeping things cool – is essential to keeping telescope and related equipment at extremely low temperatures so that they can pick up the slightly warmer rays of stellar radiation. And France was, at a political level, less vulnerable to American-inspired embargoes of advanced know-how going to the USSR.

Other experiments in the pipeline include Aelita, a submillimetre space telescope, for 1994, and a radio telescope to be flown out to the far side of the Moon in the period 1995–96. All in all, the scientific programme for 1987–97 represents a series of difficult and challenging missions, requiring high technical standards.

8

Resurrection (1969–77)

LINKUP OVER THE SNOW

New Year's Day 1969 found the Soviet space programme in disarray. Shattered and dispirited by the superb performance of Apollo 8 which splashed down in the Pacific on 27 December, cosmonauts knew that the new year would probably see their rivals walk the dusty surface of the Moon. It must have galled them. But they knew that, whoever else had fouled up, it was not for lack of will on their part. The cosmonauts would have cheerfully undertaken any mission given them.

Not that 1969 was to be a barren year. Two Venus probes got away from Baikonour on the 5th and 10th January. Lined up next was a double manned linkup. A rendezvous of Soyuz 4 and 5 was a natural progression from that of Soyuz 2 and 3 the previous October, and indeed the roots of the mission went back to the ill-fated Komarov flight of 1967. This time, both ships would be manned and the crews would transfer.

It was a mission absolutely essential for the manned moon landing and that was why it was in the programme. However, since that objective had now been displaced by the space station programme, the mission would not be hailed in terms of an essential step towards an orbital station. No one was to know that the space station objective was only two weeks old, and was dated to the Government decision of 1 January 1969. No one had a clue at this stage as to what the station would look like, or even how it would be set up, or what methods would be used — which made the ostensible aim of the Soyuz 4/5 mission thoroughly fraudulent. Still, it was a convincing explanation for what Soyuz 4 and 5 did; and it took everyone else in at the time — except for the chiefs of NASA and one of the populist British dailies, the *Express* [1]. Appearance triumphed over reality again.

The new year was only two weeks old when Soyuz 4 stood ready on its pad. It was a perishing cold night on the 13th and, had this space station flight been part of an orderly progress towards such a new venture, it is doubtful whether the Russians would have run such a mission in the coldest part of midwinter. The temperature was −22°C. Pressmen were invited to inspect the 45-m high rocket; the night was clear and starry and the snow crunched crisply under their boots. Warm air had to be pumped ceaselessly to the pad just to keep the machinery from freezing solid.

Clad only in blue overalls, Vladimir Shatalov arrived at the pad at 8.30 a.m. the following morning, the 14th. He wasted little time talking to people on the ground and straightaway took the elevator up to the warm cabin awaiting him. It swayed gently in the breeze as the count continued.

At 10.38 a.m. the gantries fell away and amidst sheets of steam and vapour, Soyuz 4 climbed skywards. A bright diamond of flame was all that could be made of it as it bent over in its climb. Georgi Beregovoi was the ground controller and his comforting voice could be heard reassuring Shatalov throughout the ascent.

This time Tass, the Soviet News Agency, showed some signs of learning from the Apollo 8 experience. Within an hour it had released a full set of video pictures of the launching and showed Shatalov reporting back from orbit.

Once on his own the lone cosmonaut settled down quickly into the routine of flight. The solar wings were sprung free; he manoeuvred his spaceship from one orbit to another,

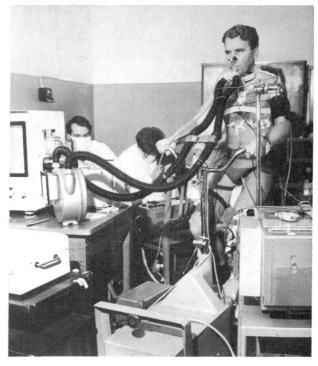

Cosmonaut Vladimir Alexandrovich Shatalov, commander of Soyuz 4, 8 and 10, is shown here during his extensive training programme in readiness for space flight.

took pictures of the Earth from the cabin, and squeezed blackberry juice out of his toothpaste tube-like containers for his dinner.

Mid-morning on the 15th, Vladimir Shatalov turned his Soyuz 4 towards the launch site to try to spot Soyuz 5 rising to reach him. At 10.14 a.m. exactly it blasted aloft with its full complement of three men aboard: Boris Volynov, commander from the 1960 group, Yevgeni Khrunov, research engineer from the same group, and 1966 engineer Alexei Yeliseyev. They quickly opened up the tunnel into the orbital module and began experiments. It was the first time three Russians had flown together since Voskhod 1 back in 1964.

Boris Volynov's first duty was to establish radio control with Soyuz 4, which he did by using ultrashort wave channels. But at this stage the mission took on a new aspect, and perhaps its main technical innovation. Instead of going for first orbit docking, as the Moon plan required, the rendezvous was spread out over a full day – as it would be on a space station run, with the Soyuz chasing the larger target of a space station. So Soyuz 5 went ahead of Soyuz 4 and orbited at 88.92 minutes, with Soyuz 4 in pursuit at 88.85 minutes.

So by 10.37 the following morning, they were only 100 m apart. Tension rose:

Shatalov: Baikal clearly on the periscope. Speed 0.25. Distance 30 m, all normal.
Ground: All right.
Shatalov: Distance 20 m, Speed 0.25.
Ground: See you well.
Shatalov: Distance 10, Speed 0.25.
Ground: Perfect.
Volynov: Just waiting for contact.
Shatalov: Final approach. Normal, Contact! Linkup. Full docking. . . no relative movement of the space craft. [2]

Approaching each other, like seagulls with wings outstretched as they escort a ship at sea, 4 had inserted its pointed probe into 5's drogue. Latches clawed at the probe, grabbed it tight, and sealed the system. Electrical connectors rammed together, joining up an internal system for manoeuvring, power and telephone.

Moment of contact was 11.30 a.m. over Soviet territory. Ground controllers listened with anxiety as the two ships high above came together and met. Soyuz 4 was on its 34th circuit, and 5 on its 18th. The complex of the two ships was orbiting at 209 by 250 km, 51.40 degrees, 88.85 minutes.

The docking – smooth and flawless though it was – was only part of a more ambitious experiment. No sooner had the cosmonauts settled down after their triumph than Khrunov and Yeliseyev struggled into their spacesuits. It was a slow process that could not be rushed. There was layer upon layer to be put on: inner garments, outer garments, heating systems, coolant, helmets, visors. Finally an autonomous backpack. Valves were checked through, seals examined. It was not that they had not practised it enough, but it had to be right this time of all times.

Khrunov pulled a lever and the air poured out of the orbital compartment. Vladimir Shatalov had already done the same in his orbital compartment from the safe refuge of his command cabin. The pressure gauge fell rapidly and evened off to zero. Khrunov described what happened next:

> The hatch opened and a stream of sunlight burst in. The Sun was unbearably bright and scorching. Only the thick filtering vizor saved my eyes. I saw the Earth and the black sky and had the same feeling I had experienced before my first parachute jumps. [3]

The spectacle of the two docked craft was breathtaking, he recalled. He emerged; Yeliseyev following gingerly behind, moving one hand over another on the handrails. They filmed each other, inspected the craft for damage, and watched the Earth roll past below. Within half an hour they were inside Soyuz 4. They closed the hatch and repressurized. They had done it. The hatch into the Soyuz 4 command cabin opened, turned like a ship's handle like on a bulkhead. Vladimir Shatalov floated through and it was hugs and kisses all round. The only thing that went wrong concerned a bottle to toast their success. It burst and the contents went all over the wall of the cabin.

Khrunov and Yeliseyev also became the first space postmen. They brought Vladimir Shatalov some letters and copies of *Pravda* for the 15th – so he could read about his own launching.

After 4 h 35 min, the ships uncoupled and went their separate ways, drifting apart into separate orbits. Boris Volynov, alone now in Soyuz 5, fired his craft out of 4's way and at 6.40 p.m. in a state of exhaustion, radioed goodnight to 4 and anyone else who was listening and fell into a sound sleep.

The linkup was a neat exercise, the EVA difficult and potentially dangerous. Factories ground to a halt throughout the Soviet Union as one telecast from orbit followed another. Tass announced formally the 'establishment of the world's first experimental orbital station' Considering it ran for only two orbits, and there was no interconnecting tunnel, this was an overstatement. But it is easy to understand the Soviet exuberance. There were several firsts; they were all new cosmonauts; and they had done it all in the middle of winter. If this was what orbital stations were all about, this was a flying start. Academician Anatoli Blagonravov:

> The time is not far off when a permanent space laboratory will be circling the Earth. Scientists will go there for a tour of duty, working in comfortable surroundings and returning to Earth when necessary. [4]

And some official statements were even more exciting still.

Getting the four men back down was almost an anticlimax. Soyuz 4, with Shatalov and now Khrunov and Yeliseyev aboard, came down the following morning, in conditions even worse than when they had left. They impacted on hard snow and winds were whistling across the snowscape, blowing up fine icy particles. Temperatures plunged to −35°C. Soyuz 4 was spotted as it came in; helicopters landed beside the craft and hustled the three men into warm coats even before giving them welcoming bear-hugs, which was extremely un-Russian.

Boris Volynov was probably glad to be where he was in the relative warmth of Soyuz 5. He asked for an extra day aloft so as to avoid the snow storms. This was refused; but he was granted an extra orbit so as to come down in calmer conditions near Kustanai.

All four men returned to Moscow on the 24 January. It had been Russia's best week in space since Alexei Leonov or the Luna 9. But the reception in Moscow turned into a nightmare. As the motorcade headed from the airport to the Kremlin reception it passed the Borovitsky gate. Gunfire erupted as a young lieutenant in uniform brandishing a gun started firing wildly at the cavalcade.

He was aiming at Leonid Brezhnev but so wildly was he firing that he got the cosmonauts' limousine instead. Its driver slumped over his wheel, dead, and bleeding profusely. Beregovoi's face was splattered with blood and glass. Nikolayev and Leonov pushed Valentina Terreskhova down onto the floor to protect her. The lieutenant was grabbed by the militia and taken off to an asylum; and that was where he was last heard of.

The awards ceremony went ahead as planned. Putting the memory of the afternoon behind them, Russia's scientists bathed in the glow of their achievement. Mstislav Keldysh promised:

The assembly of big, constantly operating orbital stations, interplanetary flights, and advances in radio, television, and other branches of the national economy lie ahead. [5]

A few Western reporters still needled him about the Moon race. There was no plan to go to the Moon at the moment, he said, but, when asked to confirm that Russia had abandoned plans to go to the Moon altogether, he would not.

TROIKA: MARKING TIME, OR FLOPNIK?

The next Soyuz flight presents real problems; and years after, no one is much the wiser as to its real objectives, failures or achievements. There are good reasons to believe that things went wrong.

Considering that Soyuz 4 and 5 were to usher in a new era of orbital space stations, the new era was suspiciously slow in dawning. Apollo 9's lunar module flew in March 1969, and Apollo 10 flew out to the Moon in May for a dress rehearsal for the landing. Leaving aside the strange intervention of Luna 15, the Americans had a clear run until that eerie and unforgettable moment on 21 July when Neil Armstrong planted Old Glory on the Moon.

August passed. Zond 7 flew to the Moon and back to the wheatfields of Kazakhstan. September passed. Not a squeak from Baikonour. The launching pads had never been more conspicuously silent. It was almost as if they had been hypnotized by the triumph of Apollo. Then came a clue. At the annual teach-in held in Kaluga on Tsiolkovsky's birthday (20 September), Boris Petrov delivered the main paper. It was called 'Manned Space Stations: the next step'. He told his audience:

The most efficient way to assemble space stations in orbit will be to take each part into orbit by booster rocket. Methods for mutual tracking of two such ships, put into close orbits, manoeuvring, docking, linkup and undocking, are being developed. [6]

Yet when the long-expected mission — now running a full ten months behind the 16 January linkup — eventually got under way, it took an entirely different track. Soyuz 6 was fired aloft at 2.10 p.m. on Saturday 11 October 1969, with a two-man crew. Tass announced that its main objective would be welding in space. Soyuz 6 was soon circling the Earth at a low orbit of 186 by 223 km.

Once again there were new faces aboard. Commander was Georgi Shonin, 34, flying on what was for some reason his only space flight. Dark-eyed, curly haired, intense, he was the last of the 1960 group to get a mission. Flight Engineer Valeri Kubasov, from the 1966 recruitment, was to emerge as one of the most experienced and capable engineers. When he and Shonin boarded their spaceship it was cold and drizzly and they were probably glad to get away.

Russian space-lab goes into orbit.

Russia tries space breakthrough.

Russians launch space-lab.

These were typical headlines in the Western press the following morning. Writers, psyched up by the headlines of the previous January, were convinced that this was the first stage of an orbiting laboratory — not without good reason either: several drawings in the Russian press in the previous week had shown two-ship linkups (like Soyuz 4/5) and also three-ship linkups. One spacecraft was linked to two others by a flexible tube.

But the USSR went to some pains to explain that Soyuz 6 was different from previous Soyuz models. It carried no docking mechanism, nor automatic rendezvous equipment; instead it carried extra fuel for 'extensive manoeuvring', and new means of carrying out vacuum-welding.

As Soyuz 6 swung over Baikonour the following morning Soyuz 7 streaked through cloudy autumn skies to join it. Another three new cosmonauts were on board; Anatoli Filipchenko, Vladislav Volkov and Viktor Gorbatko, men who unlike Shonin were to fly again.

Filipchenko was heavy, thickset, a well-built pilot, 41, veteran of supersonic planes, whose favourite pastime was speargun fishing. He was from the 1963 selection. Volkov, a superb engineer, came from a family of aircraft designers. He was a splendid athlete, excelling at soccer and ice hockey, and was nationally known. Viktor Gorbatko, who looked a little like America's Neil Armstrong, was the last of the 1960 selection to get a flight. He was an experienced parachutist and had EVA training, having stood in for Alexei Leonov in 1965 and Yevgeni Khrunov in January 1969.

There were now five men in orbit, and the ships were quite close to each other as they circled the globe. Vladislav Volkov spoke to Moscow television from orbit. He hinted darkly: 'I am responsible for communications and various other tasks, but I'm not going to tell you about them yet'. So the *Manchester Guardian* wrote:

It seems very probable that tomorrow night Russia will have completed her most important experiment and be ready to build and supply man's first home in space. [7]

'Higher and faster, up it goes!' exulted a Tass commentator when at lunchtime the following day Soyuz 8 took off through heavy rain to join the five comrades. It was

The three crew members of Soyuz 7, Anatoli Filipchenko (left), Vladislav Volkov and Viktor Gorbatko shown after the successful landing of their spacecraft. They had taken part in a strange, three-spacecraft 'Troika' mission, which seemed to achieve little other than mark the first occasion on which seven men were simultaneously in space, aboard Soyuz 6, 7 and 8. No dockings took place and the three craft remained close to each other for about a day before moving away for separate flights.

13 October 1969. On board were two veterans of the January mission — Vladimir Shatalov and Alexei Yeliseyev. Shatalov was named as the 'Commander of the Space Fleet'. The Russians dubbed it the 'Troika' after a three-horse snow sleigh.

It was a record. Never before had seven men been in orbit at once, nor three manned spaceships. They were in close orbit together. One Western paper noted that 'Moscow was quiet as the seven took to space. . . but the Russian people seem unexcited. The reaction appears to be that we have seen all this before' [8].

14 October was clearly signposted to be 'the day'. Around midday, the three craft drew to within 200 m of each other. At 7 p.m. the Western radio press reported a docking between Soyuz 7 and 8 but this was quickly denied by Tass. 'Optical and signalling tests' were being carried out. Then news dried up completely. And nothing new was heard for a day. Tass announced that the Soyuz 6 and 8 had in turn been approached to 'within a few hundred metres' by Soyuz 7. They were playing a game of cosmic tag, overtaking each other in orbit, testing navigation and manoeuvring devices. In all, 31 joint manoeuvres were completed.

At this stage, official sources began to contradict each other. Dr Yeliseyev was quoted as saying 'there would be no dockings or EVAs'. *Soviet Weekly* cautioned that 'Soyuz 6. . . has no docking equipment since it is not planned to perform any linkup manoeuvres with her' — but did not say the same about 7 or 8. Then Dr P. Lyobmirov wrote in *Sovietskaya Rossiya* to inform readers that Soyuz 6 was a 'prototype ferry craft capable of mooring itself to a space station' [9].

Later on the 15th, ground observers in Britain spotted the three craft crossing the sky in the dusk. Soyuz 7 and 8 were about 11 km apart, with 6 following 450 km behind.

Then, in the early afternoon of the 16th, Tass broke the drought of news by announcing that a major welding operation had been concluded aboard Soyuz 6 and that the crew had returned to Earth. On its 77th orbit, Georgi Shonin and Valeri Kubasov had retreated to the descent module and Georgi Shonin had depressurized the orbital module. One entire part of it had been set aside for the experiment and Kubasov could observe what was happening on closed-circuit TV. Several metals were tested under three methods of automatic welding: plasma, arc, and electron beam welding. While welding on Earth in a near-vacuum was virtually impossible to simulate, more pure vacuum conditions could be obtained in orbit. Free of air molecules in between them, metallic parts will, provided the surfaces are clean, fuse in a vacuum.

The entire device had been put together by Dr Boris Paton of the Paton Welding Institute in Kiev — probably the most advanced such laboratory in the world. It was certainly an unusual experiment, although its space station applications lay some distance in the future.

Once the experiment was done, the module was repressurized. Valeri Kubasov reentered the orbital cabin, collected the welding samples, brought them back and stowed them away. They fired the retrorockets and came home. Soyuz 6 was back after 81 orbits. Shonin and Kubasov came down in a field, covered in the first snow of winter and right beside a childrens' school. Classes broke off at once and all ran to investigate. Soyuz 7 and 8 came down at 24-hour intervals over the next two days. Within a week of the missions' brave start, they were all back on the ground.

'Soyuz jaunt could be one big flopnik!' ridiculed the *Daily Mail*. It was a typical reaction. Apart from the welding, which involved only the one ship the circus had achieved nothing new — indeed less than the January linkup. So the *Mail* concluded:

> While the Russians may have learnt a lot about techniques to assemble platforms in orbit, it is clear that their permanent space station is not as close as was thought. [10]

This impression was strengthened when *Pravda* quoted the 'deputy flight control director' as admitting: 'Unforeseen situations arose that were new for the cosmonauts and for ground control' [11]. Even Shatalov, the flagship commander, accepted that: 'Certainly there were difficulties but we dealt with them calmly' [12].

None of this of itself meant that the mission suffered a major reverse. But is it probably enough to suggest that Soyuz 7 and 8 held off from docking with each other because of suspect equipment. An 'experimental orbital station' of the January 1969 model, but with five men and linked for the period of the joint mission, say three days, would have represented a more worthwhile advance.

Once the seven were safely back, the Soviet press, stung by the Western criticism, mounted a full-scale counteroffensive. They hailed the heroes as 'the men who brought space down to Earth' and gave pages of details of cyclones tracked, minerals found, land masses tracked, typhoons spotted, and vegetation observed [13]. And, they added scornfully, any schoolboy knows that space docking is a 'relatively simple routine': navigation work is infinitely harder. Perhaps so. But if this was the case, then Soviet news management was poor, to say the least. Drawings of multiple dockings in *Izvestia* before the flight could only have lifted expectations. There were confused and contradictory statements during the flight. And if Soyuz 7 and 8 were not intended to dock, no effort was made to clarify this beforehand, unlike Soyuz 6.

Assuming that the Troika did fall short, the outcome was not disastrous. The space station was indeed some time ahead still, and would not be ready till 1971, whatever happened. Soyuz 6—8 was still a valuable learning experience. Launching, controlling and landing three spaceships in a week was a real achievement in coordination — and helpful practice for the man-on-the-Moon mission.

One further factor may give us a clue. The backup crews for the three missions were never revealed, where they had been for virtually every other mission in the early Soyuz series. Is it possible there were none? Could it be that with the Salyut station still 18 months away there was a lot of pressure from the Kremlin to run a mission, any mission, to steal some of the thunder of the all-too-successful Apollo 11?

The hardware was there. Five new cosmonauts could get flight experience. Since they had all trained for the January mission, it would be easy enough to replicate many of its features. Soyuz 6 had probably originally been intended as a solo flight, but it could become the third member of a double docking. With the collapse of the G booster in June, something had to take its place. So the Troika was hastily put together, without the time to train in reserve crews.

But these were not reasons that could be advanced publicly. Hence the confused and maladroit news management, exacerbated by problems in orbit which caused Shatalov to exercise caution and call off a docking — which only caused more problems and a three-day news blackout by Tass, a sure sign of trouble.

All this the seven men tried to put behind them when they arrived in Moscow on 25 October aboard a brand-new Ilyushin jet, the Il-62. Mstislav Keldysh told the press conference that 'Soviet manned space stations, orbiting for very long periods, will be operating in less than five years' [14]. And as if to reinforce confidence in the cosmonaut squad, and the team which had just flown the Troika, Shatalov and Yeliseyev were nominated soon after to be commander and engineer for the first space station, to fly in 1971. Vladislav Volkov was nominated backup flight engineer.

MORE GAPS

But the first space station mission was still some time away. About all that could be done in terms of orbital rendezvous had been done, and any further troika-type flights would only encourage more misunderstanding at home and abroad. Yet in 1970 the Americans, who returned to the Moon on Apollo 12 in November 1969, were planning two further visits there in 1970, Apollo 13 and 14.

So the Soyuz 9 mission was constructed to fill the gap. It was a sensible move. The Soviet duration record was only five days, as set by Bykovsky back in 1963, and since surpassed by Gemini 5 (eight days) and Gemini 7 (fourteen). The Apollo Moon missions were lasting about ten days. A duration mission was necessary as a prelude to a long flight aboard an orbital station — indeed that was the whole purpose of flying orbital stations. Eighteen days was set as the target.

As a bonus, Soyuz 9 would test out the lunar decontamination unit. The man-on-the-Moon programme was still in existence at this stage and, should it fly, some kind of decontamination would be required. The whole question was taken very seriously at the time. It was feared that lunar spacemen could pick up germs from the Moon, bring them back to Earth and let them loose on an unprotected population of earthlings. So when Neil Armstrong, Michael Collins and Edwin Aldrin came back from the Moon they were unceremoniously bundled into blue overalls and gas masks and locked up in a sealed caravan for three weeks. (Such precautions were dropped in 1971.) Another good reason for Soyuz 9 testing out the Soviet equivalent was that it had been built and unless this crew used it, no one else was likely to later, unless the G booster and its associated equipment had a sudden run of good luck.

Soyuz 9 would also develop the earth resources observations begun by the Troika. The flight would be timed for midsummer so as to give conditions of maximum lighting over the northern regions of the USSR. It seems that much more lengthy preparations went into Soyuz 9 than the Troika. At the 25 October press conference, Mstislav Keldysh indicated they were already under way: 'The biggest problem involved in building orbital stations is the ability of man to remain long in space' [15].

Accordingly in the autumn of 1969 the cosmonaut squad was divided into two groups — the Soyuz 9 mission group, and the space station assignment:

	Soyuz 9	Space Station Salyut
Prime crew	Nikolayev Sevastianov	Shatalov Yeliseyev Rukhavishnikov
Backups	Lazarev Markarov	Dobrovolski Volkov Patsayev
Reserve (Soyuz 9) or 2nd boarding crew (space station)	Grechko Filipchenko Khrunov	Leonov Kubasov Petr Kolodin

Soyuz 9 was of course limited to a crew of two, for reasons both of air supplies and the amount of physical space on board. It was Vostok 3 veteran Andrian Nikolayev's last chance to get into space. He had repeatedly failed to master the docking simulator in training and this was the last solo flight planned for some time in which docking would not be required. Flight Engineer Vitaly Sevastianov was already known to television viewers because he had his own science programme — but none of the viewers yet knew of his other identity.

It was well into the night-time after a scorching hot day when the transfer van brought Andrian Nikolayev and Vitally Sevastianov to Pad B at Baikonour. Floodlights lit up the complex as the final count began. Engines hummed and liquid oxygen boiled off in the sweltering heat.

By way of a strange counterpoint, the first man on the Moon, Neil Armstrong, was visiting Moscow that evening. He was in Star Town. Its auditorium was filled as he showed the audience a film of his flight to the Moon and gave his own personal commentary. The experience excited both envy and intense admiration. The audience were taken with Armstrong's personality: quiet but confident, friendly, but not effervescent. The film was greeted with warm applause. Georgi Beregovoi presented him with a model of Soyuz; he got a bouquet from Valentina Terreskhova. A bittersweet moment followed as he told the assembly how, on the personal request of Valentina Komarov and Valentina Gagarin he had placed the medals of their husbands on the

The Soyuz 9 capsule sits atop an A-2 launch vehicle on launch pad B at the Baikonour cosmodrome at Tyuratam. This was the first manned spaceflight to take place from Pad B, which was completed in 1966. Most Soyuz and later Progress craft have been launched from there, although not Soyuz 11, 16, 19 and 25.

surface of the Sea of Tranquility. This gesture of friendship left many tears and it seemed not to matter that it was American astronauts who put them there.

After the film show, it was time for dinner chez Beregovoi. Half-way through Beregovoi turned on the television and treated Armstrong to the televised liftoff of Soyuz 9. It probably occurred to Neil Armstrong at one stage that this was a Beregovoi prank but it was not. Valentina Terreskhova, wife of the mission commander, was with them, and she made it clear it was not.

By the 14th orbit on 2 June the two cosmonauts had manoeuvred into a stable orbit of 247 by 266 km, 89 minutes and in this pattern they remained for the full mission.

The designers of Soyuz 9 made serious efforts to provide for the material comforts of the crew. There was a sofa, a working table, a microfilm library, portholes with blinds, brass handrails, and the inevitable picture of Lenin overseeing all. The men slept in sleeping bags and were able to shave. Each man consumed 2600 calories a day, thirty types of food were stored in tubes and an electric cooker provided hot meals and drinks.

Soyuz was spun 2½ times a minute so as to distribute heat evenly over its surface. It was, of course, de-spun: for experiments, and observations of the ground were a major part of the mission. Vitally Sevastianov had been specially trained to look at snow cover in the mountains of the southern republics. A geological survey of Siberia was made on 17 June, in conjunction with aircraft. On the 12th they tracked the progress of a storm over Iran. On the 13th they were able to give a storm warning to the citizens of Novosibirsk, well in advance of the local weather service.

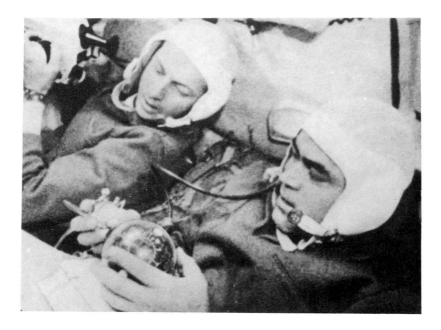

Soviet cosmonauts Andrian Nikolayev and Vitally Sevastyanov pictured aboard their Soyuz 9 spacecraft during their successful 18-day flight in June 1970. The cosmonauts suffered badly for almost two weeks after landing and this showed it was necessary to reduce this re-adaptation stress on return to Earth by various factors — including rigorous exercise.

Vitally Sevastianov made a special project of luminous clouds and later wrote a paper about them, published in May 1971. Originally they were thought to exist only over the Arctic, but he found them over Arabia too. And on Soyuz' 188th orbit they did a weather profile of the Indian Ocean combined with sounding rockets launched from the ship *Akademik Shirmov* 230 km below and a Meteor weather satellite 370 km above. The flight was paying its own way, claimed Tass. Fifty separate experiments were carried out.

But the success or failure of the flight would stand or fall on the basis of the ability of the men to withstand zero gravity. At the beginning, all went well enough. Doctors insisted they exercise at least 2 hours each day on a bicycle frame and chest expander so as to build up muscles that would otherwise deteriorate. This they did, but it was not popular, particularly as there was no means of showering afterwards.

Flight doctors went to some length to provide psychological comfort. Programmes were beamed up on radio and TV. Both cosmonauts talked to their families and Nikolayev to his daughter Lenochka on her birthday. They watched some of the World Cup soccer. They voted in the USSR general election. They played a 35-move chess game with ground control: it was a draw.

The problems began on day 12 when fatigue began to set in. The men began to look for rest periods sooner and sooner and once tried to dodge exercises: ground control found out when telemetry showed that carbon dioxide levels in the cabin were too low. They got eye irritation. They got so tired that ground control had to use a siren to wake them up in the morning. After 285 orbits it was decided to call it a day.

Andrian Nikolayev fired the retrorockets for 145 seconds over Africa. With their feet drawn together closely in the cramped cabin, they gradually felt the gentle tug of gravity as it began to draw them earthwards once more — then more and more strongly. They could see flames shoot past the window as they blazed in an arc over the Mediterranean.

Helicopters spotted Soyuz 9 descending and followed it down for a full eight minutes. The capsule came to rest in a dusty ploughed field. It had been away for a full 17 days 16 hours and 59 minutes — a new record.

Rescue teams from four helicopters surround the capsule. The two men were brought out on stretchers through the top, and transferred to the helicopters in a state of biological isolation. They were flown speedily to Star Town by way of Vnukovo airport, and not let out till 2 July, two weeks later — the same period of isolation as a Moon journey would require.

Flight debriefing was carried out behind glass partitions: telephones and microphones were used. The isolation complex had probably cost a lot to build and this was the only use it was to get. *Soviet Weekly*:

> The isolation isn't because of fears that Nikolayev and Sevastianov may have brought back strange diseases from outer space! Indeed the precautions are for the opposite reason. Doctors consider it possible that protracted space flight may lower normal immunities and they are therefore making sure that the spacemen are protected from earthbound infection until they have acclimatised. [16]

Yet Sevastianov got no such protection when he returned from 63 days in space in 1975! The biological isolation was only one of the myths surrounding Soyuz 9. The other was the actual medical condition of the cosmonauts. First reports indicated – in fact they stated outright – that both men were well and had suffered no ill-effects from the mission, and were as well as previous crews:

> The condition of health, working efficiency, and the general tone of the cosmonauts are much higher than what the medical men expected... the flight has shown that many of the worries the doctors and biologists had were unfounded. [17]

However, observation of the cosmonauts during their isolation period showed that they were 'slow to respond', 'pale', with 'their faces furrowed with wrinkles'. They tired rapidly, lost concentration, and efforts to make conversation or jokes faltered [18]. These were the medical reports, not what readers got from their papers.

Andrian Nikolayev and Vitally Sevastianov resurfaced publicly at an International Space Conference in October 1970 in Konstanz, West Germany. A new story came out there. Both men had been severely weakened by their spell in space. They could not stand for three days and their heart rates were twice normal. They took a full month to recover.

Nevertheless, these factors made Soyuz 9 a success, rather than a failure. To have proceeded directly to a space station without such a mission would have been foolhardy. The next months were quiet while Soviet engineers completed assembly of the world's first orbiting space station. It was planned to have it ready in time for the 10th anniversary of Yuri Gagarin's flight, on 12 April 1971. And to salute the occasion, the station was named 'Salute'.

SALUTE

Indications of an upcoming space station mission first appeared on 15 March 1971 when the unnamed Chief Designer told *Socialist Industry*: 'It seems to me very expedient to build in the near future an orbital space station near the Earth that would operate for a very long time' [19]. Came the Gagarin anniversary and the rumours were flowing thick and fast. Two teams of cosmonauts had already left for the pad. The tracking fleet had taken up station. The Moscow press corps were abuzz with excitement. Clearly something big was afoot.

It happened on 19 April. Late that morning Moscow radio came on air to announce the launching of the world's first orbiting space station. It had entered a low but safe orbit of 200 by 222 km, 51.6 degrees, 88.5 minutes. Salyut was given a complete telecommunications checkout on its 9th orbit, and all was in order. The next day, 20 April 1971, Leonid Brezhnev called the flight an 'important step in the conquest of space'. On the next day Georgi Beregovoi added that orbiting stations with changing crews would be the main feature of space exploration in the 1970s.

At this stage no one had a clue as to what Salyut looked like. Futuristic drawings had appeared in Soviet magazines showing all kinds of cylinders and domes linked together, but they were only sketches. In fact, in designing Salyut, Soviet engineers had used a fairly simple model to start with: they used the basic stage of the Proton payload, fitted living quarters, and added attachments to the outside. Design work had taken a year, manufacture a further year. There had been no time for tests.

Salyut was a tapering cylinder of three different diameters – 4.15 m, 2.9 m and 2.0 m. It was 14.4 m in length and weighed 18.9 tonnes. At the rear was a motor and propellant so the spacecraft could change orbit, a capability America's Skylab did not have. At the front end was the docking unit. Masts and antennae protruded. Two solar arrays sprang out from the front and two from the rear. It looked like a strange aircraft of revolutionary design.

On the inside it was a real space home. There was an abundance of room, unlike in the crammed cabin of Soyuz. Swimming into Salyut from a docked Soyuz the visitor met a spacious control panel. It faced forwards and there were two pilot seats. Lights flashed and displays hummed and control sticks permitted the cosmonauts to control and fly the whole complex. The walls were full of lockers – for food, water, scientific and repair equipment, manuals, clothes. And there were handrails everywhere for the men to move about in zero gravity.

Moving on to the main room of the cylinder, there was a compartment filled with equipment. A telescope built into the hull allowed the men to view the stars. There were three portholes so the cosmonauts could view the Earth. Sleeping bags were slung from hooks. Several exercise devices completed the internal equipment. It provided living space on a scale never enjoyed before and a range of equipment those who had flown in the small up-and-down craft could never have imagined.

In the tail of the station were a series of oxygen and fuel tanks, water containers and purifiers. Because the station was not designed to return to Earth, the designers had a free hand with their layout, not constrained by the need to streamline.

Late on 22 April, Salyut completed its 66th orbit. The temperature at night-time Baikonour was −25°C. Three cosmonauts had just arrived at the pad. The onion-shape-topped Soyuz 10 rocket stood waiting, bathed in floodlight. Alexei Yeliseyev, Flight Engineer, was holding an impromptu press conference. In their flight overalls alone, the crew would have frozen; but they wore thick leather jackets and officers' caps. Yeliseyev used a twig to draw in the snow to explain the upcoming mission to journalists. With mission commander Vladimir Shatalov beside him and research engineer Nikolai Rukhavishnikov alongside, Yeliseyev concluded: 'the night is cloudless, clear and starry. We are ready to go on up'.

Flames licked around the base of the stand. Night turned to day as Soyuz 10 rose from the pad and sped to orbit. The chase had begun.

Soyuz 10 shot into a much higher orbit than planned, but Vladimir Shatalov at once began pursuit manoeuvres. With Yeliseyev they comprised the most experienced crew that could be put together for such a mission. In six hours, Soyuz 10's long-range radar had picked up Salyut.

Vladimir Shatalov went through twelve complex computer manoeuvres. Soyuz 10 changed orbit three times and Shatalov commanded Salyut through four changes. Twenty-four hours into the mission, the two ships were 11 km apart. They were closing at 98 km/h. Shatalov cut the closing speed and braked. He commanded on the navigation lights of Salyut. Now Alexei Yeliseyev could spot it through his window. With its lights flashing, the bright white cylinder, wings outstretched, was, he recalled later, 'indescribably beautiful'. The letters 'CCCP' were clearly visible on the side.

Shatalov moved Soyuz 10 forward till they were only 200 m apart. They lined up for docking. Then, slowly, they moved forwards at 1 m/s and cut the speed again. At 2.47

a.m. on the 24 April they had contact. The ships were coupled. It was the second orbital space docking they had achieved. Alexei Yeliseyev said it was like 'a train arriving at a railway station'. They had done it: the first linkup to an orbital station – a first.

Or so everyone thought. The next the world knew about Soyuz 10 was that it was back on Earth. And it was not an easy reentry either. It took place at night. Rescue teams gasped as Soyuz 10 headed straight towards a lake. At the last moment a breeze blew it away and it came down on a pebble beach 44 m from the water's edge as frogmen stood ready with aqualungs. The three cosmonauts had been up for 47 hours 46 minutes – the shortest Soyuz mission so far, since Komarov. They were flown at once by helicopter to Karaganda. Snow lay on the ground as they held a post-flight press conference.

So what had happened? Soyuz 10 and Salyut 1 had been linked for 5½ hours, or nearly four orbits. There was no suggestion that an emergency arose. Indeed a telecast from Salyut showed Soyuz pulling away against a cloud-shrouded background of Earth. It was all very orderly. This was indeed the official story: 'The Salyut station flies on, with just one dramatic step of its mission completed' [20]. Soyuz, so the story went, was simply testing the docking mechanism, and it had never been intended to board the station. But this explanation never sounded very convincing. Official news coverage had never tried to damp down expectations of a boarding, which would have been an obvious precaution. And the landing seems to have taken everyone by surprise.

A look at the Soyuz landing lines shows something suspicious too. From Soyuz 1 on, it had always been a mission rule that retrofire should take place in conditions of maximum sunlight (presumably to ensure that electrical systems can be fully powered up just before descent), and that landing should take place at least one hour before sunset in the local landing zone, so as to give the crews time to find the landed spacemen. In practice this had always meant touchdown normally occurring between 0.1 of a day and 0.2 of a day before local sunset when the spacecraft is directly over a landing zone. All the Soyuz 1–9 missions conform to this pattern: 10 does not. It is way out. It broke the rule-book to return when it did. Indeed a landing 'according to the book' was not due until the period 16–26 May. This indicated a proposed mission duration of 23 to 33 days [21]. So why the return? There does not seem to have been a sudden or life-risking emergency. But it may be fair to conclude that there was a problem (probably on Soyuz) and that Shatalov, erring on the side of caution, decided to come home.

At one stage there were rumours that Rukhavishnikov had become ill. The Russians indignantly denied these claims. They were probably right too: he did get space sickness, it is admitted, but about half of all space fliers did in those days.

Not that much disappointment was visible when the crew were received at the Kremlin on 30 April. For the mission was basically sound. The linkup could be done again. Salyut itself was in perfect order. On 27 April it fired its rocket motor to put it up into a much higher orbit of 251 by 277 km, 89.36 minutes. From there it would be in a good position, having drifted downwards once more with atmospheric drag, to receive a new crew in the first week of June.

At this stage the State Commission did something unusual. Rather then let the assigned Soyuz 11 crew fly the next mission, it put in the backup Soyuz 10 crew instead. We know this because photographs of the Soyuz 10 and 11 pre-flight press conferences show the same six cosmonauts all the time. The crew who were bumped – Leonov, Kubasov and Petr Kolodin [22] – are nowhere to be seen and their exact role did not come to light until a training film was released (by mistake perhaps again) years later.

Salyut 1 flew on. Whatever the problems were with Soyuz 10 they were not so serious as to impede a new launch at the first available opportunity when Salyut was over the launch pad and the landing lines fitted the rule book. The launch window began on 6 June, and the landing lines were from 9 July to 21, suggesting a duration mission of at least 34 days.

SOYUZ 11: HEROES FOREVER

A *Pravda* interview on 3 June with Konstantin Feoktistov about the importance of space stations set the scene for a new flight. On the 4th, Tass reported Salyut's orbit as down to 251 by 277 km, 88.36 minutes, just in range for the Soyuz ferry.

It was nearly 5 a.m. on the Sunday morning, 6 June 1971, when Georgi Dobrovolski, 43, Vladislav Volkov, 35, and Viktor Patsayev, 37, arrived at the pad. Dawn had just broken. It was so very different from the April mission with its snowy backdrop. Now the steppes were scorched and dry and this day would be a hot one too.

Onlookers, wellwishers and launch staff pressed flowers into the hands of the departing cosmonauts. Dobrovolski was the tallest and had donned a military cap like the ones John F. Kennedy wore on wartime PT boats. Vladislav Volkov was relaxed, jaunty and cheerful as ever. Viktor Patsayev was the shyest of the three and stood quietly. Then they climbed aboard.

5.40 a.m. From his cabin 40 m up, Georgi Dobrovolski reported: 'This is Yantar (code name) and we are ready to go on up'. The count went on automatic sequence. Fuel lines were cleared, drainage lines withdrawn.

5.45 a.m. Soyuz 11 was now on full internal power. The capsule access arm retracted.

5.50 a.m. The large squad of journalists and newsmen present trained their big cameras on the booster. They stopped talking, silent in expectation. Morning sunlight shone brightly on the white rocket.

5.55 a.m. And off it went! Soyuz 11 lifted slowly off the pad. It accelerated skywards, trailing a cottony white contrail. 'Little vibration', Georgi Dobrovolski reported back. They were soon lost to sight.

6.02 a.m. 'Temperature 22°C, pressure 840 mb, all's well.'

6.03 a.m. 'Orbital insertion', Dobrovolski reported. 'Commencing separation, stabilization, antennae and solar wing deployment.' So well was the mission going that when news of the launch was broken, it was also announced that Soyuz would carry out 'comprehensive studies with the Salyut station'.

7 June, 5.26 a.m. By now, Georgi Dobrovolski had navigated Soyuz 11 across the vastness of space to only 6.5 km from Salyut. Then using the manoeuvring stick, he closed to 100 m.

5.50 a.m. Station keeping, 100 m apart. The two spacecraft flew a full two revolutions at this distance. There may have been a fault in the automatic system for, at 8.30 a.m., he was ordered to complete the operation manually.

8.45 a.m. Linkup! Salyut had completed 794 orbits, Soyuz 18. They contacted slowly and then coupled rigidly — mechanically, electrically, hydraulically.

Then began the stage where their predecessors were cheated: climbing into the station itself. Opening up the internal hatches was not as easy as it sounded, for all the pressures

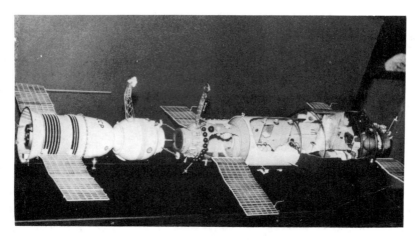

Two models depicting the spaceship Soyuz 11 just before its successful docking with the Salyut 1 space station in June 1971. The cutaway of Salyut (right) shows some detail of the working environment aboard the space station.

and valves had to be equalized and the tunnel airtight. Eventually all was ready. Vladislav Volkov opened up and floated through. He was the world's first visitor to a space base. Gingerly he swam in, moving hand over hand on the handrails. Viktor Patsayev and Georgi Dobrovolski followed: 'The station's huge: there seems to be no end to it!' the commander exclaimed. As they floated through they could appreciate and enjoy its size; their first task was to turn it into a real home.

And that is what they did. They unloaded their equipment from Soyuz and after two days they were able to close down Soyuz's systems. They pulled the hatch behind them and lived entirely in the station itself.

Salyut in the meantime was warmed up and hummed into life. Georgi Gobrovolski and Vladislav Volkov soon got used to controlling the space station from its jetliner-like flight deck. On the 8th and again on the 9th they used it to turn on Salyut's motor to raise the orbit up to 259 by 282 km — the first time a manned space station and attached ferry flew together as one unit. The men could see a bright burst of flames through the portholes. The ship shook with vibration. Ice flakes drifted off the hull like a snow blizzard as their base swung into a higher orbit.

The three-man crew soon settled into a pattern of work. There was always at least one man on duty at a time. Breakfast happened each day at 11 a.m., after which the crew ran a comprehensive check of the station's systems. From 3 p.m. to 11 p.m. they were outside the radio range of ground control. Once back they reported in. Each day they sent in a weather report.

Starting on 9 June, the crew started transmitting a daily series of television chat shows. Each day they reported back on something new they were doing. The first time they appeared in strange-looking floppy tracksuits: called 'penguin suits' they were designed to stretch certain parts of the body and freshen muscles that would otherwise decay.

Like Soyuz 9, exercise was the key to survival, though the roomy conditions made this infinitely easier. Each cosmonaut exercised two hours a day on a chest expander, a bicycle and a treadmill. They did not like it, but they knew they had to do it.

A vast programme of scientific work was begun that put previous missions in the shade. They tested radiation levels on board every day. On the 10th, Viktor Patsayev took blood samples of all the three men and analysed them. They watched through the portholes regularly to see just how much the hull was being battered by micrometeorites.

11 June: a new gamma-ray telescope was put into working order for the first time and they became the first space astronomers. Viktor Patsayev showed visitors his fish farm: tadpoles swam around in a jar. What they made of weightlessness we do not know, but their reactions were being tested. Biology was Patsayev's speciality. Salyut had a small garden with daylight provided by fluorescent lamps and nutrition from special hydroponic solutions. He was growing kale, cress, flax, Chinese cabbage, and onion. Photographs were taken each day to observe growth.

Later, space food would be grown on board. As it was, Salyut had a hot meal cooker and refrigerator. Their food had extra quantities of calcium — essential in zero gravity, which depleted the calcium in the bones.

By 15 June they had flown 134 times around the Earth in Salyut. Observations of the Earth were central to the flight. The men studied cyclones and typhoons. They fitted filters to their cameras over the USSR's land mass, to map the snow, tree disease, crops and moisture on the ground. At one stage on 14 June they did a coordinated sweep of an area near the Caspian Sea with an Ilyushin 18 flying at 8000 m and an Antonov 2 at 300 m.

On 19 June, Viktor Patsayev celebrated his 38th birthday. They had a party and ate fruit, cheeses, nuts, veal and prunes. Then they got down to work and used their 'Orion' telescope to track a star and its short-wave characteristics, including rays that never reached the Earth. On 23 June they broke the Soyuz 9 record of 18 days. They were heading into the medical unknown. They saw a sandstorm start up in Africa. In the garden, flax and kale had come up.

On 26 June the men passed the three-week mark and reported fatigue for the first time. It was little wonder. The flight log had recorded a hectic round of medical check-ups, astronomical studies, gardening, atmospheric observations, examinations of the Earth and charged particles. By 27 June the medical readouts suggested a continued deterioration in the cosmonauts' health. The instruments on board provided the doctors on the ground with unprecedented detail — blood pressure, heart rates, volume of breathing, speed of inhalation. The men were simply tiring. Baikonour ordered Dobrovolski to programme Salyut's computer so the station could fly itself once they had left.

On the 28th, ground control ordered the crew — then on their 342nd circuit — to pack their belongings and come down the next evening. They could have stayed up longer but the doctors wanted to take no chances. It would mean a landing outside mission rules, but 9 July was too far away.

Early return or not, feelings on the ground were close to exhilaration. The three cosmonauts had smashed every record in sight. The concept of orbiting stations had been vindicated. Salyut was the first space base beyond the Earth. The scientific haul from the mission would keep the scientists busy for years.

The daily telecasts had made the three personable men heroes throughout the USSR. They became the best-known space fliers since Gagarin and Leonov. The nightly shows from space entertained and enthralled viewers, not to mention one demonstration after another of the value of space research. It was clear that *this* was what space flight was all about — not lunar stunt shows. And an American answer to Salyut was still some years off. It was the good old days all over again.

A tremendous reception was being prepared for the three cosmonauts for when they came home. Excitement about the flight had increased every new day they stayed up there, as the magnitude of their achievement percolated down.

They undocked at 7.28 p.m. on 29 June. Like a pilot fish to a whale, they flew alongside Salyut for an hour. Then they drifted slowly apart. At 11 p.m. Georgi Dobrovolski fired the retrorockets over Madeira. They burned briefly and the spacecraft began to head home. Soon they would enter radio blackout. As they did, Vladislav Volkov peered out of the window and unexpectedly caught sight of Salyut sailing past, high above. The rays of the Sun glinted on the solar cells of the panels and gleamed brightly:

Volkov: All is well. So long. See you soon on Earth.
Dobrovolski: See you back on Earth. We're going into orientation now. [23]

These were the last words spoken by the crew of Soyuz 11. Seconds later their heartbeats ceased and they were never heard again. Subsequent investigation showed that the seal of the descent module broke. The air rushed out. They had no space suits. They died instantly.

The three Soyuz 11 cosmonauts, Georgi Dobrovolsky, Vladislav Volkov and Viktor Patsayev who successfully docked with Salyut 1, and completed a 24-day mission of scientific experiments.

'AN INVESTIGATION HAS BEEN ORDERED. . .'

The reentry continued automatically. The computer brought the capsule down. A helicopter saw it land. The ground control had noticed the loss of contact but had assumed only that the radio had gone wrong. The helicopter landed right beside the capsule. Its crew ran across the field to open the hatches. As the official announcement put it:

> The reentry was entirely normal. When the recovery forces opened the hatches, they found the crew in their seats, but there were no signs of life.
> An investigation has been ordered. [24]

These chilling words glossed over what must have been an appalling shock for the recovery team — seeing the capsule land intact, opening it up, to be greeted only by the stare of three dead men. It is probable no one believed their first reports.

Their shock was only an inkling of the terrible gloom that was to descend like a dark shadow on the Soviet space programme and people alike. The crew of Soyuz 11 had not just been any ordinary crew: they had done something radically new, had broken records, and had vindicated Soviet science and technology. Victory had been snatched from them in their last minutes and had been transformed not merely into failure but overwhelming defeat.

From the outset the Soviet official sources were at a total loss to explain the disaster: no effort was made even to suggest an interim explanation. The effects of prolonged weightlessness were the first and most obvious suspect: the three cosmonauts had somehow passed some magic threshold beyond which the human heart could not any longer stand the forces of gravity. So their hearts had given way.

'The outlook for manned space flight is bleak', reported a leading Western paper, echoing these fears [25]. This was only the start. The deaths of the three explorers — whom Soviet citizens had grown to admire over 24 days — left the Russian public grief-stricken. There were black-bordered protraits everywhere. Chopin's funeral march played endlessly on radio and television. Tributes poured in from throughout the world, not least from NASA and the Americans.

The ashes of the three men were interred in the Kremlin wall on 2 July. Besides the leaders of State and the cosmonaut squad, the mourners included American astronaut Thomas P. Stafford, representing NASA and President Nixon. The day was hot and heavy and blazing sunshine streamed down. The bands played to miles and miles of citizens and soldiers; portraits and banners followed the urns in solemn tribute. The endless slow pacing of shoes was broken only by the fluttering of flags, the brush of wind in the conifer trees and from time to time by the echoing gun salute.

Shock passed: sadness set in. And on that day, a defiant note could be detected. Cosmonauts and Party leaders swore that the struggle to conquer space would go on. At no stage was the achievement of Salyut lost. Boris Petrov wrote that day: 'It can be said with confidence that the 1970s will be the epoch of the development and use of long-term manned orbital stations with changing crews' [26]. The State Committee set up to investigate the accident reported sooner than anyone expected — by 7 July in fact. The cause had nothing to do with zero gravity. It stated: 'On the ship's descent trajectory, 30 minutes before landing there occurred a rapid drop of pressure in the descent vehicle, due to a failure in the ship's sealing' [27].

What happened was this: after retrofire, the service module and the orbital module were released. The jolt of the release caused a valve to open. This valve was designed to come open only at 5000 m above the ground — they were still 100 km high at this stage — to equalize pressure between the cabin and the air outside. So air rushed out, spinning the capsule around, and confusing the cosmonauts as to what was actually going on. Once they realized, it was too late, for the valve took a full minute to close by hand. The cosmonauts probably lost consciousness in ten seconds, and they became the first men to actually die in the space environment.

REDESIGN

The effects of the Soyuz 11 disaster were, in planning terms, as follows. Soyuz 12, with Kubasov, Leonov and Kolodin aboard, and due to lift off during the next launch window, was cancelled. Salyut 1 was abandoned, though it stayed aloft till October. The decision was taken to redesign Soyuz, a process which took a full eleven months.

The Soyuz redesign was a major undertaking. At a bare minimum the Russians could simply have modified the faulty valve in question. But they went much further in order to eliminate wider risks which cosmonauts had hitherto been subjected to. It was decided to put the cosmonauts into full space suits which they would wear at all critical stages of the mission, such as launch, docking and landing. If for any reason there was to be a pressure loss, the crew would still survive.

Such a decision, based on conservative notions about safety, implied serious weight and space penalties. The suits, the extra life-support systems to supply them with air power and coolant, weighed well over 100 kg for each cosmonaut, taking up critical space in the cramped cabin. Something had to give, and it was the third seat. It was simply removed. For the foreseeable future, Soyuz and space station occupancy would be based on a two-person crew, not three. This reduced all future space hours by 33 per cent straight off, and put the USSR at an immediate disadvantage compared to America's Skylab, with its three-man Apollo — which could indeed take five in an emergency configuration. It was not until 1980 that a three-man Soyuz became available once more on the Soyuz T; but this was due to the introduction of microcircuits which replaced some of the heavier equipment. The option was not available in 1971–72.

The hiatus led to other design changes in Soyuz. Some fuel capacity was dropped, largely because the Soyuz had spare capacity since it had been designed around lunar orbit flights. Less fuel was needed for Earth orbit missions. Also dropped were the solar panels. Given that the redesigned Soyuz ferry was supposed to fly independently for only two days, it seemed to make sense to rely on battery power alone for that period. But both these decisions — the fuel reduction and the removal of the panels — were serious errors of judgement.

The work of Salyut came to an end on 11 October 1971, though not before Salyut had three times raised its orbit — on 1 July, 28 July and 18 August. Flying over the Pacific on its 2900th orbit, its engines were commanded on by special signal from the ground. It was in effect a retrofire manoeuvre: and with no shielding only one outcome was possible. It broke up and burned up. Some larger parts may not have been completely consumed by the fires of reentry; but they were designed to fall well away from the shipping lanes.

Before its fiery end, Salyut had been seen a few times by ground observers. Lit up by the setting sun, it could be seen crossing the autumn sky, a silent bright, fast-moving star — a symbol of things to come. Its place in space history is an honoured one: the first laboratory, the first home in space, made the more poignant by the deaths of the three brave men who first flew aboard it.

FROM DISASTER TO DISASTER

The Soviet manned space programme now entered the darkest three years in its history. No cosmonaut left the ground for another two years. There was to be no successful round-trip space station occupation till the summer of 1974. The 24 days of Soyuz 11 were not surpassed until 1975. And the first long-term space laboratory had to wait till 1977. There was to be one near-disaster to Soyuz, and several linkups that failed. Two space stations were destroyed. Soviet space leaders watched helplessly as America completed its Apollo programme, and, more galling still, flew a successful space station programme (Skylab) — the one area of space travel the USSR had declared *mare nostrum*. Nothing went right.

What was worse was that these mishaps had little to do with the faults related to Soyuz 11. The causes of the Soyuz 11 disaster were identified within a week, and the appropriate remedies soon agreed upon. The repair work and modifications took less than a year, and on 26 June 1972, Cosmos 496 flew on a six-day shakedown cruise to test out the revised design. It went perfectly and the new Soyuz — with two seats, not three; with batteries not panels; and with smaller fuel tanks — was declared operational once more. The Russians were ready to fly in space again.

According to the best information available, Salyut 2, similar in design and concept to Salyut 1, was made fit for launch on 29 July 1972. Two cosmonauts were ready to fly in pursuit: Alexei Leonov and Valeri Kubasov, with, as backups, Vladimir Kovalyonok and Viktor Gorbatko.

Starting in early June 1972, the Soviet public were treated to a series of statements on the value and importance of Earth-orbiting stations. On 7 June, the anniversary of the Salyut 1/Soyuz 11 docking, Radio Moscow was quoting scientists as saying: 'We should expect stations to be working regularly and making complex observations in the near future' [28]. More significantly perhaps, it was announced on 22 July that the flagship of the Soviet tracking fleet, the 45 000 tonne *Cosmonaut Yuri Gagarin* had put to sea on its first operational mission. It joined the smaller *Cosmonaut Vladimir Komarov* (17 500 tonnes) and the *Academician Sergei Korolov* (22 000 tonnes).

But the days passed and the weeks passed and the summer went by and then the autumn and nothing happened. There was a flurry of 'manned launch due soon' rumours around 27 July, but they dried up as quickly as they came. Nothing. Not one statement was made that autumn about Soviet space intentions until the 24th International Astronautical Federation meeting in Vienna much later that year. Cosmonaut Anatoli Filipchenko told his audience that the Soyuz spacecraft was still undergoing 'extensive modification' [29].

We still do not know what happened. There are two stories: one of a launch failure, one of a countdown that threw up major systems failures to the extent that the mission was called off. Whatever it was, it was serious. And whatever it was, Soviet scientists could only contemplate with growing unease the impending launch of the American Skylab, then due for April 1973. Unlike the Moon race, the space station race could not be side-stepped or avoided. The USSR could not declare it was not interested – unless it wanted to pull out of space altogether.

Regardless of the 29 July incident, and the non-appearance of a new Soyuz then, the USSR not only decided to beat the Skylab deadline, but to go one better: two space stations would be prepared and would be orbited simultaneously. That would certainly put the Americans in the shade. In fact, a two-station series of flights suited the state of Soviet space planning that autumn of 1972. But to explain why, it is necessary to jump forward some years.

Following the flight of the Salyut, a design prototype of a space station, the decision was taken, the origins of which remain obscure, to build two types of orbital station: a military one and a civilian one. This was not fully realized until the summer of 1976, when a detailed analysis was made of the behaviour of the first five Salyuts. In looking at their behaviour, two very distinct categories became apparent, relating to their orbits, transmission frequencies, return capsule carried, and mission publicity [30].

	First category	Second category
Number	Salyut 2, 3, 5	Salyut 4, Cosmos 557 (29 July mission ?)
Orbit (km)	260	340
Period (min)	89.6	91.3
Frequencies (mHz)	19.994, 143.625	15.008, 922.75
Return capsule	Yes	No
Crewing	Both military pilots	Civilian flight engineer
Length (m)	21	23

Besides the fact that there were two separate patterns of flight, the quality of external publicity was also important. No photographs, mockups or displays were ever released of Salyut 2, 3 or 5, unlike Salyut 4 which was paraded at exhibitions throughout the world. General publicity of the former missions was low-key and the report of mission activities aboard Salyuts 3 and 5 would only account for some of the time the crew were spending aboard.

These at least were the facts and the patterns. On this base, it was possible to put forward a hypothesis to explain them. This hypothesis was that the first category of flights had a military orientation. The lower altitude is more suitable for military observations. Military manoeuvres on the ground did coincide with the manned phases of their operations. The unique use of military-only crews, a pattern never used before or since, fits this explanation. And finally, the failure to release any design drawings suggests that there was at least something the world was not to know. And what was the function of the mysterious return capsule? So it seemed that only one explanation was possible: that there existed two Salyut programmes, running parallel: one military and the other civilian.

Another point which was not known in 1972 – but which was clear by 1977 – was the exclusive nature of the crews flown aboard the military series (a programme which ended in 1977). With two exceptions (Viktor Gorbatko and Anatoloi Berezovoi) none of the 'military' Salyut cosmonauts flew again after 1977, and the group seemed to disappear from the ranks of active cosmonauts. We know that the backups and reserves for the Salyut 3 and 5 missions were common to both and rotated through both programmes — but not through any of the others. This was all the more strange as they included men who never got a second flight, unlike many of their contemporaries. All this proves nothing sinister, but it does point to a special group in the cosmonaut squad, assigned to cover a certain type of mission. But why run a separate military programme at all?

The answers to this question are not directly known. For the years 1972–77, the manned programme ran in two separate streams — one military and the other civilian. For the military one to have started in 1973, a go-ahead would have been necessary in 1970, or even earlier, perhaps in 1969 when Salyut was initiated. Perhaps the military felt entitled to a share of the space action after the dismal failure of the Moon programme; perhaps even the cost of the civilian programme was underwritten by the military, who exacted their own price in return.

The military Salyut programme would have worked on the assumptions that (1) military reconnaissance could and should be provided by the human eye in orbit, and that cosmonauts could make a major contribution to this science; and (2) that military hardware could be tested out in orbit. If one looks at the American programme at the same time, this becomes a very reasonable proposition. From 1961 to 1965 the US Air Force had its own man-in-space programme, the X-20 Dyna-Soar project. It was an experimental rocket plane that looked like a mini-shuttle (indeed the title is short for 'dynamic soaring'). Then in 1965, the project was replaced by the Manned Orbiting Laboratory, MOL. Two men would go into orbit on a Gemini spacecraft which was attached to a cylindrical laboratory atop a Titan 3 rocket. They would transfer into the laboratory for two weeks or so, carry out military reconnaissance and experiments, and return in Gemini. A special team of astronauts was even recruited for the missions, and its members eventually flew the early Shuttle missions of the early 1980s [31].

Costs spiralled and dates slipped and MOL was cancelled in 1969. But the point was this. In the late 1960s, both superpowers believed that there was great value in orbital military space reconnaissance, and both devised similar programmes to meet that perceived need. MOL and military Salyut were actually not very different in terms of size and performance.

A dual civilian and military Salyut programme was therefore very much rooted in the conventional space philosophy of the day. Salyut 1 can then be seen in retrospect as a prototype station upon which the two parallel designs were based. So, by early 1972, two such programmes did exist and the crews were allocated accordingly:

Crew	Military	Civilian
A	Pavel Popovich Yuri Artyukin	Alexei Leonov Valeri Kubasov
B	Boris Volynov Vitally Zholobov	Vladimir Kovalynok Alexander Ivanchenkov
C	Lev Demin Gennadiy Sarafanov	Vasiliy Lazarev Oleg Markarov

Crew	Military	Civilian
D	Vyacheslav Zudov Valeri Rozhdezhvensky	Alexei Gubarev Georgi Grechko
E	Viktor Gorbatko Yuri Glazhkov	Anatoli Filipchenko Nikolai Rukhavishnikov
F	Anatoli Berezovoi Valeri Illarianov	

These allocations, which subsequent chronology would suggest were made in the spring of 1972, are important, for they governed all the crew allocations to Salyuts 2—5, including the 29 July mission and Cosmos 557, and still had implications for deciding who flew aboard Salyut 6. Salyut crewing policy has always operated on a leapfrog principle — crew B would stand in for A, D for C and so on. Thus the order of flight would be A, C, B, D, and so on.

THE SQUAD IN 1972

At this stage it is worthing looking again at the state of the cosmonaut squad. By early 1970, no fewer than 84 cosmonauts had been recruited — 20 pilots in 1960, four women (since disbanded), 12 senior pilots and engineers (1963—64), four Voskhod, 20 Young Guards, and 12 engineers from 1966—68. Twelve scientists had been recruited in 1968—69, but with the loss of the third seat after the Soyuz 11 disaster there was no prospect of them flying so that group was disbanded.

But due to death, retirements, natural attrition and the accomplishment of specific missions, the 84 had by 1970 shrunk to a fraction of its former size. About 32 were left, dominated by the 1963 senior pilot group and the 1966—68 engineer group. This left some gaps; so in 1970 new recruitment began once more. This was done not so much with the upcoming Salyut flights in mind (existing recruitment could take care of that), but with a view to meeting the needs of later generation Salyuts.

Two groups were recruited in 1970 — six pilots aged 26 to 30 and six engineers aged 30 to 35. The six pilots included:

Vladimir Dzhanibekov
Yuri Romanenko
Leonid Popov
Anatoli Berezovoi.

The six engineers included Boris Andreyev (who left without having flown, in 1980) and Alexander Ivanchenkov.

Vladimir Dzhanibekov was a tall, big, sandy-haired fighter pilot who had trained pilots of the Indian Air Force, through the medium of English. He was in fact a skilled English speaker and a Shakespeare lover and expert. In his spare time he was a hi-fi builder, radio ham and electronic expert. Yuri Romanenko was a boyish-looking fighter pilot who spent his youth in Arctic sea ports where his father was ship's captain. He applied to the cosmonaut team after meeting Gherman Titov. Anatoli Berezovoi was a handsome, moustache-wearing pilot. Boris Andreyev was, like his wife Tamara Vasilevna, a Bauman Institute graduate; Alexander Ivanchenkov, or 'Sacha' to his friends, was a cheery, thin, dark-looking computer expert from the Moscow Aviation Institute.

A further four design engineers were recruited in 1972–73. They were:

Valentin Lebedev
Valeri Ryumin
Vladimir Aksenov
Gennadiy Strekhalov

These were senior spacecraft designers. Valentin Lebedev, born in 1942, smiling, tall and bald, was one of those who redesigned Soyuz after the disaster. Vladimir Aksenov had been in the Korolov design bureau since the Sputnik of 1957: he specialized in life-support systems and was intimately involved in manned flight from Vostok on. Strekhalov joined the design group only in 1965, though he started life as a coppersmith. Valeri Ryumin, later to become one of Russia's best known space fliers, was the tallest by far and barely fitted into the cramped Soyuz cabin. With a big mop of wiry black hair, he had trained as a Red Army Tank commander, and was well used to small spaces. Yet it was his experience as a communications officer on one of the fleet training ships that led him into the Salyut design office first and the cosmonaut squad soon after.

So around 1972 the USSR had a team of about 50 cosmonauts with a wide mix of experience, age and background – from the Young Guards to the senior pilots, from computer specialists to designers who had to fly the ships they built.

THE CHALLENGE TO SKYLAB

In early to mid-1972, with Soyuz redesigned, the Soviet space plan appears to have been based around a civilian Salyut in mid-1972 and a military one in 1973, one alternating with the other until about four or five had flown. Each station would be visited twice. Because the military station would be in a lower orbit, in order to get the best imaging of the ground, its lifetime would be short: so there would be two two-week visits spaced out by about three months. By contrast, the civilian Salyut, in a much higher orbit, could fly for longer missions, perhaps extending up to 100 days.

By around 1976 or so, four Salyuts would have flown and a substantial body of experience built up. This would pave the way for a second-generation Salyut, with two docking ports, larger crews, automatic refuelling, and duration flights of up to six months.

The failure of 29 July 1972 was the first, and perhaps least significant, interruption in these plans. The first of the military Salyuts was due to fly in April 1973, and arrangements proceeded as per schedule. But this was the same month as America's Skylab (though that in fact slipped into May). The Soviet planners decided to bring in the station that was backup to the 29 July launch and fly it at the same time as Skylab and Salyut 2.

The USSR would thus have two stations in orbit to America's one! Thus the scenario as it looked in early April 1973:

3 April: launch of Salyut 2
mid-April to mid-May: occupation by Pavel Popovich and Yuri Artyukhin
1 May: Skylab launch, followed a day later by Apollo
11 May: launch of Salyut 3 (civilian)
mid-May to mid-June: occupation by Alexei Leonov and Valeri Kubasov.

Landing windows for the first Salyut were from 17–27 May and for the civilian one from 7–19 June. Although the military flights were generally in the two-week class, this one might be exceptional, in order to match Skylab and the various landing lines.

Not that the USSR was under any misapprehension as to what Skylab was all about. It was a big project. The Americans had, in an uncharacteristically crude manner, simply converted the upper stage of the Saturn V into the giant empty shell of a space station. To the front they fitted a docking adaptor and a solar observatory based on components of the old lunar module. Its weight was no less than 90 tonnes, length 36 m, volume 361 m^3. It would fly nearly 400 km high. The astronauts got a wardroom, showers, even their own bedroom. The interior was so vast that it would be used to test out the Manned Manoeuvring Unit rocket backpack – which had been planned for use outside in open space! Three Apollo missions were set to fly up to it – one of 28 days and then two of 56 days. Both targets were way beyond the Soyuz 11 achievement. It was a dramatic and ambitious project, worthy of the nation that built the Hoover Dam and the Moon project; and the USSR felt it deserved a convincing response. Certainly their political judgement, so often wrong, was not at fault here.

So it was that on 3 April 1973, Baikonour reverberated to the rumble of the D-1 putting aloft Russia's second space station, Salyut 2. It soon entered orbit of 215 by 260 km, 51.6 degrees, 88.9 minutes.

During the 20th orbit, Salyut's motor fired and the station raised its perigee 15 km, placing it in perfect orbit for a rendezvous on 9 April. Observers stood by for Soyuz 12.

On 8 April, however, a further burn took place on the 83rd orbit, raising the orbit to 261 by 296 km, 89.9 minutes. This was high for a rendezvous, unless the Soyuz could manoeuvre to new high altitudes. The new orbit still gave rendezvous windows every five days – 14, 19 and 24 April. These manoeuvres puzzled observers and confusion was compounded by the fact that they could not pick up Salyut's signals – they had not yet realized that Salyut was transmitting on different (military) frequencies. Either way, a series of statements of Cosmonautics Day, 12 April, on the value of orbital stations, only added to the feeling that a manned launch was not far away.

It seems that 14 April was to be the critical day. A manoeuvre was planned for when Salyut 2 crossed the Atlantic en route to overflying the waiting Soyuz crew on the pad at Baikonour. The plan was that a signal would be sent by the ground tracking ship up to Salyut 2 to tweak it into exactly the right orbit.

The signal was sent from the tracking flagship *Cosmonaut Yuri Gagarin* then at sea off Newfoundland. However, far from gently nudging Salyut into the right orbit, the manoeuvring engine turned on and concluded its burn in a violent explosion, throwing Salyut into a mad tumble, ripping off the solar panels, blowing away the antennae, and crippling the station's power supplies and communications. Salyut turned end over end, and, soon, ground observers could spot it flashing in the sky as one side, then another, shone in the sunlight. Had cosmonauts been on board, the explosion would have destroyed their living quarters and killed them outright.

The explosion was at once recognized as terminal to the mission. Within hours, the *Yuri Gagarin* had sailed for Havana, Cuba. At Baikonour, cosmonauts Pavel Popovich and Yuri Artyukhin climbed out of their cabin, dejectedly took off their heavy spacesuits and stood down.

The 14 April blast raised the orbit still further, but because it was unstable it was clear that Salyut 2's orbit was not going to last long. Decay in fact occurred after 55 days and Salyut 2 fell out of the sky on 28 May. The real question was then: how would the Soviet Union explain its untimely demise?

Soon after 14 April the USSR actually engaged in one of the few instances of spreading disinformation about a mission. On 18 April it was stated that it was never intended to man Salyut 2. Salyut 2 was, the world was told the next day, testing equipment for the joint Soviet–American space flight! But on 28 April, the conclusion of Salyut 2's mission was officially announced: 'The information gained will be used in creating new space vehicles' [32]. The word 'successfully' was not used in the end-of-mission statement.

Still, the tone of Moscow's announcement was far from depressed, as if they knew they still had another card to play. For Moscow's sake it was just as well, for the postponed Skylab launch was just 16 days ahead. In fact, the second Salyut of the series lifted off on 11 May, watched anxiously by its slated crew, Alexei Leonov and Valeri Kubasov. It reached orbit – a standard civilian Salyut, one of 214 by 243 km, 51.6 degrees – but that was the most it could do. The first transmissions from the craft as it sailed high over the Pacific Ocean told the ground that it had been crippled by a massive systems failure.

So total was the failure, and so immediately obvious, that the station was hastily given a Cosmos designation (Cosmos 557). It crashed to Earth on 22 May. It is still not known exactly what happened.

The appearance of Cosmos 557 did not pass unnoticed in the West, not least because of the nature of its orbit, its size when observed from the ground, and its use of the traditional manned frequencies, like Salyut 1. Initially it was mistaken for an unmanned Soyuz – perhaps flown up to inspect the doomed Salyut 2? Another theory was that it was a backup to Salyut 2. It was not until later, when the dual military/civilian nature of the programme was clear, that it emerged that there were two separate programmes brought together in time in the hope of upstaging Skylab.

America's station nearly went the way of Salyut: one of its solar panels was ripped off in launch and the other jammed shut. It was underpowered and overheated. In a heroic mission, astronauts Conrad, Kerwin and Weitz docked with the station on 26 May, spacewalked along its hull, used a giant clippers to free the jammed panel and erected a protective cover over the overheating central section. The power surged in, the station cooled to the bearable, and they themselves went on to fly 28 days aboard. In the autumn, astronauts Bean, Garriott and Lousma collected tons of information and research on a 59-day mission. In the winter, novice astronauts Carr, Gibson, and Pogue set up an 84-day record [33]. Skylab triumphed: Salyut was in ruins.

So by early June 1973 the Russians had lost three orbital stations in the space of a year. It was now two years since a Russian had even flown in space. Ironically, it was the Americans who offered a way out.

AMERICAN LIFERAFT

1972 was a year of *détente* between the United States and its Communist adversary, following the improved relations between the US and China that resulted from President Nixon's visit there in 1971. Although the reasons for *détente* are not strictly relevant here, it is worth mentioning some factors in the equation. These include the USSR's desire for Western technology, the United States' need to sell wheat, and a grain shortage in the Soviet Union. After Frank Borman and Neil Armstrong visited Moscow and after some Soviet cosmonauts visited the United States, a space journalist floated the idea of the joint American—Soviet space flight. No one could think why not.

Pressure for a joint flight was stronger from the United States to start with, a position which was ultimately to be reversed. Early in the 1970s NASA was losing one mission after another to Congressional budget cuts. Five lunar missions were cut, as was a second Skylab. The problem was that the spaceships and hardware had already been built.

From NASA's point of view, a joint flight held three distinct advantages. It used up at least one of its surplus spaceships. Second, there would be few funding difficulties, as the President and many members of the Congress saw the exercise as politically desirable. And third, with Apollo ending in 1974 and the next programme (the Shuttle) not due till 1978, it would at least bridge a gap during which no Americans would otherwise be flying in space.

So it was that in February 1972 NASA and the Academy of Sciences agreed on an Apollo docking with a Salyut in 1975. It would be the first Salyut with two docking ports — Soyuz would arrive at one end and Apollo at the other. A detailed programme was agreed in April 1972 [34].

Salyut would go up on 10 June 1975. Soyuz would follow on 11 June. Apollo would be launched on the 14th and dock on the 15th. Three American astronauts would work aboard Salyut with two Soviet colleagues for three days till the 18th. The Soyuz crew would remain aboard while Apollo would fly independently and then return.

The plan was ratified in Moscow on 24 May 1972 by President Nixon and Prime Minister Alexei Kosygin. Yet only a month later the USSR withdrew the Salyut part of the mission. A two-port Salyut would simply not be ready in time, they said. The linkup would have to be between Apollo and a two man Soyuz instead. This was a much less ambitious project. Shatalov and Yeliseyev were touted as the pilots.

NASA announced its crew to man the Apollo—Soyuz Test Project (ASTP as it was now being called) in January 1973 [35]. Commander was to be Thomas P. Stafford of Apollo and Gemini fame; and the other members were Donald K. Slayton, the only Mercury astronaut who had never flown, and newcomer Vance Brand. But the USSR held off a final crew announcement.

In retrospect it is easy to see why. Their main crews were tied down in the upcoming double Salyut mission. The crews were finally announced on 4 June — after it was clear there would be no space station mission. The prime crew was announced as Alexei Leonov and Valeri Kubasov, who had been waiting for a mission together for two years.

The spring disasters compelled a rethink in the space programme. The next station would not be ready till the summer of 1974, and it would be a military one. The military crews were simply reallocated till then. ASTP would follow in July 1975, a year later still. That still left a hiatus till the summer of 1974, or a total of three years since Salyut 1. For reasons of morale if nothing else this gap would have to be bridged.

So a four-stage requalification programme for Soyuz was ordered up. There would be two unmanned tests and two manned. Of the two manned tests, one would be a two-day test of the new redesigned Soyuz ferry on its own. The second would be an eight-day solo scientific test flight, carrying an astronomical package similar to that fired aloft on Cosmos 557, called 'Orion'. These tests were scheduled for July 1973 and October 1973, before the winter.

Once again, new training groups were formed. No fewer than eight men were assigned to Apollo–Soyuz, as follows:

Prime: Alexei Leonov and Valeri Kubasov
Reserve: Anatoli Filipchenko and Nikolai Rukhavishnikov
Backup spacecraft: Vladimir Dzhanibekov and Boris Andreyev
Reserve: Yuri Romanenko and Alexander Ivanchenkov

And for the Soyuz requalification, the assignments were as follows:

Soyuz 12 prime: Vasili Lazarev and Oleg Markarov
Reserve: Alexei Gubarev and Georgi Grechko
Soyuz 13 prime: Pyotr Klimuk and Valentin Lebedev
Backup: Pilot not identified, Vitally Sevastianov

Pyotr Klimuk was the first of the Young Guard to get a flight and a member of this group stood in for him, although he never flew in the end. Valentin Lebedev got his assignment within months of joining the cosmonaut team – proof indeed that this crew had been put together at short notice.

The first unmanned requalification flew from 15–17 June 1973 and went perfectly under the cover of Cosmos 573. The manned flight was planned for a month later and tracking ships took up position on 15 July. Rumours of an impending launch circulated, but Soyuz did not fly [36]. At the end of July the fleet dispersed. The second Skylab manned mission took off on 28 July and attention switched once more to Houston, Texas.

Soyuz 12 finally did lift off on 27 September, just two days after Bean, Garriott and Lousma came down. The two month delay probably had little to do with the Skylab schedule or any desire not to be flying at the same time as their rivals: more likely there had been a serious countdown hitch at Baikonour in July forcing a two-month delay.

Vasili Lazarev (1960 group) and Oleg Markarov (1964) had been selected for this demanding mission. Their task was to put the redesigned Soyuz through its paces and come back alive after two days. They were to restore confidence to a faltering programme. If successful, space station flights could begin anew the next year; if not, there would be a serious question over the USSR's ability to fly manned operations around the Earth at all. Although both members of the crew were new cosmonauts, they had more experience than that bare fact might indicate: both had stood in as backups — to Voskhod 1 and Soyuz 9 — important flights by any standards. Lazarev had been nearly ten years in training — having applied for the 1960 group and then twice being selected, in 1964 and 1966. He had unusual skills: a flair for high performance aircraft and expertise in aviation medicine. Oleg Markarov was a 1957 graduate from the Bauman Institute, where he met and married another engineer.

They boarded their capsule wearing new lightweight space suits, suits that were tight, stylish, and a close fit. Liftoff was 1.18 p.m. and Soyuz 12 went into an initial orbit of 194 by 249 km, 88.6 minutes, but at 7 p.m. Vasili Lazarev took the craft up to 326 by 345 km, 91 minutes — the highest Soyuz had ever gone.

The crew spent nearly all their time testing the manoeuvring system and navigation methods and the basic functioning of the craft. But they did have some time to run tests with cameras and spectographic filters to look at below-ground-level ores and water, drought and disease, and the maturity of crops.

In the launch announcement Tass made it clear that only a two-day flight was planned, sensibly avoiding undue speculation resulting from the flight's brevity. So it was that on 29 September Vasili Lazarev brought his craft down to a featherbed-soft touchdown in a clear autumn field 600 km southwest of Karaganda.

OBSERVATORY BEYOND THE EARTH

The two men, jubilant with their modest triumph, were flown at once to Moscow to be greeted by Vladimir Shatalov. Confidence was creeping back. But it was a sorry state of affairs for the USSR when a two-day test flight of a six-year-old spacecraft was considered an achievement. Russia had at this time only 5000 man-hours in space, compared to America's 16 000. Russia had flown 34 cosmonauts on 19 missions, the American 64 astronauts on 29.

Still, the pace was beginning to quicken. One problem which needed to be solved if long duration flight was to take place, was the ability of Soyuz's systems to function in long periods in orbit when linked up to an orbital station. How would the capsule endure the hot and the cold, the micrometeorites, the vacuum, and how would its stored fuels hold out? To test this out, Cosmos 613 was launched on 30 November. It was recovered on 1 March after 60 days, flying 270 by 385 km, the height selected for a civilian station.

The second stage of the manned Soyuz requalification took place later than planned. Scheduled originally for October before the winter snows, Soyuz 13 had slipped two months because of the delays that had grounded Soyuz 12. Soyuz 12 soared into a wintry Kazakhstan sky on 18 December with two of Russia's youngest cosmonauts on board, designer Valentin Lebedev and Young Guard Pyotr Klimuk. Both were 31. Klimuk was the first of the Young Guards to fly: his credentials were unsurpassable. He had been one of the youngest members of the Communist Party at 20 and a cosmonaut at the tender age of 23. His active involvement in constituency political affairs also helped him get the assignment.

Pyotr Klimuk and Valentin Lebedev were not the only men in space, for they joined America's Skylab 4 crew, then a third of their way into their marathon 84-day mission. It was the first time two crews of separate nations had ever been in space at the same time, though they never had direct contact.

Soyuz 13 rapidly manoeuvred into a stable orbit of 225 by 272 km. It brought with it two key experiments: Orion 2 and Oasis 2. Both were derived from Salyut 1 tests, and both were to have flown on the stations of the previous spring.

Orion 2 consisted of two telescopes, one standard and one ultraviolet, designed to study both the Sun and the stars. Together, said Moscow they constituted 'a powerful observatory beyond the Earth's atmosphere'. Oasis 2 was a biological container in which chlorella and other plants were cultivated. It was a closed eco-system. It looked at the possibility of biological processes producing protein for a long flight.

Moscow announced that the flight was completed on 25 December, though not before the cosmonauts had spent some time using their telescopes to try to pick up Comet Kohoutek as it rushed towards the Sun. They came out of orbit early on the 26th. Reentry took place over the Caspian Sea and took 8 minutes. The parachute popped open on schedule and the next 14 minutes were the most hazardous of the flight. In the landing area, a snowstorm had been whipped up by strong 8 m/s winds. Low, snow-filled clouds darkened the landing area. The blizzard meant that the ground crew could not see what it was doing, and the temperature was $-8°C$. Contact with the cosmonauts was lost.

This ugly situation did not last long. The cone-shaped capsule came to rest in a snow-drift. Its beacon guided in the rescue crew, who airlifted out Klimuk and Lebedev. They were decorated for bravery in the Kremlin on the 29th.

SALYUT 3: MEAGRE HARVEST

Now that the requalification was apparently completed, observers awaited the early launch of the Salyut 3 station. But it did not appear till 25 June. It was probably planned for earlier; for, if not, Soyuz 13 could have been held off till springtime rather than face such hazardous weather. All the same, another Soyuz mission was flown in April 1974, to become the final part of the four-stage retesting process. Cosmos 638 orbited for three days at 195 by 326 km from 3–6 April. The need for this last test is obscure.

But there was nothing wrong with the launch of Salyut 3 in June. It settled into the low orbital designated for military stations at 219 by 270 km. Observers stood by to await the long-expected manned linkup.

This time they were not disappointed. 'It was a soft docking!' reported back veteran Pavel Popovich early on 5 July. With fellow crew member Yuri Artyukhin he had guided his Soyuz 14 through space for 32 hours with pinpoint accuracy. They had lifted off at night on the 3rd and took over a day to close in. Both were aged 43: Popovich, the veteran of the Vostok 4 flight of 1962, and Artyukin, graduate of the Zhukovsky Academy in 1958 and cosmonaut since January 1963.

By 8 July Tass was able to report that Salyut 3 was in full working order. The cosmonauts were studying the Earth, solar radiation and the polarization of sunlight. Creature comforts on board included a refrigerator, TV, tape recorder, casette library, exercise conveyor belt, and collapsible writing table. A large boom TV camera was erected outside the craft but the results were hazy and fuzzy. Apart from that, reports on what the crew were actually doing were scarce.

There is some reason to believe that the actual design of Salyut 3 (and 2 and 5 as well) was somewhat different from its civilian counterparts, particularly since no identifiable pictures of this version were ever published. From official sources alone it is known that the military version is 2 m shorter and that it consists of two cylinders rather than three. The transfer unit, presumably, is missing. This suggests that there is a docking unit at the rear port and that the fore port was taken up by the recoverable capsule which appears later in the story.

Soon after, it was announced that the crew were half-way through their flight. The first scheduled landing window was 15—27 July. The only experiments which were announced had to do with a solar telescope, a spectograph to examine the effects that aerosols had on the atmosphere, bacteria cultivation and water recycling.

Early on 19 July, on day 16, Pavel Popovich and Yuri Artyukin clambered into their Soyuz 14 ferry and at 9.03 a.m. cast off. They were back on the ground by lunchtime only 200 m from the prearranged spot.

All had gone like clockwork. It was the first time the USSR had completed a full space station mission. The bad memories of previous years began to recede. At the time few people paid much attention to the lack of information about what the crew were actually doing, or why details of Salyut had not been released. Getting through an entire mission from one end to the other was considered an adequate justification in itself.

'PRACTISING NIGHT LANDINGS. . .'

Suspicions that there would be further developments associated with Salyut 3 proved correct when, late on 26 August, Soyuz 15 took to the skies. The sun was setting and the silhouette of the gantries cast long shadows across the evening Baikonour landscape.

Two new cosmonauts were soon in orbit, and mission commander Gennadiy Sarafanov, 32, at once put Soyuz 15 into a chase orbit of 254 by 275 km, 89.6 degrees. As the pursuit got into its stride, the Soviet publicity machine pulled out all the stops. *Soviet Weekly* was a typical example:

> New visitors for space station. All is going well with the latest Soviet manned space shot, as Soyuz 15 pays a visit to the Salyut 3 station which has been orbiting since June. [37]

There were pictures and films galore. Pen portraits of the crew appeared all over *Izvestia* and *Pravda*. Sarafanov was the second member of the Young Guard to get a flight — he too (like Klimuk) had joined that unit at the age of 23. His flight engineer was, by way of contrast, 48. Lev Demin, who had been a military research officer since 1956, was one of the engineering intake of 1963. He was probably one of Salyut 3's designers. At a personal level, interest focussed on the fact that he was a grandfather: his married 26-year-old daughter Natalya had a baby boy, Vladimir. He was the oldest man to fly, and after the flight he was to emerge somewhat improbably as the President of the USSR Stamp Collectors' Association.

The blaze of publicity indicated a longer flight than Soyuz 14. The landing window was in fact from 15—25 September, giving a mission of 19—29 days: the intention may well have been to equal Soyuz 11.

Even as the Western press was digesting all this data, the Soyuz 15 mission was in serious trouble. As always, the main part of the mission was carried out automatically. Information on the trajectories of both Soyuz and Salyut was fed into the onboard computer: the computer then commanded the engines to fire to bring Soyuz into line for docking. But despite repeated firings, Sarafanov and Demin looked on in mounting frustration as Soyuz failed to close the distance. More and more fuel was being used up and Salyut was not even in sight. The computer data and the resulting orbits simply were not matching.

So, early on the 28th, Sarafanov called off the rendezvous. Like a submarine on silent running and awaiting depth charging, he had to power Soyuz down to save electrical power. Soyuz 15 eventually came down just before midnight. It was drizzling in the recovery zone 45 km from Tselinograd and the fresh rain sweetened the smell of the ripening corn of the country's bread basket. Cloud cover was low and helicopters made out the blinking lights of Soyuz 15 descending. The rescue crew met the cosmonauts 17 minutes later.

No one knows exactly what went wrong. At the time, the crew were said to be testing out a new manual means of rendezvous. Then, later, they were said to be testing out a new automatic means of rendezvous designed to pave the way for automatic spaceship docking and refuelling! In the end, computer trouble and fuel shortage proved decisive.

Soyuz 15 could probably have been written off as a random interlude, were it not for the fact that over the next ten years no fewer than four similar rendezvous failed in a similar fashion. Fuel shortage contributed to three of these failures. This was to remain a basic weakness in Soyuz, which was a spaceship originally designed for a man-on-the-Moon programme and not as an Earth orbit chase vehicle. The consequences of this fundamental change in purpose were now being faced.

In the period immediately following the crew's return, the Soviet press devoted an unusual amount of effort to covering up the failure of the mission. This time it was more than usually unconvincing. Three theories were advanced by Tass. No docking had ever been intended, it was claimed. Then, the purpose of the mission was to test the psychological compatibility of a 32-year-old and 48-year-old in orbit. Finally, even more incredibly, they were 'testing' emergency landings by night!

On 23 September a capsule was undocked. It returned to Earth and was recovered. On 24 October, Salyut 3 pushed its orbit back up to its operational altitude of 268 by 299 km. On 25 December, after 2950 orbits, *Pravda* announced that the mission had been abandoned. At the end of January 1975 the station burned up over the Pacific Ocean.

Analysed in scientific terms alone, the results were meagre. The short period of human occupancy (two weeks accomplished, over five weeks planned) indicated that Salyut 3 was less a manned orbital station than an automatic space station to be visited occasionally by cosmonauts.

Salyut 3 did carry what was described as 'a TV system designed to orientate the station to the Earth for long periods to obtain information on natural resources' [38]. It is possible that the flight was principally designed as a test of military surveillance systems. The first crew set the system in order and let the TV system take over once they left. And when all the data was collected it was parachuted down in the recovery capsule – one probably derived from the Cosmos programme. In this sense, Salyut 3 may have been more successful than Tass would have cared to explain.

Yet even as the Salyut 3 mission was drawing to a close, the Apollo–Soyuz project was coming closer and 1974 was a year of hectic activity. July 15, 1975 had been agreed as the launch day. The Americans were busy constructing the docking unit – a 3.15 m long, 1.42 m diameter, 5907 kg box-shaped tunnel. Cosmonauts were regular visitors to Cape Canaveral and Houston; American engineers and astronauts were seen in Star Town. Together they worked on the problems of pressures, optical and radar methods of navigation, and docking and tracking.

What with all the Salyut and Soyuz mishaps, the USSR felt that success was at a premium in the upcoming ASTP. They must be seen to be at parity with the United States. Nothing was to be left to chance. While the Americans allocated six astronauts and one spacecraft, the Russians allocated eight cosmonauts and three Soyuz. One was for a technical test before the flight; one was for the mission itself; and another was to stand by as reserve.

The pre-mission technical test took place from 2–8 December, 1974. It was flown by Anatoli Filipchenko and Nikolai Rukhavishnikov and designated Soyuz 16. They flew the 142 hours profile planned for the ASTP and carried out 20 experiments, mostly relating to the docking tunnel, atmospheric pressures, and frequencies. The Soyuz 16 was tracked by the NASA network and communicated through Mission Control Houston.

THE GREAT COMEBACK

By the end of July 1975 Apollo-Soyuz had been carried out with goodwill all round and supreme efficiency on the Soviet part. Not only that, but two long duration missions had been flown, both breaking all previous Russian records. The Soviet space programme was riding high once more and indeed all the objectives of the first-generation Salyut had been fulfilled.

In December 1974 such a radical transformation hardly seemed possible. But the dying days of 1974 saw a new station put aloft, the Salyut 4. Its initial orbit was 235 by 270 km, but by 5 January it had lifted itself up to a circular orbit at 355 km. It was the first civilian Salyut since Cosmos 557 and Salyut 1, and was much improved.

Salyut 4 carried three large solar panels on rotating levers – the third being on the top of the body like the sails on a yacht. Inside, the main control panel had one seat, not two. Salyut 4 carried a garden, an Earth-observation camera, a water recycling unit, and a solar and ultraviolet telescope. The Earth camera, set in a huge cone in the floor of the main cabin, was the bulkiest single instrument and looked not unlike a hospital scanner.

It was a full two weeks before two cosmonauts climbed aboard Soyuz 17 to set out in pursuit. No sooner were they in their cabin than fog enveloped the launch area and the rest of Baikonour. It was a thick clammy fog and no one could see a thing. They went ahead anyway. It was 10 January. Soon they had left the mists and fogs behind and dawn greeted them as they entered orbit.

Alexei Gubarev was 43, a senior pilot from the 1963 intake. He had an explosive temper and liked to run spaceflights exactly his own way. Normally this would have disqualified him right away, but he had combat experience from the Korean War and superb navigational skills, and after what happened to Soyuz 15 they were very much in demand. Georgi Grechko, also 43, was a small chubby man with small eyes and asiatic features. He was quite the opposite of Gubarev: gentle, even-tempered, humourous, smiling and a favourite with Western correspondents. He was a senior designer and had helped build the Luna 9 Moon probe in the Korolov design bureau.

Alexei Gubarev judiciously used his thrusters to bring Soyuz 17 across 1500 km of open space into Salyut's docking nose. They nudged together and soon the crew were aboard and settling into a routine of work. In no time they had grown green garden peas in their garden, tracked forest fires in Africa, and pointed their telescope towards the Sun, the stars and galaxies. They watched the hatching of eggs in the biological container. 100 separate experiments were planned and carried out.

By 3 February, they had broken the 24-day record of their comrades Dobrovolski Volkov and Patsayev. Some minor medical problems had arisen. Both men suffered from colds and fatigue, the latter due to Gubarev's insistence on running the station timetable without too much reference to Earth.

Several new experiments worked out quite well. The water regeneration device meant they needed to carry less water aloft — they simply recycled the station's moisture for their own drinking. The 250 mm telescope took views of the Crab nebula and the star Vega. And the biology experiment carried bacteria, fruit flies and frog spawn. The final part of the flight was a survey of the land mass of the USSR, then in the grips of winter. A map of snow cover was compiled. The crew came down on 9 February after 30 days aloft. A large ringsail parachute lowered them gently onto the flat packed snow.

For Alexei Gubarev and Georgi Grechko it was a triumphant return. The jinx had been broken. Salyut 4 was the first flight for many years that actually broke new ground. They had stayed up a full month, collected a vast body of data, and done it all in rigorous winter conditions. No wonder the flight was called 'the great comeback' [39]. And even if their condition was described only as 'quite well' when they landed, they soon recovered fully.

FALLING LIKE A STONE

After the success of Soyuz 17, the next flight was expected to double the new record The launching of 5 April gave landing windows of 26 May to 7 June (for a mission of between 51 and 63 days). It may have been in their minds to break America's second longest record, which was then 59 days. Chosen for Soyuz 18 were the veterans of Soyuz 12, Vasili Lazarev and Oleg Markarov. They surely deserved a long flight after their earlier two-day hop.

Soyuz 18 lifted off on schedule and curved over towards the northeast. The strap-ons fell away and disappeared from sight. At 120 km the time came to drop the core stage and fire the upper section. But the explosive bolts failed to fire: the whole rocket began to tumble violently end over end!

Vasili Lazarev reported the problem at once, but ground control would not believe him. For some reason, telemetry did not indicate a fault. 'Abort, abort!' he screamed, 'cut us free!' Only after further pleadings and swearing was Soyuz blasted free from the gyrating rogue rocket. Soyuz began to fall like a stone.

Down it came and the G forces got harder and harder. It was a straight vertical descent, quite unlike a normal reentry. Just then Lazarev, realizing the craft was heading for China, began to ask for a predicted landing spot. $4G$, $5G$, $6G$. Three helicopter pilots were already in a Peking jail for a number of years for landing the wrong side of the border. $8G$, $9G$, $10G$. The cosmonauts' flesh sunk deep into their cheekbones. Each man now weighed a tonne. 11G, 12G, 13G. 'We do have a treaty with China, don't we?' pleaded Lazarev. 15G. Radio contact was lost. 16G — past the Soyuz design limit 17G: each cosmonaut now weighed a tonne and a half. 18G: the cosmonauts blacked out and the G meter jammed, bent.

The cosmonauts slowed down from 17 000 km/h to 200 km/h in four minutes. At last the G forces eased. The parachute popped out and filled. They were heading into the remote Altai mountains, a near-desert populated only by herdsmen on horseback. The sun had just set. Their troubles were only just beginning.

After 16 minutes aloft, Soyuz 18 touched down in snow — but at once began rolling down a steep mountainside. It bumped and jogged, and Lazarev and Markarov were violently thrown around. It crashed and smashed over the ground, and the two men screamed as they were flung about and battered. The capsule was heading towards a precipice.

They would certainly have died if it had plunged over into the valley, but the parachute lines snagged and tangled in some conifer trees and thorny bushes — and, miraculously, held. The two men, bruised, bleeding and with broken bones, climbed out in the darkness. What would they do? They were badly injured and needed help. Yet the chances were that they were in the Peoples' Republic of China. At best they faced an uncertain future. After an hour, a group of villagers who had witnessed the drama, approached with torches and lights. It was bitterly cold. To the enormous relief of Lazarev and Markarov, they spoke Russian. The border, however, was close [40].

Next day they were airlifted out. Lazarev came off much the worst of the two — reports said he was suffering from broken ribs, internal bleeding and concussion. He never flew again. The USSR told everyone that the crew were fine (which they were not) and explained the failure as being due to poor checking by the launch crews (which whilst designed to reassure American engineers preparing for ASTP probably had the opposite effect).

The failure of Soyuz 18 — later called charmingly the 'April 5th anomaly' (one wonders what Lazarev made of that description) — presented real problems [41]. Soyuz 18 was to have come home long before the Apollo–Soyuz flight, in fact by 7 June at the latest. The earliest the Russians could now get the next mission aloft was 24 May, which would give a return time of between 24 July and 6 August. This would mean running the mission during the Apollo–Soyuz flight. And they could not wait further, for the food and other supplies on Salyut 4 had a limited shelf-life. To add to the complications, July was the month of the commissioning of the new control centre to replace the old one at Yevpatoria in the Crimea.

The new control centre was in Kalinin, a city 200 km northwest of Moscow on the rail line to Leningrad. Quite why it is located there is a mystery. Although near Moscow, it is not part of the Star Town complex and in fact is some distance from it. Still, it provided size and sophistication not available before, with long rows of desks, screens and panels. At the bottom of the room, like at a cinema, were wall screens projecting images from launch control and the spacecraft, along with displays, diagrams and maps.

The State Commission on Space Flight weighed up the risks and decided it would fly Soyuz 18B during the Apollo–Soyuz. Preparations for a replacement mission went ahead frantically. The Soyuz 17 backup crew were pressed into training. Plans to spacewalk, part of the original brief, were dropped, as adding too much to the training load given to

Pyotr Klimuk and Vitaliy Sevastianov. They finished training on time and were in orbit on schedule on 24 May.

Later that evening Salyut could be seen crossing the western sky, a bright curving light in the dusk. Two minutes later a dimmer, faster light could be seen racing in pursuit. Late on the 25th, only one bright light could be seen: they had made it. It was the first time the Russians had ever put a second crew on an orbital station.

By 26 May Salyut had completed 2388 orbits and its two new crew members were bringing it back to life. By the 31st, they had circularized its orbit at a steady 350 km and had got the water recycling plant going again to the extent that they were getting 2 to 4 litres a day from it.

By early June, Klimuk and Sevastianov were fully into the mission routine. They exercised no less than two and a half hours a day — mainly on a bicycle, sent back regular television broadcasts, tried to locate oil deposits and shot star spectograms of Cygnus. The flight became so routine that it dropped lower and lower on the Moscow evening news and the day's events on Salyut were only mentioned at the end. But routine was, after all, the purpose of the flight.

By 24 June they had broken the record set by Gubarev and Grechko. No fewer than 30 pea plants had sprouted in the greenhouse. By 4 July Salyut had clocked up 3000 orbits and Klimuk and Sevastianov were busy forecasting the summer weather.

What the cheerful mission reports did not tell anyone about — and few knew about it till the flight was over — was the green mould problem. Transmissions picked up by American monitoring stations heard the two men complain from late June onwards that the station's humidity system was breaking down.

What was happening was simple but unpleasant: there was too much humidity in the air. As a result, the windows fogged up (a problem known to the Americans in Apollo), and, worse still, a green mould began spreading from the floor upwards. In early July, Vitally Sevastianov complained that it was half way up the wall. It must have made it uncomfortable to sleep in dampish sleeping bags. Pyotr Klimuk asked several times for permission to come home. He was refused every time. The need to set up a duration record was more important than mere physical discomfort. Every six days they asked to come home and each time they were told to soldier on. By the time the green mould had got near to the ceiling the eyes of the world had shifted to another enterprise altogether.

'IT'S A GOOD SHOW, TOM!'

In early July, preparations for the long-awaited Apollo-Soyuz mission reached a climax. There had been endless exchanges of astronauts to Russia and cosmonauts to Houston. The Americans had never really got used to the cold of Moscow's winter. The Russians looked — and were — extremely uncomfortable in the humid heat of the Houston summer. The Americans even got used to being bugged in their rooms in Moscow: it amused them more than angered them. At one stage in their rooms they complained loudly about the lack of coathangers: next morning they miraculously appeared.

Alexei Lenov and Valeri Kubasov flew down to the cosmodrome on 3 July. Soyuz 19 was moved out to the pad on 12 July, and the backup vehicle the next day. The

Americans flew their T-38 training aircraft, practised aerobatics, and rehearsed their Russian language lessons.

Press interest in the flight reached a level not known since the days of the Moon landings. In the West there was amusement and a certain disbelief at the notion of the old rivals getting together. Western news coverage was made easier by the principal characters involved — greying old-timer Donald Slayton getting his first flight aged 51, the straight-talking, completely bald Tom Stafford; and joking, easy-going Alexei Leonov providing a real-life Russian personality.

The Soviet press was obliged to advertise and announce the whole thing in advance. They made the best of this and announced plans to broadcast the launch live as 'a novel departure from the Soviet tradition'. Well they might. They made a virtue of necessity and ran the show with all the razmatazz of an American network doing the same thing. Full flight details were released some weeks ahead. Some early off-the-mark state enterprises even marketed Apollo-Soyuz cigarettes and perfume as exclusive one-off brands.

The flight got smoothly under way on the afternoon of 15 July. Alexei Lenov took Soyuz 19 up into a clear blue sky. A vanishing cottony vapour trail was all that could be seen over the steaming pad when it was announced that Soyuz 19 had safely reached orbit. The next step depended on the Americans.

NASA's astronauts were in fact asleep when Alexei Lenonov and Valeri Kubasov entered orbit. Once awoken, they watched a videotape of the start of their comrades' mission. They dressed, were driven to the pad and boarded what was to be the last Apollo. Like the Skylab missions, Apollo ASTP used the smaller Saturn IB rocket rather than the Saturn V moonrocket, but it used the Saturn V tower. It was perched on pad 39 on a special trellis tower. Long flames could be seen coming from the base of the Saturn and reaching down to the ground like a gas flame on a cooker upside down. Then it lifted skywards.

Late that night, the rendezvous chase was under way across the entire hemisphere. Apollo was 6000 km behind and closing fast. At 200 km altitude it was flying unusually low for Apollo, so low that Donald Slayton gasped, with probably just a little poetic licence: 'Those thunderclouds down below nearly reach up to us'.

By midday on 17 July, Apollo command module pilot, Vance Brand, peering through his docking module window, had spotted Soyuz 50 km away, with its red, green and white lights flashing. He braked Apollo's closing speed with a burn of 0.2 seconds. By 5 p.m. Universal time they were 150 m apart. Pictures taken by Apollo showed the winged Soyuz against the curving background of the Earth's horizon. Soyuz rolled, to align the communication systems. 'Remember to turn off your engines!' joked Leonov, as Apollo headed in for capture and docking, which took place over western France.

Not long afterwards Tom Stafford and Deke Slayton began the lengthy procedure of depressurizing the docking module to Soyuz's level. The cameras went on, pointing down the tunnel. It was like a pit rescue when men entombed for days are about to be pulled out.

So it was that at 8.17 p.m. the hatches opened and the smiling figure of Alexei Leonov could be made out in his communications soft hat and light overalls. He stretched forward his hand and the immortal and long-awaited handshake in space at last took place. Deke Slayton followed Tom Stafford into Soyuz where they joined Alexei Leonov and Valeri Kubasov for a dinner of borscht out of toothpaste tubes. The crews exchanged gifts, flags, toasts and pleasantries. Alexei Leonov played the perfect host. The good-natured *bonhomie* was interrupted by a brief message of congratulations from Leonid Brezhnev and an embarrassingly long telephone call from President Gerald Ford.

The two spacecraft stayed docked together for two days. There were four series of crew transfers. Tom Stafford took Moscow TV viewers on a tour of the Apollo cabin. Press interviews were given. There were some (fairly limited) experiments.

The hatches between Soyuz and Apollo were closed for the last time on the 18th. The spaceships separated the next day. Apollo drew 50 m away from Soyuz so as to eclipse the Sun, thereby enabling Soyuz to photograph the solar corona. They then redocked in a manoeuvre which had its moments, because the first time only one docking latch caught. Soyuz slewed around several times before docking hard again. Then they separated finally.

The landing of Soyuz on the morning of the 21st went as smoothly as the rest of the flight. Taking heart from the success of earlier live coverage, Soviet TV fitted cameras to their large Mil recovery helicopters. One of them picked up Soyuz high over the town of Arkalyk just after the parachute opened. Other cameras followed it down in the seven-minute descent. A stiff wind blew it across the brown steppes like a glider on a cross-country race. A whoosh of dust blew up as the retrorockets fired. It was over.

Mission control in Kalinin applauded wildly. The two cosmonauts emerged, signed the side of their capsule in chalk, chatted to pressmen, and were flown off. When mission doctor Yegorov heard that they had got only 15 hours of sleep since take-off six days earlier he ordered them to bed at once.

For the Russians, Apollo-Soyuz gave them parity with Apollo in the eyes of the world after six years of setback and disaster, during which time the Americans had truly conquered the Moon and flown three times to their own orbiting Skylab space station. Under the full glare of the world's press, the USSR had flown a mission to high standards of technical competence and had not been found wanting.

Apollo continued in orbit till 24 July. The instrument section of Apollo had been con-verted to fly a wide variety of Earth resources experiments and astronauts Stafford, Slayton and Brand spent the rest of their mission gazing down on icebergs, sand erosion in the Sahara, the Pyramids of Eygpt, anchovy fisheries, and carrying out electric furnace welding.

The *USS New Orleans* took the last Apollo out of the Pacific Ocean. Only a few minutes after the three astronauts had walked across the flight deck of the aircraft carrier, they were in the intensive care unit, poisoned. As soon as the parachutes had opened, astronaut Vance Brand had thrown a switch to dump any unused fuel still on board. But instead of venting outside, the fumes were blown back into the cabin. All three astronauts began to lose consciousness. Tom Stafford and Deke Slayton managed to get oxygen masks on, but Vance Brand was too late. Tom Stafford managed to revive him, but they only stopped coughing and spluttering once the hatches were opened up and the fresh sea air of the ocean blew in. The medium-term effects of the toxic poisoning were severe and the astronauts were not declared out of danger till the 28th. They left hospital on the 29th.

Apollo—Soyuz was a technical dead-end, though it did show how two countries operating very different technical systems could work together. Despite allegations to the contrary, the Russians probably learnt little about the American space programme and its technology, and nothing they could not have found out through the open technical literature. The Americans, by contrast, got a grandstand view of how the Soviet Union ran its space missions, warts and all.

Although the Americans had to design and build a special docking module, the adventure probably cost the USSR more financially. After all, they built no fewer than three spacecraft for the flight. There were numerous advantages to the Americans: it bridged a gap that was to last seven years betwen Skylab 4 and the first Shuttle; it enabled NASA to hold on to many good engineers and astronauts who would have otherwise left because of the lack of prospects for their work; and the Earth resources package on Apollo 18 would alone have justified the flight. But Congress would not have funded it were it not for the international aspect.

So Apollo–Soyuz probably owed more to a number of factors at work in the two separate programmes at the same time, than to any high talk of *entente cordiale*, though without that, of course, it could not have happened. After 1979, when American–Soviet relations took a nosedive, 1975 seemed to take on a certain period charm and innocence compared to the Cold War that followed.

General Alexei Leonov and his wife watch US President Ronald Reagan address the Soviet people on television on 1 January 1986. The president's address was followed by that of Mikhail Gorbachev to the American nation broadcast on both United States and Soviet television. Alexei Leonov was commander of Soyuz 19, the Russian part of the Apollo–Soyuz link-up in July 1975 – the first international space mission.

TURTLES ALOFT

The Mil helicopter crews which picked up Leonov and Kubasov were instructed to stay in the area to await the return of Soyuz 18 whose crew had, of course, been forgotten about amidst all the excitement. On 16 July, during a lull in the Apollo–Soyuz mission, they had spoken to Alexei Leonov as Soyuz 19 crossed their path 120 km below.

On 21 July — with the green mould problems now much worse — came the long-hoped-for moment when the cosmonauts were given permission to land. It was day 57. They had flown 900 orbits and they had spent their last days looking at solar wind, the northern lights, and Earth resources. They had photographed 8½ million square kilometres of Soviet territory. So great was the volume of research that it took them three full days to pack up. Boris Petrov announced that this would be the last manned flight to Salyut 4 and if they left anything behind it would stay behind.

Pyotr Klimuk, now aged 33, and Vitally Sevastianov, 40 (both had celebrated birthdays in orbit) eventually came down on 26 July. They had flown 63 days in a courageous mission and endured some hardship. It was the second-longest space flight ever.

By the end of July, Soviet scientists could afford themselves a certain degree of self-satisfaction. Visible parity with the United States, Salyut 4 achieving all its mission objectives, and two duration flights — all in the space of six months. After four years of disasters and problems, the worst was well over. As if to underline it all, Vitally Sevastianov was back on Moscow television with his own programme within a week of his return to Earth.

However, the flight of Salyut 4 was not yet over — indeed it was to fly in space a full 770 days, right up to February 1977, or well over two years. 770 days was, after all, the amount of time required for a manned flight to Mars. At this stage — August 1975 — the Soviet space programme was getting set for its second generation of Earth-orbiting stations, which would have two docking ports. This meant that, theoretically at least, it would be possible to keep space permanently occupied. One ship could arrive at one port while another could return from the other. This in turn opened up propects for regular refuelling of the station. Or put it another way, refuelling would be essential to keep occupation going.

Having looked at the mathematics and the logistics of keeping crews up in space, Soviet scientists concluded that Salyut itself would only be able to supply its occupants with enough air, water, food and fuel for about three months at a time. Thus was recognized the need for devising some kind of unmanned ferry that would rendezvous and dock automatically, bringing up fresh supplies.

Work began on it in early 1974 and Soyuz 15 had in fact tested the prototype automatic rendezvous device — an inauspicious start. The automatic Soyuz was to be called 'Progress' — an unimaginative title in the 'October 25 Machine Tool Factory number 17' tradition. Based explicitly on Soyuz, the orbital and command modules would be merged and the life-support systems would be removed. Progress would be dumped after it had delivered its cargo, and no return trip would be intended.

However the second-generation space station would not be ready till 1977 so the Progress was not essential until that date. The gap till 1977 was to be bridged by a second and last military orbital station, for which two prime and two backup crews had been trained. This would be the main focus for manned space activity till then, and these launches were set for the second half of 1976.

Rather than wait till the military mission was over, space planners decided to take advantage of Salyut 4's continued presence in orbit. Because of the green mould (the Salyut interior must have been unimaginable at this stage!) there was no possibility of manning it again, but there was no reason not to test out the technology that would be associated with the new Progress craft.

A two-stage test of the elements that would be flown on Progress was then commissioned. In both cases, recoverable Soyuz capsules were flown, but the prime purpose was to test the autopilot that had given trouble on Soyuz 15.

Cosmos 772 flew on 29 September 1975, on a three-day solo mission. The new autopilot behaved as it should, the capsule was recovered and the data was analysed. The second test, Soyuz 20, was targeted for Salyut 4 itself and took off from a wintry Baikonour on 17 November 1975.

Soyuz 20 was a rigorous test of the Soyuz/Progress autopilot. Two full days were devoted to the chase manoeuvres which took the following format:

Initial orbit	199 by 263 km
Rev. 11	254 by 286 km
Rev. 22	328 by 355 km
Rev. 34	350 by 359 km

One of the principal designers of the new system appears to have been Konstantin Feoktistov, for from Soyuz 20 onwards his name featured more and more in the Soviet press in articles associated with these new missions. Soyuz 20 was advertised explicitly as a cargo vehicle and the rendezvous on autopilot was, according to Feoktistov, 'a great new success for Soviet space nagivation'.

Once Soyuz 20 had docked, the USSR shut up completely about Soyuz 20 and Salyut 4. November went into December, December into January, January into February. There was not even an acknowledgement that the station still existed, and enquiries about Salyut were not even replied to. Then, out of the blue, at the tail-end of a news bulletin on 16 February 1976, came the news that Soyuz 20 was back on Earth. It had come down in the snow after 91 days aloft.

Soyuz 20 then was more than the test of the Progress autopilot. It did two other things: it tested the ability of the Soyuz capsule to survive 90 days in space without its fuel and thermal protection decaying. This test was essential if the long-duration Salyut was to work and if Soyuz was to tie up at one end so a crew could stay aboard a number of months. And second, it was a serious biological mission.

Soyuz 20 carried several turtles, 20 species of higher plants, drosophila fruit flies, cacti, corn and vegetable seeds. For the same reasons as they were used on Zond 5, turtles were considered reliable indicators of how men would survive space flight. Soyuz 20 again showed the traditional Soviet approach of not flying men until lengthy animal tests had been run first. Yet even while the data was being analysed, preparations were being made to put up the last of the military orbital stations. Like its predecessor Salyut 3, it was to encounter its share of difficulties.

SALYUT 5: BAD AIR

Four crews were allocated to Salyut 5, which reached orbit on 22 June 1976:

Crew	Prime	Backup
1	Boris Volynov	Vyacheslav Zudov
	Vitally Zholobov	Valeri Rozhdezhvensky
2	Vyacheslav Zudov	Viktor Gorbatko
	Valeri Rozhdezhvensky	Yuri Glazhkov

Boris Volynov's last and, so far, only command had been Soyuz 5 in 1969. Vitally Zholobov was a moustached oil engineer. Zudov and Rozhdezhvensky were both Young Guards. Zudov was a highly qualified parachutist and flier of military transports. Rozhdezhvensky was an expert on EVA (extra vehicular activity), something probably related to his experience as commander of the Baltic Sea fleet's diving rescue service. And Yuri Glazhkov (engineer, Young Guard) was a candidate for a Science degree for a thesis on EVA.

Although both flights planned were to be military ones, the Academy and the Space Commission decided to add a number of more civilian objectives. It was decided not simply to run two two-week missions. One reason could have been to avoid drawing attention to the manner in which Salyut 5 differed from Salyut 4 but was similar to Salyut 3. (At this stage it was not possible to detect the fact there were two separate types of programmes under way.) Second, there was good reason to persist with developing lengthier missions and perhaps break the hurdle of three months represented by Skylab 4.

Spacewalking was also added to the mission objectives. No Soviet cosmonaut had spacewalked since 1969 and it was a glaring gap. The EVA was scheduled for the end of each mission and the purpose was to retrieve materials left on the outside of the hull, materials which would have been exposed to radiation and micrometeorites [42].

Salyut 5 came at a time of extraordinary American achievements on Mars. Viking 1, after a year's journey, entered Mars orbit on 19 June. A month later its robot lander hovered down to a soft landing on the sandy deserts of the windswept planet and began to send back breathtaking pictures of an Arctic-like environment. Viking 2 followed on 3 September, touching down after a nerve-racking descent. Anything that would take the spotlight off these remarkable accomplishments would be welcome.

Soyuz 21 was planned as a 66-day mission, starting on 6 July and coming down on 10 September. The second mission, planned for 14 October, would fly to 27 December for a 73-day target and if the crew were able for it, 8 January, which would give a target of 85 days, or a day beyond the American record of 84 days. Both could be accomplished within the six-month design life of Salyut 5. But these dates remain only speculation as to what could have been done, for neither of these missions achieved them.

Boris Volynov and Vitaliy Zholobov were in orbit on 6 July and by midday on the 7th they had brought their Soyuz ferry to within 400 m of their twinkleing target. 'Hard dock', Boris Volynov reported on a crystal clear radio line as the two ships clunked together 40 minutes later.

As with the earlier Salyut of the military type, Salyut 3, there was noticeably much less data available on what the crew were doing. There were some major Soviet military manoeuvres in eastern Siberia in late July and spotting them could have been an important part of their work.

But there were scientific experiments. The cosmonauts had a guppy fish on board in a tank and they spent much of their time observing how it reacted to zero gravity. They had fish eggs in another aquarium. They tried to assess pollution in the atmosphere and whether aerosols destroy ozone. They forecast the weather and their advice was eagerly awaited, for Europe was in the throes of a severe drought all summer. Farmers scanned the skies in vain searching for signs of relief.

More significantly, Salyut 5 carried the first full battery of materials processing equipment into orbit — a prototype of the first space factory. Zero gravity and the exterior vacuum of space would together provide an ideal environment for testing out pharmaceuticals, magnets, electronics, optical glasses, tools and ceramics. A processing plant could manufacture specialized industrial equipment to a standard not possible on the ground. To operate it, the crew simply swung particular items for testing out through an airlock on the side of the main cabin. Salyut 5 carried four such experiments — Sfera (for melting lead, tin and cadmium); Krystall (growth experiments with potash); Diffusia (for making alloys); and Reaction (which melted nickel and manganese). The two cosmonauts soldered 15 mm wide stainless steel tubes.

SUDDEN RETURN

Then suddenly Radio Moscow announced that the cosmonauts were preparing to return to Earth. Normally this announcement is the prelude to six days of packing up and switching the station to automatic operation. But Boris Volynov and Vitaly Zholobov were on the ground no more than two hours later — near Baikonour itself (most unusual) and at night (like Soyuz 15). They had been up 48 days.

Boris Volynov and Vitally Zholobov held their post-flight press conference at Baikonour next morning. They reported that their flight had been 'interesting but complicated', the normal codeword to indicate that problems had arisen. Then *Izvestia* reported that they had suffered 'sensory deprivation'. And there was none of the usual fanfare that normally greeted returning cosmonauts after completing a successful mission. It was low down in the news reports and received little mention after about four days.

Other hints and reports leaked out to explain what seems to have been a hurried return. The most plausible explanation seems to have been that there was an 'acrid odour' in the air supply system, and subsequent events were in fact to bear this out. A bad smell, possibly poisonous, was a reasonable explanation of a hurried evacuation. But whatever it was appeared to be fixable, for it did not stand in the way of a subsequent mission to the station.

NORTHERN AUTUMN

Even as this work went on, an independent manned flight was in preparation. A backup spacecraft had been left over from the three allocated to the Apollo–Soyuz test project. It had waited on the pad in case Soyuz 19 had not come up to expectations. Now it was decided to fly it on a solo, once-off Earth resources mission. The docking tunnel was removed and replaced by a massive purpose-built camera from the German Democratic

Republic (GDR, or East Germany). Its bulk actually filled more space than the old docking unit.

The camera, known as MKF-6, weighing 205 kg, was the most advanced of its type in the world and was built by the Carl Zeiss factory in Germany, which had been manufacturing high-quality optical equipment since the nineteenth century. During the Second World War, no self-respecting Field-Marshal or U-Boat captain was seen without Zeiss binoculars around his neck.

The MKF-6 was to take pictures of the ground in strips 165 km wide in six light bands, using colours that could be stereoed together. Each cassette of film could take 16 million square kilometres. The pictures were to be analysed by cartographers, by river engineers, by geologists and by agricultural experts to assess the autumn crops. If the MKF-6 worked well, then it could be used on the next orbital station, Salyut 6.

It was the first time that foreign equipment had flown on a Soviet manned space flight, and only a day before it took off the Soviet Government announced it was inviting the other Socialist countries to send cosmonauts to the USSR for training. This decision was one that produced mixed feelings. Those favouring an expansion of international space links supported it; as did those who wished that the benefits of Soviet technology should be more widely available. There was a substantial lobby against it, however. For the trainers, it would mean training a whole series of cosmonauts, only half of whom would fly (each country sent two for one flight), and they would only fly once. This was wasteful. For mission planners, it meant running a succession of missions up to Salyut that had no engineering justification. So space flight planning was once again being determined by political considerations.

But those opposed to this development of the Intercosmos programme simply had to put up with it, for soon after, air force officers from Czechoslovakia, Poland, and the German Democratic Republic appeared for training in Star Town. Vasili Lazarev was put in charge of training, and Vladimir Shatalov, now responsible for crew assignments, put them in place for a series of flights due from 1978 on.

The Soyuz 22 flight took place against the background of quiet warm autumn weather with abundant sunshine and excellent lighting conditions. The commander was Valeri Bykovsky, on his first flight since Vostok 5, and engineer Vladimir Aksenov.

They flew into orbit on 15 September and rapidly manoeuvred into a circular orbit of 251 by 257 km, 65 degrees. It was the first time the 65 degrees pattern had been used since Voskhod 2, and it brought Soyuz over northern latitudes for the first time. It also overflew NATO's 'Operation Teamwork' in Norway at the same time ($64°N$) but that may have been coincidental.

Once Soyuz 22 was in orbit, Vladimir Shatalov announced that it would be short, solo mission — conscious that unless this were made there would be speculation that it was supposed to have some relationship with Salyut 5. Experiments began soon after arrival in orbit. Bykovsky and Aksenov turned their camera eyes on the Baikal–Amur railway in eastern Siberia and forests near the Yenisei. They looked at tidal zones in the Sea of Okhotsk; the salinity of the Caspian Sea; and acid rain in the GDR.

They came down on 23 September after eight days and with 2400 photographs. The fine weather had held, clear skies had prevailed, and it had been an 'Indian Summer' across the Soviet Union. Lengthening autumn shadows could be seen around the Soyuz 22 capsule when it came to rest on a field in the steppe.

BLIZZARD!

Salyut 5 remained aloft. Analysis of Soyuz 21 data suggested that the fault in the air regeneration system could be dealt with. There were compelling reasons to return to the station: the onboard camera was continuing to take film of military value and it was desirable to get it back. It would need to be packed into a special return capsule.

The next launch window opened late at night on 14 October, with landing windows scheduled for 28 October to 9 November (for a short mission) or 27 December to 8 January (for a longer one). Since Soyuz 21 had failed to reach its 66-day target, it was probably tempting to try to push Soyuz 23 to up to 85 days. Floodlights bathed the Baikonour cosmodrome in creamy light when Soyuz 23 went aloft and shot through the darkness. Watching cosmonauts shielded their eyes against the glare.

The flight proceeded normally the next day. Then Moscow fell silent, and bulletins on the two men – Vyacheslav Zudov and Valeri Rozhdezhvensky – dried up. It was a sure sign that things had gone wrong, and wrong they were. Very early on the 16th, Moscow announced that the crew had abandoned the linkup, had powered down the spacecraft, and would land at the first available opportunity.

An electronic failure had developed not long before the scheduled linkup. Vyacheslav Zudov had done his best to get Soyuz into a docking position by manual control, but had run out of fuel. At 3 a.m. he told a tense mission control that it was no use continuing further.

Zudov and Rozhdezhvensky knew that they would be coming in for a night landing, but they had no idea just how dangerous it would be. All during the day the weather had got worse in the recovery area. Snow began to fall, gales whipped up the snow, and temperatures plummetted. Late on the 16th temperatures were down to −17°C and falling.

The heat shield of Soyuz 23 was still red hot when its parachute lines came open and its beacons began flashing. But the six Mil helicopters already up in the air could not see a thing. They bucked the winds but despite full searchlights all they could see were flurries of snow. The winds whistled as Soyuz 23 was blown downwards – and it was crashing right down into a salt lake! It was Russia's first splashdown and it could not have taken place in more atrocious conditions.

Zudov and Rozhdezhvensky must have realized quickly that they were not in a snow-drift but adrift on a turbulent, choppy lake. They struggled out of their spacesuits into cold-water survival gear. After an hour, the prowling Mil helicopters found the Soyuz. Frogmen were dropped into the icy waters and attached flotation collars. They tried to get a line to the capsule but they failed. Amphibious vehicles tried to get through and they failed too. The cosmonauts got colder and colder as the rescue teams continued to flounder in the snow-swept darkness. And the winds howled on and on.

Eventually, after a long five hours, and with a sense of desperation, a line was secured, but the helicopter was unable to pull the capsule out of the water. Instead, capsule and helicopter were blown across a frozen swamp. Finally they restored control and the helicopter landed on solid ground. The cosmonauts, shaken, frozen and exhausted, climbed out of their capsule, were pushed into a helicopter and whisked away.

Ten hours after splashdown, mission control heard that the two men were safe. It was the nearest close escape since Voskhod 2 came down in the Urals. Zudov and

Rozhdezhvensky were decorated for bravery — as were the crews who rescued them. They deserved their medals.

VALVING THE AIR

Recovery of film cartidges from Salyut 5 was obviously an important mission objective, for Soyuz 24 was launched on 7 February 1977. Under the circumstances, this was not expected, for the next Salyut was due to fly in June, then only five months away.

Weather conditions had improved compared to those of the recent ill-starred flight. Patches of snow lay on the ground around the pad as Viktor Gorbatko and Yuri Glazhkov went aloft. They docked smoothly on revolution 19 the next day.

Mission controllers had long since decided to drop both a duration flight and space-walking as mission objectives. With Salyut 6 coming up, this could be done later. Soyuz 24 was limited to an 18-day tour. Since the recovery of the film was the principal objective of the mission, ground control would be satisfied if this was achieved. But what about the 'acrid odour' that had forced down Volynov and Zholobov the previous summer?

Western suspicions that bad air had caused such an early return was confirmed when the new cosmonauts failed to board Salyut 5 straight away. They spent a whole day still in Soyuz 24 before heading down the tunnel. This never happened before or since. Then, on the 21st, they carried out an entirely novel exercise — they completely renewed the air supply by dumping all the existing air out one end of the station and flooding in fresh air from the other. Not that Soyuz 24 was all about bad air and film cartridges: the cosmonauts repaired the computer on board; they grew mushrooms; they photographed glaciers.

The metallurgical experiments started by Zholobov and Volynov were pressed back into use. Steel pipes were soldered — and they later withstood pressures of 500 atmospheres. Seeds left behind during the summer were watered, and they duly sprouted. Fungus was grown on board: strangely, it grew into the most unpredictable of shapes rather than the normal. Gorbatko and Glazhkov used the on-board telescope. And they tracked atmospheric pollution.

Soyuz 24 made an uneventful return to Earth on 25 February. Viktor Gorbatko and Yuri Glazhkov came down in cloudy weather, strong winds and sub-zero temperatures, but they were quickly spotted and recovered. On the following day Salyut 5 ejected its film capsule. It was recovered at once, containing, presumably, data that was too bulky to go down in Soyuz and, presumably, so valuable that it required a special mission to collect. The swift return of the capsule meant that very newly-collected information could be analysed virtually immediately.

Salyut 5 burned up on 28 August 1977 after 14 months aloft. For the first time in many years, the skies were now officially empty of Soviet space stations. But the experience gained during the period of 1971—77 had been put to good use and the next Salyut would be a radically new step forwards. With a five-year life, two docking ports and provision for unmanned resupply, it would take space development into new areas never before imagined.

The years 1971—77 of the long haul back were slow, disappointing and frustating. Several real achievements had been marred by mishaps, recurrent failures and plain bad luck. But the lessons had been studied and analysed and put to good use for the next big step forwards. This time neither the cosmonauts or the designers — nor their paymasters, the Soviet public — were to be disappointed.

9

Into deep space

Whilst the centrepiece of the Soviet space programme during the 1970s was the establishment of Earth-orbiting space stations, the Soviet Union also conducted programmes for the exploration of the Moon, Mars and Venus. However the Moon exploration programme was abandoned for the time being in 1976, and no spacecraft was sent to Mars after August 1973. A successful series of Venera probes were sent to Venus throughout the period and showed no signs of abating even into the 1980s.

The Moon programme had its origin and purpose in the manned Moon race of the 1960s, and when that race was over and lost it too seemed to lose its *raison d'être*. The attempts to explore Mars were so chronically unsuccessful that not only were missions to the Red Planet suspended, but the USSR chose not to send any probes to the outer planets to match America's Pioneer 10 and 11 and Voyager 1 and 2. As a result the Russians did something they had never done before: they conceded defeat and resigned themselves to a second-place role in one area of the exploration of space that they were unable to carry out for themselves. The Americans were permitted unchallenged superiority and by the mid-1980s their probes had travelled the length and breadth of the solar system. Pioneer and Voyager had sped past Jupiter and swept past the rings of Saturn, and Voyager 2 even aimed for flybys with Uranus and Neptune. The world held its breath as one astonishing series of colour images unfolded after another, revealing strange worlds previously only guessed at.

Why was this? How did the USSR, traditionally the front-runner in every field of space exploration, manage to find itself in second place to its rival? It was all the more peculiar in the case of the Moon. When Apollo 17 astronauts Eugene Cernan and Jack Schmitt left the Taurus-Littrow site in December 1972 they knew they would be the last Americans to walk on the Moon for at least two decades, perhaps three. The Russians had the place to themselves from that moment on.

Several things, it seems, happened. It seems fair to speculate that in the 1970s there was much less money available to the Soviet space programme, compared to the 1960s, when no project was considered too ambitious or too expensive and few seem to have been turned down. The Academy of Sciences had to make do with less. Just as, in the United States, space spending was squeezed out by military, social and environmental projects, so the same probably also happened in the USSR. The debate on social priorities is less open in the USSR, but is none the less real. The critics who attacked NASA's projects in the United States as wasteful and unproductive probably had their counterparts in the Soviet Union: they too would have pointed accusing fingers at prestige projects that were low on scientific and economic returns. They would have argued that the country could not afford trips to the asteroids at the expense of weather satellites that were of more urgent domestic need.

Such criticism may well have been sharpened by the failure of the Soviet Union to win the manned Moon race. The Russians had made a heavy investment in the race, had lost, and had little to show for it. One of the main lessons they took to heart from this failure was not to compete directly with American projects — for fear of further unfavourable comparisons being drawn if things went wrong once more.

So in the context of reduced space spending, hard choices had to be made and painful decisions implemented. Some of these may have been made around the time of the reshuffling of Soviet space priorities that took place in January 1969. At that time the Salyut space station project replaced the Moon programme as the main thrust of Soviet cosmonautics. It was a visible project, economically attractive, and offered a real opportunity to get ahead of the United States in an area that was not the Americans' top priority.

If the space station project was to be the principal line of development, then the growth of military and applications programmes came second. The purposeful and regular expansion of the Meteor, Moloynia, Ekran and Raduga series all indicated a systematic attempt over a long period to develop applications satellites that would provide a known, or at least, predictable, economic return.

Flights into deep space came a poor third. They offered no tangible economic return, they were expensive, and they would be competing with a series of American missions that were lined up for several years ahead. Numerical evidence shows how deep space probes became less important. Twenty-three Moon probes were launched from 1959 to 1970, but only seven in the period 1971–76, and none thereafter for a decade. Eight Mars probes were launched from 1962 to 1973 and none for well over a decade thereafter. In fact these figures are an underestimate because they do not include launch failures. These were very prevalent before 1970, and only one is known of in the period from 1971 to 1984.

Venus probes alone kept up their former pace. There were nine launchings from 1961 to 1970, and a further nine from 1971 to 1983. The Venera series alone survived the purge that began around 1969. And noticeable by their absence are the planets not explored in this later period. America launched a probe to Mercury in 1973, and four to Jupiter and Saturn in the years 1972–77. The Russians tried nothing at all.

It is possible to speculate on the reasons for the virtual disappearance of the Soviet deep space programme. The reasons are somewhat different in each of the four cases under examination – the Moon, Mars, Venus and the outer planets. The Moon programme in effect was run to its natural conclusion – the hardware of Luna 24 of 1976 was little different from the Luna 15 that had circled the Moon in 1969. In effect, it was decided to fly missions that had already been designed and built. More positively, the later Luna series was complimentary to Apollo and could do things Apollo could not do. The lunar scooper, moonrover and orbiter did represent a credible 'alternative' programme to Apollo – and indeed was all the more necessary if the Russians were ever going to persuade people that there was no need to explore the Moon with dangerous missions that risked astronauts' lives.

The same was true up to a point with the Mars soft-landers. They were already in design in 1969 (two had been built) and for a country that had already made attempts to soft-land on the more difficult territory of Venus, soft-landers for Mars were both rational and logical. Using the D-le booster, which could send five-tonne probes to the Red Planet, a soft-landing could be achieved by the USSR long before the United States. In 1969 the Americans were capable only of smaller, flyby photographic probes. Its own Mars soft-lander, Voyager (renamed Viking) was originally planned for 1969 but that date was to slip and slip again. But it does not seem that any Mars probes were authorized after the end of the soft-landers – which would be after 1973. Because a planetary probe has a lead-in time of about four years, there was little point in cancelling anything that had already started: but if one was looking for economies it made sense simply not to run missions after a certain finite period in the future.

Venus alone remained a priority in a low-priority programme. First, it was the nearest planet and presented the fewest problems in terms of tracking and distance. Second, the USSR did have a good track record of success in exploring Venus, and this was something which could be used to advantage. Third, it was a low priority inside NASA. American plans incorporated only three probes to Venus in the 1970s – Mariner 10 (1973) and two Pioneer Venus probes for 1978. The Americans regarded Venus as biologically a dead loss – it was a boiling acid bath, whilst Mars offered chances of life and Jupiter and Saturn were virtually unknown. Any Soviet emphasis on Venus was not going to be challenged unduly by the United States. And finally, the preservation of a Venus programme (with two launches in each window) may have been consolation to scientists who saw all their other plans frustrated: it did at least keep some kind of deep space programme in existence.

Thus can one explain the nature of the Soviet deep space missions of the 1970s, or the lack of them. The need for economy, the desire to use up existing designs and hardware but not start up new programmes, the determination not to compete directly and at the same time with similar American missions – these three factors played their part. But they do not fully explain the lack of deep space missions. Even if the Americans had the plans for the outer planets, the USSR could have run low-cost flights that did not directly compete, like an asteroid rendezvous. Here, technical factors intervened.

TRACKING AND NAVIGATION

The Academy of Sciences knew in 1969 that NASA and its interplanetary section the

Jet Propulsion Laboratory (JPL) in California planned two deep space probes in 1972–73. Called Pioneer 10 and 11 they were small (260 kg), carrying only cameras and limited instrumentation. Pioneer 10 was to fly past Jupiter while Pioneer 11 was to take in Saturn as well. Two heavier, and much more sophisticated, probes were to follow in 1977.

Although the D-le would have been well capable of sending up a probe of at least this weight — it could send 5000 kg to the near planets, or about 500 kg to the more distant ones — this was not the problem. Difficulties with long-distance tracking were decisive.

Any flight to the planets would require a first-class tracking network, reliable long-distance navigation, and the ability of spacecraft to function over long periods in the intense cold of deep space. All these three demands created problems.

First, the USSR did not have a deep space tracking network of NASA's quality. NASA had several large dish antennae at strategic points around the world — in California, Africa and Australia. The USSR could not hope to provide the same coverage, with its land bases only in the northern hemisphere and the mobile naval tracking fleet.

Second, the Soviet record in long-distance space navigation was poor. Venera 1 and 2 had both packed up en route to their target; the same fate had befallen Zond 1 and 2 and Mars 1. The Americans had never had the same trouble. Long-distance space navigation depended on precise computer programming and the spacecraft's ability to track stars and the Earth and to point itself in the correct direction. The Americans were early to develop micro-circuits, or chips as they came to be called, and these had the advantages of lightness, flexibility, and sophistication. American computer technology became more and more advanced, spurred on by Apollo and the vast amounts of data its missions had to handle at critical speeds. By 1969 American analysts came to the belief that Soviet computer technology had fallen some distance behind their own, and that a gap of about two or three years had opened up. In retrospect, this assessment may have been about right. This gap was to double in the mid-1970s.

So the Russians may have realized that even if they were to launch their deep space probes successfully — and with the problems of the D-le sorted out in 1971 their chances would have been good — it would have been likely that their probes would not have managed to track their way across the cold emptiness of deep space to their targets and return useful data. In the early 1960s and with blank cheques from Khrushchev such a risk would have seemed worth taking, but in more cost-conscious times this was no longer the case. Flights to the asteroids and beyond would have to wait till better times.

IN THE SHADOW OF BLACK SEPTEMBER

When Luna 15 was smashed to pieces in the Sea of Crises in July 1969, Russia's elaborate plan to upstage Apollo by the first automatic recovery of lunar soil came unstuck. That produced its own disappointment and frustration. But Soviet scientists felt obliged to go on. First, because the series could produce a credible automatic programme for the exploration of the Moon; and second, because the series was important if the Soviet man-on-the-Moon programme was to be completed after all. Such hopes still existed up to the summer of 1971.

Inside the third generation of the Luna programme (Luna 15–24) were three separate models: the moonscooper, the lunar rover and the orbiter. They all used common components and the same base, and many of the parts were identical to those of the Soyuz lunar module design. The base was 4 m wide, consisting of four spherical fuel tanks, four cylindrical fuel tanks, nozzles, thrusters and landing legs. Atop the structure rested either the sample return capsule, or the lunar rover, or the instrument cabin for lunar orbit studies.

The successors to Luna 15 were ready to fly just months after the disaster in the Sea of Crises. The first probe in the programme, a lunar orbiter to scout out landing sites for future missions, was sent up by D-le on 14 February 1970. It crashed into the Pacific Ocean. Success was to elude the planners and designers until 12 September 1970 when Luna 16 was launched. Like Luna 15 it headed out moonwards on a slow four-day coast. Indeed right up to the landing, its characteristics were identical to that of Luna 15.

Despite the great media interest which Luna 15 had attracted, Luna 16 went virtually unremarked by the Western media. This was a pity, for Luna 16 was a remarkable technical achievement by any standards. But its flight coincided with what became known to the world as Black September. Four airliners were seized in the space of a few hours by Palestinian fighters: the aircraft were hijacked to a remote airstrip called Dawson's Field in Jordan. King Hussein's army moved in to crush the troublesome Palestinians who had taken refuge in Jordan ever since the Arab–Israeli War of 1967. Bloody and vicious fighting followed: the world looked on mesmerized.

Luna 16 entered Moon orbit on 16 September at an altitude of 110 km, 71 degrees, 1 h 59 min. Two days later it braked into an elliptical course of 106 by 15 km. Its final path was 15 by 9 km, identical to Luna 15's last erratic orbit and so low as to only barely scrape over the peaks of the Moon's highest mountains.

A descent was inevitable. Early on the 20th, as Luna 16 skimmed over the eastern highlands of the Moon, the retrorocket of the 1880 kg craft blasted on: Luna 16 began to fall. The critical stage had begun. Luna 16 was now over flat lowlands. Sophisticated radar and electronic gear scanned the surface, searching for a suitable landing place. The engine thrust was carefully modulated to prevent the craft from either falling too fast or drifting to the side.

At 20 m the retrorocket cut off and small vernier engines came into play. The craft was aligned, and the descent speed cut to zero. At 2 m, sensing the nearness of the surface, these too cut out. Luna 16 dropped silently to the airless surface, bouncing gently on its landing pad. It was down, safe and sound, on the Sea of Fertility, and the local lunar dawn had just risen. The surface was barren, flat and stony and marked only by a few small craters. Within hours, the USSR had announced its third soft-landing on the Moon – but said no more. Ground observers picked up strong signals, and suspected something as afoot.

They were not wrong. A quarter of a million miles away, a long drill arm swung out from Luna 16 like a dentist's drill on a support. It swung well clear of the base of the spacecraft, free from any area that might have been contaminated by the gases of the verniers. The drill head bored into the lunar surface and then scooped the grains of soil (weighing 100 g) into the container attached to the drill head. Like a robot in a backyard assembly shop, the drill head jerked upwards, brought itself alongside the spherical recovery capsule, and pressed the grains into the sealed cabin.

By the 21st, Luna 16 had spent a full day on the Moon. There was still no official indication as to its purpose. Jodrell Bank reported still more strong signals. In fact what

Luna 16 was doing was checking out its exact landing coordinates so as to give the best possible return trajectory.

27 hours after landing, explosive bolts were fired above the Luna 16 descent stage. On a jet of flame the upper stage shot off and headed towards the white-and-blue Earth hanging in the distance. It curved over, motor still purring, its radio pouring details from the four aerials poking out the side. The Sea of Fertility returned to the quiet it had known for eons. The descent stage was the only forlorn reminder of the brief visit.

The ascent from the Moon was so accurate that no course change was needed. The returning rocket — capsule, instrument container, fuel tanks and motors — reported back from time to time as it headed for a straight nose-dive reentry. The tiny capsule separated from the instrument and rocket package, plunged into the upper atmosphere, glowed red and then white as temperatures rose to $10\,000°C$ and as it hit forces of $350G$. Helicopters were already in the air as a parachute ballooned out. The capsule hit the ground and beacons began sending out a bright bleep! beep! signal as rescuers rushed to collect their precious cargo.

It was transferred to a plane and flown at once to Moscow to a laboratory for analysis. How the scientists ever got the soil container open is a mystery for the entire outer skin of the capsule may well have been welded by the intense heat of the fiery return. Once open, the golden grains of moondust poured out — loose lumps of blackish powder like very dark wet beach sand.

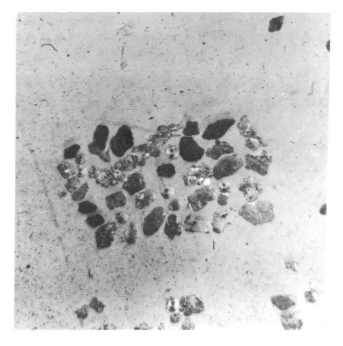

Samples of Moon rock brought back to Earth by the remarkable spacecraft Luna 16 that soft-landed on the lunar surface on 20 September 1970, and collected samples of the lunar regolith. This mission, heralded as the beginning of the 'decade of the space robot' went largely unnoticed by the West as the news media were preoccupied by the 'Black September' hijackings of four airliners to Dawson's Field in Jordan by Palestinian terrorists.

It was a tremendous triumph. The Luna 16 mission had gone perfectly from start to finish. The tricky stages of soft-landing, drilling, and take-off were just like the text book said they should be. 'It's the decade of the space robot!' heralded the Soviet press. The USSR made great play of how such flights were cheaper than manned flights like Apollo, how they did not expose humans to danger, and how versatile space robots could land just about anywhere. Lunar observatories would follow, and according to Georgi Petrov there would be a manned space station in orbit around the moon capable of sending down robot probes to the lunar surface [1].

For NASA and Western observers the real significance of Luna 16 lay elsewhere: it confirmed what many, but not all, of them had suspected was Luna 15's real purpose, namely that it was a real challenge to Apollo 11 a year earlier.

Russia did have good grounds to celebrate Luna 16. Some of the remarks about its low cost and versatility were exaggerated, and the sample of 100 g was tiny compared to the samples obtained by Apollo, each mission of which brought back well over 20 kg. But Luna 16 did represent a meaningful no-risk low-cost alternative to the Apollo programme, and in its small way contributed to the ultimate political undermining of Apollo in the eyes of American scientific sceptics and cost-conscious congressmen.

ROVING IN THE SEA OF RAINS

Any advantage that was gained by the success of Luna 16 was turned to double advantage just two months later by Luna 17. The moonscooper, pushed to the back pages by the eruption of political violence in the Middle East, had made little public impact. The same could not be said of its successor, put up on 10 November 1970.

Luna 17's mission was, at least for its first six days, apparently identical to that of Luna 16 and 15. A four-day coast out to the Moon was followed by lunar orbit insertion at 85 km, 141 degrees, 1 h 56 min. On the 16th, the onboard motor lowered the orbit to an altitude of 17 km.

Luna 17's target was nearly a hemisphere away from that of Luna 16. The entire western face of the Moon is dominated by a huge dark 'sea' which is called the Ocean of Storms. In its northwest corner is a semi-circular flat bay called the Sinus Iridium, or the Bay of Rains.

After only two days in orbit, and reflecting the bright sunlight of the setting sun, Luna 17 skimmed in low over the Jura mountains. The rocket fired. Luna 17 hovered as its radar searched for a suitable site. And down it came, as softly as a parachutist on a wind-free day. The long shadows of the structure stood out starkly towards the darkening east.

For two hours, Luna 17 reported back its position. Russia coolly announced its fourth soft-landing. A return capsule would be fired back to Earth the next day. Or so everyone thought.

Not so. Although this was not known at the time, the entire upper stage, which on Luna 16 was the return rocket, had been converted into a flat platform. On it rested the first vehicle ever designed to explore another world. It had eight wheels, looking like pram wheels, which supported a shiny metallic car in the shape of a bath-tub, covered by a kettle-style lid. Out of the front peered two goggle-like television eyes. Above them peeped a laser reflector and two aerials. It was an unlikely-looking contraption, on first impression more the outcome of a Jules Verne or H.G. Wells type of sketch rather than a tool of modern Moon exploration. But the wheels were ideal for gripping the lunar surface and less prone to failure than caterpillars. The lid could be raised backward to the vertical and on the other side were solar cells to recharge the batteries in the Sun's rays. There was genius in its simplicity.

The most dangerous part of the vehicle's journey was probably getting off the platform and onto the lunar surface. Two ramps unfolded at each end, so it could travel down the other way if one exit was block. The vehicle, to be called 'Lunokhod' or 'moon walker' weighed 756 kg. Its wheel base was 2.21 m by 1.6 m. With Lunokhod still sitting on the landing platform, ground control commanded the dust hoods to fall off its TV eyes. A television picture came back at once, showing the wheel rims, the ramp down to the flat bright surface, and the silhouette of the landing ramps. At this stage there was nothing for it but to signal to Lunokhod to go into first gear and roll down the ramp — and hope for the best.

So it was that at 7.28 a.m. on the morning of 16 November 1970, and carrying the hammer and sickle, a red flag and a portrait of Lenin, the moon vehicle edged its way down the ramp and rumbled 20 m across the lunar surface. Its tracks were the first wheel marks made on another world. Its TV cameras showed its every move. At one stage Lunokhod slewed around to film the descent stage which had brought it there. On day two it parked itself, not moving at all, lying there so that its lid could soak in solar energy for its batteries. On day three it travelled 90 m, and 100 m the following day, overcoming a 10 degree hill. On the fifth day, with lunar night not long off, it closed its lid, settled down 197 m from Luna 17, and shut down its systems for the 14-day lunar night. A nuclear power source would supply enough heat to keep it going till lunar daybreak.

The remarkable automated lunar roving vehicle Lunokhod 1, landed by Luna 17 on the Moon's surface in November 1970, which functioned for nearly a year, travelled over 10 km and sent back more than 20 000 pictures. It was a brilliant achievement in automatic space exploration.

The Soviet – and Western – press took to Lunokhod with an affection normally reserved only for friendly robot television personalities. There was unrestrained admiration for the technical achievement involved, for it was a sophisticated automated exploring machine. *The Times* of London called it 'a remarkable achievement'. 'A major triumph' said The *Scotsman*. The *Daily Mail*, in a front page editorial entitled 'Progress on pram wheels' gave Lunokhod's designers an effusive message of congratulations [2]. It was the main news story for several days.

TO THE PROMONTORY OF HERACLES

The control centre for Lunokhod was, like much else in the venture, a scene straight from science fiction. Five controllers sat in front of television consoles where lunar landscapes were projected on screens. The crew of five worked together like a crew operating a military tank. There was a commander, driver, engineer, radio operator and navigator.

Night-time on the Moon. Temperatures plunged to $-150°C$, and stayed at that level a full two weeks. Lunokhod, lid closed, and glowing warmly from the heat of its own nuclear radioisotope, rested silently on the Sea of Rains. It was bathed in the ghostly blue light of Earth as the mother planet waxed and waned overhead. Even as it stood there, laser signals were flashed to Lunokhod from the French observatory in the Pic du Midi and from the Semeis Observatory in the Crimea. They struck the 14 cubes of the vehicle's laser reflector and bounced back. As a result, scientists could measure the exact distance from the Earth to the Moon to within 18 cm.

To the east of Lunokhod rose a ridge and the sharp rays of dawn crept slowly over its rugged rocks early on 9 December. Had the moon rover survived its two weeks' hibernation? Within minutes, ground controllers knew it had. It raised its leaf-shaped lid and at once began to hum with life. Four panoramic cameras at once sent back striking vistas of the moonscape, full of long shadows as the Sun gradually rose in the sky.

After a day recharging, Lunokhod set out once more. The drivers on the Earth soon got into their stride and had the mooncar swivelling around, reversing, and traversing craters and slopes at will. One day it travelled 300 m, more than it had achieved in its first five days in November. And just before Christmas the camera eyes spotted in the distance a far range of mountains. It was the far peaks of the Heracles Promontory, part of the vast bay encircling the Sea of Rains.

For ground control it was just like being there. From the cosy warmth of their control post they could direct at will a machine a quarter of a million miles away. This prompted romantic notions in the minds of the earth-bound. Radio Moscow promised 'more Lunokhods, faster, and with a wider range'. Petrov spoke of mooncars that would collect samples and bring them to craft like Luna 16 for transporting home. Others would install packages on the Moon and carry radio telescopes around to the far side where there was radio peace free from earthside interference. Other probes would reach the lunar poles.

Such notions did not seem like daydreaming at the time. As the project proceeded, it became apparent that Lunokhod was not just a playful bathtub-on-wheels but quite a sophisticated machine. It carried a soil analyser called 'Rifma' which bombarded the surface with X-rays and enabled ground control to read back the chemical composition of the basalt-type soil. And from time to time a mechanical rod jabbed into the soil to test its strength.

Lunokhod did not only look moonwards. There were two telescopes on board — one to pick up X-rays beyond the galaxy and another to receive cosmic radiation. On 19 November it recorded a strong solar flare that could have injured cosmonauts had they been on the Moon at the time.

Lunokhod therefore contained within it several concepts: an exploring roving vehicle; a rock-testing mobile laboratory; and an observatory able to capitalize on the unique air-free low-gravity environment beyond the Earth.

Come the new year, 1971, Lunokhod was back in action once more and on 18 January drove back to the Luna 17 that landed it there. A spectacular photograph of the landing vehicle with ramps, and wheel tracks all about, reminded the world that Lunokhod was still there prowling about the waterless sea of the Bay of Rains.

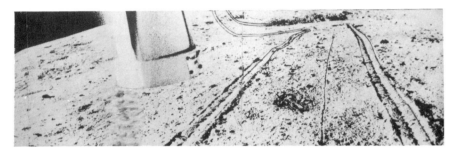

The TV cameras aboard Lunokhod 1 record the tracks made by its wheels in the soft lunar dust of the Sea of Rains.

By the fourth lunar day — 8 February 1971 — scientists were able to compile a map of that part of the Bay of Rains adjacent to Luna 17. On 9 February the mooncar survived a lunar eclipse when temperatures plunged from +150°C to −100°C and back to +136°C, all in the space of three hours. In March the craft drove around a 500 m wide impact crater in ever-narrowing circles. Lunokhod nearly came to grief on 13 April. It got stuck on a crater slope, and it needed full power on all the eight wheels to get it out again. It used up so much energy that it had to sit silently on the surface for some time, simply recharging. Later that month it ventured into a crater field full of boulders over 3 m across. Because of a nearby crater impact, all the black lunar dust had piled up against one side of the boulders as if a hurricane had swept through the area.

Early on 5 August, American astronauts David Scott, James Irwin and Al Worden flew directly over the mooncar in their Apollo 15 command module and Lunokhod's magnesium alloy frame glinted in the Sun. As it drove slowly, plodding across the moonscape, the two different Moon explorers were in striking contrast to each other.

Then suddenly, whilst hard at work on 4 October, Lunokhod's 'heart' — its isotope power source — gave out. Telemetry reported a rapid drop in pressure inside the hermetically sealed cabin. The wheels halted, the TV pictures faded, signals ceased. It was the end.

Considering that Lunokhod had been designed to function for only three months, and had worked for nearly a year, its mission was a cause of much congratulation. It was the USSR's most brilliant achievement in the field of automatic space exploration. Crude in design, superbly built, with a reliability the perfectionist buffs in NASA would have envied, it endeared itself to the public at large and became the most exciting robot of its day. In statistical terms alone, its achievement was impressive. It had travelled 10.54 km, covered an area of 80 000 m², sent back 20 000 pictures, and X-rayed the soil at 25 locations. A month later Radio Moscow announced that a new mooncar was being designed [3]. And why not?

THE TORRID GULF

Luna 16 and 17 represented two pieces of a three-part programme that involved soil samplers, moonrovers, and lunar orbiters. Warnings of a new Moon probe first appeared in January 1971 when predictions of 'low-flying artificial satellites' were made that would fly 'fairly soon' [4]. Sure enough, Luna 19 was launched on 28 September 1971, and entered circular lunar orbit of 140 km, 40 deg 35', 2 h 01 min, on 3 October. Four days later it was confirmed that Luna 19 was an orbiting mission. It settled into steady orbit of 127 km.

A lunar orbiting mission lacked the appeal or interest of a soil sample or rover. But it was valuable and important nonetheless. The mission lasted till 3 October 1972 and 1000 communication sessions were held. Luna 19 reported back on magnetic fields, mascons and meteoroids, and sent back televised pictures of an area 30S to 60S and 20E to 30E. In February 1972, it swept over the Torrid Gulf near the crater Eratosthenes and filmed rock-strewn plains above which reared a volcanic-like summit. In order to take such pictures it had dropped into a new orbit of 77 by 385 km, 131 minutes on 28 November.

Strangely, no concluding report on Luna 19 was ever issued. The report of 3 October 1972 said that the mission was 'nearing conclusion' and no photographs of this Luna were ever released, though there was no reason to believe that it was anything other than successful [5].

The same cannot be said of its predecessor, Luna 18. It appeared on 2 September 1972 and was a soil collector. After a perfect journey to and around the Moon, it fired its braking rockets over an area near the Sea of Fertility on 11 September. The small thruster rockets tried to guide it into a suitable landing site, but the fuel supplies gave out and it crashed.

Not even Radio Moscow felt able, or thought it worth its while, to invent a cover-up story. Something like 'testing new landing techniques' may have been considered, but this time they came straight out and admitted that the landing had been 'unlucky' in a 'difficult and rugged' upland area.

The intentions behind Luna 18 became clear when its backup vehicle was sent aloft on 14 February 1972. Luna 20 fired its engines to come in for a landing late on 21 February. This was the critical stage and it had gone wrong twice before.

Luna 20 was coming down right on top of mountains. The Sea of Fertility lies on the right of the Moon's visible face, and Luna 16 had landed on one of its flattest parts. About 70 km to the north, hills rise and there are soon mountains 1500 m high. Where Luna 20 was aimed was in a plateau between two peaks, less than 5000 m from where its predecessor had come to grief on a sharp slope. The area is called Apollonius. It was tougher than anything the American lunar module would have tried. But Luna 20 made it, whether through luck or skill we do not know.

And so it came to rest, hemmed in by towering mountain peaks. Signals at once indicated to relieved controllers that it was safe and secure. Within seven hours, aided by a small television camera, its drill was hard at work scooping up lunar soil. The whole operation took 40 minutes. The rig encountered stiff resistance at 100 mm and operations had to stop several times because it overheated. When it reached 150 mm the samples were scooped into the return capsule to await the long journey home. The on-board computer fired the engines up early on 23 February and the return vehicle climbed away from the lunar peaks. Two days later it headed into reentry.

An appalling blizzard hit the recovery area during the day. Helicopters spotted the tiny capsule − parachute, antennae and beacon deployed − heading straight into the Karakingir river. Would the precious samples be lost at this stage? Luckily the capsule came to rest on an island in the middle of the river, landing in a snowdrift and trees. But getting it back was easier said than done. The gale was too severe for the helicopters to land. Four cross-country vehicles tried to get across on the ice but it cracked so they called it off for fear of falling in.

The capsule of the automated spacecraft Luna 20 lies in the snow after its successful touchdown in Kazakhstan. Despite its landing during an appalling blizzard, helicopter observers spotted the tiny capsule and after severe gales had prevented recovery by helicopter and cross-country vehicles had tried in vain to get across dangerously thin ice, the precious lunar samples were eventually recovered.

They retrieved the battered and burnt capsule the next day when the wind abated. Its contents were opened at the Academy of Sciences before the end of the month. They were surprisingly small − only 50 g. But it was Moon all the same, this light ash-grey dust 3000 million years old. The records state it consisted of anorthosite, olivine and pyroxene.

With Luna 19 still in orbit, Lunokhod just closed down after its record stint, and the second series of Moon samples back, Soviet scientists had good reason to glow. They had presented an alternative to Apollo, one that would last beyond the end of the last of the Apollo missions of December 1972. There was more to come. According to Radio Moscow: 'Only the first few steps in a very wide and continuing lunar programme have been taken. Future missions will concentrate on the lunar uplands' [6].

BACK TO THE SEA OF CRISES

Apollo ended in December 1972. It was Apollo 17's commander, Eugene Cernan, who balefully drew attention to the fact that they would be the last Americans on the Moon till the early 21st century. Apollo's Moon landing programme had lasted a brief three years, during which the Americans had landed twelve men on the Moon in six locations, and recovered no less than 380 kg of moonrock. The last missions had been impressive: the Apollo 17 mission had spent three days on the Moon, two astronauts had spent 11 hours each walking on the Moon, and their lunar rover had taken them far from their lander. Their leaving of the Moon was characterized not so much by a feeling of triumph at what they had achieved as a feeling of sadness at the promise of the post-Apollo programme that had been cancelled due to lack of public support.

The original post-Apollo programme planned at least three more landings, including missions to such exciting places as the crater Copernicus. NASA also proposed a mission that would fly two astronauts into a lunar polar orbit for a month on a mammoth mapping survey. This too had gone by the board. So had even more ambitious notions like a month-long lunar shelter adapted from the LM ascent stage, with a relief LM to pick up the crew. The sole survivor of the post-Apollo programme was the space station Skylab, designed to fly in 1973. Next after that was the Space Shuttle, whose in-service date was 1978: it was linked exclusively to flight in low Earth orbit. No one forsaw a return to the Moon before 2001. So when Apollo 17 splashed down in December 1972, the Russians had the Moon to themselves for at least three decades.

When Luna 21 headed moonwards on 8 January 1973, the launching was seen very much in terms of cashing in on NASA's disappointment in the Congress's suppression of the post-Apollo programme. In fact, the timing was coincidental. The second mooncar, for that was what Luna 21 carried, had taken a full year to design after Lunokhod 1 had terminated its programme. Luna 21 weighed 1814 kg and its moonwards flight was problematical. False telemetry signals nearly aborted the mission, and then Lunokhod 2's solar lid opened during the moonwards coast, without being asked to do so.

On its 41st Moon orbit, Luna 21 began its descent from an altitude of 16 km. The target was Lemmonier crater, only 180 km from the valley just visited by Jack Schmitt and Eugene Cernan. Off the edge of the Sea of Serenity, the Lemmonier crater cut into the edge of the rocky Taurus mountains. Luna 21 would come down in a relatively flat area surrounded by the high rims of the old crater.

And so it did. Luna 21 touched down on 16 January 1973, and Lunokhod 2 rolled down the landing ramps not long afterwards. The touchdown was at one-fifth the speed of a parachute-landing and was the gentlest ever. Lunokhod 2 at once made a trial journey over the surface.

Lunokhod 2 was a distinct improvement over its predecessor. It was 100 kg heavier. It could travel at twice the speed. It had twice the range. There was an extra TV camera and some new scientific instruments, most notably a photometer to detect ultraviolet light sources in our galaxy.

Lunokhod 2's programme was as follows: it was to sit on the Moon for the first two days, charging up its batteries. Then it was to inspect the descent stage, to which it would not return. Finally it would head south to the mountains 7 km away and it would explore them as long as its lifetime permitted.

This it did, and in one of its early sessions the bug-eyed roving vehicle went 1148 m in six hours – much faster than anything achieved before. On the second lunar day (February 1973) the robot headed south towards the mountains, prowling through craters and ridges. It climbed one hill of 400 m, with its wheels at one stage slipping up to 80 per cent. From the top it sent back an eerie photograph of the Taurus peaks glowing to the north, 60 km away, and the thin sickle of the Earth rising just above. One day it travelled 1.6 km. As it travelled it measured and analysed the lunar soil.

On its third lunar day, Lunokhod 2 reached a rille at the edge of the Lemmonier crater. The rille – a valley similar to but smaller than the Hadley rille explored by Apollo 15 – was 50 m deep and 400 m wide. Lunokhod was steered gingerly along the edge of the rille which was 14 km long. It was not easy, and Lunokhod faced and overcame the hazards of loose soil into which its wheels sank and large boulders with which any collision would be fatal.

It was expected that Lunokhod 2 would continue its work for several months, but on 4 June came the sudden announcement from Radio Moscow that 'the programme had been completed'. No explanation was given, but it seems fair to assume that the rover did not survive the lunar night of May/June. The Russians seem to have been disappointed but there is little reason why they should have been.

Lunokhod 2 travelled 37 km, sent back 86 panoramic pictures and 80 000 television pictures and had covered four times the area of its predecessor. It had investigated not only crater floors but much more difficult geological features like rilles and uplands. One of its most interesting findings actually had nothing to do with the lunar surface, but the suitability of the Moon as a base for observing the sky. Whilst it would be excellent during the lunar night, during the daytime the lunar sky was surrounded by a swarm of dust particles, a kind of atmosphere, that would make telescopic observations difficult.

LUNOKHOD – PROTOTYPE OR EXPERIMENT?

What next after Lunokhod 2? The two moonrovers had been outstanding successes, the first operating well beyond its design lifetime and the second providing major advances in range and speed. Yet Lunokhod 2 was the last Lunokhod, and in 1977 the Russians admitted publicly that the programme had been abandoned as too expensive. At the time, this seemed the least likely outcome of the lunar rover programme. Throughout the period of Lunokhod 2's operation, the Soviet press was full of glowing plans for the future of lunar exploration. Several articles appeared in the months April to June 1973 and all pointed to a vigorous programme of lunar exploration. These are some examples:

> Stationary lunar laboratories will perhaps appear, capable of carrying out a broad range of scientific research in astronomy, seismic and soil analysis for long durations.
> — Vsevolod Avduyevsky, *Izvestia*, January 1973. [7]

There will be a lot more such mooncars in use in many areas of the moon in the coming period.
— M. Dhcherbakov, *Soviet Weekly*, 11 March 1973. [8]

Teams of Lunokhods will be operating on the moon. They will collect soil samples which vehicles of the Luna 16–20 type will return to Earth.
— Academician Boris Petrov, 25 March 1973. [9]

What we need are small and cheap long-lived automatic lunar stations for seismic and magnetic studies.
   To land an unmanned probe on the far side of the moon or in its polar regions is a challenging problem. . . which would require a relay satellite in lunar orbit.
— Georgi Petrov, *Soviet Weekly*, 21 April 1973. [10]

These are not the only statements and there are others like them forming part of a coherent pattern. Most of them were made in the period of January to June 1973. The USSR made very few such statements about its Moon programme after that date, even though three more Moon probes were to follow. Indeed in their last major item on their Moon intentions, moonrovers were linked not so much to the Moon but the Mars:

Deployment of Lunokhod-type automatic stations is a tremendous step forwards in space research, in the study of planets of the solar system.
   Such automatic devices will be of particular importance for the study of Mars and other planets. Mobile, they will be able to engage in the detailed study of the numerous martian surface areas.
— Academician Anatoli Blagonravov, 2 June 1973. [11]

Yet these were to prove empty promises. Undoubtedly there were many scientists who would have liked such adventures to take place. Indeed there is evidence that a lunar farside orbiter was built (but not launched) in early 1978. But none of the hypothesized missions actually flew. And June 1973 was about the worst possible time for the advocates of lunar research to be looking for approval for a post-Lunokhod programme. Two space stations had fallen out of the sky in the previous five weeks. The Soyuz programme was years behind schedule. Moonrovers were irrelevant to the main thrust of Soviet space exploration, namely orbital stations. Lunokhod and the moonscoopers had their origins in the days of Apollo and were designed as its rival. Apollo was over now, and they too served little further purpose or advantage.
   It was a full year before the next Moon probe, Luna 22, took off. It was a direct replacement for Luna 19, whose mission had apparently ended early in 1973. Luna 22 went up on 2 June 1974, and entered Moon orbit at a standard altitude four days later. Late that month it swooped down to 25 by 244 km for special photography, before going back up again to 181 by 299 km.
   Over the next year, Luna 22 regularly altered its orbit, displaying both versatility and reliability. In April 1975 it was in an eccentric orbit 1000 km out. Then in September 1975 it dipped to a mere 24 km over the surface before returning to a higher orbit. The termination of the mission was announced in November 1975.

So what was it doing? The next — and last two probes — were soil collectors, and targeted for the Sea of Crises, a well-known and very flat part of the Moon on its eastern edge, one which hardly needed detailed photographic investigation at this stage. So Luna 19 and 22 can only have been doing one of two things: either mapping gaps in the Russian Moon maps or mapping landing sites for possible future missions. Luna 19, it is known, made detailed maps of the southern highlands of the Moon.

THE LUNAR FARSIDE MISSION

The USSR's last two Moon missions in this series were in November 1974 and August 1976. Luna 23 tried to land in the Sea of Crises but was severely damaged in the course of the landing. The soil collecting gear was wrecked, although the descent stage was able to continue transmission for a further three days.

A replacement mission was organized. Indeed, Russia's determination to get back samples from the Sea of Crises seemed nearly obsessive, as this had also been Luna 15's target, and the Sea is not thought to be an area of outstanding geological interest. Luna 24 actually came down only a few hundred metres from the wreckage of Luna 23, and at the exact place of Luna 15's targeting spot. Touchdown was on 19 August 1976, and all went well this time. The drill was a radical improvement on its predecessors and was able to drill to a depth of no less than 2 m. It brought up samples weighing 170 g. The upper stage of Luna 24 blasted off for Earth the next day and the capsule came down in summertime Siberia near the tundra town of Surgut, a recovery area never used before or since.

With this impressive demonstration of the ability to drill and recover deep samples from the surface of the Moon ended Russia's Moon programme for a decade. This gap has never been officially explained. Indeed a Novosti publication of 1983 stated blandly: 'We believe that future vehicles on Mars and Venus will use all the best features of the design and technology tested by Soviet automatic moon probes' [12] — as if the Moon had no other place in the Soviet cosmic mind than to be a testing ground for spaceships destined elsewhere for more worthy objectives. Far from it, as the race to the Moon from 1962 to 1969 testified.

After 1973 the Soviet literature shut up about the Moon, and publicity about Luna 22, 23 and 24 was minimal, and actually, hard to find. There was one break in the silence though. Several reports reached the West, and they were summarized in *Spaceflight* magazine of June 1978 as follows:

Polar orbiting craft, and improved orbital vehicles designed to produce geochemical maps of the whole lunar surface and a complete and accurate photographic atlas of the moon will be sent up between now and 1983.

By the end of the 1970s a Soviet unmanned Luna-type spacecraft will return to Earth rock and soil samples of the lunar far side. [13].

And as if to confirm this report, a photograph appeared in 1984 showing the Venus probe Venera 12 in assembly in its hangar in March 1978. The point of interest was not Venera 12, but, standing tantalizing in the background, a Luna spacecraft capable of returning rock samples from the Moon!

How can one explain these strange events? It seems that the Moon programme of the years 1970–76 represented the ultimate development of the hardware designed and planned in the late 1960s, and which was related to the man-on-the-Moon effort. These missions were let run their natural course, and their last mission was to have been Luna 23 in 1974. Only its failure permitted the launch of its backup two years later.

However, it seems also fair to surmise that serious consideration was given to a number of follow-on missions in the period around 1973, not least because of the success of the Lunokhods. Otherwise the glowing predictions of Petrov and others would never have appeared in print, since their publication means they must have had some official *imprimatur*. So one can presume that approval was given for a small number of follow-on missions in the late 1970s, including a farside soil recovery. This would have been an impressive achievement, but well within the capabilities of the Luna 24 class of vehicle. So why did it not fly? It could have been that the same pressures which in the United States killed off the post-Apollo unmanned programme were also at work in the Soviet Union. After all, 1979 was the year in which NASA finally abandoned, after years of trying, attempts to persuade the Congress and the President of the need for a low-cost Polar-orbiting chemical mapping satellite. Perhaps the politicians of both East and West, concerned to keep space spending within limits, wanted to hear least of all about the one part of the heavens on which each country had already spent the better part of a fortune.

The inactivity of the years after 1976 was a far cry from the triumphs of the Lunokhod and the Luna 16. Indeed, the Russians had at one stage – long after the Moon race was lost – been talking about new manned flights to the Moon. Georgi Petrov was quoted, not long after the return of Luna 16, as saying:

It is now time for the establishment of permanent space stations in orbits ranging out to near that of the Moon.

As for a manned moon base, much more valuable would be a manned space station in orbit around the moon, capable of sending robot probes down to the surface. [14]

And in 1979 a Soviet space official spoke of lunar space stations from which cosmonauts would descent in small expeditionary ships. So although the automatic Soviet space exploration programme suffered a long hiatus, the Moon ambition was not completely dead. It would be surprising if it were. And with the development of advanced space stations in the mid-1980s, and 'Star' modules with large cargo and tugging capacity, a lunar orbiting space station becomes more and more feasible. A lunar base is then only a small step away.

DOWN IN ELECTRIS

The USSR's early efforts to explore Mars had been unhappy ones. The attempted Mars launchings of 1960 had ended in a catastrophic and fatal pad explosion. Mars 1 had made a long journey out to the Red Planet in 1963, but communications had failed. Zond 2 was also silent as it swept past Mars in 1965. Out of five attempts, only two had actually got away from Earth, and neither had achieved their objectives.

Perhaps sobered by these disappointments, and realizing the scale of the problem of maintaining long-distance communication, the USSR decided to miss the launch window of 1966—67. Instead it waited until the next launch window of 1969 when the new D-le launch vehicle was available. This could put up a very large craft indeed. The maximum possible payload to Mars was five tonnes. This enabled Soviet scientists to think well past flyby probes to not merely an orbiter but a lander as well. They could then achieve the hat-trick of the first soft-landing on the Moon, Venus, and now Mars. This was an attractive proposition since the continued postponements affecting America's Voyager project meant that their rivals would be unlikely to fly such a mission before 1973 at the earliest.

Two spacecraft were prepared for launch, on 27 February and 3 March 1969. Each weighed 3495 kg, which was less than the permissible five tonnes but the launch window was not a very favourable one and extra fuel had to be carried in the escape stage. The D-le was going through its most difficult phase and when it dropped what would have been Mars 2 into the Pacific Ocean the second launch was cancelled so that the faults in the booster could be rectified before wasting more precious cargoes. So far the score was seven attempts, five complete failures [15].

It was such an abysmal performance that, in comparison, American efforts could only appear better. So they did. The American preference in the early 1960s for using equipment that was sophisticated rather than simple, lightweight and complex rather than crude, began to pay off in interplanetary flights. American equipment began to achieve a degree of reliability just when demands of reliability were at a premium, on the long interplanetary flights.

Mariner 4, put up the same time as Zond 2, gave an early indication of these qualities. Much smaller than the Soviet probes at around 260 kg, Mariner 4 was still functioning when it passed Mars after an eight-month journey in July 1965, and, as it flew past, its camera clicked 21 historic pictures of the surface. Gone were dreams of canals, vegetation, and an atmosphere that would make living on Mars as easy as strolling on Earth on a bright summer's day. Exploded were the myths — nurtured for over a century — of a civilization that had constructed watercourses to take cool arctic waters from the Martian poles to distribute them to hungry farmers living on the Martian equator. For Mariner 4 found a planet that was barren, riddled with craters, and blessed with an atmosphere that was only one per cent as stong as Earth's.

The Americans returned to Mars in 1969 with two more spacecraft, Mariner 6 and 7. With four vane solar paddles, they looked like windmills with a box in the middle. They looked not unlike Mariner 4, but details on their capabilities showed how much American engineering had improved in just five years. Data came back at 16 200 bits per second now, compared to 8.3 before; 200 pictures were sent back rather than 21.

The planet the probes revealed was even more bleak than had been thought before. Mars was cold, dry and nearly airless, and the atmosphere was almost all carbon dioxide. Mariners 6 and 7 passed over crater after crater of a landscape as desolate as that below an aviator overflying the Western Front during the Great War. Ice clung to the crater slopes.

These triumphs largely passed the world public by, for they took place barely days after Neil Armstrong and Edwin Aldrin had walked on the Moon and nothing could ever compare with that ecstatic moment. NASA was less easily overwhelmed, and at once ordered up a further two Mars craft whose job would be to map the planet in detail from pole to pole. Mariner 8 and 9 were prepared: they were 1032 kg in weight on account of the need for an engine and fuel to put them into Mars orbit.

These developments must have been observed in the USSR with growing apprehension, but May 1971 was to see a peak of both Soviet and American efforts to explore Mars, with the Americans flying orbiters and the Russians flying landers. On 9 May Mariner 8 lost altitude on take-off and crashed into the Atlantic Ocean. The next day a D-le Proton booster left a large object in low Earth orbit, which quickly burned up. Cosmos 419 was actually the last planetary failure of the D-le.

There the run of bad luck ended. Mars 2 swung out of Earth orbit on 19 May and Mars 3 on 28 May. American's Mariner 9 just beat the end of of the launch window by a day on 30 May. The Soviet missions were not long under way when Russia revealed that soft-landings were intended. That was not all, as everyone subsequently found out.

Both probes were big. Each was a cylindrical doughnut 3 m high. A huge dish antenna was lashed to each side. Two solar wings stuck out the side of the craft like butterfly wings. The main body was full of pipes and lines and aerials and rods and tubes. From the bottom peeped out a retrorocket. On the top sat the precious dome-shaped cone of the landing capsule.

Throughout the summer and autumn the three probes sped towards Mars. At the end of July Mars 2 was 17 million kilometres from Earth and Mars 3 followed 2 million kilometres beind. Then came trouble. At the end of October, the smallest of the three probes, America's Mariner 9, began warming up its cameras as if flexing its muscles for the climax of its journey. And what those cameras saw at the beginning of November meant that the Mars they were journeying towards was very different from the planet they were expecting. Far from being the quiet and cold planet with spring gradually warming the southern hemisphere, the whole planet was convulsed in a raging dust and sand storm. The likes of it had not been seen since 1937 or 1956. Not a thing was visible — just swirling red and brown clouds.

Mariner 9 fired its 44 cm wide nozzle for 14 minutes on 14 November and swung into orbit, each revolution lasting 12 hours. The bad weather did not bother it terribly — it just waited for the dust storm to settle, which it did in January 1972. Mariner 9 went on to map the planet and was an oustanding success. But, for the Soviet probes heading in for a landing, the effects of the dust storm were nothing short of calamitous. The time at which the landing capsules would be released was already built into the computer programme — and could not be changed.

Mars 2 reached the planet on 27 November. Four hours before arrival the cone-shaped capsule separated from the mother ship. At the fantastic speed of 6 km/s the little cone hurtled into the thin Martian atmosphere. Shock waves formed and gases heated the capsule to thousands of degrees. Mars 2 crashed through the air and was soon over the deserts of Mars. At still supersonic speed, a giant parachute unfurled.

What happened next no one knows. Mars 2 did not survive the descent with intact instruments though it is known that it did reach the surface. A pennant with the Soviet coat-of-arms was on it, and we know that it must have arrived. It was the first direct human contact with the planet Mars.

The second craft, Mars 3, headed on. On 2 December the descent capsule blasted free of the mother ship to begin its perilous descent. There was no way ground control could intervene because it took 15 minutes for signals to reach the spacecraft and the same again for them to return. All had to be done by advance programming and autopilot.

The entire process of supersonic entry and landing took only three minutes. Out came the Mars 3 parachute, with the speed at Mach 1. The heat shield, still glowing red hot, was dropped. The radio transmitter started pouring out a flood of data to Earth. But far from swinging gently beneath its canopy, the descending capsule was being buffetted by the ferocious winds of the planet-wide sandstorm that was roaring. Tiny grains of sand slammed into its side.

20 m above the surface a tiny rocket pulled the parachute free so that it would not fall on top of the 450 kg descent capsule. Another rocket on its top fired briefly to lower speed to the survivable.

At 16.50.35 Mars 3 reached the surface. It was down in the southern hemisphere at 45°S in a region called 'Electris'. Four petals opened and the domed shape of the capsule rested there on the sands of Mars. Antennae popped out, aerials searched sky-wards, TV cameras began scanning. The video came on at 16.52.05 and began to transmit a picture at once.

And then it was all over.

At 16.52.25 Moscow time Mars 3's voice disappeared into the crackle of outer space and was lost forever. We do not know if the sandstorms with their tiny but ferocious grains of sand blew it over or rendered it inoperable. Or — the explanation put forward many years later — the orbiting and transmitting section of the Mars 3 orbit module malfunctioned. But imagine the maddening frustration: a successful soft-landing, the first ever, and then silence.

Still, it was quite an achievement to get that far. The navigation and engineering problems in even soft-landing were far from modest. And the experiment as a whole was far from over. The two mother ships had gone into Martian orbit and a wide range of research began:

	Mariner 9	Mars 2	Mars 3
Apoaxis (km)	17 916	24 938	190 333
Periaxis (km)	1 389	1 380	1 500
Period	12 hr 34 min	18 h	11 days
Inclination (degrees)	64.3	48.54	N.A.

The large volume of data returned from orbit partly offset the disappointment of the soft-landing failures. Both probes continued their transmissions until September 1972. Both sent back pictures. The first one from Mars 3 showed the thin crescent shape of the planet beckoning in the far distance from the apoaxis of its orbit.

The two Mars probes carried instruments with exotic names like spectrometers, photometers, cosmic ray detectors and ion traps. They found mountains on Mars as high as 22 km. They found hydrogen in the atmosphere. They calculated the surface temperature on Mars as an icy −15°C. They found the dust storm whipped up granules of sand as high as 7 km into the sky. Both probes dipped out of their natural orbits as a result of Martian mascons.

Neither Mars 2 nor 3 was as successful as Mariner 9: its detailed mapping photographs were spell-binding and showed the planet to be much more varied than could ever have been imagined. Mariner 9 found rilles and giant canyons. Its cameras picked out what seemed like ancient river beds. Finally it found 20 volcanoes. Nix Olympica took every-one's breath away: a giant volcanic pile, it was twice the size of Earth's Everest.

THE MARS FLEET

An unparalled assault on Mars began in 1973. No fewer than four craft were involved. Spurred on by the near-success of Mars 2 and 3, this launch window also represented the last chance the USSR had of beating the United States to a soft-landing with prolonged transmissions from the surface. America's Voyager project had slipped to 1971, then 1973, and now 1975. It had grown enormously complex and expensive, and, as if to shake off the bad luck and difficulties with which it was associated, it was renamed Viking.

To everyone's surprise — and probably not least the Russians themselves — all the four attempted launches went perfectly. They took place on 21 and 25 July and on 5 and 9 August, the last one only hours before the window closed. Never before had so many spacecraft set out for one planet at one time. Even if only half the probes worked, a real success was inevitable.

The fleet of four actually included two groups of probes. Because the launch window was not a favourable one, somewhat less than the full payload could be flown. As a result, the designers could either build landers or orbiters, but both were not possible in the one probe as they had been in 1971. So Mars 4 and 5 were orbiters, and 6 and 7 were landers. The orbiters would serve as relay stations for the landers.

But fate was very cruel to the Russian Mars fleet as it approached the Red Planet in the spring of 1974. So much so that the Russians themselves described the outcome as 'disappointing' [16].

Two probes were total failures, and failures of the type that could have been expected ten years earlier. Instead of firing its engines so as to enter Mars orbit, Mars 4 neglected to fire at all. It coasted past. Mars 7's landing probe separated prematurely, and missed the planet altogether by 1300 km. Mars 6 underwent an experience similar to Mars 3. Its probe was successfully cast off and it went through the entry phase and opened a parachute. Data was returned — indeed it flooded in for a full 150 sec. And then Mars 6 fell silent. 'Contact was lost', said the official sources and that is probably all they knew. It was just before touchdown.

Only Mars 5 achieved any degree of success. It entered Mars orbit with a periaxis of 1300 km and an apoaxis of 32 586 km. It sent back a modest amount of information. The photographs it took were comparable to Mariner 9's and showed volcanoes, river beds, craters and canyons. And like Mars 3 and 2 it sampled the atmosphere.

But taken as a whole, the Mars expedition of 1973 was a disaster. It came at a low point in the manned programme as well. The financial controllers turned on the Mars designers with a vengeance. Even with everything going in their favour, they blew it. Those who had argued for a scaling down in the deep space missions around the time of the 1969 decisions were vindicated. They were told that Mars 7 would indeed be the last Mars spaceship for some time. So it was. The launch windows of 1975, 1977, 1979, 1981 and 1984 were untroubled by emissaries from the Baikonour cosmodrome.

The sense of defeat was reinforced when the American Viking project matured in 1975. Each of the two probes was much more sophisticated than the Mars probes, even

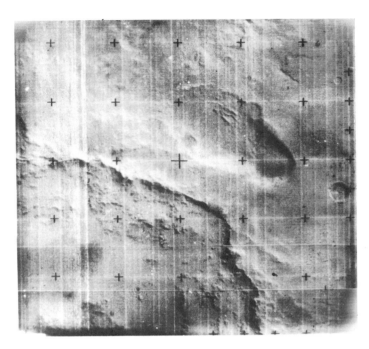

This photograph received from the Soviet probe Mars 5 shows an area 100 km square of the Martian surface. It shows the western part of a large crater having a diameter of about 150 km and a depth of 3 km. Near the centre of the picture an irregular-shaped depression about 25 km long can be seen.

though they weighed less (about 3400 kg). Rather than releasing a probe on approach, the entire Viking entered Mars orbit. The orbiter spent a month selecting a suitable landing site — not an academic exercise since JPL's original designated sites turned out to be dangerous and had to be altered. This period of waiting could also have been used to ride out dust storms — an option not available to the hapless Mars 3.

Viking 1 came down in a field of boulders on the seventh anniversary of the Moon landing: 20 July 1976. Viking 2 followed a month later. Both spacecraft were lucky, and had either landed just a few metres from where they did they might have overturned, so rocky were the two landing spots.

But people did not remember the good luck. They remembered instead Viking digging up the soil with its mechanical scoop. They remembered instead the daily weather reports, given faithfully every day until the spring of 1983. They remembered the on-board soil laboratory, and excited scientists poring over the strange results when the Martian soil was exposed to water. They remembered the sweeping panoramas shot from orbit and the eerie colours of sunset on the red world in the coldness of space millions of miles from our own world.

The battle for Mars was a less important one for the Russians than the Moon, but defeat was no less decisive. Their technology, reliability and planning was simply not adequate for the task in hand. Not until the 1980s did the Russians begin to think of Mars probes once more. The first reports of new planned programmes began to emerge in 1981 and hardened up several years later. They took the form of proposals for a five-tonne orbiter that could leave Earth in the window of July 1988 for a rendezvous with Phobos, Mars' tiny moon, setting down a beetle-like Mars-hopper that could probe around the surface. And a look at the logistics showed how a sample—return mission could be accomplished in 1998 using two five-tonne spacecraft, rendezvousing in Mars orbit and eventually firing a 85 kg capsule with Mars rock back towards Earth. With the unhappy memories of the early seventies receding, in the goodness of time, new ideas and designs could safely go into the making [17].

THE LURE OF VENUS

Despite the cutbacks in the Mars and lunar programme that began to bite in 1974, plans for the exploration of Venus remained apparently unaffected. Indeed the USSR went on to build up a special expertise in the exploration of Venus. Its probes were both more ambitious and more successful than the American ones.

The revelation that Venera 3 had been designed to soft-land in 1966 gave the clue to the mission of Venera 4, put up on 12 June 1967. A companion mission, Cosmos 167, did not achieve orbit five days later, and by then the Americans had launched a rival in the form of Mariner 5. Few of the launchings were noticed by the world, then immersed in the Middle East War.

This could not be said when on 18 October, Venera 4 reached Venus. Western observers had been following the mission by way of the large dish at Jodrell Bank. Early that morning, Venera 4's signals had ceased on final approach. Then, as the light of dawn cleared the cold October sky, entirely new signals were picked up, coming directly from the surface of Venus. It was the first soft-landing on another planet and the transmission lasted 94 minutes.

Or so it seemed. What was actually happening was more complicated. Venera 4, shaped like a milk bottle with solar wings, a dish aerial, and a bucket-shaped landing capsule on one end, had sped towards Venus with extreme accuracy. Some hours before arrival the 383 kg capsule had been separated from the mother ship to begin its own descent. The atmosphere braked it, and thick parachute lines opened. The capsule swung underneath its canopy as it came down through thick layer after thick layer of swirling clouds. Instruments began at once sending back data on temperature, pressure and the chemical composition of the atmosphere.

The pressure built up and up — 10 atmospheres, 15, 20 — until at 22 atmospheres with still 25 km to go before the surface, the capsule cracked open like an egg and was smashed to tiny bits. Venera 4 never reached the surface intact: the signals heard at Jodrell Bank had been those sent back during the descent only.

The data returned was invaluable, though hardly encouraging from the point of view of human habitation. Even 25 km above the surface, temperature was 280°C, pressure 22 atmospheres, and the atmosphere was largely carbon dioxide with only one per cent oxygen. If that was what it was like there, what kind of hell lay below? And these pessimistic views were confirmed by Mariner 5 the following day when it passed by at 3991 km. It too found high temperatures and pressures. It was rapidly becoming clear that Venus would not be the object of early human colonization.

MOUNTAIN PEAKS?

Because of the way Venera 4 had been crushed by the terrible atmospheric pressures it was decided to reinforce the parachutes on its two successor probes, scheduled for 1969. Each canopy would be much smaller — $15m^2$ rather than $50m^2$ — in the hope of getting the capsule to the surface quicker before it could be either crushed or boiled. Whatever happened, it would be a race against time.

Venera 5 headed off the pad on 5 January 1969 and Venera 6 followed on 10 January. Both weighed 1120 kg and carried 405 kg descent capsules, 1 m wide. It was a time of intense activity at Baikonour, with two Soyuz launches less than a week away.

Course corrections by tiny manoeurvring engines put Venera 5 on course for touchdown on 16 May, and Venera 6 the following day. It was a minor distraction from America's Apollo 10, whose three astronauts were due to leave for the Moon the next day.

Alas neither probe was any more successful than their illustrious predecessor. Not that they did not behave any way other than their computer programme ordered. The probes duly separated at 25 000 km out and crashed into the atmosphere at 11.18 km/s. By the time the atmosphere had slowed them down to 210 m/s the parachutes had opened and their radios were hectically radioing back as much information as they could.

As they descended the pressures and temperatures rose. The probes strained, groaned, and eventually broke up. Venera 5 was crushed 12 km above the surface and Venera 6 16 km. At one stage the Russians actually claimed that they had reached the surface and explained the high altitude readings by saying that they had landed on the top of mountain peaks! But it was wishful thinking. Transmission times were 53 minutes and 51 minutes respectively. By reducing the diameter of the parachute by two-thirds they had come much closer to that elusive touchdown: one day they would get through. The USSR issued a list of the probes' findings: the atmosphere was 93—97 per cent carbon dioxide, inert gases 2—5 per cent and oxygen a meagure 0.4 per cent.

America's next Venus probe was not until 1973. This was due partly to the concentration by NASA on other targets like the Moon and Mars, and partly to the very unappealing nature of Venus itself. Such considerations gave the Russians all that more opportunity to achieve their long-cherished goal of a soft-landing. Being the nearest planet, it presented the least engineering problems; and shining as the brightest star of all stars in the twilight skies, it was the least easy to forget.

TWILIGHT STAR

So it was that two probes were prepared for 1970's launch window — on 17 and 22 August respectively. Only the former got away (Venera 7), and the latter became known as Cosmos 359. Venera 7 went first into Earth orbit, fired its upper stage to reach escape velocity at 7.59 a.m. and by 10 a.m. Earth had receded 40 000 km into the distance. It was due to arrive on 15 December, and on the 18th of that month, Radio Moscow reported with regret that it had not improved on the performance of its predecessors. It had parachuted down, transmitting for 35 minutes, and had then fallen silent. Too bad. Would a soft-landing ever be achieved? How much longer would this furnace-like planet continue to elude them?

So things rested for six weeks until one of the ground controllers decided to go over the signals made during the descent and after and picked up by the receiving aerials. It must have been a tedious ear-straining job, but she listened in patiently and with extraordinary concentration to the cosmic crackle – the squeaks, the static, the beeps and the pips.

And there it was! Ever so faintly, barely discernible, was a strange signal! It started soon after Venera 7 had cut out, but it was unmistakeable. It lasted 23 minutes and it was the voice of the landing probe actually on the surface. So they had done it after all!

The signals were consistent and showed the temperature constant at 475°C and the pressure constant at 90 atmospheres, so the probe could only be steady, on the surface and at rest. The 495 kg probe had sat there, cooking gradually in a temperature well able to melt lead or zinc. Then it had succumbed.

It was a joyous moment – the first real soft-landing on another planet. Years of persistent toil had at last paid off. Since Lunokhod 1 was at the time driving on the Moon, the USSR was in the position of receiving information from two celestial bodies simultaneously. And the reason for the weak signals, it transpired, was that the antenna had got out of alignment and had been pointing partly away from Earth. As a result, the signal strength actually picked up was only 1/100th of what was being sent out.

A repeat mission was prepared for 1972. Venera 8 was launched on 31 March 1972, and another probe was identified by some at the time as a failed pair (Cosmos 482). Its journey out went practically unremarked. After 117 days it approached Venus, then a slim early-morning crescent low on the eastern horizon 108 million kilometres away. The probe separated at 41 696 km/h. Aerodynamic braking reduced that to 900 km/h. When the parachute – only 2.5 m in diameter this time – opened 60 km above the surface a refrigeration system was turned on to blow cold air at −8°C around the instruments so they might survive longer.

After that things could only get hotter, and they did. Venera 8 sent back readings throughout the descent, thumped down on the surface, and broadcast for a full 50 minutes. A separate and deployable antenna ensured there was no repeat of the poor signal strength of the previous mission. The main finding of Venera 8 was that the amount of light falling on the surface was similar to that of a cloudy and rainy day on Earth – a finding vital for the preparation of the next mission.

Venera 8 represented the limit of the Venera 3–8 type of spacecraft and a new generation of Venus explorer could be prepared using the D-le booster. As a result, the weight of the probe could be increased from 1180 kg to 5000 kg.

DRILLING THE RED HOT ROCKS

The preparation of a new type of Venus probe took three years, and as a result the launch window of 1973 was missed, the first time since 1961 the USSR had missed a launch window. America's Mariner 10 coincided with this gap and that was an extraordinarily successful venture. It was a small hexagonal box with two giant TV eyes on top and two solar panel wings. Only 503 kg, it sped quickly to Venus and passed by at 5760 km in February 1974.

Mariner 10 was actually en route to Mercury and was using Venus as a 'gravity assist' to get itself there. Televising Venus was a major mission objective: for eight days it filmed the clouds circling around and dispersing and building up again. Because the cameras used ultra-violet filters the cloud formations could be identified through the murky haze and the planet as a result looked much like Earth's blues and whites when viewed from half-way to the Moon.

The two new-generation probes were ready for launch in June 1975. Venera 9 got away on 8 June and Venera 10 on 14 June. The overall structure was much the same as before — a transporter and a lander. Venera 10, for example, weighed 5033 kg, including an entry probe of 1560 kg on its top. The actual lander was 600 kg. The main spacecraft was a cylinder, with engine at base and two solar wings, with endless pipes, rods and arms protruding. The lander looked like a mixture of a kettle and pressure cooker welded together sitting on a metallic ring. Two cameras peeped out like the periscopes of an early submarine.

Venera 9 approached Venus on 20 October. Early that morning it released the ball-shaped entry probe. Now lightened, the transporter continued on for two days, fired its engine, and became the first spacecraft to orbit the planet, with a periaxis of 1400 km and apoaxis of 112 000 km. It stood by to act as a relay station.

The entry probe plunged straight into the atmosphere. At 65 km the worst was over, the protective shield was jettisoned, and a metallic parachute opened. The lander fell to 50 km, when the parachute was discarded. This was the radically new design step. The lander would now fall unaided but for a disc brake — fast enough to get it to the surface quickly, yet hopefully not too fast to damage it.

After 75 minutes the capsule was on the surface, its impact cushioned by shock absorbers. Then the real work began. Caps dropped off the camera covers. A density meter jabbed into the soil. Dr Mikhail Marov, Head of the Science Team working on the mission, described what happened next:

> The lander touched down at 8.28 a.m. Moscow Time. Within 15 minutes we had the first pictures. We were surprised at their sharpness. We expected the pictures to be dark due to the thick clouds and the dust, and we hardly expected to discern separate objects. Instead the panoramic views showed a curved horizon 300 m away with the light sky and the dark surface clearly separated. [18]

There were rocks and rocks everywhere — sharp and round and curved on a dark black surface. They were the first pictures from the surface of another planet.

Venera 10 touched down on 25 October some 2200 km away. It too was a triumph. It reported pressure at 92 atmospheres and temperatures of 465°C. Mission mapper Boris Nepoklonov noted: 'Venera 9 came down on a plateau 2500 m above average planet level, showing us scattered large rocks on a mountainside. Venera 10 was on an old mountain formation' [19].

The strips of photographs were released to the press at once, unprocessed and unenhanced. They were not as good as the American Mars pictures that were to follow, but the nature of the surface was quite clear. It was an engineering achievement of major proportions.

LIGHTNING

Repeat missions were flown in 1978 by Venera 11 and 12. They were launched in September and arrived in December. Neither of the transporter craft entered Venus orbit, but flew past the planet instead. Strangely, no TV pictures were sent back from the surface. No explanation was forthcoming and it seems the surface package failed entirely on both probes.

The missions were otherwise highly successful. The atmosphere was sampled many times during the descent, and quantities of inert gases were found. One instrument called 'Groza' was designed to detect electrical activity. It found more than it bargained for: Venera 11 counted 25 strikes of lightning a second, and Venera 12 picked up 1200 strikes. 15 minutes after touchdown a massive thunderclap reverberated around the whole planet.

Carbon monoxide was found by the gas chromatograph. And Venera 12 transmitted 110 minutes on the surface before succumbing to heat, pressure and the acid air. Their landings were matched by two American missions – Pioneer Venus 1 and 2. One was a lander (with three sub-probes) and the other an orbiter. A substantial amount of data was returned and the orbiter identified canyons, craters, plateaus and mountains.

So by 1979 Venus was known in some detail and was no less hostile than originally feared. The next steps were to map the planet properly – with a radar that could pierce the thick clouds – and to identify the chemical composition of the surface.

For the Americans, this was easier said than done. NASA had no chance of getting approval for an expensive lander, but did hope for a Venus Orbiting Imaging Radar, or VOIR. But during the Carter administration (1977/81) space spending reached rock bottom and the project was vetoed year after year. (President Reagan, who took office in January 1981 and who was prepared to put money into military space activities, eventually approved a scaled-down Venus Radar Mapper (VRM) in 1983.) So the USSR once more, for the moment, had a clear field.

Russia was both able and willing to take advantage of this hiatus. Indeed the point was rammed home at the very time that the American space shuttle 'Columbia' was going through an exasperating series of countdown failures and hitches in November 1981. Venera 13 left Earth orbit on 30 October 1981, and with what seemed like effortless ease Venera 14 took off on a curving path to the evening star on 4 November.

DRILLING RIG

Venera 13 was the first to arrive. A parachute took the 700 kg craft down to 47 km and the airbrake took it the rest of the way. Venera 13 was aimed at the rolling Plains of Phoebus, and somewhere near there it came to rest, raising, as it did so, a cloud of dust. The camera lens cover at once fell away onto the steaming surface and the probe began work on the cauldron of the hell planet.

A mechanical ladder straightaway extended to the surface and began to analyse the rocks using screw drills. The system had to work against time, and there was the possibility that the whole probe might collapse under the pressure any time. But within minutes scientists had a read-out on the composition of the soil: 45 per cent silica oxide,

4 per cent potassium oxide, 7 per cent calcium oxide. The general composition was basalt.

Remarkable though these findings were, they had none of the dramatic impact of the pictures taken by the cameras of Venera 13. They sent back eight separate panoramas, scanned in red, green and blue. The cameras revealed a rolling stony plateau and the curved horizon in the distance. Scattered on it were stones, pebbles and flat rocks. Many looked like the type of flat pebble that could be picked up off a beach and skimmed across the waves. And looking skywards, the cameras found a bright orange sky and not a blue one. By the time the experiment was over, earthlings had a realistic view of what it would be like to stand on the surface of Venus.

Venera 14 came in for landing on 5 March over a thousand kilometres away. It was just as successful and it touched down on a low-lying basaltic basin. The pictures were quite different. They showed a flat cracked surface like icing on a chocolate cake. The more geologically professional description of Radio Moscow was that it was 'wrinkled brownish slate like sandstone'.

And as with Venera 13, the mechanical drilling arm reached down for samples, scooped them into a hermatically sealed chamber and subjected them to X-ray and fluorescent analysis. This internal chamber operated at a temperature of $30°C$ and a pressure 1/2000th that of the air outside.

The Venera 13 and 14 missions were triumphs by any standards. The scientific data returned were unambiguous and the pictures were a feast to geologists' eyes:

	Venera 13	Venera 14
Landing date	1 March 1982	5 March 1982
Pressure (atm)	89	94
Temperature ($°C$)	457	465
Transmission time (min)	127	57
Location	$7.5°S$, $303°$ longt.	$13.2°S$, $310°$ longt.

The transmission times were better than expected, for the design life was only 32 minutes: all the photographic and soil analysis work had been scheduled for that time period.

Venera 13 represented, along with Venera 14, the limit of the surface lander's potential for at least a number of years. Nevertheless this did not prevent further designs of landers being ordered. Two were commissioned in a joint Soviet—French mission to Venus and Comet Halley, codenamed Vega.

In the meantime, an entirely new type of Venus probe was prepared and sent on its way in the summer of 1983. Venera 15 was put up on 2 June and Venera 16 on 17 June. Each weighed about 4000 kg and an ungainly-looking sideways-looking radar mapper was installed where normally a lander would be carried. The two spacecraft duly entered orbit around the planet on 10 and 15 October 1983 respectively, each orbit taking about 1440 minutes, flying at an altitude of 1000 to 65 000 km. Within weeks, radar images of the Venusian surface were flooding in, to the delight of designer Vyacheslav Kovturenko.

The missions of Venera 15 and 16 lasted a full year, and by the time they concluded 120 million square kilometres had been mapped. 1000 spectrographs had been taken and a thermal map compiled.

Vega 1 and 2 were duly launched in December 1984. They streaked towards Venus on the most sophisticated mission to the planet ever. The ultimate purpose was to intercept Comet Halley in 1986 and all manoeuvres had to be characterized by pinpoint accuracy.

500 000 km above Venus on 9 June 1985, Vega 1 released its descent module. It coasted down towards the surface, which it reached two days later. The 100 kg lander returned data throughout the descent and after touchdown. For two hours it analysed the rocks of the Mermaid Plains [20].

More spectacular was the deployment of a snow-white balloon aerostat. Released at 55 km above the surface during the descent, it had a diameter of 3.4 m, and it began a 47-hour journey in the Venusian atmosphere. 12 m below the balloon was a gondola, full of instruments reporting back on temperature, winds, and the composition of the atmosphere.

By all accounts the balloon had a bumpy ride. The little aerostat was caught in vortices that whirled around at 200 km/r, and tossed it up and down in air pockets. Over the Aphrodite Mountains, the balloon plunged a full 1400 m before steadying its fall. After two days, following a journey of 9000 km, the balloon reached the daylight side of the planet, where the heat expanded the envelope to bursting point.

Vega 2 was equally successful on 16 June 1985, deploying both a balloon and a lander. Both mother ships steered past the planet at 39 000 km, altered course, and set out in direction of the comet as it swung in from the depths of the solar system. Vega 1 and 2 duly intercepted the Comet Halley in the first days of March 1986. Both probes beamed back surrealistic blue, yellow and purple images of the strange, illuminated cosmic snowball.

AROUND VENUS IN 80 DAYS?

Russia has demonstrated a fascination with Venus bordering on the obsessional, and since 1961 only two launch window opportunities to go to Venus have been missed. However in late 1986, the USSR announced that it would be holding back its Venus programme for the time being so as to concentrate on Mars missions.

Nevertheless, Venus is a planet that Soviet space probes will return to. Strange designs of new probes have appeared from time to time. Some came to light in 1984 and they included balloon-like cabins with windows and giant aerials that would float around the atmosphere held under a ringsail torus airship-type design. There were also rumours of roving vehicles and five-tonne landers that would transmit for a week.

A design study of a manned Venus mission appeared in the Soviet magazine *Science and Life* in 1982. The model was unusual and it looked more like an airship patent from the 1890s than anything else. 20 m long, it was the shape of a wasp: a manned capsule up front, an accordian-like fuselage, and a propeller at the rear. The concept was based on expanding and contracting the fuselage size according to altitude. The designer suggested an altitude of 39 km (if filled with steam); or 48 km (if filled with methylalcohol); or 100 km (ammonia). With an electrical supply of 5 kW it would propel itself around the atmosphere at 48 km/h. Despite its unusual nature, the design does make sense and is in line with principles familiar to earthly science [21].

Perhaps one day in the not-too-distant future a crew of cosmonauts will board a purpose-designed Venus craft in Earth orbit, fire its motor, and head out in a curving trajectory towards the shining crescent that people have known since the start of civilization as the evening star. When the cosmonauts return two hundred days or so later, they will have completed the first interplanetary flight by flying by Venus: the conquest of the solar system will have begun.

10

Living in space (1977–85)

The flight of Salyut 5 over 1976–77 marked the end of the first phase of the manned orbital space station programme. Historically too it marked the end of Russia's first twenty years in space, for 1977 was the 20th anniversary of the first Sputnik launching. The next stage was the establishment of a semi-permanent orbiting space sation. It was a more radical step than was realized at the time, so it is worth tracing the origins of this development [1].

It was obvious in the period 1973–74 that the first type of Salyut had only limited potential. Only one ferry could dock with it, and then return. The men had to go down the same way as they came up, evacuating it and closing it down before the next mission. And since Soyuz could stay in space only 90 days at the most, the best that could be achieved was occasional visits to such a space lab.

But setting up space stations was not about visiting: it was about the permanent occupancy of space. This required not so much a larger station, but more important, one with a docking port at either end. A new crew could board at one end as the old one was leaving. So Salyut had to be redesigned. Even so, this was on its own not enough. A quick look at the logistics showed that to support a person in space required the regular supply of quantities of air, food, water, propellant, and replacement parts. Some kind of unmanned cargo ship was called for and the design bureau approved a specification in 1973. With unusual lack of imagination, it was called simply 'Progress'.

Soyuz itself was showing its age. The reduction of crew size from three to two had produced its own problems in terms of performance, and there were also the repeated docking problems. Happily the advent of microelectronics offered a solution to both.

Lightweight electronics saved space, and gave the Soyuz computerized controls. Work on the new Soyuz, which would carry a crew of three and use automated systems, began in 1974. It was called Soyuz 'T' — T for transporter. Not a good week for innovative nomenclature.

Two other technical developments were initiated at the same period. First, both because of America's large Shuttle programme, now due to fly in 1978, and because of their own expected ferrying needs in the late 1980s, work began on a Soviet space shuttle. Reentry tests were planned for 1976 and orbital tests of scale models for 1980.

Second, the versatility of an orbital station could be greatly enhanced by the use of additional specialized modules that could be attached to the station. Thus was the 'Star' module conceived, thought to be the brain-child of cosmonaut and designer Konstantin Feoktistov. A test flight was prepared for 1977, with operational use set for some years later. And so the mid-1970s saw the USSR gear up for the replacement of its original space station by a two-port modernized station; a new-look Soyuz; a cargo spaceship; and an experimental module. One of the extraordinary features of the new upcoming space station, to be Salyut 6, was that by the end of its lifetime it was flying spaceships that were only being designed when it first went into orbit [2]. Such a rapid pace of technological innovation had hitherto been the preserve of only NASA.

THE POLITICS OF CREWING

This period marked the emergence of Konstantin Feoktistov as one of the many chief designers, along with Chalomei, Bushuyev and Simeonov. At 47 Feoktistov was able to represent the generation that came after Korolov. His white-haired, immaculately dressed figure always appeared from this time on in film clips about space missions, and most of the authoritative statements about Soviet space intentions which appeared in the press were issued by him.

It also marked the ascendancy of Boris Petrov until his death in 1981. Author and promoter of the Intercosmos programme, it was he who persuaded the Soviet Government to authorize the series of manned flights with other Socialist countries that began in 1978. Each of the Comecon countries was invited to send two cosmonaut trainees to Star Town and one from each group would be selected to fly.

Such missions would serve a dual purpose. If Soyuz was to be regularly resupplied and visited by manned spacecraft, why not use the copilot's seat to best advantage? And to the Soviet leadership, anxious to impress upon its allies the virtues of their Soviet associations, nothing could be better than offering them the spare seat.

Thus emerged a crewing policy whereby Salyut would be manned by a resident all-Soviet crew and would be visited by crews that included a Soviet Commander and guest flight engineer. How long would such resident crews stay up there? Soviet doctors laid down a 'not more than 50 per cent' rule: endurance missions could not go on more than 50 per cent longer than the longest previous mission. These limits were thought to be safe. Accordingly, three long-stay missions were planned for Salyut 6: they would be of 90–100 days', 140 days', and 175 days' duration.

The proposal to fly guest cosmonauts was not a popular one. Cosmonauts who had waited long and trained hard for their own mission did not take kindly to being bumped by relatively untrained cosmonauts from other countries. And their training would be short. Candidates from Czechoslavakia, Poland and the GDR appeared in late 1976 and they were due to fly within 18 months. But the Russians simply had to put up with it. Vladimir Shatalov was now responsible for crew selection and training and probably had to keep his views to himself. Vasili Lazarev was put in charge of training the new arrivals.

The new Salyut would place unprecedented demands on the cosmonaut corps. Most of the 1960s selection had retired, and so had a number of the 1963 and subsequent groups. The military pilots associated with Salyut 3 and 5 were stepped down (Berezovoi and Gorbatko excepted). To fill these gaps, mission assignments would go to some of the younger pilots selected in 1970 – Dzanibekov, Romanenko, Popov, Berezovoi; and also to the design engineers selected in 1972–3 – men like Lebedev, Ryumin, Aksenov and Strekhalov. Even so, additional cosmonauts were recruited in anticipation of further missions. These included Vladimir Titov, aged 28 when recruited in 1976 as part of a new group of pilots. In 1978, five well-qualified engineers were selected: Viktor Savinyikh, Vladimir Solovyov, Alexander Serebrov, Alexander Alexandrov and Igor Volk. Vladimir Titov was no relation of the other, older, more famous Titov: it is simply a well-known Russian surname.

The first three long duration missions were going to be critical for the setting up of long-term orbiting stations. Each of the crews was going to be asked to fly longer and further than ever before and carry a huge workload, as well as take on board visiting Soyuz crews and Progress freighters. The first such crew was selected in early 1977:

| First crew: | Vladimir Kovalyonok | Backup: | Yuri Romanenko |
| | Valery Ryumin | | Alexander Ivanchenkov |

The first group of visiting Intercosmos crews was also selected:

Czechoslovakia:	Alexei Gubarev	Backups:	Nikolai Rukhavishnikov
	Vladimir Remek		Oldrich Pelczak
Poland:	Pyotr Klimuk	Backups:	Valeri Kubasov
	Miroslav Hermaciewski		Zenon Jankowski
GDR:	Vladimir Dzanibekov	Backups:	Oleg Markarov
	Sigmund Jaehn		Eberhard Köllner

One feature is already apparent, and that is the selection of inexperienced cosmonauts for the resident flight, and more veteran men for the visiting missions. It might have been expected to have been the other way around, but the rationale appears to have been that the shorter missions were actually more demanding and required more experienced pilots.

LAYING THE GROUND WORK

By the summer of 1977 work was proceeding at a feverish pitch on the new station and its related components. The Progress ferrycraft was nearly ready. It was based on the Soyuz. The insides had simply been torn out, and replaced by a much larger freight compartment. Two Progress models were constructed: a tanker and a freight-only model. The tanker could carry about 1000 kg of fuel and 1300 kg of general cargo; the freight-only model would carry 2300 kg of dry load. And that cargo could be anything: fresh water, post, new equipment, repairs, air, food, clothes, books, film, experiments. At one stage even a guitar was sent aloft. Soyuz 20 tested some of the Progress equipment in 1975 and Cosmos 772 completed a three-day Progress test in the same year.

The new Soyuz T was taking a little longer. Sometime before the new Salyut 6 flew it was apparent that it would not be ready in time for the new station, or at least during the first few missions. The delay was almost certainly due to the slow development of the new microcircuits, but it was not the only change being carried out. Solar panels were introduced with an area of 11.5 m². There was a unified propulsion system, meaning that fuel could be transferred from the main engine to the attitude control jets and vice versa. The orbital module was to be cast off in orbit, before retrofire, thus saving some reentry thrust. The on-board propellant was increased from 500 kg to 700 kg, giving an extra margin.

The first flight of the Soyuz T was 29 November 1976, with an 18-day shakedown cruise. Problems still had to be sorted out, and a further 11-day test was flown by Cosmos 1001 on 4—15 April 1978. A 60-day endurance test was then run by Cosmos 1074 starting on 31 January 1979. The extreme caution shown in introducing this model of Soyuz showed again the extent to which the USSR was anxious to make safe its new spacecraft.

The third part of the jigsaw was the Star module. This was further ahead and was ready to fly even before Salyut 6 itself. When it did fly it was to cause quite untold confusion and mystery: indeed the USSR would not admit for many years that Cosmos 929 was anything other than an ordinary Sputnik designed for scientific research. But within days of its launching, it was clear that something odd was going on.

Cosmos 929 went up at 9 a.m. on 17 July 1977. It went into an orbit of 227 by 275 km, 51.6 degrees. Ground trackers at once identified it as of space station class, weighing not less than 16 000 kg and having solar panels. During one pass in the evening twilight it was seen to flash brightly, its panels glinting in the Sun as it turned over.

So why was it not called Salyut? Had it failed? To the contrary, two sets of signals were hooting away loud and clear, and on Salyut frequencies. And from the manoeuvres that followed, it was clear that far from anything being wrong, it was under close ground control and performing as instructed.

During the first month of its flight, Cosmos 929 fired its engine four times. By 7 August its orbit was so low that it was skimming the upper layers of the atmosphere. Then on 19 August a recoverable capsule was sent down. Two days later, as if to confound everyone, the main spacecraft blasted itself into a high orbit of 314 by 329 km. There it stayed for some time.

Some kind of mystery craft was aloft. It was large, had a powerful engine, two types of telemetry, and a recoverable module like the military station. There was no sign of it being manned but unlike Salyut 2 there was no sign of a fault. Then suddenly on 19 December a blast of the motors sent the craft up to an unprecedented 440 by 448 km. On 2 February 1978 it was deorbited over the Pacific, away from the shipping lanes [3].

By then most people had lost interest in Cosmos 929 because it had been overtaken by Salyut 6 which was stealing all the headlines. Still, speculation abounded amongst those who would never close a file on a mystery mission until all was told. One interesting explanation came in an article called impressively 'The prospects for Soviet orbital construction in the summer of 1977' by Nicholas Johnson, which linked Cosmos 929 to a failed Proton launch on 4 August. Cosmos 929 was, he argued, the first spacetug, and it was to tow a special module (to have flown on 4 August) up to the upcoming Salyut 6 to set up a multi-complex space station just in time for the 20th anniversary of the Sputnik launching on 4 October [4].

Far-fetched? Probably. But his understanding of Cosmos 929 turned out to be more accurate than people thought. The USSR had talked publicly for some time of flying specialized modules up to space stations, and Cosmos 929 was actually the first of them. It was a combined spacetug, freighter, specialized module and recovery craft – an extraordinarily versatile machine and a radical innovation. Cosmos 929, it later transpired, was its first, and highly successful test.

Even as this was going on, the real space station was nearly ready. On 29 September a D–1 rocket put Salyut 6 into orbit. Autumn was in the air. On 4 October the Sputnik anniversary passed. The third decade of the space race was just about to begin.

FOUR-TIME FAILURE

Inconveniently, the orbital path of Salyut 6 did not suit a 4 October launch on the exact anniversary date. Salyut was still manoeuvring to its operational altitude of 336 by 352 km, which it reached on 7 October. Two days later, the two cosmonauts selected for the mission arrived at the pad. It was still dark and liftoff was scheduled for 5.40 a.m. Fully helmeted and suited they clambered out of the transfer van, and carrying their life-support boxes, walked gingerly across the concrete apron like scuba divers about to take the plunge.

Both the jaunty, cheerful commander, Vladimir Kovalyonok, and the tall, black-haired engineer, Valeri Ryumin, were very much aware of the importance of their mission. They chatted to the pressmen and drew their attention to the fact that this was the same pad from where Sputnik 1 had been launched twenty years earlier.

Nor were these historic parallels lost on the Soviet media. Moscow television showed the cosmonauts heading skywards in their Soyuz rocket with hammer and sickle flags flying proudly on the apron. Soyuz 25 headed into orbit 27 minutes behind Salyut. After course adjustments on orbit 3 and 5 it was below and behind Soyuz and closing fast. The crew rested that night and prepared for docking. Down on the ground, Kettering Grammar School had picked up Soyuz on the standard frequency and listened to the voice exchanges between Soyuz and the ground.

They were glad they did. On revolution 17 they heard Kovalyonok call off 'three metres a second and closing fast', and then 'two metres a second'. They waited for the next fly-around, expected to hear the pressures between Soyuz and Salyut being equalized. But they picked up no such reports on revolution 18. What was going on? At the same time – though Kettering could not know it – American ground trackers measured Soyuz and Salyut so close as to be indistinguishable.

Revolution 19. The last pass before Soyuz 25 went out of Kettering's range. The students picked up Kovalyonok and Ryumin going through a systems check of Soyuz. Far from having docked, they were still on their own. A silence descended on the mission in Moscow. Eventually after 14 hours it was announced that the docking had been cancelled and the crew were returning to the Earth. The craft was being powered down to conserve energy.

They were down the following morning near Tselinograd, having been in space 2 days and 46 minutes. They were exhausted, frustrated and depressed. They were at once flown off to Baikonour to begin the process of finding out what had gone wrong. Whatever it was, the men themselves were not to blame. They had rendezvoused perfectly – and indeed had spent revolutions 18 to 24 only a few hundred metres from the station. Four times they had closed in to dock. And four times they had failed to get a connection. Each time they had operated all the mechanisms, and still no capture.

It was an experience identical to what American astronauts had found on Apollo 14 and Skylab 2: a stubborn refusal of the mechanisms to couple. On both occasions the Americans had simply rammed their ships together and it had eventually worked. Kovalyonok tried this again and again, but to no avail. So the big question was: did the fault lie on Soyuz or the station? They hoped the former and feared the latter. If Salyut's docking port was defective, the Russians had just launched a defective orbiting station.

RESCUE JOB

Mid-November: a contingency plan had been prepared. They would fly the next Soyuz up to the other docking port. Then they would send a cosmonaut spacewalking to inspect the other docking port and try to locate the fault. The backup spaceship was made ready, with its crew, Yuri Romaneko and Alexander Ivanchenkov.

So far so good: it would be the first Soviet repair mission in space. But neither man had been in space before. Vladimir Shatalov must have thought long and hard before he took an unpopular but ultimately correct decision. He pulled Ivanchenkov out of the flight and substituted the more experienced Soyuz 17 veteran Georgi Grechko. Older, longer in the business, a spaceship designer himself, better he did the spacewalking than a novice, even if he had only four weeks in which to get ready.

Georgi Grechko and Yuri Romanenko must have worked flat out for the next four weeks to prepare their mission, upon which the future of Salyut depended. For the first time they were able to use the huge new hydrotank in Star Town. Like a giant swimming pool, it contained full-scale mockups of the Soyuz and Salyut which were placed on the bottom before the tank was filled with water. It had glass sides so that observers could see everything that was going on. Romanenko and Grechko donned scuba suits built to the same size as spacesuits and repeatedly practised exiting from the EVA hatch, inspecting the faulty docking drogue and returning. The tank had its limitations but it was the nearest that they could get to zero gravity on that kind of scale on Earth.

Each man gradually got to know another he had not before teamed up with. The younger Romanenko must have found the presence of a more experienced engineer and designer reassuring, while he knew his own piloting experience would stand him in good stead.

They blased off on 10 December. It was a night-time launch and they met the dawn as they came over the Pacific Ocean. They settled in for the day-long chase of their target.

Ground control was crowded early the following morning as Romaneko steered Soyuz 25 in for docking at the second port. Konstantin Feoktistov stood behind the control consoles, checking each one in turn. Engineers, frowning and anxious, studied incoming

The smiling face of cosmonaut Yuri Romanenko, commander of Soyuz 26, who, with fellow cosmonaut Georgi Grechko, docked with Salyut 6 in December 1977 and stayed aboard the space station for (at the time) a record-breaking 96 days.

data. Large wall displays charted the main information. The cameras were switched on to show the gull-shaped Salyut in the middle of the screen, larger each minute. Mission doctor Alexei Yeliseyev had his earphones on and was listening to the crew's every report.

Automatic control brought the two craft within 10 m of each other. Yuri Romanenko then took over, and, wasting no time at all, nudged Soyuz forward for the last little bit. 'Full pressure. . . full electrical coupling!' he reported. They had done it! There were sighs and signs of relief all round, and the ground control emptied out like a parliament once a crucial vote is taken and over. Then routine went on again.

Kettering Grammar had picked up the cosmonauts on radio. They phoned Reuters news agency at once: Reuters told them Moscow had still not made any announcement. First again. And within hours an exuberant Yuri Romanenko and Georgi Grechko were aboard the Saylut, crawling through the rear end which had hitherto contained only equipment and motors. Now the motors were on an outside ring away from the docking tunnel, which was an awkward arrangement but one which worked.

HOME FROM HOME

Salyut 6 was no bigger than its predecessors, but the internal design was much improved and Georgi Grechko must have been struck by the changes of design that had taken place since his sojourn aboard Salyut 4. Dominating the large equipment module was the cone-shaped BST 1M telescope located on the floor, and also recessed into the floor was the MKF 6M multi-spectral camera. Storage tanks and food lockers were recessed into the walls. So too were a treadmill weighing device, and sleeping bag beds. As they moved into the forward part of the station the cosmonauts found the large control console with displays and blinking lights.

There was a water recylcing plant, full of pipes, blocks and cylinders; a barrel arm for rotating the solar panel on the roof; and finally in the airlock hatch were storage containers for the spacesuits they would soon be needing. Salyut 6 on its own was 15 long, 4.15 m in diameter at its widest, weighed 18.9 tonnes, and the solar panels had an area of 60 m². The manoeuvring engine had a thrust of 300 kg. Habitable volume was 90 m³, nine times more than their Soyuz ferry.

On the outside the station's separate modules had been welded together. A multi-layer blanket had been put on to protect the skin. Radiators had been added to disperse the heat. The small portholes had been sealed by rubber. The only other breaks in the structure were an electric welding furnace, called Splav-01, and a refuse hatch.

For Yuri Romanenko and Georgi Grechko it was to be their home and the designers had made some efforts to improve creature comforts. One such device was a shower made out of a collapsible polythene cabin. A pump would be used to squirt in water at one end and extract it at the other. The American Skylab shower had been an all-round disaster, taking one and a half hours to erect. The astronauts hated it: there was never enough water and it left them covered in soap bubbles.

For their first week on board, Yuri Romanenko and Georgi Grechko settled in, turning all the systems on till they were humming. They evacuated and mothballed their old Soyuz. They took viewers on a tour of the station, with their colour camera. They tested the 'Delta' navigation system and swung the station through different attitudes.

Perhaps the most important change compared to the previous missions was in the length of the working day. On earlier missions there was a constant need for contact with the ground. This meant that one cosmonaut had always to be up, and this proved to be very tiring. Now there were teleprinters on board which meant that there could be the automatic telexing of information from Earth up to the station and vice versa. As a result, the crew worked Moscow Time, like the ground, and the telexing could be taking place when the crew were sleeping. This made the work much easier, and after a week in space the crew were in a position to carry out the vital spacewalk that would determine the entire future of the mission.

'NO SCRATCHES'

They went into the airlock hatch and got into their new spacesuits. They were quite different from the earlier suits: they were only one-piece and the astronaut climbed in through a zip in the rear. It was a standardized size, for use by future crew members of different shapes and sizes. The helmet was clear glass. The system had an independent air and communication system, and only a tether was necessary to connect the cosmonaut to the station itself.

It was midnight early on 20 December by the time they were ready and had tested their suits for faults and leaks. Grechko emerged first, and Romanenko was to remain behind in the depressurized airlock to monitor readings from Grechko's suit. At least that was the idea.

Grechko emerged when Salyut was cruising over the Cook Islands in the Pacific. He was nearly blinded by the sunlight. Gingerly he grasped the handrails alongside the hull and edged his way along to the docking port. By the time he got there the Sun had gone down. It was pitch black. He looked down and he could see the pin-prick lights of African and European cities glowing in the dark. The Moon was setting and he could see the stars. From the inside of the station it was simply impossible to comprehend the vastness of a sky like this.

Soon he was over the USSR and in live contact with the ground. He set up a bright arc lamp so he could inspect the docking unit. With him was an equipment box of tools spanners. And in no time he could see that there was little visibly wrong with Salyut's docking port:

> The butt end is brand new — just as when it was machined tooled. There are no scratches or dents or traces. The cone is clear: not a scratch. The lamps, sockets and latches are in order. [5]

He tested all the plugs, sockets and rods and they all worked perfectly. It must have been the Soyuz that had been at fault. Grechko beamed the camera onto the docking system so that the images could be transmitted to the ground for them to see. They were in a state of exhilaration. 'Come back in!' Grechko was ordered. He grabbed the handrails and headed back — and got the fright of his life.

Yuri Romanenko had spent the past hour in the airlock, suited up and watching instruments, and seeing none of the action. Curiosity got the better of him. He poked his head out of the hatchway and pushed himself gently out just for a look at the view. He expected his tether to pull him back — but it did not. He must have never attached it! He was heading rapidly into open space, on the verge of becoming his own one-man satellite of the Earth. His air might last an hour or two before it ran out. He began thrashing wildly to try to attach his tether somewhere, just anywhere.

Georgi Grechko had just reached the main part of the airlock module to see his comrade in dire distress. He pushed off from the hull, floated towards him, judging his movement ever so carefully, reached out and grabbed his line, and pulled him in. Seconds later and it would have been too late. Sweating madly and their hearts pumping, they climbed in. Never again!

They were debating about whether to tell ground control about this *faux pas* when they were confronted by a more serious crisis. They ordered the valve which depressurized the airlock to close — but it would not. The instrument panel showed it as open and jammed open. They could repressurize the airlock as much as they wanted but the air would still go gushing out into space through the valve. They were stuck in the vacuum and their spacesuit air was running out even as they discussed what they could do next.

Mission control was shocked to hear of this development: the cosmonauts should have been back in Salyut long ago. They talked and argued and decided they simply had to repressurize and hope that the instrument reading was wrong.

The pressure held. They climbed back into the main part of Salyut, took off their suits, headed for their sleeping bags and slept for ten hours. The worst was over. The mission was saved.

DOUBLE LINK-UP

Ground control was not told of Romanenko's little adventure until they were back on Earth. He made his confession to the post-flight press conference and did so in such a charming and disarming way that no one felt they could reprimand him.

The successful spacewalk paved the way for a linkup with the front docking port which now had a clean bill of health. The Czechoslovakian visiting mission was not yet ready, so the first visiting crew would be an all-Soviet one. Vladimir Dzanibekov and Oleg Markarov were taken off the East German crew assignment (their places were taken by Bykovsky and Gorbatko) and told to prepare for Soyuz 27 in mid-January. They could then bring the old Soyuz 26 back and leave the rear docking port free for the first cargo ship. It could only come in at the rear port.

Having recovered from their EVA, Romanenko and Grechko got on with their more routine work. They exercised regularly. They checked each other medically each day. They watched forest fires in Africa. On 26 December two supertankers collided off Africa and they reported on the resultant oil slick. The cosmonauts worked six days a week and established a pattern of Sundays off. They played chess, using magnetic counters. They read books, and Georgi Grechko kept up his English. They had video casettes if these diversions were not enough.

They needed their recreation. They found it hard to sleep at night with the relentless noises of an orbiting station. In the daytime the humming and clicking of the motors, relays, equipment and filters did not matter as much: but at night it kept them awake and they were always alert for the sound that might tell them something more serious had happened.

Actually keeping the station running used up much of the time. Every five days they had to replace the air units. They were chemical and soaked up carbon dioxide, eventually becoming saturated. The water regeneration systems had to be renewed and each cosmonaut needed about 3 qts of water each day.

As for food, they were eating mainly from cans. There were ten dehydrated items which they could put into hot water. A typical day's menu was:

Breakfast: White bread
             Cottage cheese and blackcurrant jam
             Canned ham
             Cake
             Coffee

Dinner: Vegetable soup
                 Canned chicken
                 Plums
                 Nuts
                 Biscuits and cheese

Evening dinner: Black bread
                  Canned steak
                  Fruit juice
                  Cocoa

Vitamin pills were obligatory. But the food tasted blander than on the ground – somehow there was a difference. The crew also got a craving for some items like honey and spices. Above all they desired onions, garlic, horseradish and mustard.

On 1 January they became the first Soviet crew to move from the old year to the new while in orbit. They crossed the time zones fifteen times in one day. And they were never far from the twenty portholes on board. Georgi Grechko gazed down on the icy peaks of the Himalayas and this is what he told the ground: 'Our cities in the northern hemisphere are snow-clad but their outline can be clearly seen. In the south, hot summer has set in. Snow has melted in the mountains and the rivers have dried' [6].

Four days later, tadpoles hatched out in the fish containers brought on board. Unlike earthly tadpoles, which swim randomly, they used to swim in spirals. On the biological front they were also growing chlorella which could serve as a source of food. On 6 January as they flew over Japan they spotted 3.7 km tall Mount Fujiyama rising through the clouds. Two days later they activated an experiment called 'Medusa'. Two sets of containers were set up, one outside the station and the other inside. Each contained amino acids and the other basic building blocks of life. The two would be retrieved and compared, the external one being particularly interesting from having been exposed to the rawness of space.

Meanwhile preparations had continued at rapid speed on the ground for the first-ever double space linkup – the joining of two manned craft to one orbital station. If successful it would mark a landmark in the development of orbital stations.

10 January. Midday. Cosmonauts Vladimir Dzanibekov and Oleg Markarov arrived at the launching pad. It was a clear winter's day and very cold.

2.19 p.m. Salyut 6 passed over Baikonour. Every tiny detail of its trajectory went into Soyuz' computer.

2.26 p.m. The Soyuz rocket shook and shuddered and headed skywards, gathering speed all the time. Within minutes Soyuz 27 was in orbit.

The final part of the chase was in darkness. Vladimir Dzanibekov picked up the space station visually at 1500 m and saw its docking lights blinking at 300 m. He went in entirely automatically and the two ships clunked together. The mishap of the previous October might never have happened.

Romanenko and Grechko had retreated to their own Soyuz 26 and battened down the hatches, just in case the docking was violent and the pressure was lost. They need not have worried. Dzanibekov and Markarov were on board within hours and it was a cheerful reunion. And why not, for the docking port was now operational and the first-ever three-ship linkup was now history. Tass crowed:

> For the first time in the history of astronautics a manned scientific research station has been created in terrestrial orbit consisting of an orbiting station and two space-craft. [7]

The complex weighed 32 tonnes and was 30 m long. The process was not as easy as it looked, for the engineers were afraid of the structural strain that two spacecraft would have: they feared it might make it unstable. Unanticipated metal fatigue had after all destroyed the career of the Comet 1 civil airliner in the 1950s. So, in an experiment aptly named 'Resonance', the crew had to jump up and down to a metronome beat relayed up from the ground, so as to see if they set up any unanticipated strains. They did not.

On 15 January Dzanibekov warmed up the old Soyuz 26 to prepare to bring it home. They swopped their own custom-built couches from Soyuz 27 into 26 and vice versa. And they did a final day's work, the four men together. Several televised broadcasts showed them happily at work in the main cabin, clipboards in hand and communications cords snaking all about.

On the 16th they undocked from Salyut 6 and pulled slowly away. Dzanibekov and Markarov circled the Earth twice, blased the retrorockets, and went into blackout over the Caucasus Mountains. They touched down in the snow 20 minutes later. Their six-day mission had proved conclusively that manned orbiting stations could be met in space, crews put on and taken off, all with the efficiency of a train timetable.

FERRY AHOY!

Dzanibekov and Markarov, flush with their triumph, arrived in Star Town on 20 January to be greeted by Konstantin Feoktistov. Only hours before, television pictures relayed on Moscow Television had shown a new Soyuz rocket on its way to Salyut. For early that morning the first of the Progress ferrycraft had set off in pursuit of the orbital station.

This was a critical moment. Progress had been tested only twice before. There was a danger of collision if Progress came in too fast. For this reason, two precautions had to be taken. First, two external camera trackers had been installed on the outside of Salyut. Second, data from Progress read out automatically on Salyut's TV. That way the crew would know if something was wrong and they could intervene.

Progress's slow pursuit took two full days, and Romanenko and Grechko eventually picked it up against the background of the Earth when it was 10 km away. It was moving rapidly against clouds. Soon its contours came sharply into focus. It moved in and docked smoothly. Within hours Romanenko and Grechko had opened the transfer hatch and were unpacking the robot visitor.

First, and always first, came the personal items. The families of cosmonauts always used these opportunities to write to their away-from-home fathers and husbands. Families could now send up letters and even small parcels. It did wonders for morale and, with visiting crews, return letters were now possible as well. This did much to break down the psychological isolation of orbit. Newspapers helped too.

Not the least welcome of the Progress cargo was underwear, fresh clothes and bed linen. The ferry also carried bread, fruit, more film, seat straps and medicine. There was a small electrical glass furnace experiment. To help with Earth observations, there was something so basic that no one had thought of putting it on Salyut in the first place — an atlas.

PUMPING UNDER PRESSURE

But that was the easy part of the Progress operation. The more difficult part — refuelling — lay ahead. On 30 January the cosmonauts pumped air on board from Progress into Salyut's air tanks, under pressure. Transferring volatile fuel around under pressure, in zero gravity was tricky, dangerous and difficult. Still, it had to be done. Salyut's own fuel, used to boost up its orbit whenever it fell lower, was nearly used up. The craft was being frequently reorientated for observations, and these manoeuvres were dear on fuel too.

Salyut had six fuel tanks — three of them hydrazine and three of them nitrogen tetroxide, pressurized by nitrogen at 220 atmospheres. This nitrogen had to be pumped out so as to let the new fuel in. All this required a formidable amount of electrical power — in fact 1 kW — or most of the station's available energy. So that this could happen, the station was powered down, and all the other experiments were turned off. And to conserve power, refuelling was spread over four days.

Romanenko and Grechko took up position at the control panel. They had to be ready to respond to any problems that might arise, like leaks or airlocks.

First they brought pressure inside Salyut's fuel system down to 3 atmospheres. Then they purged the system with helium. Finally, pushed in by the 8 atmosphere pressure in Progress, the new fuel was pumped aboard. They could listen to it gurgling and flowing in. After six shifts, the operation was complete. It had gone perfectly, and on 5 February a last purge was carried out to prevent Progress spraying Salyut when it undocked. Finally on the same day, and noting that there was still a fair amount of Progress's own fuel still aboard, Flight Director Alexei Yeliseyev blasted Progress's engine to push the whole complex into a higher orbit. It was the first-ever use of a spacetug.

They were not finished with Progress yet. They loaded it up with rubbish like leftovers from food, containers, boxes, paper, in fact anything they no longer needed. Then they sealed the hatch, and commanded Progress 1 to undock. Progress withdrew to 16 km away. Then ground control activated its backup rendezvous system and commanded it return to the station, which it obediently did.

Finally on 8 February its engines lit up for the last time and it was deorbited into the North Pacific Ocean, away from shipping lanes. It had passed all its tests with flying colours and vindicated its designers. In the space of three weeks, Progress 1 and Soyuz 27 between them had given the USSR an operational space station system. The failures of earlier flights receded into the distance.

Dumping rubbish into Progress let some Westerners — anxious to defend the much delayed American Shuttle — decry Progress as a 'throwaway supply ship', inferring that it was, if anything, a step backwards. It certainly was that, but it was based on a proven Soyuz design. Development costs were therefore low, and, more important, it worked.

How to dispose of rubbish was indeed a problem. America's Skylab astronauts expressed the view that unless special measures were taken, astronauts were in danger of circling the Earth in the polluted debris of their own rubbish. Salyut cosmonauts also dumped rubbish out of their airlock hatch. At one stage, ground control told Grechko that they could see flying saucers closing in on the station. He looked out — and found the station was being enveloped in plastic bags which they had dumped overboard just a few orbits before. They only got away from them when they changed orbit.

On 11 February they had spent two months in space, and with still a month to go they broke the 63-day record of Pyotr Klimuk and Vitally Sevastianov set in 1975. The previous day had been the 150th anniversary of the birth of Jules Verne and Georgi Grechko hosted a special press conference to mark the occasion:

> Hello, everyone. Today is Jules Verne's anniversary. There's hardly anyone who hasn't read his books, at least among the cosmonauts. He was a dreamer and a visionary who foretold flights into space. I'd say this flight was predicted by Jules Verne. [8]

Like Leonov, Georgi Grechko brought his drawing block with him into space. With coloured pencils he made drawings of clouds in the upper atmosphere, or aurorae, and Venus rising over the horizon.

SPACE FACTORY

The USSR had paved the way for welding experiments in space, starting with Soyuz 6 and continuing on board Salyut 5. After Progress 1's arrival the cosmonauts were able to complete assembling an electric furnace going under the name of 'Splav-01'. Once all the components had been put together, they were placed in the airlock.

Spalv-01 weighed 23 kg and could heat metals up to temperatures of $1100°C$, with a computer controlling accuracy within $±5°C$. For the first experiment, which lasted 14 hours, the station was powered down and allowed to drift, both to save energy and so as not to disrupt the work of the furnace. Capsules of copper, indium, aluminium and magnesium were put into the furnace and crystallized. The airlock was then repressurized and the samples were recovered. A second experiment was then run in soldering and welding aluminium and tungsten. The samples were retrieved and placed in containers for later recovery on Earth. The great advantage of the new manned ferry and automatic cargo ship system was that the scientists could examine the results and then send up new materials in the next ferry.

More processing experiments were to be flown on Salyut 6 later on, and in 1980 the American magazine *Aviation Week and Space Technology* made the following comment:

> 'Extensive space processing on Salyut 6 has the potential of providing the USSR with a technical lead on the US' [9].

On 20 February Romanenko and Grechko brought their large telescope into action for the first time. It was the largest telescope of its kind ever flown in space – indeed it used up a substantial proportion of the equipment module. Its detector crystals were cooled by liquid helium to a temperature of −269°C. And like any Earth-bound astronomer they sighted it with a small built-in telescope sight.

And it opened up the universe to them. Through it they could spot and photograph Mars and Jupiter, the star Sirius, the Orion nebula and interstellae gas clouds. And using it to look towards Earth gave even more spectacular vistas.

Things did go wrong from time to time. At one stage the radio broke down and they lost sound channel completely. They had to turn on the television and use gestures and drawings to explain what was going on! And then there was the great fly escape. Fruit flies escaped from their container. Romanenko and Grechko spent hours chasing them around trying to catch up with them and mop them up with a vacuum cleaner. They got most of them, but a few would still come out to buzz around their ears whilst they slept.

By now they were well into a routine. Relaxing each seventh day. Sleeping, eating, housekeeping. They hated the mandatory two hours' exercise each day. It cut down the time for experiments which was why they had gone up there in the first place. It was uncomfortable and left them sweaty and tired. The shower took hours to erect and take down and there was not enough water coming out. But they also knew that their bodies could never return to Earth unless they exercised. Still, it gave them headaches and fatigue. By the time they received their second set of visitors to the station on 3 March they were not in the best of humours.

COMRADES ABOARD

They must have had their doubts about the nature of the Soyuz 28 mission. Originally the international missions had been planned to promote cooperation and take up redundant seats when the old Soyuz capsule had to be flown down and a fresh one brought up. But Romanenko and Grechko were nearing the end of their mission anyhow. There was no need to replace Soyuz 27, and in fact they planned to ride it home. Soyuz 28 would come up for eight days and return. There was no engineering necessity for the mission: in other words, it was being flown more for political reasons than anything else.

Running international missions was not of itself an unuseful exercise − but running missions which had no other justification was indeed questionable. And the USSR went to great lengths to get the Intercosmos cosmonauts into the air as soon as was feasible. The training period was sometimes as little as 15 months, and the new men bumped Soviet cosmonauts who had been waiting for flights as long as 12 years. Instruction seems to have been minimal. Few got practical experience in running missions from ground control. And once the mission was flown, the two cosmonauts were sent straight home: there was never any question of a second mission.

More worrying perhaps were the reasons involved in crew selections. Guest cosmonauts were vetted for their political reliability. Czech cosmonaut Vladimir Remek was son of his Government's deputy Defence Minister. Poland's Miroslav Hermaciewski was brother of an Air Force General. It was a standard East European joke at the time that if it was not for such severe criteria the crew would defect and arrange to land in West Germany!

This is not to suggest that the East European pilots were incompetent: far from it. They worked hard, mastered their lessons, were able fliers, and would not have been put on board if they were not. Vladimir Remek's training including a diet, in the course of which he had to lose 20 kg — otherwise he would be unable to fit into the tiny Soyuz cabin.

So why the rush to get the Intercosmos pilots airborne? One reason was that the Americans also had an international manned programme in the pipeline. The United States' equivalent, Spacelab, was a small manned space laboratory to be flown in the cargo bay of the Shuttle, and the first Spacelab mission had been set for 1980. Spacelab was being built by the European Space Agency, ESA, partly because NASA could not get the funds for Spacelab on its own. But part of the deal was the ESA could nominate astronauts for NASA to fly aboard Spacelab. In fact, the first Spacelab mission was to slip until late 1983, when NASA flew a West German, but that could not be known at the time. Intercosmos meant beating Spacelab, and the fact that there were eight Intercosmos countries meant that eight Intercosmos flights were slated for Salyut 6, departing in order of political loyalty. The Rumanians, the most disloyal of all the Eastern Bloc countries, had to wait till last. [10]

The planners of the Salyut 6 mission may well have resented the intrusion of the Intercosmos missions, but they had to grin and bear it. The Americans were not beyond reproach either, and in 1983 President Reagan was busily and magnanimously offering seats in the Shuttle to Brazil and Canada. A share of the space action was fast becoming part of the superpower game. And security checks on the ESA astronauts were rigorous: a British candidate astronaut was dropped in 1984 simply because he had been an acquaintance of someone involved in a minor security scandal.

Soyuz 28 docked with Salyut's rear docking port on the evening of 3 March. Vladimir Remek and Alexei Gubarev were given a warm welcome aboard and they celebrated through the night. Georgi Grechko spent much time comparing notes with Alexei Gubarev, with whom he had flown on Salyut 4 four years earlier. Pictures of Leonid Brezhnev and Gustav Husak were sellotaped to the walls before the TV cameras. Fraternal greetings flowed to and fro.

A number of joint Soviet–Czechoslovakian experiments were devised for the mission. 'Chlorella' investigated how seaweed could be used to develop a closed ecological system. They used the 'Splav-01' furnace to smelt glass, silver and copper for the Academy of Sciences in Prague. There were eight other experiments, whose strategic value was uncertain.

Alexei Gubarev and Vladimir Remek undocked over Lake Baikal on 10 March. Retrofire was over the South Atlantic and they were down near Arkalyk within half an hour. Within weeks they were being fêted as heroes throughout Czechoslovakia. Streets were named in their honour and they were opening schools and talking to youth groups and meeting factory workers throughout the summer.

Their return gave Romanenko and Grechko the breathing space they needed to re-organize Salyut and prepare for their own return. Tension rose — they would be returning after being aloft longer than anyone before them. Exercise periods were doubled for their last week in space. They used their penguin suits all the time.

Closing down the orbiting station sounded simpler than it was. A precise inventory had to be made of what was still on board. Systems had to be turned on automatic. All research results had to be stowed carefully on Soyuz 27. On 15 March they fired the Soyuz engine for a quarter of a second to check if it was still operational.

Aboard the Salyut 6 space station (from right to left) Yuri Romanenko and Georgo Grechko, the crew of Soyuz 26, prepare to open the first post office in space with the assistance of the two visiting cosmonauts Alexei Gubarev and Vladimir Remek from Soyuz 28.

The two men rose early on 16 March, had breakfast, and surveyed the interior of Salyut for the last time. It had been their home for three months and it had served them well. They scribbled a note for the next crew, slammed the hatch and strapped themselves into the descent cabin.

CARRIED AWAY

It was getting dark near Tselingorad when their blackened capsule, beacon aflashing, was spotted coming down under its single parachute. It was on time and in the right place. Shadows of the ground crews and the helicopters stood out long in the spring snow. The five Mil helicopters, their engines roaring as they raced their throttles, their blades whirring, closed in and landed a safe distance away. They turned off their engines. Calm returned to the snowscape. There was only the crunching of boots on the snow.

They placed ladders against the capsule. Doctors raced to the top and opened up. They were greeted by two grinning faces. Romanenko and Grechko were eased up, onto stretchers, and carried into the waiting helicopters. Their smiles and grins stretched from ear to ear. Relieved and elated, they were breathing real fresh air for the first time in a quarter of a year. How wholesome it was, how natural in its coldness! The quiet words of welcome were muffled in the snow. The Mil engines roared and they were carried away. They were someone else's business now.

They had good reason to celebrate. The flight was 96 days and 10 hours, no less, and twelve days beyond the Skylab 4 record. Grechko had reached a personal record of 124 days in space.

But in one sense the experiment was only just beginning. How would they readapt to our heavy planet? The men were forbidden to walk unaided, not that they could not have done so, but for fear of in some way straining their hearts. Everything they found heavy. Their beds were heavy. Lifting a cup of tea was a challenge akin to weight-lifting. Sudden movements brought nausea. This might have caused worry, except that there was nothing wrong with their sleep nor their appetites.

By 20 March they were able to go for a walk together. Soon they were talking to different scientific groups that had prepared and followed their flight – the engineers, the spacesuit designers, the astrophysicists. By early April they had put back the weight they had lost in orbit and had shaken off the sensations of the flight. They eventually rid themselves of the tendency of trying to 'swim' out of their beds in the middle of the night!

Head of the Medical Team Dr Anatoli Yegorov attributed the medical success of the mission to their ability to go on working, to regular exercise, the size of Salyut itself, and psychological compatibility. Yuri Romanenko and Georgi Grechko became good friends during the flight and their friendship was to endure. Grechko's humour probably kept things going when times got hard.

On 10 April they returned to Star Town. There was a reception in the Kremlin, medals speeches, and toasts. A large press conference followed, attended by experts from different aspects of the flight. Early in May they joined the Soyuz 28 crew then touring Prague and Bratislava.

By early 1978 Soviet cosmosnauts had spent 600 days in space aboard the six Salyuts, compared to the 500 days of Skylab. But the achievement of Georgi Grechko and Yuri Romanenko was more than the number of hours flown: they had demonstrated the ability to live and work in space, to refuel, to take on visiting ships and crews, to inspect damage, to weld materials in the vacuum, and to take Salyut to its limits. There had been problems, but the systems had passed their tests. The bad old days seemed behind them at last.

So they were. Soyuz 26 began a period of virtually unbroken success in which one record was to be broken after another, and one frontier after another pushed back. The years of persistence were paying off.

OFF AGAIN!

Evaluation of the first set of missions was complete by mid-May and the decision was taken to proceed with the next long-duration mission. An added incentive was the long summer evenings because they gave good lighting conditions in the more northerly parts of the USSR.

Who would fly the next mission? The hiccup of Soyuz 25 and the drafting in of Georgi Grechko had upset the original crewing schedules. So some rearranging was done. The crew commander selected was Vladimir Kovalyonok (of Soyuz 25) and the flight engineer was the man Georgi Grechko had bumped – Alexander Ivanchenkov. This was fair for everyone, except Valeri Ryumin, who had been with Kovalyonok on Soyuz 25. He was put down as backup with Vladimir Lyakhov, which meant that they would in turn be in line for the third long-duration mission the following year.

The challenge they faced was to extend the last mission by 50 per cent, to around 140 days. They really would be on their own this time, with no American experience to guide them. Physically very different — Kovalyonok was short and square-faced while Ivanchenkov was thin and long-faced — their temperaments were similar: determined, and insistent on achieving excellence in whatever they were asked to do.

Kovalyonok and Ivanchenko took off on a warm summer's evening, only a week before the longest day in the year. It was 15 June. A new navigation system had been installed on Soyuz 29 called 'Igla' or 'needle'. It was switched on 22 km from Salyut and took care of the final phase of the rendezvous.

It took them a week to get Salyut back into shape and operational once more. They worked a more relaxed schedule than their predecessors — a five-day week rather than a six-day week; nine hours sleep a night rather than eight; and a schedule from 8 a.m. to 11 p.m.

From 23 to 26 June they ran a three-day smelting experiment on mercury and cadmium. They closed the Soyuz, turned off the thrusters, and let the station drift to prevent irregularities in the metals. It so happened that they found themselves in an orbit in which the Sun simply rolled low on the northern horizon and never set and they could look at it without the need for filters.

A MESSAGE FROM GENERAL JARUZELSKI

Martial law was imposed in Poland in December 1981, under the guidance of strongman General Woiciech Jaruzelski. He was an unforgettable figure — small, with an abrupt marching manner, shiny leather jacket with wide lapels, reflective black glasses. His martial law regime was to earn him Soviet trust on the one hand and the antipathy of Poland's free trade union, Solidarity, on the other.

But that was far into the future. On 27 June 1978, when General Jaruzelski arrived at Baikonour cosmodrome as the Polish Government representative, Poland was a quiet undemonstrative ally of the USSR and a lot more reliable than the troublesome Czechs or Rumanians. There was no indication of the turbulence yet to come.

General Jaruzelski had gone to Baikonour to bid goodbye to Poland's first cosmonaut, Miroslav Hermaziewski, who had been teamed up with Pyotr Klimuk. The General must have been well satisfied with what he saw: Soyuz 30 lifted off smoothly and on 28 June its crew were boarding Salyut through its rear port.

There was, technically speaking, no need for the flight, and they came back in the same Soyuz 30 that put them up there. But a batch of experiments was put together anyway, by the Polish Academy of Sciences and the Warsaw Institute of Air Medicine. The most important, called 'Sirena', involved 14 hours of smelting pure glass. It was to be run at night, so that the process of development would not be interfered with by wakened cosmonauts moving around the station. But Miroslav Hermaziewski was so worried about whether the equipment was working that he got up several times during the night to check, with the result that he may have ruined the outcome!

They were back on the ground after a week on board, coming down inconsiderately on a field of maize on the Rostov State Farm. Hermaziewski was franker about his feelings during reentry than his Soviet colleagues normally were: 'You sit in the landing capsule and you see nothing but flames all around. . . you trust the machines, you trust the technology, but in your heart of hearts you still have that nagging doubt' [11].

MEDUSA

What was probably more valuable in the long run to Kovalyonok and Ivanchenkov was the regular supply of cargo from Earth. Progress 2 rose to join them on 7 July and was alongside a day later. It brought 50 days' worth of supplies of food, water and air, as well as letters, and, for Ivanchenkov, his guitar which he had requested.

At this stage, new advantages of the Progress began to show up. Salyut 6 had run out of film: Progress 2 brought up 100 kg of new film. One of the main instrument panels had blown: Progress brought up a replacement. And a new internal furnace called 'Krystall' was sent up. Propellant was transferred, almost as a matter of routine at this stage.

By 29 July they were ready for a spacewalk, not so much with repairs in mind this time but the retrieval of the 'Medusa' experiment. An old theme of science fiction writers had been contamination and they had drawn up horrifying scenarios of alien spaceships crashing on our planet and spreading their infections like man-eating fungus. There was a scientific basis to the general proposition, and the purpose of 'Medusa' was to test just how living organisms could survive raw space.

'Medusa' consisted of living tissues and organisms left in capsules on the outside of Salyut. It was the role of cosmonauts to retrieve the experimental container and see if life had survived or not. It was also the first time they had put their nose outside the door in 45 days.

They emerged in pitch blackness over the Pacific. The sky rolled around their heads like the dome of a planetarium. Alexander Ivanchenkov turned off his miner-style lamp so as to get used to the darkness. He could see the stars march through the heavens, the lights of Earth's cities below, and the flash of fireballs and meteors crashing into the atmosphere.

Turning on his lamp, Ivanchenkov, with his companion beside him, removed all the samples from the side of Salyut's hull, and replaced them with new samples. As well as 'Medusa' there were radio-sensitive plates to register micro-meteorites. The two cosmo- worked hard by night and day and after 45 minutes ground control told them to come in when they were ready.

They did not. There was simply too much to watch and see — the grandeur of their space island floating over the oceans, rich blue seas and rugged brown mountains. Out there they had the whole universe at their feet. They could turn and fly and somersault as free as a bird and there were no walls to collide with. They made the most of it and came in just in time before their next pass over a ground station.

The spacewalk was a great morale booster and it lifted their spirits no end. There had been no problems, no dangers and it had gone like clockwork. Soon it was back to work. The furnace burned away and by 2 August they could display a beautifully finished 12-faced crystal to the ground.

2 August was a red-letter day: Russian cosmonauts finally overtook America's grand total of 937 days in space. The same day, Progress 2 was released and sent crashing into the Pacific. No sooner had this happened than Progress 3 was on its way, arriving 10

August. It would give them another two months on board. This Progress carried no propellant and was dry cargo only. Its manifest declared its contents as being 280 kg food, 190 l water and 450 kg oxygen.

Unloading Progress and keeping the systems going used up much of their time. Despite that, Kovalyonok and Ivanchenkov had difficulty getting to sleep at night and had to resort to drugs. Other problems tended to be minor. Ivanchenkov lost weight until supplies of cheese arrived on Progress; he had earache, cured by an alcoholic drink; and both had headaches until they spring-cleaned the air purifiers.

Cosmonauts Vladimir Kovalyonok (left) and Alexander Ivanchenkov, the crew of Soyuz 29, in an off-duty moment.

When the Americans designed Skylab they planned a wardroom for eating and recreation that did not have a porthole. The astronauts rebelled and insisted one be cut into the hull. They never regretted it and the three crews spent hours in fascination watching the ground pass below them. They were never far from that porthole.

Salyut was no different. Kovalyonok and Ivanchenkov spent hours simply gazing at typhoons, the seas and the underwater sea beds, glaciers and mountains. Kovalyonok spotted a big iceberg drifting north from Antarctica, trailing clear fresh water against the blue green sea. He noted the gradual advance of desert land in Africa. The crew never tired of their global geography lesson every 92 minutes, all in the richest of colours. Indeed the on-board 192-grade colour chart was not subtle enough for the variety of shades they encountered.

CLEAN SHEETS

Progress 4 improved on their comforts. It arrived on 6 October, with sausages, fresh milk and chocolate; boots and slippers; electric razors; clean sheets; and partitions so they could make their own bedrooms. Their station in the sky became more of a home each day.

A second international crew came aboard at the end of August. Soyuz 31 took off on 26 August, carrying Valeri Bykovsky and Sigmund Jaehn of the German Democratic Republic (GDR). There was something historical about this, even if the Russians never themselves mentioned it. The old wartime German A-4 was one of the reasons why anyone was in space in the first place. Germany had written the title page to post-war space travel and might even have conquered space had the Thousand Year Reich lasted as long as had been planned. Von Braun might have got the Americans to the Moon, but it took the Russians to get a German into space.

And, war or not, the Germans had retained their skill in optics and cameras. The Carl Zeiss works were in East Germany and the Russians looked to it for high quality optical equipment. Salyut's own optics were designed there and the ground survey camera was based on the Soyuz 22 camera test of two years earlier.

Sigmund Jaehn brought Practika cameras up with him and it was no coincidence that the best pictures of the Salyut 6 missions belong to the Soyuz 31 flight. Jaehn took some memorable pictures of the delicate shades of orbital sunset gently bathing Salyut as he and Bykovsky slowly drew away for their return. Antennae sparkled in the soft sunlight.

Bykovsky and Jaehn took their seats out of Soyuz 31 and switched with 29. They powered up its engine and fired it for a full 5 seconds. Bykovsky, riding his third mission home, took Soyuz 29 down on 3 September. They were ahead of their landing crews and were already on the ground and out and about, chiding their rescuers with remarks like 'what kept you?' when they eventually did arrive.

140 DAYS

Kovalyonok and Ivanchenkov now faced the final stage of their flight on their own and they still had two months to go. Their first task was to take advantage of the fact that they had a fresh Soyuz on board. However it was attached to the rear docking unit, which they needed for the next Progress. It had to be moved. So on 7 September they climbed into Soyuz 31 and undocked.

They backed away 200 m from Salyut and began a careful aerial ballet. They commanded Salyut 6 to turn through 180 degrees. Slowly the giant station swung around in its path, nudged along with little orange thruster bursts. With the forward port now facing them, Kovalyonok eased Soyuz back towards the station. It was the first time a ferrycraft had undocked and redocked: yet another display of its capabilities.

Most of September was spent mapping the Earth, using the telescope to study the stars and the Moon, and welding. On the 15th they decided to brave the shower once more to get clean. Kovalyonok used a mask and goggles to try to deal with the problem of soap stinging the eyes.

Not long afterwards they heard that the 'Medusa' spacewalk had been a success. Feoktistov called up to tell them how the meteorite plate they had brought in (and which

The Soyuz 29 capsule makes a 'soft-landing' in Dzhezkazgan carrying the crew members of Soyuz 31, Valeri Bykovsky of the Soviet Union and East German cosmonaut Sigmund Jaehn, after their successful mission aboard the Salyut 6 space station.

Bykovsky had carried down) was covered in tiny microscopic craters: it was as if it had been raining, he said.

By the end of October 1978 it was time to come home. By all accounts the humour of the crew was good and morale high. Kovalyonok commented on relationships between the two crew members:

Heated discussions are unavoidable — a space flight is not a society reception and we all have our points of view, so there are disputes. But during the 140 days we never took breakfast or dinner or supper separately — that fact tells a great deal. [12]

On 2 November they plunged through the atmosphere and floated down to Earth. Kovalyonok climbed out unaided, picked up a handful of soil, stood up and waved it in the air — and promptly fell back into doctors' arms. They put him into special restraining couches. But he showed them gravity had not beaten him, and their grins showed just how pleased they were with their 139 days, 14 hours and 48 minutes. A plane brought them to Baikonour and lunch of tomatoes, bread and grapes — and a cup of tea. But more than anything else, said Ivanchenkov, they loved the intoxicating fresh air of mother Earth and the breeze of wind in their faces.

By 4 November they were walking and the next day the doctors told them there would be no more breakfast in bed – they could find their own way to the canteen. They had some weight to make up: Kovalyonok had lost 1 kg and Ivanchenkov 1.8 kg.

On 16 November they were in Moscow, and President of the Academy of Sciences Alexandrov staged a press conference in the lecture hall of Moscow University – an enormous Chicago-like skyscraper in the Stalinesque style. Academicians Gazenko, Petrov, Sagdayev and Logimov were all present – a roll-call of Russia's leading space planners. And when the mission doctors and debriefing team had finished with them they were sent to a resort in the Caucasus Mountains to write a full mission report.

THE HALF-YEAR BARRIER

The fact that Kovalyonok and Ivanchenkov were in better condition than Grechko or Romanenko showed that the measures taken to combat weightlessness were working. Technically it could be done. The key to it was pacing the flight – neither overworking the crew nor leaving them unoccupied, but finding the right balance between work and leisure. So it was that in late 1978 consideration began of a third and last mission to Salyut 6. The aim would be to take a mission to 175 days, a full month further. There would be two Intercosmos linkups, from Bulgaria and Hungary. The crew chosen was, predictably, Vladimir Lyakhov and Valeri Ryumin. Backups were Leonid Popov and Valentin Lebedev. It was to be an epic mission – but not in the way the designers had intended.

The mission review began on 15 January 1979 and was completed in about three weeks. By February, the two Bulgarian trainees, Georgi Ivanov and Alexander Alexandrov, had completed their training. By the end of the month, winter was losing some of its hold and the two Soviet cosmonauts boarded the Soyuz 32 on 25 February. Lyakhov was easy to identify – smaller, shorter and chubbier than the tall Ryumin. He had never been in space before and Ryumin's experience was the two-day aborted Soyuz 25 linkup two years earlier.

Ground control played music over the loudspeakers to the crew as they counted down. Take off was at 2.54 p.m. local time. They lost the strap-on boosters after 2 minutes. The second stage fell away at 170 km and Soyuz 32 was already way above the atmosphere. Third stage cut-out was at 225 km.

'Yest Stikovka!' reported Vladimir Lyakhov a day later as the Soyuz probe snapped into place in Salyut's docking tunnel. They had made it, and after floating down the tunnel the first thing they did was turn on the lights because everything inside was pitch blackness.

The smell of pine forest had been stashed in air containers. The cosmonauts turned on Salyut's venting system and soon they had freshened up the whole interior. They soon got into the swing of things and established the patterns of a working week. They planted cucumbers, onions, parsley in the garden.

REPAIRS AND LEAKS

Repair work was the first priority and the new crew were sent up with screwdrivers, vices and pliers. It was not as easy as it sounded and the first attempt to unscrew a panel went badly wrong. Lyakhov spun round and round, not the screw! An attempt to fix their broken tape-recorder was more successful, using a fitter's soldering iron.

Progress 5 came up with 2300 kg of cargo and arrived on 14 March. Just under half was rocket propellant. The rest included fresh water, a fire-warning system, a new tele-type unit, and a walkie-talkie unit so they could communicate with each other while at other ends of the station. The fire alarm was sensitive enough to be set off by cigarette smoke. Lyakhov had been a heavy smoker until he entered cosmonaut training and if he resumed his former bad habits he would be found out.

Unloading Progress took four days: there were 300 separate items to be taken out of 27 containers. For personal interest there was a 9 kg parcel of letters, newspapers and gifts from home, family and friends.

Then the problems began: the western press suddenly began to report there were fuel leaks on board. Alarms sounded.

In fact there was a fuel leak. A membrane had broken and had been contaminated with nitrogen. As a result, pressurization of the Salyut system had been partly lost. They could not fire the main engine.

There was only one thing for it: the errant tank had to be isolated. So on 16 March, they spun Salyut round and round to force out the fuel and the contaminated fuel was forced into an empty tank. Once this was done, the valve was then closed and purified for new fuel. The contaminated tank was then opened at the other end to vent into open space to shake out the bad fuel.

And this is what Western observers, or the CIA spacewatchers in particular, picked up. They speculated that Salyut was in serious trouble and venting badly. Radio exchanges sounded tense (sometimes they were). Either way it made a good story: Salyut was in dire straights. But as the mission wore on, and the crew remained alive, the story lost credibility. It was not to be the last time a Salyut crew had its obituary written prematurely.

Progress 5 did bring up a television for the crew and as a result they were able to pick up direct broadcasts from the ground. First of all they were sent up a video of their own launching. In fact, the principal value of the on-board TV was to be psychological, for it enabled the crew to talk direct to their families and vice versa. But there were many other practical benefits related to their performance on the mission: on the planning side there could be teleconferences with the mission directors; and statistical and computer data could be gone over together. In addition, they had 50 video casettes on board, including films, concerts and cartoons.

After a month, the crew took their first shower. There was a new ring in it to collect stray water, so the overall process was better than the earlier attempts. Several days later, Progress 5 was cast off and deorbited. Before it left, it burned its engine to leave the complex in its ideal orbit of 91.4 minutes, ideal for the upcoming launch window.

BURN OUT

Bulgaria is one of the smallest of the East European Socialist countries. It has always been the most loyal to the USSR, partly because of a shared Slavic history. For Bulgaria the flight of Soyuz 33 was set to be of tremendous symbolic importance, rather than as some Poles and Czechs had made it — the subject of underground jokes.

The Soviet commander was Nikolai Rukhavishnikov, veteran of Soyuz 10 and 16, the first civilian Soviet space commander. Flight engineer was Georgi 'Gosho' Ivanov — a tough, moustached aviator who could have also passed as a Balkan mountain partisan.

Surrounded by a gaggle of Bulgarian officials, politicians and functionaries, Rukhavishnikov and Ivanov arrived at the launch pad at 6 p.m. local time on 10 April 1979. It was a fresh, blustery day with winds gusting at 18 km/h. After that things got worse and the wind speed picked up to 40 km/h. No spaceship had ever been launched in such bad conditions before. The crew swayed back and forth, sensing the gusting, but the launch went ahead anyway and it was dark when they took off. After ten minutes they had left the Earth's unpredictable weather behind.

Mass rallies were held throughout Bulgaria to celebrate. Pavel Popovich spoke to crowds on the streets in Sophia. A special song was composed. Bulgaria, tiny Bulgaria, was the sixth of the world's nations to have a man in space.

Docking was due at 9.15 p.m. on the 11th. At 8.30 p.m. the two spaceships were so close together they were in the same time zone and Yeliseyev — who was directing the mission — could talk to both crews simultaneously. On the display screen the scarlet (33) and blue (Salyut) lights had nearly joined.

8.40 p.m. Yeliseyev sent up the final data for the docking manoeuvre.

8.45 p.m. Closing distance was now 3000 m.

8.54 p.m. Final manoeuvre: 8 second burn.

Rukhavishnikov fired the engine. It burned for four seconds — and then flickered and then died. It just sputtered out. The propulsion system suffered a total failure.

8.55 p.m. Soyuz 33 whizzed past the space station. 'Something's gone badly wrong!' whispered Ryumin to Lyakhov — they had both been watching through the portholes. Soyuz 33 disappeared from sight.

Fortunately Soyuz had a reverse system, otherwise they would have been truly marooned. Yeliseyev ordered them to come home at the first available opportunity. He had no choice but to do so. And if the fuel tanks were at fault, then the reserve system might not function either. Lyakhov and Ryumin could not sleep that night for they were thinking how they could somehow set out in their own Soyuz 32 to rescue their comrades.

A complication for Soyuz 33 was that they could trust the reserve system for only one firing. Normally a Soyuz coming home from the space station would be expected to deorbit in two burns — the first one at 350 km, and the second at 220 km. It then goes into a gliding reentry. But one burn only and at 350 km meant a plunging vertical descent. But there was no other way.

On their 31st orbit, Rukhavishnikov fired the backup motor. It should have run for 213 seconds, but it did not shut down. He had to turn it off himself. Soyuz 33 plunged earthwards. G forces built up — 4G, 8G, 10G. Contact with ground control was lost. Inside, it was 'like being in a blowtorch', said Rukhavishnikov as Soyuz was subjected to the full ballistic descent. The capsule shook and shook around: there was 'the roar of a burning chimney fire', he recalled.

But they made it, and were coming home under a cloudless sky with a blazing full Moon. It was now mild and calm, unlike the previous day. An airplane pilot spotted the glowing red of the heatshield underneath the capsule and a flashing beacon on top. Flight control relaxed when the crew reported through and told them the parachute was out and they were alive and well. They were a little distance from the recovery area — not surprising considering the type of descent — and the aircraft pilot directed the helicopters to the site. Soyuz 33 touched down and rolled over onto its side. The two men lost no time getting out.

They were whisked away to the 'Hotel Cosmonaut' in Baikonour. They were quite exhausted. All Rukhavishnikov could manage was to comment that the flight seemed like it lasted a month. The next day he told a press conference that their situation had been much too much like Apollo 13 for their comfort. He was probably right. Soyuz 33 was the closest the Russians had come to a disaster since the launch abort of April 1975, and the nearest they ever came to getting a crew stranded in orbit.

PROBLEMS — POLITICAL AND LOGISTICAL

The failure of Soyuz 33 created all kinds of problems. First there was the fault in the engine itself, which was serious enough, made worse by the fact that the guilty parts had burnt up on reentry and could not be examined. Analysis of the fault would have to be based on telemetry alone. Second, Soyuz 32's own safe lifetime would expire in June. So they would have to either bring the crew back then, thus cutting short the mission, or send up a replacement Soyuz by then. This could be either manned (if the fault had been isolated) or unmanned if it had not. Third, there was the political issue. The Bulgarian had not reached the space station, so should the unfortunate Bulgarians have a second shot at it? Would they relaunch the same crew, or their backups (Yuri Romanenko and Alexander Alexandrov)? If they did would there be repercussions from other Eastern European countries?

By mid-May it was clear that work on the faulty engine would take some time yet. The controllers felt sufficiently confident that they could keep Lyakhov and Ryumin up there, but not confident enough to fly a new crew as well. So they would replace the ageing Soyuz 32 with an unmanned Soyuz 34, even though this laid them open to criticism that it might have the same flaws as the hapless Soyuz 33.

As for the Bulgarians, they were sent home and got no second chance. They must have been disappointed. But it would have put them in an invidious position for them to have been given two flights. And the Hungarians, next in line, would have to wait a full year. They were probably delighted to get the extra training time.

Western observers had little to go on when they tried to assess the situation. The authoritative British aviation magazine, *Flight International*, announced confidently 'Russians plan new Soyuz linkup' [13]. It was not aware, and could not have been, of the seriousness of the Soyuz 33 failure, which most people attributed to causes similar to those which afflicted Soyuz 15, 23, 25. And the idea that Lyakhov and Ryumin might be expected to stay aloft for the whole summer without any visitors at all had not crossed their minds. But the Russians for their part were struggling with these problems on a day-to-day basis too, a situation familiar to NASA, which was well used to coping with in-flight emergencies.

Progress 6 was sent up to the orbital station on 13 May, and docked two days later. After refuelling, Progress 6 fired its engines like a spacetug to place Salyut in the right orbit to receive a new visitor.

On 2 June Hungarian news sources were told officially that the upcoming Hungarian flight was off. In order not to disappoint the Hungarians, Moscow let it be known that the Soyuz design fault was 'serious', with the counterproductive result that the Western media concluded that the cosmonauts were stranded. Curiosity only deepened when on 6 June Soyuz 34 was launched – with no one on board. It closed in on the station and docked on 8 June, just hours after Progress 6 had left.

Lyakhov and Ryumin more and more took the view that the Soyuz 33 engine failure was one of those occasional random and worrying failures that do arise from time to time. The engine was traditionally extremely reliable, and this was the first such failure in 4000 firings. Progress 6 and Soyuz 34, which had identical designs to the faulty engines, showed no indication of the problem, whatever it was.

As it was, the cosmonauts decided to use the situation to best advantage. Soyuz 32 would become the first cargo ship to return from the station to the ground, unlike the Progress ferries which burned up. So they packed it with 180 kg of the results of their experiments – 29 welding samples, 50 canisters of film, and biological specimens. Soyuz 32's capsule was back on the ground on 13 June.

This hectic pace continued. The next day the crew climbed into Soyuz 34, undocked and flew it around to the main docking port. This left the rear port free for Progress 7 which went up on 28 June. It brought up fuel, freight, a radio telescope, a political briefing on the SALT-2 Treaty, and a book on the history and geography of Moscow city. The Progress 7 engine then fired a total of 191 seconds to boost the complex to an all-time high of 411 km.

SEARCHING THE UNIVERSE

Ever since Galileo, humans have relied on the eye to scan the heavens, using eyepieces and telescopes as the principal means of increasing the sum knowledge of the skies. After Galileo had come Herschell in Germany and Rosse in Ireland. They had noted the planets, mapped the nebulae, and glimpsed distant galaxies. But in the 1950s, scientists realized how the visual world was only a tiny fraction of the universe and what it had to say. Radio signals, invisible to the eye but audible to the electric and electronic world, could tell infinitely more. So there were built the giant radio dishes of Jodrell Bank and elsewhere, mostly in the 1950s and 1960s.

The next task of Lyakhov and Ryumin was to assemble the first radio telescope in space, called the Cosmic Radio Telescope 10 (KRT-10), given the title '10' because it was 10 m in diameter. They assembled its component parts like a model aircraft kit throughout the central line of Progress, like a closed umbrella. The base was attached into Salyut's rear docking port.

On 18 July 1979, Progress 7 drifted away, careful not to brush against the radio telescope in its tunnel like a dipstick in a car oil filter. No sooner had Progress disappeared from sight than the telescope was commanded to unfurl, which it did just like an umbrella popping open. So from the rear port could now be seen a wire mesh not unlike a spider's web.

KRT-10 worked together with the 70 m dish of a Crimean observatory. By doing so, the combined systems used a base line which could be as wide as the diameter of the Earth itself. It went into action at once and homed in on pulsar PL 0329, the Sun and the Milky Way. It was an innovation of great significance. The only snag was that it gobbled up so much electric power that it could be used only on alternate days.

The radio telescope experiment was completed on 9 August. It was cast off so as to free the rear port for future dockings. Lyakhov and Ryumin had now been up for nearly six months and their return had been fixed for some ten days later. They had, after all, been in orbit since February, and had watched the seasons turn and warmth and greenness spread over the northern hemisphere for a spring and summer.

KRT-10 cast off alright — and promptly snagged in the optical sighting device on Salyut's rear. The station was now pulling along in its wake a wobbling useless metallic wire mesh. Salyut was shaken around by its manoeuvring jets to jolt it free.

It remained stubbornly stuck.

PLIERS AND CLIPPERS

There was only one thing for it — and that was to spacewalk and cut it free. But it was late in the mission and the cosmonauts were very tired. The radio in the airlock was broken. The telescope was at the far end of the station, away from the airlock. The spacesuits were past design lifetime. But in the meantime some other cosmonauts tested out the idea of a spacewalk in the hydrotank in Star Town and said it could be done.

Lyakhov and Ryumin were not so sure. They loaded all their research results into Soyuz 34 so it could return without them if need be. Each man wrote a last letter to his family and put it on board.

The spacewalk was agreed for 15 August. All the work would have to be carried out away from ground contact because of the broken radio. But out they went. They ran into a problem right away: the airlock hatch jammed. It took twenty minutes to open. By the time they got it open it was night, and they had to wait another half-hour, for mission rules forbade any night-time work.

They waited and rested — Ryumin outside the hatch, Lyakhov just inside. Weightless or not, Valeri Ryumin admitted he was scared as he contemplated the drop 300 km below. So he took his mind off potential phobia by watching the pinpricks of stars in the night sky. Then dawn marched over the horizon and he could get to work.

He clambered down the hull of Salyut and played out the 20 m safety line to its limit. He reached the far end. Sunshine glared directly into his eyes. It got hotter and hotter. Condensation steamed. But he reached the snag and cut away with his clippers. It cleared and he gave it a final *adieu* with his boot. Success! The radio telescope drifted slowly away. Soon it was hundreds of metres off. As he returned to the airlock he picked up the cassettes left by Kovalyonok and Ivanchenkov a year before.

After an hour and a half Ryumin struggled back in, alive, exhausted and elated. He reported his success to ground control. They stood in applause, so loud it deafened his earphones. Yet another in-flight problem had been dealt with in real time.

This spacewalk was the last major activity of the mission. The next few days were centred on closing the station down. 19 August was the 175th day of the mission, and

Soyuz undocked at 11.08 a.m. Vladimir Shatalov advised them of the weather in the recovery area:

Cloud base: 1000 m
Visibility: 20 km
Wind: 5 m/s

Floating gently to earth, the descent module of Soyuz 34 brings Vladimir Lyakhov and Valeri Ryumin, the crew of Soyuz 32, safely back after their highly successful 175-day flight aboard Salyut 6. Because it was feared that the Soyuz 32 capsule had exceeded its design life, an unmanned Soyuz 34 was used to bring the crew back to Earth.

Alexei Leonov was in charge of recovery operations. He ordered all air corridors in the area closed. Electricity lines were all disconnected. As retrofire was reported, he scrambled 15 helicopters and 11 aircraft. They waited.

It was not long. The TV helicopter spotted the capsule coming down under a red and white parachute. The bottom was blackened and the windows covered in soot. The capsule came down in flat harvested cornfields and at once rolled on sharp stubble. Ground crews were beside the capsule three minutes later and helped Lyakhov and Ryumin into flat lounge chairs.

Ryumin was in the better shape and was able to walk. A doctor pressed flowers into his hands, but he could barely find the strength to hold them though he loved the smells and adored the fresh scent of the harvest air. His friend Lyakhov was dazed and could not balance. They were both carried to a giant inflated tent which was quickly erected behind the capsule. It looked like one of those Antarctic cabins and was ideal for medical examinations.

Safely landed after a 175 days in space, the crew of Soyuz 32 — Vladimir Lyakhov and Valeri Ryumin are tended by doctors and ground crew; their Soyuz 34 capsule lies nearby.

The full medical report on the mission was made available in April 1980 and was written by mission doctor Robert Dyakonov and senior medical expert Dr Oleg Gazenko. The two cosmonauts were in no worse conditions than the first Salyut 6 crews. Bone calcium loss was 8 per cent, compared to 6.8 per cent on Skylab and well within safety limits (20 per cent).

Lyakhov and Ryumin were, meanwhile, guinea-pigs for new measures of readaptation They were encouraged to swim in the pool of the 'Hotel Cosmonaut' at Baikonour. They underwent massage to rebuild their muscles. Within four days they were jogging and playing tennis. On 9 September they were allowed to rejoin their families for holidays in the Crimea. The six-month barrier was down.

SOYUZ TRANSPORT

Salyut 6 flew over the Baikonour cosmodrome on 16 December. If a Soyuz launching is planned, it normally takes place 30 minutes after the flyover, or 60 minutes later in the case of Progress. But not this time. No less than 73 minutes later, an A-2 rocket headed off the pad into the wintry skies. This was something different. The new spaceship entered orbit, shot ahead of Salyut, and, three days later, approaching from up front slid into dock. No one was aboard. Tass called the new machine the 'Soyuz T'.

At first glance, Soyuz T looked similar enough to the old Soyuz. The solar panels were back, which was the most obvious change. But once the observer looked inside, there the resemblance ended. First of all, there were three seats. Life-support systems were miniaturized. Second, the control panel was quite different. It had computer displays and the whole system was geared to operation via computer. Soyuz T used all the microchip technology that came in during the 1970s, and which could not have been envisaged in Korolov's time [14].

Soyuz T was the first to fly the new 'Argon' computer with a 16k capability — it was able to fly the mission on its own and provide instant readouts to both the crew and the ground.

Third, the engine system was simplified. The main engines and the thrusters were now to run off the same system, which was turbine-driven. Fuel was also saved by releasing the orbital module before reentry. Overall, Soyuz T was 200 kg heavier. It was designed to be faster, more efficient, safer than the old Soyuz, and, not least of all, was designed to eliminate the type of faults that had prevented four previous dockings.

Soyuz T's search, rendezvous and docking went flawlessly and the manoeuvre stretched over three days. Soyuz T undocked on 23 March 1980 and then went through two days of tests on its own. It was back on the ground in a night-time landing on the 15th. Flight time was 100 days 9 hours. It went so well that it could now be considered operational.

But what was going on with Salyut itself? Only three resident missions had been planned for the station, and these had now been carried out. The next Salyut would not be ready till 1981, and Salyut 6 still seemed to have plenty of life in it. So a fourth resident mission was planned, to fly a similar length to the last. A crew was selected — newcomer Leonid Popov (pilot group 1970) and designer Valentin Lebedev of Soyuz 13. Launch was set for 9 April.

In preparation for the new mission, a progress freighter was sent up in advance. This was new. Progress 8 went up on 27 March and docked at the rear end two days later. Soon after, its engine trimmed Salyut's orbit to await the new crew.

But there was turmoil in the training centre. In mid-March, Valentin Lebedev was exercising on a trampolene in Star Town to keep up his fitness. Something went wrong: he smashed his knee and was rushed to hospital. He must have known at this stage he would be grounded, and he was. The State Commission had a problem in finding a replacement. The new mission had no backups because it was an unplanned bonus mission. It needed the most experienced person available. That was Valeri Ryumin — just back from half a year in space. He was asked. He agreed. We do not know how he felt, nor his family, nor his fellow cosmonauts. But on 9 April he was back in orbit on Soyuz 35 and en route to Salyut once more.

RUBBER BOTTLES

Leonid Popov — an austere-looking jet pilot — guided Soyuz into Salyut 6 and they docked solidly. They floated into the more spacious Salyut, only to pick up a message left for them by the previous crew. Ryumin had never dreamed he would be leaving himself his own note! A TV-broadcast to Earth was transmitted. Ryumin produced an enormous cucumber which he said he had found in the station's garden. It had grown during their absence.

The biologists were stunned. How could such phenomenal growth take place? Then Ryumin coyly admitted it was a plastic imitation. The biologists were furious at being taken in, but the doctors were delighted at Ryumin's high spirits.

It took two weeks to get Salyut ship-shape again. Clocks and light-bulbs had to be fixed; new batteries were needed; water tanks were changed. Air and fuel was pumped aboard from Progress 8. It was then sent spinning away to a fiery end on 25 April.

The next six weeks were to be frantic — like a train schedule, according to *Pravda*. Progress 9 set off on 27 April. It brought a biological centrifuge aloft, air filters, and a system for pumping water directly on board, called 'Rodnik'. All drinking water (180 kg) was now transferred in pipes, instead of in 5 kg rubber bottles, bottle by bottle. Again, this was another example of step-by-step improvements on each new flight, improvements not conceived when the flight began. Progress 9 left on 20 May.

The next Soyuz was already flat on its rail-transporter being pulled along to the pad. This was the long-awaited Hungarian flight: Valeri Kubasov (of Apollo–Soyuz fame) and Bartalan Farkas. Backups were Vladimir Dzanibekov and Bela Magyari. Launch was on 26 May. The visitors spent seven days aboard Salyut and carried up a record 21 experiments, though for Popov and Ryumin the highlight may well have been cans of Hungarian goulash.

Some of the 21 experiments were out of the usual. One was an electronic aptitude test to measure reaction times and fatigue in orbit. Another was the manufacture of interferon. It was thought to possibly hold the key to a cure for cancer: extremely expensive to produce on Earth, the process was easier in zero gravity. They smelted copper, aluminium and arsenide.

Kubasov and Farkas returned in the old Soyuz 35 on 3 June. They had already unloaded most of their equipment by the time the helicopter crews arrived. And in the now-familiar game of cosmic musical chairs, Ryumin and Popov above them were bringing the new Soyuz 36 around to the main docking port.

'Soviet space crew heads for docking' flashed the newspapers from Moscow on 5 June. Someone was a bit late with the previous week's news, was the first reaction. Then on closer examination, it was revealed that a new Soyuz was up in space — the first manned

Participants in the joint Soviet/Hungarian space mission, the crew of Soyuz 36, Valeri Kubasov and Bertalan Farkas, sign their names on the side of the descent module following the tradition.

version of the Soyuz T. The new launching – the second manned flight in ten days – took everyone by surprise. Aboard Soyuz T were Yuri Malashev and Vladimir Aksenov, the latter from Soyuz 22. Yuri Malashev was a classmate of Vladimir Lyakhov and Vladimir Kovalyonok and from the 1967 selection. Tall, cheery, with close-cropped hair, he looked like the average American athlete. And they kitted up in new lightweight suits with zips, elbow and knee joints, and individually-fingered gloves that could, at least according to the designers, pick out a match from a pack.

It was the first operational test of the Soyuz T. It was not all plain-sailing either. The brand-new Argon computer brought Soyuz T2 to within 180 m of Salyut's rear port, and then promptly broke down! Once again, Soviet cosmonauts faced failure, and, with the station still in sight, Malashev's pulse shot up to 130/min, with Aksenov not far behind at 97. But Malashev was not contemplating failure. Without asking, or indeed telling anyone, he took over manual control and pressed Soyuz T2's nose into its port. They had made it.

Malashev and Aksenov spent three days on the Salyut. More was not considered necessary at this stage since it was a test of the T's systems first and foremost. They left on 9 June and spent a couple of hours on a photographic flyaround of the ageing station. They then came out of orbit, touching down at local midday. In a small but important move to improve visibility, the exterior cabin windows, soot-blackened after reentry, were dropped off, thus enabling the crew to see properly as they came in.

Soyuz T was now operational, and the order was given to put it into production at about three a year. Meanwhile, aboard Salyut, Popov and Ryumin settled down into a quieter period. They smelted materials, turned their telescopes on the stars, and they used the long daylight conditions to make observations of the northern parts of the USSR.

HANOI TO HAVANA: THIRD WORLD GREETINGS

Christmas 1972. Peace talks between the United States and North Vietnam failed. President Nixon and Secretary of State Kissinger ordered in B52 bombers from their bases in Guam and the Philippines. Like giant heron birds they strained for height, belching smoke from their eight engines. Each carried tens of tonnes of bombs.

As they neared Hanoi, coast watchers spotted the contrails high in the sky, each trail preceded by the black speck of each bomber. A shaky telephone line alerted the nearest airfield. Several bullet-scarred MiG-21s emerged from their camouflage netting. They roared along the pot-holed runway and were airborne.

One was piloted by 25-year-old Pham Tuan. He headed off in pursuit of the B52s. The MiG-21 was fast and he felt the G forces pushing him back into his seat. The B52s were high up and hard to catch. Eventually he got one in his sights, afar off, fired a heat-seeking missile, and headed for home. As he did, there was a blinding flash. The B52 was going down, trailing a thickening plume of black smoke. That was the last he saw of it.

Some other B52s were brought down that day. The rest did terrible damage, flattened parts of Hamoi, destroyed houses and hospitals. Pham Tuan came back a hero: destroyer of an ugly, death-dealing B52.

Now it was 23 July 1980: Pham Tuan, now 33, was pressed into his seat, heading for orbit on Soyuz 37 with Soviet Commander Viktor Gorbatko. Backups were Valeri Bykovsky and Buy Than Liem (who was to die in an air crash in Vietnam in 1982).

Gorbatko and Pham Tuan spent a week aboard Salyut 6, which had just earlier received a fuelling visit from Progress 10. For the Vietnamese, the main mission objective was to map tidal areas of Vietnam, silting and flooding, and the wartime effects of defoliation on the jungle.

The sudden appearance of the Vietnamese was a surprise, as the Cubans had been next in line for a flight. In fact no one would have known it was coming up at all had not Vladimir Lyakhov mentioned it casually in the course of the pre-flight press conference. The two Vietnamese only arrived in May 1979, a year earlier, and long after the Cubans. Perhaps the Cubans were not yet ready for their flight. Or perhaps there were political reasons. A Third World B52 slayer, orbiting at the time of the Moscow Olympic Games, Games which the Americans had boycotted, was a counterblast to American imperialism. And it was good news for the Vietnamese too, for they had been getting a bad press all summer because of the mass exodus of the boat people and refugees.

Gorbatko and Pham Tuan returned on 31 July in the Soyuz 36 brought up by the Hungarians. Popov and Ryumin continued smelting, and spent August taking pictures of crops ripening throughout the USSR and trying to predict crop yields from what was often a temperamental harvest. Ryumin celebrated his 41st birthday in orbit on 16 August — the second time he had been away from Earth for the occasion. The flight was drawing to a close, but there was still one more Intercosmos visit planned. For Ryumin, this 1980 flight must have been a contrast to the lonely vigil he had put in a year before; for this time there were no fewer than four visiting crews.

The crew of Soyuz 38 was Yuri Romanenko and Arnaldo Tamayo Mendez and they flew up to Salyut on 18 September. Mendez became the first black person in space. He

Jubilant on their successful return to Earth, the crew of Soyuz 37, commander Viktor Gorbatko and researcher-cosmonaut Pham Tuan of North Vietnam are interviewed by the Press.

Twenty-five years after he had worked as a shoe-shine boy in Cuba, researcher-cosmonaut Arnaldo Mendez, the first coloured man in space, chats with fellow veteran cosmonaut Yuri Romanenko. Together they formed the crew of Soyuz 38.

spent some time conducting 27 Cuban-designed experiments, and some of which involved the behaviour of sugar in the weightless environment. Sugar was central to the Cuban economy. And whenever he could, he went sightseeing at the portholes to try to spot his home country in the midst of the blue Caribbean Sea.

Soyuz 38 returned on 26 September. It came down in the dark and helicopters had to turn on their searchlights to locate it. It did not take long. The Soyuz 38 was later presented to the people of Cuba and became a permanent exhibit in the museum in Havana.

There was no need for a new spaceship as Popov and Ryumin were themselves coming home. A final freighter craft was sent up on 28 September. Three days later Popov and Ryumin broke the previous 175-day record. They accelerated their own preparations for return and exercised ferociously.

Leonid Popov and Valery Ryumin came home on 11 October after 185 days — over 6 months. It was a triumph. Ryumin pulled himself out of the cabin, strolled across to the reclining chairs, and declared that he was ready to fly to Mars! He, at least, had banished weightlessness with a vengeance. Of the past 18 months of his life, he had spent less than 6 months on Earth. He was the most-travelled man in history, and the accolades heaped on him in the months that followed he richly deserved.

MISSION ACCOMPLISHED?

The return of Popov and Ryumin meant that Salyut 6 had accomplished not only the three basic missions that had been planned, but also a lengthy bonus flight. The question was, what to do next?

The next space station, Salyut 7, was still at least a year off. Two groups of Intercosmos cosmonauts remained to fly: Mongolia and Rumania. Also in the queue was the redesigned Star module, a follow-on to Cosmos 929. Could these components of the space programme be flown before Salyut 7?

It was hard to say. Many parts of Salyut 6 had worn out and needed repair. Going by the reports of Popov and Ryumin, Salyut 6 would not be able to support a full further six-month flight. So a compromise was worked out. A two-week repair mission would be flown up to Salyut in late 1980, and it could also be the first operational three-man Soyuz T mission. Then in March 1981 there would be a medium-length resident crew on Salyut, with the last two Intercosmos visitors. The station would then be abandoned from the point of view of human occupation, but kept aloft for a 'Star' test. Once again, these decisions were the product of operational planning, with the planners responding to changed circumstances as the needs arose.

Already mission planners were casting their minds towards Salyut 7. This new station would develop in two stages. The first resident mission would be a duration one, pushing the limits back beyond 200 days. The prime crew selected was Anatoli Berezovoi (1970 group) and Valentin Lebedev, now recovered from his knee injury. Backups were Vladimir Titov and Gennadiy Strekhalov. That still left the question of visiting crews, and visits would clearly be desirable both because of the duration of the flight and the need to bring up fresh spacecraft. In September 1980 an agreement was signed between the USSR and France to add that country to the Intercosmos protocol and offer France a seat on a Soyuz.

It was logical enough, for France was the Western country with the most long-lasting scientific contacts with the USSR. De Gaulle had visited Baikonour (1966); French equipment had flown on Lunokhod (1970), Mars 3 (1971) and subsequent Venera craft.

The arrangement suited both sides well. From the Soviet point of view, it provided access to Western technology, and particularly, French expertise in cryogenics. From the French point of view, it demonstrated French independence, able to choose at will and pick between the two superpowers. Not only that — and France kept close links with NASA all this time — France also became the driving force behind the European space effort. It was the second largest payer of the European Space Agency (ESA) and the principal funder of the all-European rocket Ariane, set up as a commercial challenger to the Shuttle in 1983.

So in September 1980 two French cosmonauts arrived at Star Town, both air force pilots. They were Patrick Baudry and Jean-Loup Chrétien. Yuri Malashev and Alexander Ivanchenkov were later selected with Jean-Loup Chrétien as prime crew: backups were to be Young Guard commander Leonid Kizim and 1978 engineer Vladimir Solovyov, to prepare along with Patrick Baudry.

But Salyut 7 would be able to take more than one visiting crew. With the Intercosmos programme for the time being exhausted, other alternatives could be considered. There were all kinds of exotic possibilities, like flying Palestinians, or Nicaraguans or Pioneer scouts; but other considerations intervened. The most important of these was a development that was taking place in the United States. The USSR had not failed to note NASA's new policy of encouraging female participation in Shuttle recruitment. Six women astronauts joined the NASA squad in 1978.

It was only a question of time before one flew on the Shuttle: Rhea Seddon had been suggested for such a flight in 1982/3. No Russian women had flown since Valentina Terreskhova in 1963. They were still *personae non grata*, and in March 1980, Yuri Glazhkov told readers of *Soviet Weekly* magazine:

> Cosmonautics is still in its infancy and life aboard spacecraft is extremely wearing, demanding and physically difficult. . . including perhaps dangerous situations.
>
> That being so, we feel the time is not yet right to impose such a strain on women. [15]

But, with NASA prepared to impose such strains, the Soviet attitude underwent a complete reversal in the space of a matter of months. The call went out in 1980 for more women cosmonauts. There was no contest, for the only real contender was 32-year-old Svetlana Savitskaya. Her credentials were better than those of most of her male colleagues.

Svetlana Savitskaya was a sky-diver at 16, she had three world parachute records at 17, and she was world aerobatic champion at 22. She was dubbed 'Miss Sensation' by the British press after a display she gave in England. She went on to fly planes at four times the speed of sound, did design work, and made one terrifying parachute drop from 14 252 m (44 000 ft), only opening the ripcord 500 m above ground. To add to all this, the cheerful daredevil had a father who was an Air Marshal of the Soviet Union. Short-haired and plain, she lacked the glamour of Terreskhova but had all the skills expected of a cosmonaut of the eighties.

Another woman cosmonaut, Irina Pronina, was selected to train with her, but she must have known she would have little chance of actually flying. Leonid Popov, just back from space, was selected as her commander, and newcomer Alexander Serebrov (1978) as flight engineer. So by late 1980 fourteen men and two women were in training for the first set of Salyut 7 missions.

The second step in Salyut 7 would be the long-cherished dream of permanent occupancy. This meant that when a resident crew was about to leave, a new crew would be boarding through the other docking port. That was the target for 1983, and would be facilitated by the operational use of the 'Star' module. After that time, the Russians would always have someone in space. The Americans would be still shuttling away with a hedgehopper spacecraft that would not stay up for more than a week at a time.

Permanent occupancy seemed less and less of a problem as the results of the 185-day Popov and Ryumin flight were analysed. Both men had gained weight on board – Popov 3.2 kg and Ryumin 4.7 kg. They also gained height as their spinal fluids expanded: Ryumin grew from an already tall 184 cm to 187 cm. And, thanks to Einstein's law of relativity which said that the faster you travelled the slower you aged, both men came back 4.5 milliseconds younger than they would have been had they stayed on Earth!

The scientific results of the flight, published in 1981, were also excellent. In terms of volume alone they were impressive. The cosmonauts welded 196 samples, took 550 photographs, 40 000 spectograms, and spent hundreds of hours on astronomy. They had replaced 50 items of equipment. Even the plants had done better: orchids had bloomed, and an arabdopsis plant had flowered. Like Captain Nemo's ship *Nautilus* of Jules Verne, future space crews would live in a green world that they would harvest themselves. And by doing their own repairs, growing their own food, recycling their own air and water, the space station would be less and less dependant on the Earth for its existence. And that was what living in space was supposed to be all about.

REPAIR WORK

Although Popov and Ryumin had returned on 11 October, mission planners were able to get the new Soyuz T repair mission ready by 27 November, very late in the year. Indications of a new mission came when, on 16 November Progress 11 refuelled Salyut entirely under automatic control. Chosen for the new mission were Leonid Kizim and Gennadiy Strekhalov, both of whom were preparing for long-duration Salyut 7 flights. The third crew member was three-times veteran Oleg Markarov. Kizim was a short, businesslike Young Guard commander. Strakhalov was one of the designers of Soyuz T and had been with it since the blueprint stage. He had two inventions to his credit.

The crew of three reached Salyut on schedule the next day and the computer worked faultlessly. They quickly boarded the station and began work. It was the first three-man launch since Soyuz 11 in 1971 and the first time the USSR had three people on a station on a resident basis since Skylab.

The first and main problem that they tackled was the hydropump which circulated antifreeze to keep up the temperature on board. It had simply given out and had never been designed with repair in mind. They had to take the whole system out, which meant using a metal saw to cut it free. The most important thing was to ensure that the anti-freeze did not spill out and deluge the station. It did not, and the replacement job worked.

The hydropump was not the only problem. Kizim, Strekhalov and Markarov repaired an electricity commutator and the electronic telemetry system; onboard timers; and a refuelling system transformer. The two engineers then spent a full week inspecting every nook and cranny of the station to prepare a full report on its flight worthiness.

The work completed, the three men spent their second week in space on a total of ten experiments. They brought up the first holographic camera to be used in space to produce three-dimensional images.

Kizim, Strekhalov and Markarov dropped away from Salyut in the early morning of 10 December. By mid-morning they were parachuting down to a Kazakhstan snow-scape. First to spot the craft was a group of Cossack horsemen. They galloped across the snow to meet the crew. The old and the new stood together; the tiny capsule that had whirled around the world at 8 km/s, and the horse, transporter of humans for four thousand years.

The three men were in far worse shape than the long-duration crews: they had worked non-stop on board and had failed to exercise. But on a two-week mission they suffered little harm. Progress 11 undocked the next day and burned up after 70 days in space, the longest time any Progress was in space.

FINAL VISIT

Soyuz T3's crew gave Salyut 6 a clean bill of health for a final visit, and preparations began immediately in the new year. Progress 12 went aloft on 24 January and refuelled the Salyut automatically. Soon after, problems developed. One of the solar panels stuck, thus reducing the electricity available inside Salyut. Temperatures fell to 10°C from the normal 21°C. The new crew would have to fix this problem.

Chosen for the last mission were veteran Vladimir Kovalyonok and 41-year-old geodesist Viktor Savinyikh. They had entered training for this mission only in December; it must have been rushed because earlier statements had made much of the fact that the controls of Soyuz T took 18 months to master. Winter had thawed out at Baikonour when, on 12 March, Vladimir Kovalyonok and Viktor Savinyikh rode the elevator to climb aboard Soyuz T4. It soared skyward and an evening later they were aboard. Within hours they had fixed the solar battery and temperatures aboard were once more comfortable. They unloaded Progress 12, but by the time they finished they had run into the problem of where to store all the equipment that was now aboard.

The remainder of the flight of Soyuz T4 was, to the outsider, fairly predictable.

The Mongolian crew went up from 22–30 March on Soyuz 39. The commander was Vladimir Dzanibekov and his copilot was 34-year-old Jugderdemidiyn Gurragcha, an army captain. The Russians in Star Town never mastered his name and nick-named him 'Gurr'. The crew brought up a record 30 experiments, several of which concentrated on mapping the inaccessible desert regions of Mongolia. The last of the old Soyuz — number 40 — flew up to Salyut 6 on 14–22 May. The commander was to have been Yevgeni Khrunov. A mysterious figure, he was one of the youngest members of the 1960

Soyuz 39 cosmonauts Vladimir Dzanibekov (left) and Mongolian Jugderdemidyin Gurragcha who remained aboard the Salyut 6 space station for just under 8 days in March 1981.

selection. He did not fly initially till 1969 and was long due a second flight. But with only a few months to go before piloting Soyuz 40, he pulled out. It is not known why. His place was hurriedly taken by Leonid Popov, who flew with 28-year-old Rumanian Dimitru Prunariu. Their most interesting experiment was an attempt to produce solar cells in orbit using silicon monocrystals.

The flight of the last ordinary Soyuz marked a milestone. Even as it returned the first of the redesigned Star modules was aloft. And, more significantly, the Americans were back in space.

'WHAT A WAY TO COME TO CALIFORNIA!'

The American space shuttle had been due to fly in 1978. Air-launched tests aboard a Boeing 747 jumbo jet in 1976 had been so successful that NASA had even set a launch date for 31 March 1978. But one date after another had slipped . . . to 1979, then 1980, then 1981.

Four shuttles were built, in addition to the prototype, called the 'Enterprise', which was not supposed to fly into space. While the gliding tests had worked well, one problem after another had to be ironed out, with the main engine the chief culprit. Then the real blow came. As the first operational shuttle, the 'Columbia', was being transferred to Cape Canaveral — again atop a 747 — thousands of its exterior tiles fell off. 'Columbia' arrived, looking like a ship that had been battered by a tidal wave.

Now, *Columbia* had 34 000 tiles and if just one of them came off from a vital place during reentry, the whole structure might burn up. Each tile was individually computer-designed, and the replacement work dragged on and on. The tiles were brittle. Made from sand, silica and plastic foam, they were bonded by bathtub glue and they had to withstand the vibration of take-off and landing too. On such mundane household materials was a revolution in space travel built.

To pilot the first do-or-die flight of the *Columbia* were two brave test pilots: Robert Crippen, and four-times Apollo and Gemini veteran John Young. The shuttle was a revolutionary design and was a quantum jump forward. It took five years to design and seven to build. The main craft looked like a DC-9 airliner atop a zeppelin-like cylinder (the fuel tank) and two ordinary-looking solid rocket boosters. It was to take off like a rocket, fly like a spaceship and land like an airliner. It stood 56 m on the pad and weighed 2040 tonnes. The orbiter, which could take a crew of seven weighed in at 84 tonnes and was 37 m long with a 24 m wingspan. It came down like a brick and landed at 335 km/h.

NASA's problem, however, was that it had nothing to shuttle to. It had taken the best efforts of NASA could muster to persuade President Nixon to accept the project at all, in 1970, and its price was the cancellation of three Apollo missions. But Reagan could no more see his way yet to approving a space station for the shuttle to use than had his predecessors Ford and Carter. So NASA accepted that, for the time being at least, the shuttle would only carry cargo into orbit in its big cargo bay. By 10 April 1981, as Vladimir Kovalyonok and Viktor Savinyikh circled the earth, all was ready and NASA counted down.

But computer trouble caused delay after delay and NASA had to scrub the launch two days to 12 April 1981 which, as luck or coincidence would have it, was the 20th anniversary of Gagarin's historic first mission.

Millions held their breath as Young and Crippen reached the awesome moment when the boosters finally lit up. First came on the dull orange light of the main engine, only a small intimation of the huge power of the solid boosters which then roared to life. The shuttle shook and the solids took it away in only three-tenths of a second. The white and orange flames grew to over 1 km in length. The boosters dropped away at 40 km and the External Tank took the shuttle up like a plane and it curved into orbit over Gibraltar.

Young and Crippen rolled and flew the *Columbia* for two exhilarating days before hitting the reentry button over Guam on Mach 24. By the time they reached the coast of California they were down to Mach 7. They were flying like a plane, head-first into reentry, gravity pulling them forwards. Orbital thrusters soon became useless: the shuttle now responded instead to moves on the ailerons.

'What a way to come to California!' shouted Crippen as *Columbia* crossed the coast, dropping fast. It glided over the coastline and swung over the orange and wine valleys, and John Young searched for the dried-up-salt lake beds of Edwards Air Force Base inland. He found them, steered *Columbia* over the mountains, and floated in. It was a truly glorious moment. The reticent John Young could not restrain himself and bounded out of the hatch to tell the whole world.

SILENT STAR

Cosmos 929 had from July 1977 to early in 1978 tested out the idea of a specialized work module to be built onto a Salyut station. With Salyut 6 nearing the end of its manned operational life, this was a perfect time to conduct a lengthy test of an advanced pre-operational version.

The chosen vehicle became known as Cosmos 1267, launched from Baikonour on 25 April 1981, just before local dawn. There was nothing official to mark out its existence as something special, but Western observers, hardened and ready to identify anything peculiar, pounced soon enough.

The orbit was a low Salyut one: 200 by 278 km, 51.6 degrees, 89 minutes. Its frequencies were the same as Cosmos 929. Ground tracking showed that it was at least as bright and as large as Salyut itself. But its orbit was a long way behind. If it was going to catch up for a rendezvous, it would need at least a month to do so. And that is what it did. Cosmos 1267 closed in, slowly but surely. It released a descent module on 24 May and docked with Salyut's forward port on 19 June. Only then did the Soviet press reveal its identity and purpose.

By that time, Salyut 6 had been deserted, and for the last time, by human crews. Vladimir Kovalyonok and Viktor Savinyikh had come down on 26 May after 75 days, the shortest Salyut 6 mission. When a few days later President Leonid Brezhnev gave them their awards at a ceremony in the Kremlin, he told them: 'Now we will have to embark on the next step — to put into orbit permanent orbital research stations with changing shifts of crews. Cosmonautics will be busy: there is fascinating and vital work to be done' [16].

Salyut 6's own record had been impressive by any standards: there had been five main expeditions, 11 visiting missions, and 12 Progress supply flights [17]. This accounted for 27 dockings. Salyut 6 was manned for 676 days. 1330 separate experiments had been carried out. Three crews had made spacewalks. 15 000 photographs had been taken. The BST 1M telescope had been kept at sub-zero temperatures for the duration of the flight. Emergencies had been faced, fought, and dealt with. All the years before Salyut 6 could now be put down to experience, and the space programme had at last come of age.

One of the last things Kovalyonok and Savinyikh had done was to leave a small docking module attached to Salyut. This small docking module or collar enabled Cosmos 1267 to dock. And so the prolonged test of the 'Star' systems began, with the complex kept in a constant orbit of 350 by 380 km.

So quiet were official sources about Salyut 6 that in January 1982 the Russians felt obliged to issue a statement to the effect that Salyut was still in orbit! Its fate had not yet been decided, they said, but it was still going strong. But they had largely themselves to blame for the speculation. After the return of the Soyuz T4 crew, information about Salyut dried up. The silence was broken only by an interview given by Konstantin Feoktistov in early July 1981:

Modules performing diverse functions will be a common sight in space. Some will be a fitted out space laboratory to enable research by specialists. Others will perform merely technical duties. There will be laboratory modules and even whole plants for manufacturing. Large modules will be available for cosmonauts to rest in. Space stations will be large enough to accomodate the entire staff of a scientific laboratory who could use the station to place other satellites into desired orbits. [18]

Feoktistov himself dreamed of returning to space. There were rumours that he managed to get himself assigned to at least one mission (Soyut T3) only to fail a medical.

So much for Salyut 6 and Cosmos 1267. A new Salyut could not be long off, though there was some uncertainty as to exactly when it would appear. In August 1981 Alexei Yeliseyev announced that it would be the following year at the earliest, and in December the French were told that their upcoming joint flight, slated for mid-1982, would fly up to the old Salyut 6 if Salyut 7 were not available.

The delay, it later transpired, was due to the need to commission a new launch control centre at Kalinin. Three were now in use, thus making it possible to control a Salyut, Soyuz and Cosmos simultaneously. In January 1982 Vladimir Shatalov announced that 16 people were now in training for the next set of missions. Soon after, pictures appeared of a new type of spacecraft in the hydrotank in Star Town. Was this the elusive 'Star' module?

Despite the suggestions of delays, Salyut 7 was off the pad on 19 April 1982, just eleven years to the day since Salyut 1. By late April it had reached operational height. Salyut 6 could now safely be dispensed with. No manoeuvres were conducted between 22 October 1981 and its decay on 28 July 1982 when with the mysterious Cosmos 1267 still attached, the 35 tonne complex was deorbited, to crash into the Pacific. It was an obscure end to the most successful space mission the Russians had ever flown. The Soviet press gave it a perfunctory obituary and less than it deserved. 'Salyut 6 says goodbye' was the best headline it could muster [19].

'STARTING ALL OVER AGAIN'

By the time the next Soyuz mission was ready to go, it was close to a year since the last Russians had been space. It was the biggest mission gap since 1976. The arrival of American Shuttle had been more and more evident all the time. In November 1981 *Columbia* had returned to space for a two-day mission, and in March 1982 Jack Lousma and Gordon Fullerton had taken it up for an eight-day flight. They tested a remote arm for deploying satellites, and because the principal landing site was waterlogged they came down over Truth or Consequences, New Mexico, onto White Sands airfield high up in the mountains.

The Salyut 7, for which sixteen cosmonauts had trained, was little different from its predecessor, at least externally. Two rendezvous antennae were added, one docking target removed. Three furnaces were put on board, and they were called 'Kristall', 'Magma F' and 'Korund'. The BST 1M telescope was replaced by the SKR-02M spectrometer and an X-ray telescope called RT4M, or 'Sirena' for short.

As Salyut 7 orbited, crew members Anatoli Berezovoi and Valentin Lebedev waited for their moment to come. We know quite a lot about how they felt, not only before their flight but during it, because Valentin Lebedev kept a diary. After they returned, *Pravda* had the good sense and openness to publish it. They and their backups (Vladimir Titov and Gennadiy Strekhalov) left Moscow on 28 April: 'When we were driving off I looked at the balcony and saw my mother wiping her eyes. I waved but she didn't see' [20].

11 May. Valentin Lebedev confided to himself that he feared the 200-day flight, not because of its dangers or hardships, but because of 'sudden doubts you might have that you might not be able to live and work alone with a colleague for so long – what if you show some weakness of character or stroke of bad temper?'

They went up on 13 May. After their first day they went to sleep – Lebedev in the descent module and Berezovoi in the orbital module. When they awoke early on the 14th, Lebedev could not find his colleague – all there was in the module was two spacesuits hung up on the walls. But Berezovoi had taken refuge in one, so cold was that night.

They docked on 14 May. Lebedev, who had flown before, had great difficulty in keeping his commander away from sight-seeing at the windows. Sickness afflicted them, like any new crew, and Berezovoi kept talking in his sleep. The French mission was not due till the end of June, so Berezovoi and Lebedev spent some time getting Salyut into order. On 17 May they launched a small sub-satellite, Iskra 2, through the airlock. It was a bit of one-upmanship on the Shuttle, which was specifically designed to launch satellites from orbit, but had not yet done so. Progress 13 came up to the station on 23 May. When it left it used its motors to lower Salyut's orbit as the upcoming three-man mission could not travel up as high as the two-man crews.

This was not the only complication of the Soviet–French flight. In February 1982 the prime commander went down with flu and then a suspected heart condition. Yuri Malashev was replaced at short notice by Vladimir Dzanibekov. Training went on, and the crew were given special dark track suits and mission badges (hitherto largely only an American embellishment). The uniform was actually similar to the Red Army Tank Corps.

Then the political climate worsened [21]. Socialist President François Mitterand (elected in May 1981) took a hard anti-Soviet line, in contrast to his centre-right predecessor Valery Giscard d'Estaing. Hostility to the Soviet invasion of Afghanistan and the deployment of SS-20 missiles created an anti-Soviet climate. Eminent scientists appealed to Mitterand to call off the flight. He contemplated doing so, but did not. The compromise was that the flight received minimal media attention, and the media duly obliged. But the French trainees — called, neutrally, 'spacionautes' (neither astronauts nor cosmonauts, another compromise) went on training and practising Russian. Both were bright, chatty test pilots and they were determined to do a good job of work.

Lebedev and Berezovoi had meanwhile been weather forecasting and mapping cotton and grain fields around the Volga. They were into a work pattern and began to resent the thought of new arrivals. Lebedev's diary tells it best:

> We're waiting for our guests nervously. Our relationship has settled. What impact will the new people have on us? The two of us have got used to each other and we're getting along well in our work. Now it's as though we'll have to start all over again. We've eaten all our soups. All we have now is porridge, wheats, and canned food. The bread is inedible. There's nothing left to feed the Frenchman — we'll hope they bring up something themselves.

HAUTE CUISINE

'Polyot normalyo!' reported Dzanibekov as Soyuz T6 lifted off the pad just after mid-summer's day. It was 24 June. They were alongside next day. Then the gyro broke down. Soyuz was still 900 m from Salyut.

Dzanibekov seized manual control. Perhaps he was afraid he'd be ordered home, because he wasted no time manoeuvring T6 forwards, and did not even turn the TV system on. They docked over Africa, 14 minutes early, and independent of ground control.

Dzanibekov, Ivanchenkov, and Jean-Loup Chrétien clambered on board — the Frenchman bringing up crab soup, lobster, hare and cheese, with orange and strawberry lollies. He wanted to bring wine and garlic. The former was forbidden (though strangely Salyut 7 did carry vodka, allegedly for medicinal purposes) and the latter was disallowed because the air purifiers could not cope with it. Lebedev:

> Everyone then went to bed except me. I took a thick mail envelope and hid away in the transfer compartment reading my mail. I had a great time. . . Lyusha and Vitalik had written lots of letters.

The French visit heightened the atmosphere:

> Jean is a funny man. He brought a quasimodo face mask up with him and when I approached the instrument panel a hairy image came out at me. I screamed! There was laughter all round.

Frenchman Jean Loup Chretien surrounded by ground crew after the successful landing of the Soyuz T6 capsule on which he joined Soviet cosmonauts Vladimir Dzhanibekov and Alexander Ivanchenkov.

Soyuz T6 brought up several experiments. An ecograph was used to get TV images of the inside of the heart, like a scanner. 'Cytos-2' looked at bacteria. There were three welding sessions: the thrusters were turned off and the crew took long-duration photographs of the Earth and the sky during orbital night-time.

Dzanibekov, Ivanchenkov and Chrétien landed near Arkalyk on 2 July. There were decorations all round and the earlier doubts were forgotten. The two French spacionautes returned home. Jean-Loup Chrétien was made an air defence Commander — the Russians being their postulated enemies during their military exercises. Patrick Baudry got a nomination to be the first Frenchman to fly on the American Shuttle as part of the ESA programme, and thus became the first spacionaute to be trained by both superpowers.

Progress 14 came up to the station on 12 July and stayed till 10 August. During its visit the cosmonauts spacewalked two and a half hours to inspect the exterior of the station:

The night before I did not sleep at all. I kept thinking of my home, of the flight, of my friends, of my work. I should have dozed off a little, but I did not. Tolya (Anatoli) did not sleep well either.

I turned the lock handle, and bright sunlight flooded in. Space began to suck everything out like a giant vacuum cleaner. . . there were washers and nuts and a pencil.

My first impression was that of a huge Earth and the real irreality of everything that was going on.

There was the dark velvet of the sky, the blue halo of the Earth, lakes, rivers, fields and cloud clusters. It was dead silence all around. Nothing to indicate speed. No wind whistling in your ears. No pressure. It was serene and majestic.

AROUND THE WORLD FOR 200 DAYS

By mid-July fatigue had set in. Lebedev told his diary that the most difficult thing was not to lose one's temper either with one's colleague or with the ground. You have to keep calm because if there is a row, any crack in the relationship between the crewmen can only grow wider. Even so, the strain was growing:

> July 16. It is more and more difficult to fly on. But watching the Earth calms you.
> July 26. The days are harder to bear.
> September 6. Will I ever be back on Earth, with my own people? I find it harder and harder to fall asleep. I am lying like a young girl, dreaming of all and sundry. I fall asleep after midnight.

The image of the long-distance space traveller is the fearless forty-niner, the let's-stay-up-and-fly-further hero. But the reality is a story of loneliness, of fear, and homesickness. Either way, however, the sheer routine of running a station diverted their attention from these problems for the rest of the time:

> A pair of scissors is the most indispensable thing on board. Each of us has one tied by a long cord to his pocket and uses it every minute, preparing the food or doing the repairs — the first need everywhere is to open packages or cut tapes.

Routine used up so much of the time that even some scientific work became wearying:

> Sept 6. Today I at last finished plotting the fracture of the geological feature from the Caspian Sea to Lake Balkash.

Four days later sprouts began to shoot up in the garden: there were cucumber, radish, peas and wheat.

> Sept. 10. It's nice touching the sprouts with the palm of your hand — they tickle you.

Then in late summer came the second visiting team:

> Aug. 20. At last we see the transport ship 5 km away, coming towards us like a bright star. The Sun lit it up from underneath. Next to it I saw a tiny star — a real one. It was all very beautiful.

Leonid Popov, Svetlana Savitskaya and Alexander Serebrov spent a week aboard Salyut 7. Svetlana, the second woman in space, was the star of the show, and the mission even received modest coverage in the Western press. There were regular telecasts of the five cosmonauts swimming around in weightlessness.

> Aug. 26. They are going to land tomorrow. I'm not at all upset, but we stay. We have our own job to get on with — the earliest we can hope for a landing is in two months.

Popov, Savitskaya and Serebrov returned in Soyuz T5, leaving them the fresher T7. They then left the station and took T7 round to the front docking port. They took Salyut 7 back to its operational altitude of 350 km.

Two more cargo ships resupplied them – Progress 15 which arrived on 20 September and Progress 16 on 2 November. On 18 November they launched another Iskra sub-satellite through the airlock.

WILTING

The next landing window was early January, but by early December it was clear that the crew would not last that long – at least not psychologically. Despite exercise and a five-days-on, two-off routine, they were needing no less than 12 hours' sleep each night. Berezovoi and Lebedev expressed a strong wish to be with their families by the new year, which meant a return at least two weeks before that. They requested a night landing on 10 December and the doctors and flight directors approved. The men's humour perked up at once.

Dec. 9. I wonder how things are down below? We've got so used to being here in this little island in space – just think of going back into the real world again.

Soyuz T7 came down at 00.03 Kazakhstan time. That was when the trouble started. The Soyuz rolled over down a slope: Lebedev crashed out of his seat belt onto Berezovoi. When the battered men crawled out it was freezing cold. They saw they were being rapidly enveloped in thick bands of fog. Visibility was about 1000 m and decreasing rapidly.

They heard the search helicopter hovering somewhere overhead. Its pilot picked up the Soyuz beacon and tried to land. It came down nearby but it was a heavy landing in a dried-up river bed and it lost a main wheel. It guided in the medical helicopter to a safe landing. Now snow was falling.

Things could only get worse. They did. Temperatures fell to $-15°$C. It was a recipe for disaster, and the pilot of the wrecked command helicopter ordered the other helicopters to scatter. The press helicopter was blown 150 km off course by high winds and came down only to wait 10 hours to be rescued. The journalists missed their story.

Back at the Soyuz, Berezovoi and Lebedev – who were theoretically supposed to be under the most intensive and delicate medical care – were huddling together to keep warm. They had wisely kept their spacesuits on. The medical team found them in an hour, but conditions were so atrocious that the medical helicopter could not fly them out. A big transporter was summoned from 50 km away. It had huge wheels for heavy cross-country work and a rear section originally designed to carry a platoon of soldiers.

Post-flight debriefing had long since gone by the board as the rescue team battled blizzard, fog, and a penetrating icy wind all in the dark. Only the radio kept the operation together at all. After hours of waiting, the cross-country teams eventually arrived. Berezovoi and Lebedev spent their first night back on Earth in the bumpy rear cabin of a troop transporter. But they were too tired to care. It was all over now. Getting the rest of the way back to base was someone else's responsibility.

And Berezovoi and Lebedev were back with their families by New Year's Eve as promised. Flight control was now only beginning to analyse the results of the experiment and the 211 days aloft. There were 20 000 photographic plates to examine, and in 1983 an Earth Resources Centre was set up in one of the southern republics to handle the data. Pictures from Salyut 7 helped to locate oil and gas fields. They guided the route for the transcontinental gas pipeline and the Baikal–Amur railway. The cosmonauts' weather forecasting alone saved a billion roubles a year in terms of advance warning.

Four months were to elapse before the next mission got under way: phase two had, as its goal, the permanent occupancy of space.

DISAPPOINTMENT TO NEAR DISASTER

Central to this second stage was the notion that a resident crew would be replaced by a new crew while still in orbit. Tours of duty would last about four months – the amount of time calculated to produce maximum productivity and minimum fatigue. A new resident crew could be settled in and the old one could then fly home from the other docking port.

Such an achievement would place the USSR demonstrably well ahead of the Shuttle, though such direct comparisons were invidious. In November 1982, Shuttle STS-5 had launched the first payloads from its cargo bay. In April 1983, a second Shuttle, *Challenger*, entered service. The Americans planned to move to regular monthly launchings of fare-paying cargo.

The first resident crew on this second stage was composed of Vladimir Titov, 36, a new pilot selected in 1976, and veterans Gennadiy Strekhalov and Alexander Serebrov. It was by any standards a strong team; and it was backed up by Vladimir Lyakhov, who had 175 days behind him, and two newcomers – Alexander Alexandrov (no relation of the Bulgarian) and Alexander Volkov (no relation to the Soyuz 11 flight engineer). It would be a three-man resident crew. The crew would be relieved in mid-August by a second set of cosmonauts, thought to include Leonid Kizim and Vladimir Solovyov. Before that, though, there would be a visiting mission, and the crew selected was thought to have been composed of Vladimir Vasyutin, Viktor Savinyikh and Savitskaya's backup, Irina Pronina, who was being primed for the first woman spacewalk, which would be another first. So it was to be an action-packed year.

Star Town was busier than ever. For each mission, a prime crew, a backup crew, and a reserve crew were selected. Many were drawn from the team of pilots selected in 1976 and a group of engineers selected in 1978. A new squad of cosmonauts was appointed in December 1982 who would be needed in upcoming missions. Of these 15 flight and research engineers, three were women.

These missions would be made possible by the first operational use of the 'Star' module. With a mass of 20 tonnes it was heavier than Salyut itself. It had two modules – a smaller forward one which was recoverable (6 tonnes) and a larger main module, based on the Salyut central section, weighing over 14 tonnes, which was not. Both contained fuel and supplies and the cosmonauts could enter both.

A Proton booster carried the module aloft on 2 March 1983. It was labelled Cosmos 1443. As usual, the Russians were coy about its purpose, and said nothing further until it had docked with Salyut 7 on 10 March. Such reticence about the module continued and its design was not released until the late summer, and only then in one of the less-well-known Soviet technical periodicals.

Very early on 20 April, the Novosti press agency in London published pictures of the Soyuz T8 crew. It was all a terrible mistake, far from being in orbit as Novosti thought, they were all still asleep at the cosmodrome! They did not fly till lunchtime. Spring was at an advanced stage and Soyuz T8 took to the skies in bright, warm and sunny weather freshened by gusting winds. A blaze of publicity greeted the new flight. Moscow TV ran a 20-minute special programme from Baikonour and captured the tension of a difficult and challenging mission.

Though they did not know it, Titov, Strekhalov and Serebrov were up to their heads in trouble. The rendezvous radar, which swings out of the side of the craft, simply failed to deploy. It stuck stubbornly in. No radar, and the crew were flying blind.

Titov, however, was not the kind of man to let this ruin the mission. He asked, and got, permission to fly the first-ever all-manual chase and rendezvous through space. And this seemed to work, for by orbit 17, Titov was able to bring Soyuz T8 to within 80 km of Salyut 7. Flight control remained nervous about the idea, but so far so good.

Soviet media coverage had, meanwhile, stopped abruptly. The flight disappeared from the news. In hours everyone realized it was in trouble.

Titov flew on. He burned the motor 50 seconds on orbit 17 and by orbit 18 he had Salyut in sight. Nearly there! Could he pull it off against all the odds — a space rendezvous without radar? Final approach. He nudged Soyuz forwards. Just then, Soyuz went into darkness. Pitch black enveloped the Soyuz, and the Salyut/Cosmos complex. Titov commanded on the searchlights to illuminate the target.

Soyuz T8 was drifting in towards the Salyut. But Titov found it harder and harder to get his bearings and estimate his distance in the dark. He could see he was getting closer and closer, but how close? There was a danger of collision and impact. 300 m, 200 m. Too fast, too fast. Titov fired his motor once more, to pull away just for the moment. He had got as close as 160 m from Salyut.

By the time they emerged into light they were a full 4 km away. Titov then reported back on the fuel situation. The gauges indicated the tanks were nearly dry.

They soft-landed safely on 22 April. The Politburo was hosting a reception in the Kremlin at the time, and defence minister Dmitri Ustinov was handed a note to tell him of the safe soft-landing. He squeezed past shoulders to tell everyone. The relief was visible to all.

This setback was a bitter disappointment. It was the fifth such rendezvous or docking failure, and the whole purpose behind Soyut T was to eliminate the possibility of these failures. But there was nothing for it but to press on. The backup crew — minus Volkov who was dropped to save weight and gain fuel — was pressed into service and launched on 27 June, a mere three days after the return of the NASA Space Shuttle. This was its seventh flight and it attracted attention for flying America's first woman astronaut, Sally Ride.

There were no hitches this time and the crew of Vladimir Lyakhov and Alexander Alexandrov were aboard the next day. Alexandrov was slight and thin, and contrasted with his well-built commander. Alexandrov was an experienced designer who had been refused admission to the cosmonaut squad in 1965. He had been accepted in 1978 and his wife was a flight controller. Pictures showed him relaxing with his wife and family in the woods outside their country cottage near Moscow.

It took them a full three weeks to unload Cosmos 1443, which was doubling up as a cargo carrier. There were 600 items to be unloaded with a total weight of four tonnes. To speed up the process, the module was fitted with mechanical railcars so unloading scenes must have made the men look like coal miners.

The relief flight was − owing to the late start − not now due to start until mid-October, following the visiting mission due at the end of September. But there was a logistics problem to be overcome in the meantime. A resupply mission was needed, and this could only come in at the rear port. Cosmos 1443 would have to go and Soyut T9 flown around to the front so as to leave the rear free for a new Progress.

So on 14 August Cosmos 1443 was undocked, ushering in a period of extreme confusion. First, the Russians called the Cosmos a 'tug' because it had boosted up the station's orbit. Second, they called it a 'freighter' that was returning to Earth. Third, they announced that it had sent down a 'module', and said it in such a way as to imply that the rest of Cosmos was still attached to Salyut. Then a week later it was blandly announced that Cosmos 1443 was alive and well and in independent flight. It was 'conducting exhaustive manoeuvring tests'.

Much of the confusion was due to the failure of the Soviet press to publish as much as a diagram of what Cosmos 1443 looked like. However, one did appear in the magazine *Soviet Industry*, first in outline, and then with detailed cutaways. But it got no further than that, and it is possible that some sections of the Soviet media were not aware of them, hence the clumsy efforts at explaining what the module was doing. The 'Star' module, it transpired, was based on the central section of Salyut. At one end was a docking probe and navigation equipment so that it could dock with the forward port of Salyut. At the other end was the return capsule. It looked not unlike the old American Gemini capsule with a long tower rocket at the end. It did in fact incorporate an important feature of the unusual design of Gemini as configured by the American Air Force to fly with their Manned Orbiting Laboratory of the 1965−69 period: the heat shield at the bottom doubled up as an entry hatch from the rest of the craft. The 'Star' carried two solar panels, able to provide 3 kW electricity. The manoeuring engines were slotted into the top of the hull section like water-courses, and there were four such motors: again, an unusual design feature.

The length of 'Star' was 13 m and weight 20 tonnes. The volume of the main compartment was 50 m³. The return module could bring back 500 kg of supplies − or in an emergency ferry five cosmonauts home. In fact, this new design gave the Russians a flexibility they had hitherto lacked. Such modules could be fitted as new crew areas, or specialized laboratories; they could operate in free flight and dock again; they could bring the results of experiments back to Earth; they could fly a whole station crew back; they could fly as a 'super-progress freighter'; or could be adapted as a spacetug. Cosmos 1443 was designed to explore a number of these concepts in the course of its six-month flight [22]. One of its most important manoeuvres was to man-rate the recovery module.

14 August 1983. Cosmos 1443 undocked, its recovery module filled with 500 kg of melted ampoules.

16 August. Soyuz T9 undocked and flew around to the front docking port.

17 August. Progress 17 cargo ship launched.

19 August. Progress 27 arrived with 2000 kg of food, fuel, air and water.

23 August. The recoverable 'freighter' module separated and recovered near Arkalyk.

17 September. Progress 17 burned up.

19 September. The main component of Cosmos 1443 deorbited.

Leaving aside all the traffic movements, Lyakhov and Alexandrov had a busy time. They had photographed nearly a million square metres. 4000 photographs were taken in the first eight weeks alone and were being processed by over 700 institutions. They had located shoals of fish as their station swung over the oceans.

FIREBALL

Then things began to go badly wrong. The trouble began during the second week of September. During refuelling of Progress 17, the oxidizer line suddenly sprang a leak. Lyakhov and Alexandrov speedily evacuated the station, sealed themselves inside Soyuz and closed the hatches. They prepared for emergency return, but after a number of hours, flight control had managed to reassess the situation. Only one oxidizer line had gone; there was no danger of an explosion; at worst the station would lose 50 per cent of its manoeuvring ability. They climbed back in.

The cosmonauts had barely recovered from this episode when one of the three solar panels went out of action completely, for a reason then unknown. But the consequence became obvious soon enough. The internal temperature fell to 10°C, and more seriously the humidity level rocketed to near 100 per cent. Besides being unpleasant, the damp conditions made the electrical systems prone to shorting.

These two incidents forced an abrupt change of plan to the visiting mission due on 27 September. The original crew were taken out, and replaced by Vladimir Titov and Gennadiy Strekhalov at less than two weeks' notice. There were several reasons. First, the Cosmos module had brought up some spare solar panels. Now Titov and Strekhalov had been trained to fit these in the course of the Soyuz T8 mission as a routine assignment. Because that mission had failed, and because Alexandrov and Lyakhov had not undergone specific EVA training to do this, the work had not yet been done. But now it was required as a matter of extreme urgency, and they were much the best trained people to do the work. Second, the planned visiting mission had become much less the experimental flight it had been scheduled to be because of the deteriorating state of the space station itself. The experiments that had been assigned to Vasyutin, Savinyikh and Pronina could wait till another day.

The Soyuz T10 mission was scheduled for 27 September and up to two weeks were set aside for what promised to be a risky and dangerous operation. Not only would Titov and Strekhalov be required to attach the new solar panels, but they would be asked to inspect the damaged oxidizer line at Salyut's rear. EVA was, and is, a dangerous exercise, and, as is known from the diaries of both Ryumin and Lebedev, the cosmonauts feared it.

Titov and Strekhalov were aboard Soyuz T10 at the launch pad two hours before the scheduled liftoff at 00.38 local time. At T−2 minutes the main gantries had fallen back. There was full pressure in all tanks. Only the sounds of 'everything normal' broke the static of the airwaves.

T−25 seconds. Fire on the pad! A valve jammed at the base of the A-2 rocket. A small fire had broken out and more fuel gushed out of the lines spreading the flames even further. It was only a question of time before the whole explosive rocket would go up in a bang.

T−20 seconds. At this stage the emergency rocket on top of Soyuz should have fired the Soyuz craft free of the about-to-explode inferno. But it stayed there, unmoving. Were the cosmonauts aware of what was going on? No one knew. Ground controllers watched helpless. Unless they got them out of there at once, it would be too late. Still nothing happened. The fires began to roar and flash. Ground controllers began to react: they realized the fires must have cut the wiring that would activate the escape tower. There was only one resort left, and it was a slow and clumsy one: it involved two controllers counting down simultaneously in two separate rooms and simultaneously ordering radio-controlled escape. And it took a full ten seconds! The rocket would surely blow by then.

T−10 seconds. The fires were raging, and the rapid-thinking controllers began their countdown. *Dyehssyat. . .dyevyaht. . .vossyeem. . . .* It seemed like a lifetime: would they ever get down to zero? *Syehm. . .shehst. . .pyaht. . . .* The cosmonauts must now have realized they were in dire peril. *Chyeetiryeh. . .tree. . . .* They had to hit the radio ignition button at exactly the same time. . .*tvah. . .odin. . . .*

T−0 seconds. Whoom! A gigantic bang engulfed the whole launch site. The ground just shook and shook. People were blown over. Flaming debris careered through the air. Controllers underground felt like they had received a direct bomb hit. Hearts raced. . . . They must have been too late to save the cosmonauts. Yellow, orange, red flames could be spotted through billowing black, grey and white clouds that mushroomed and swelled outwards and upwards. There was hot air being blown outwards into the night and the charcoal smell of burning metal. Wreckage was still falling. Huge billows of smoke rose from the furnace centre of the inferno and the intensity of its violence.

And above all the smoke, shot a pinprick of light! It trailed tiny flames and was lost in the clouds. The escape tower! Yes, the system had worked and worked when it mattered. The tiny rockets on the tower hurled the capsule free, every hundredth of a second bringing it further from the violence of the explosion, every instant nearer safety. It fired for only five seconds, but that was enough to get it clear of the fireball. At 1 km altitude, four petals unfolded from the base of the Soyuz. The tower took the orbital module away. The equipment module was hurled free by explosive bolts. The Soyuz heat shield was shot free. The air pressure system registered low altitude, thereby firing the cap off the parachutes. Every second counted here. Less than a thousand metres in altitude and falling fast, those parachutes had to come out fast for they had no height to play around with.

The system was designed only to be survivable, not for comfort. Titov and Strekhalov got about five seconds air worth out of the parachutes before the capsule hit the ground. Despite cushioning by the Soyuz landing rockets, they were bruised all over from the bumpy impact. A rescue team pulled them out. They were too shaken to talk and were given vodka to restore their nerves. They were bundled off in an ambulance which sped past what was left of the burning launch site 4000 metres away. Their spaceflight had lasted about 20 seconds. The launch pad was utterly wrecked. They were lucky to be alive.

DEAD IN THE WATER

Flight control advised Vladimir Lyakhov at once about what had happened and that he and Alexandrov would have to stay up there while the problems were sorted out. This might take some time. The inside of Salyut was more and more uncomfortable, and oxidizer was spilling out into space. Salyut 7 was 'dead in the water', according to the Pentagon, aware not only of the problems on Salyut but that the rescue crew had nearly been killed trying to go into orbit to make repairs [23].

Several Western papers made the most, not only of the 27 September incident, but the fact that the Soyuz T9 was now well beyond its 100-day limit. Was the crew's return vehicle unuseable?

The *New York Post* ran a sensational story called 'Trapped in Space'. The British *Sunday Express* said Lyakhov and Alexandrov were stranded and 'in a precarious state'. Their only hope was rescue by the American Shuttle: but the Russians were too proud to ask for American assistance, preferring that their men died [24].

The truth was, as always, more mundane. Kettering Grammar School, still on the job, used its short-wave radio to pick up the crew chattering away. They did not know Russian but they could tell by the tone of their voices that they were not listening in to the desperate or the dying.

Flight control were working flat out to get the flight back on a level keel. The cosmonauts were given a new programme of work with the emphasis on technological experiments. On 9 October they spotted the first autumn snowfall sprinkling the terrain of the USSR. The new work programme, in fact, gave the cosmonauts a new sense of purpose, and according to official sources, stopped and reversed the psychological decline. By 12 October, Moscow felt confident enough to announce details of a Soviet–Indian flight planned for the spring.

A Soviet–Indian flight had been talked about for many years. India, like France, liked to be independent of the superpowers and yet on good terms with both. Unlike France, India had an urgent need to modernize its technology and do so quickly. Other factors which contributed to the political possibility of the flight were New Delhi's historic border quarrels with China and Pakistan, both of which were on poor terms with the USSR. For this reason, a Moscow–New Delhi understanding was of mutual assistance.

The USSR had already launched two Indian Earth resources satellites, so an Intercosmos flight was a logical sequel. The prime crew was named as Yuri Malashev, Nikolai Rukhavishnikov and Rakesh Sharma; and backups were named as Anatoli Berezovoi, Georgi Grechko and Ravish Mulhotra. The choice of flight engineers – neither of whom had flown since 1979 – was unexpected.

The future of the existing mission was decided on during a ground-to-air teleconference held on 16 October by mission director Viktor Blagov. He told the crew that they would not be in a position to launch another Soyuz. Could they stay up another month? And would they risk flying home a 150-day-old Soyuz? And lastly, would they be able to attach the two spare solar panels themselves, even without the specialized training?

NORTHERN LIGHTS

Progress 18 was launched on 20 October to give them enough supplies for their last month on board. It stayed with the station for the period 22 October to 17 November.

The cosmonauts prepared for their spacewalk and repair mission. They were tired, at the end of an exhausting vigil in orbit, one that had hit snag after snag. But they rose to the challenge. Alexander Alexandrov opened the hatch:

It was a tense, emotionally charged experience. Only a thin suit separated you from the rawness of outer space. The Earth below was dark, like a shadow play. If we dropped small objects like nuts or bolts they looked like stars. [25]

The spacewalk took 2 h 50 min, and they returned two days later for another of 2 h 55 min. They wore new three-piece lightweight suits, an advance on those carried on Salyut 6. Vladimir Lyakhov became the first Russian to make three space walks. They had to pull the 1.5 m by 5 m panels out by means of a winch and attach them to the existing panels and then ensure current was connected.

The Soviet press hailed the adding on of the solar panels as a giant step towards huge orbital space complexes. It did increase the amount of power available to Salyut by 50 per cent. If Moscow was carried away in exaggerating the value of the spacewalk, the West ignored it altogether and as a result failed to appreciate its significance. It was a first, it was the first example of creative engineering construction in orbit, and if a Shuttle crew had done it, it would have been so hailed.

18 November marked the end of the operational phase of the mission. 350 experiments had been conducted and there were samples, tapes and films to be brought back. Vladimir Lyakhov and Alexander Alexandrov undocked on 23 November after 150 days in orbit. Salyut's new panels glinted brightly in the glow of Soyuz' searchlights. The landing was at night and in fog: no pictures were available, but the crew were in good condition and taking walks in the woods around Baikonour a week later, wrapped up in fur coats and Astrakhan hats.

The post-flight press conference was one of the best-attended in many years. It was held on 12 December and Western journalists were anxious to query the cosmonauts and the flight directors about the problems which arose during the mission. Much to their surprise, the Russians admitted there had been a fuel leak. Yes, a booster had exploded on the pad. Lyakhov:

We were told at once. Our flight programme was expanded and lasted longer than expected. But we were never in danger and could have returned at any time. [26].

More intriguingly, the Russians used the occasion to reveal a breathtaking plan of turning the Soviet Polar north from darkness to light during the winter months by the use of space stations. In 1967, the Russians had caused an international furore by announcing plans for turning some of their larger rivers, which flowed — uselessly in their opinion — into the Arctic, towards more southerly and water-starved climes to irrigate the southern deserts. Was this scheme in the same class? Whether it was or not, this was how the Soviet space directors saw the future. They had lost none of the determination, sense of purpose, or romantic dreaming they had the day that they had started.

We are at the stage of transition from the present space stations visited periodically by crews replacing each other, to a multi-sectional orbital permanently habited complex.

It will be a single system of structures of a large size orbiting between 200 and 40 000 km, linked to Earth by cargo and passenger ships.

The complex will include specialized research laboratories, comfortable living modules, powerful energy plants, a refuelling station, and even construction platforms.

It will watch the atmosphere, agricultural crops, spot forest fires, and prospect for minerals. It will monitor ships and aircraft, send out TV programmes, produce electronic and optical and medico-biological materials and preparations unobtainable on Earth.

Looking further ahead, there will be vast projects to illuminate the long solar nights with reflected sunlight. [27]

DOCTOR ABOARD

Salyut 7 was not to remain unoccupied for long. On 8 February 1984, Soyuz T-10 arrived, crewed by Leonid Kizim, Vladimir Solovyov and Oleg Atkov. The most significant crew member was Oleg Atkov: a medical doctor, he was the first Soviet doctor in orbit for twenty years. Soon after they had manned the station, it was announced that the mission target would be a new record of 240 days. The presence of Dr Atkov meant that the response of the crew to long-term weightlessness could be monitored on a daily basis by a medical expert *in situ*. From reports reaching the ground, Atkov was quite insistent on running a full medical check each day. He was one of a group of scientific specialists given cosmonaut training from 1978 on in a new model of recruitment. It went as follows: specialists in particular disciplines (like medicine, metallurgy etc.) were taken out of their work for six months of basic training for space flight. They were then returned to their normal work, but were liable to be called up at only a few months' notice for a flight, depending on the nature of the flight chosen. The Soyuz T10 crew was put together as late as September 1983.

The new crew inherited at least some of the problems of their predecessors. The most serious of these was the oxidizer fuel leak. In late April 1984 Kizim and Solovyov began a series of spacewalks to inspect the faulty line with a view to drawing up a repair programme. Five spacewalks were made that April and May, but the decisive one came in early August 1984 when, using tools which had been designed in the interim and flown up to them, they eventually isolated the fault and completed a full repair.

Two visiting missions were flown up to Salyut 7 during their occupation. The first was from 3 to 11 April and was the Indian Intercosmos mission. The cosmonauts who took part were Yuri Malashev, Rakesh Sharma and Gennadiy Strekhalov. Nikolai Rukhavishnikov withdrew some months before due to illness. Sharma was chosen because of his quick ability to master Russian, but the selectors should not have been surprised for he arrived for training with a full command already of Punjabi, Hindi, English and Telagu! The flight was a success. There were eleven passes over India itself, which made possible Earth resources surveys of the Himalayas, mainland India and the islands off its coast. Sharma experimented with Yoga to combat weightlessness; and brought up to his colleagues mango bars and curry.

The second visit was more spectacular and lasted from 19 to 31 July, a full twelve days. Aboard were Vladimir Dzanibekov, 1978 engineer Igor Volk and Svetlana Savitskaya. This was her second space flight. Late on 25 July Radio Moscow announced that the crew were on the verge of new experiments and promised tantalizingly that they would 'give listeners full details in the morning'. So they did. Vladimir Dzanibekov and Svetlana Savitskaya went out to walk in space for three and a half hours. It was the first space walk by a woman, and Svetlana was assigned the task of testing out the first electron hand welder in outer space. The equipment weighed 30 kg and had a full console. With the welder she cut, and welded and soldered metal plates, and then, to finish off, applied a coating. It was nothing less than the full-scale welding task of the type that would be used in the future to cement together the different parts of an orbital complex.

Svetlana Savitskaya clearly relished the work and returned to the cabin exhausted but jubilant. Her success came hard on the Americans who had been readying Kathryn Sullivan for what they had hoped would be the first EVA by a woman. At the time the Shuttle was temporarily grounded due to trouble in the main engines.

The Salyut 7 crew of Kizim, Solovyov and Atkov came back to an autumn Earth on 2 October 1984. They had been aloft a record 237 days — 26 days longer than the longest previous mission. They had flown over 110 million kilometres, spent 22 hours on EVA, and accepted two manned and five unmanned visiting craft. More important than the

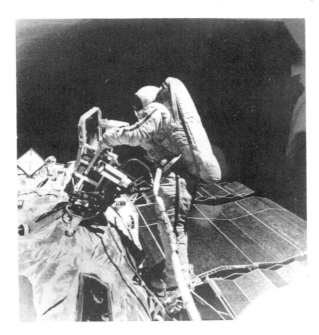

The first spacewalk by a woman took place during the Soyuz T12 mission. Here Svetlana Savitskaya carries out tests on a portable electron welding torch during her three-and-a-half-hour EVA with fellow cosmonaut Vladimir Dzanibekov.

Aboard the space station Salyut 7, Svetlana Savitskaya floats weightless, as Soyuz T12 commander Vladimir Dzanibekov offers her a biscuit. Third member of the crew, Igor Volk, sits in the background.

statistics was the sheer ability of the men to endure such a lengthy mission, function effectively, and carry out difficult repairs. Within a few days the cosmonauts were walking again and at the end of October they returned to Moscow.

SKYWRECK

Some observers had expected a replacement crew to be aboard before the T-10 flight came home, but mission directors made it clear that they did not yet feel ready for such a step. Running long flights put severe strains on tracking crews and mission control, and they needed to be stood down.

Out of the blue came the announcement on 2 March 1985, that Salyut 7 had been abandoned. It was made on just one broadcast on the North American service of Radio Moscow, and not repeated elsewhere.

Salyut 7 was in fact in serious trouble. In early January, the solar panels had lost their lock on the Sun and the station had drifted hopelessly out of alignment. Simultaneously the water system had sprung a leak, flooding some of the station and shorting some of the electrical circuits. And with the loss of solar energy, the station lost heat. The leaked water froze to ice. Radio contact was lost. Salyut 7 was a ghostly wreck.

Mission directors faced a dilemma. Salyut 7's backup had been so cannibalized for repairs and so many of its components flown into orbit that it was no longer viable. A new station was still a year away and a 12- to 18-month gap in missions was not acceptable. There may have been some political pressure from the new Soviet leader, Mikhail Gorbachev, who had made it clear that technology was one of his top priorities.

So a rescue mission was put together. Two crew members were selected: four-times veteran Vladimir Dzhanibekov and Soyuz T-4 veteran Viktor Savinyikh. They had only a month's training, much of it spent in the hydrotank in Star City, practising spacewalks. They were launched aboard Soyuz T-13 on the 57th manned Russian spaceflight on 6 June 1985.

Two days were taken to close in on and dock with the derelict space station. Rendezvous was accomplished entirely manually, using computers linked to laser optical devices. They clambered into the station. It was frozen, the air stank, and there was a strong smell of damp. Every few minutes they had to retreat into Soyuz to warm up.

It took Dzhanibekov and Savinyikh a full ten days to get the station back into basic order. Savinyikh rotated the panels back into position, thawed the station out, and reconnected the electrical systems. Batteries were replaced. Radio and TV contact with the ground was restored. The gamble paid off, and on 2 August the two cosmonauts went on a five-hour EVA to add new solar panels. Salyut 7 was shipshape once more [28].

The two cosmonauts spent the summer on a series of Earth-observation experiments and providing a weather observation service. They unloaded the Progress 24 freighter which arrived on 23 June. This paved the way for the arrival at the station on 22 July of an entirely new type of spacecraft.

Cosmos 1669 was described as a 'support satellite' based on the Progress design. It was to remain with the station until early September. Cosmos 1669 was thought to be similar to what the Americans were then designing for their space station, whose in-service date

The crew of Soyuz T13, mission commander Colonel Vladimir Dzanibekov and flight engineer Viktor Savinykh receive tuition from their training instructor I. Sukhorukov in the Gagarin Cosmonauts' Training Centre.

With all engines on their A-2 launch vehicle firing, the Soyuz T13 capsule lifts clear of the launch pad on the 6 June 1985.

had been set by President Reagan for 1992. NASA was planning a series of free-flying platforms carrying specialized scientific equipment. Capable of independent flight, they would dock with the station from time to time. Data would be collected, repairs effected, and the platform would fly off to continue its work, returning later. Cosmos 1669 carried research equipment, and had its own solar panels to enable it to fly independently.

Cosmos 1669 heralded a new series of operations that concluded just before the 28th anniversary of the launch of Sputnik 1, on 4 October 1985. Soyuz T-14 flew up to the station on 17 September carrying 54-year-old Georgi Grechko, the oldest Russian in space, and two new crew members, Vladimir Vasyutin and Alexander Volkov. They spent a week on board, carrying out experiments into materials processing, astrophysics and Earth studies.

This was the prelude to the first-ever replacement of the crew of an orbital station. Soyuz T-13 came back to Earth on 26 September, carrying flight engineer Georgi Grechko, but bringing back Vladimir Dzhanibekov, who had been 112 days in orbit. His colleague, Viktor Savinyikh, was left on board to continue his long orbital flight, now accompanied by Alexander Volkov and Vladimir Vasyutin, the last-mentioned now commanding the station. The crew replacement operation made the concept of the permanent orbiting station with changing crews a reality at last.

Barely was Soyuz T-13 back on Earth than the Soviet Union launched the first of its Star modules in over two years. Cosmos 1686 docked with Salyut 7 on 3 October. It was a multi-purpose laboratory combining an astronomical observatory, a greenhouse of biological experiments, and a technological workshop for the manufacture of semiconductors and extrapure medicines. The entire complex was 35 m long and nearly 50 tonnes in weight. The goal of an operational working space laboratory with changing crews had at last been achieved.

MIR SUPERSTATION

Setbacks still lay ahead. The new station commander Vladimir Vasyutin was noticed by his colleagues to be listless, fatigued, uninterested in his work, and to spend long hours simply gazing out the window. This was the very stuff of the science fiction writer: the mission commander collapsing under a nervous breakdown. Viktor Savinyikh and Alexander Volkov reluctantly reported his deteriorating psychological condition to the ground. Mission control at once ordered the mission to be terminated. The three cosmonauts evacuated the station and parachuted into the winter snow on 21 November. Vasyutin was rushed to hospital: it was the first time a mission had been cut short due to illness.

Viktor Savinykh (left), flight engineer of the Soyuz T13 crew, pictured here with Vladimir Vasyutin (centre) and Alexander Volkov from Soyuz T14 after their successful return to Earth from their mission aboard Salyut 7.

As it was, a new station was now almost ready to replace Salyut 7. Before it flew, the world was to suffer a horrific reminder as to just how dangerous spaceflight could be.

The new year, 1986, was only 28 days old when the American Space shuttle *Challenger* once more took to the skies above Cape Canaveral. 73 seconds into flight the entire vehicle exploded in a gigantic eruption that filled the skies with billowing white smoke. The cataclysm took the lives of Dick Scobee, Michael Smith, Judith Resnik, Ellison Onizuka, Ronald McNair, Gregory Jarvis, and teacher Christa McAuliffe.

America was plunged into grief. The subsequent investigation tore NASA apart, revealing faulty equipment, warnings unheeded, and short-cuts that had been taken. The redesign work was set to last two and a half years and NASA was virtually grounded.

The successor to Salyut, a new station, was launched from Baikonour spaceport at night on 20 February 1986. Called Mir (Peace) it startled observers by featuring no fewer than six docking ports. The station itself had no scientific equipment, only control mechanisms and living quarters. Research apparatuses would be flown up in specialized modules which would attach themselves to these docking ports. Each cosmonaut had an individualized cabin with bunk, couch and table.

Soon after, cosmonauts Leonid Kizim and Vladimir Solovyov took the plane down to the cosmodrome for the first mission to Mir. For the first time, their names were given to the press two days before blastoff and the launch was covered live. They flew up to Mir on 13 March and settled into Mir two days later.

Kizim and Solovyov were a pathfinder crew: their function was to iron out problems, difficulties and hitches on Mir before a permanent crew came on board. But there was more to come.

Soyuz T-15 left Mir on May 5. But it did not return to Earth. Kizim guided Soyuz T-15 3000 km across space and fired its thrusters to switch from one orbit to another. Late on 6 May, having traversed the emptiness of space, the two cosmonauts arrived aboard the old Salyut 7, bringing with them 300 kg of cargo. On 28 May they emerged from Salyut 7 to erect a 15 m aluminium frame. On a second spacewalk three days later they welded its trusses together with an electron ray welder gun.

Even as they did so, a new spaceship arrived at Mir. The new craft was a modernized version of their own Soyuz, called Soyuz TM (modernized transport). Soyuz TM carried a new navigation unit, power system, extra cargo space, and advanced communication systems. Soyuz TM1 arrived on 23 May and returned after five days.

Soyuz T-15 continued its virtuoso performance on 25 June. Kizim undocked from Salyut 7, activated the radar, and set off once more in pursuit of Mir in a lower, faster, transfer orbit. With Solovyov he then spent a further three weeks aboard the Mir before coming down on 16 July after 125 days in orbit [29].

The orbital transfers were a spectacular exercise in space navigation. Soviet scientists began to talk of an 'archipelago' of space laboratories, with crews transferring from one to another as occasion demanded. In August 1986, Salyut 7 was fired into a 480 km high orbit where it would be inspected by a visiting team of cosmonauts in five years' time.

BUILDING THE STATION

Snow flurries filled the air as Yuri Romanenko and new cosmonaut Alexander Laveikin boarded Soyuz TM2 on 5 February 1987. Searchlights bathed the night-time launch pad and two and a half hours later the cosmonauts ascended on a pillar of orange and red flames as the Soyuz rocket sped aloft towards Mir. The mission heralded a long flight which would see the arrival of the first of four large 21-tonne research modules. The first such module, an astrophysical observatory, was duly launched on 31 March 1987.

The cylindrical laboratory, called Kvant (Quantum) took six days to close on the station. The docking took a nail-biting six days in which the linkup came close to disaster on more than one occasion. At the first attempt to dock, the automatic control system

Their 125-day flight completed, Soyuz T15 cosmonauts Leonid Kizim (right) and Vladimir Solovyov relax with the ground crew. Their descent capsule landed northeast of the town of Arkalyk on 1 July 1986. The crew docked with the Mir/Progress 26 complex and also transferred to the Salyut 7/Cosmos 1686 combination during their mission.

broke down when the module was only 200 m distant. Kvant drifted away, apparently out of control. Several days were spent as ground controllers wrestled with the problem, anxious to try again yet wary of any collision that might endanger the cosmonauts.

After further attempts, a soft docking was at last achieved. The module was linked to Mir/Soyuz TM-2, but the tunnel with Kvant was not hermetically sealed. 40 mm separated the two vehicles, enough to make a crew transfer impossible. There was only one thing for it: a spacewalk. On 12 April 1987, cosmonauts Romanenko and Laveikin threaded their way down Mir to inspect the erring tunnel. They asked ground control to separate the modules to the limit of the connection between the drogue and probe connecting the stations. With a jemmy, Laveikin forced an object out of the tunnel, with Romanenko floating beside him with a tool box. After five attempts, the offending article was removed — a dirty rag! Romanenko and Laveikin backed off and requested ground control to command a full docking. The spaceships clunked together perfectly. After five hours' outside, Romanenko and Laveikin returned to their cabin, triumphant.

Kvant then dropped its rendezvous pack and engine motor to free the rear of Mir for further supplies. Progress 29 duly arrived at the end of April 1987, bringing fuel, food, water, supplies, and more solar panels for Mir. By this stage the orbital complex consisted of four modules, and weighed 58 tonnes. Orbital construction had truly begun.

Kvant became operational in June 1987: a shortage of electrical power had prevented it going into service any earlier. New solar panels were ferried up by Progress 30 in May, and on 16 June Yuri Romanenko and Alexander Laveikin completed two long spacewalks in the course of which they assembled a 2.5 kW panel. It was placed in position rolled up: Yuri Romanenko pulled a ring and it unfolded like a concertina. Not only did the new panel provide enough power for the cosmonauts to use the Kvant observatory, but it provided electricity for the new Korund materials processing furnace aboard Mir. 48 such experiments were planned, and by 1995 the USSR was planning to produce 35 kg units of superconductor wafers on industrial units in orbit.

A visiting crew arrived on July 24: Mir's red and green navigation lights blinked in the darkness as Soyuz TM3 was guided in by Alexander Viktorenko. The TM3 mission had been intended as a short visit by a Soviet–Syrian crew – the Syrian engineer aboard was Mohammed Faris – but instead took the form of a limited crew exchange. Irregularities had shown up in Alexander Laveikin's heart and it was decided to replace him with veteran Alexander Alexandrov. The unfortunate Laveikin was back on Earth by 30 July with Viktorenko and Faris.

Romanenko and Alexandrov flew on until the very end of the year, Romanenko becoming the holder of the space endurance record on 25 October. The two cosmonauts' lonely vigil began to draw to an end on 21 December.

Light snow covered the Baikonour launch pad as Soyuz TM4's engines lit up to send the relief crew on its way. On board TM4 were three cosmonauts: veteran Vladimir Titov, newcomer Musar Manarov and test pilot Anatoli Levchenko. It was also announced that Levchenko was training for being pilot on the upcoming Soviet shuttle, and this flight would give him (like Igor Volk in 1984) some advance idea of orbital conditions.

Romanenko, Alexandrov and Levchenko left Mir on 29 December 1987, and plunged earthward in a high arc over central Africa. Ferocious blizzards enveloped the landing site near Arkalyk and buffetted the little capsule as it sailed down for 16 minutes under a bright red parachute. The search teams, based on the area state farm, fanned out to await the returning cosmonauts. No sooner had Soyuz come to rest in the snow than a blast of wind blew it over on its side. Plans to evacuate the crew to a medical tent had to be abandoned: instead, they were carried direct by stretcher to a helicopter and whisked away for onward flight to Baikonour.

Anatoli Levchenko's work was far from over: he was straight away put behind the controls of a waiting TU-154 airliner which he was required to fly to Moscow and back. The purpose: to simulate the ability of shuttle pilots to fly airplanes in level flight after a period of weightlessness.

Television pictures showed Romanenko grinning as he chatted to friends and doctors in the helicopter cabin. He had been in space over 326 days, flown 5149 orbits, and covered 135 million miles. He was greeted by his comrade Alexander Laveikin. They were soon eating a good meal on the plane and Romanenko found he could sit up and stand once again. It was dark when the cosmonauts reached Baikonour: the immediate post-flight debriefing was dispensed with as their families rushed forward to greet them on the airport apron.

Romanenko spent the early new year recovering at a health resort in the Caucasus, returning to Moscow on 20 January. He hotly denied Western media claims that he was suffering severe depression or worse, and he described the gradual process of readaptation to gravity. The very real achiements of the long mission – in the areas of space medicine, earth and stellar observations, and industrial manufacturing – were overshadowed by announcements of new missions in the pipeline. Glavcosmos director Alexander Dunayev told the press the final preparations were under way for a shuttle launching. A spacetug was being built too. Plans were discussed at around the same time for the first Soviet

The three crew members of the Soyuz TM3 mission are pictured here at the Gagarin Cosmonauts' Training Centre. Syrian researcher-cosmonaut Muhammad Faris (right) is shown with fellow Soviet cosmonauts Alexander Viktorenko (left) and Alexander Alexandrov.

Ready for launch the Soyuz TM4 crew of Musakhi Manarov (top of steps), Anatoli Levchenko (centre) and Vladimir Titov pose for the cameras before boarding. The crew docked with Mir/Kvant on 23 December 1987 and six days later Levchenko returned with Yuri Romanenko after his record breaking 326-day flight.

Yuri Romanenko, commander of Soyuz TM2, who remained aboard the Mir/Kvant complex from February to December 1987.

moonbase in the Ocean of Storms to be built sometime 'on the threshold of the third millenium' New modules were being made ready to fly up to Mir.

Almost forgotten amidst the rising excitement were the two cosmonauts who had arrived on Mir in December 1987. By February 1988 Titov and Manarov had completed two months in orbit and had unloaded the supply ship Progress 34. Their target was the first-ever marathon year-long mission which would not see them back on the blue planet until 1989. The colonization of near-earth space had begun.

THE NEW SUPER ROCKETS

The final, catastrophic launching of the G booster in 1972 led to the termination of a programme that was to have put Russians on the Moon. The failure to conquer problems of fuels, engines and vibration was a serious defeat for Soviet rocketry. It was, after all, the first time that a major project had been commenced, pursued and then ultimately abandoned.

Yet the need for a large launch rocket remained. The existing Proton rocket had a maximum capacity of 21 tonnes, and while it was adequate for the construction of a modularized space station, really large structures in the new century would require a more powerful booster and payload. Soviet scientists were already attracted by projects for power stations in the sky and these would involve the ferrying up of substantial construction equipment. Commerical space stations with crews of up to a hundred — something well down the line from experimental scientific laboratories — would be heavy and complex structures.

The origins of Energia

In building a successor to the G booster, Soviet designers sought to combine a heavy-lift booster that would lift large payloads into orbit, with a vehicle that would carry aloft a large space plane. In doing so, several key decisions were taken, appropriate to this being the first new flagship rocket since the Proton design of 1963. First, it was decided to make the transition to liquid hydrogen engines. The second, pivot stage, was to be a liquid oxygen/liquid hydrogen engine. Second, it was decided to make the first stage reuseable. Giant shrouds were placed on top of the four strap-on rockets that were clustered round the first stage. When the strap-ons were cast aside they would flower open, slow the vehicles, and let parachutes open so the stage could float down to the desert below. The core stage was also designed to be recovered in three parts. Communist Party General Secretary Mikhail Gorbachev visited the Baikonour Space Centre on 11–14 May 1987. Accompanied by Defence Minister Sokolov, he inspected launch pads, assembly workshops, military facilities, and the administrative centre of Leninsk. In the course of the visit, the first by a General Secretary, it was announced that he had inspected a 'new multi-purpose heavy-lift rocket capable of putting into orbit large space modules and reuseable space shuttles'.

Excitement grew when, on the evening of 14 May 1987, it was announced that 'preparations were under way' for the launching of the new rocket. One day later, at 21.30 Moscow time, and after a day of countdown delays, darkness turned to light as the most powerful rocket ever built (Table 1) rose slowly into the sky, illuminating gantries, observers and towers for miles around. It picked up speed and headed into distant skies.

The first Energia heavy-lift launch vehicle on the launch pad at the Baikonour cosmodrome in May 1987. The first flight of this new generation of rockets capable of carrying a payload of between 100 and 150 tonnes into low Earth-orbit (depending upon the number of strap-on boosters used) on 15 May 1987 was a great success. Unfortunately the Soviets were unable to place a payload in orbit because of a ridiculous mistake. The engine on the payload ignited correctly, but in the wrong direction. Instead of reaching space, the payload came back to Earth!

Table 1. Energia

Weight	2 000 tonnes
Thrust	170 million horsepower
Height	61.3 metres
Payload	100 tonnes (low Earth orbit),
	32 tonnes (Moon), 27 tonnes (Mars)

Owing to an orientation failure, the third stage engine failed to place a small cargo in orbit and it burned up over the Pacific. But this was regarded as a minor setback in the context of a glorious, flawless, first flight.

Academician Yuri Marchuk in a Tass interview listed the objectives of Energia as to put in orbit:

—   heavy communications satellites
—   interplanetary stations destined for deep space
—   experimental solar power stations
—   versatile orbital complexes and large size modules [30].

Some commentaries stressed how Energia would be the basis of a reusable shuttle system; others that it would fly aloft 'the blocks from which cities in space will be built' [31].

Energia was a quantum leap forward both in design and performance. It eliminated at a stroke the limitations imposed by the 21 tonne (Earth orbit) and 5 tonne (interplanetary) capacity of Proton. It thus made possible both a shuttle and space city and the dispatch of very large cargoes. This potential was quickly recognized in the United States, and by July 1987 NASA and the US Department of Defence were examining a new heavy-lift booster for commissioning in the mid-1990s. However, early studies presaged a new rocket in the 68-tonne class, much less than Energia's capacity.

New medium-lift rocket

The Soviet Union made it clear that the existing fleet of A, D and F boosters would continue in service, even though the A booster represented 1950's technology. Most Western attention centred on a new medium-lift booster which the Pentagon dubbed the SLX-16.

Unlike Energia, the SLX-16 was introduced without either advance notice or subsequent publicity. Three reasons explained the secrecy. First, the SLX-16 was expected to fly mainly military cargoes. With a 15 tonne payload, it filled the gap between the 7-tonne payload of the A-2 and the 21 tonnes of the Proton. For example, the multiplicity of short-duration photoreconnaissance missions on the A booster could be replaced by a small number of new-generation long-stay spycraft. The same was true of other military payloads — and this process of transition was something the USSR was in no hurry to advertise. Second, it was thought that the stages and engines of the SLX-16 used equipment common to Energia, details of which could not be divulged before Energia flew. Third, it was thought that the SLX-16 would be the booster for the projected small space plane, Kosmolyot, due in the 1990's.

The first SLX-16 test is considered to have taken place as a suborbital test in March 1985. The first orbital flight was on 21 June 1985, when debris was stranded in an orbit of 197–340 km, 89.88 minutes, at an inclination never used before (64.4 degrees). Seven more launches took place over the next two years (see Table 2).

Table 2. SLX-16 launches

			(degrees)	(km)	(period, mins)
Cosmos 1697	1985	Oct. 22	71.0	850.854	101.97
Cosmos 1714		Dec. 28	71.0	163.853	94.78
Cosmos 1767	1986	Jul. 30	64.9	197.206	88.52
Cosmos 1786		Oct. 22	64.9	190.2565	113.29
Cosmos 1820	1987	Feb. 14	64.8	180.252	88.82
Cosmos 1833		Mar. 18	71.0	848.851	101.92
Cosmos 1844		May 13	71.0	848.854	101.94

It seems Cosmos 1714 was intended for the orbit found by Cosmos 1697, 1833 and 1844. Cosmos 1844 was put up the day before the Energia launch: Mikhail Gorbachev was at the cosmodrome at the time and may well have seen the launching.

The SLX-16 is believed to be two-stage, with the first stage recoverable, like Energia (Table 3). Height may be 70 m, with the Kosmolyot payload. In order to make the first stage reusable, there would need to be a circular unit between the two stages for parachute stowage. There would be fins on the bottom of the first stage, and advanced nozzle engines of 10 000 psi.

Table 3. SLX-16

First stage	LOX and kerosene
Second stage	NO_4 and UDMH
Liftoff weight	400 000 kg

In the absence of definitive information, or indeed admission that the SLX-16 exists, it is difficult to project its future use. Nevertheless its testing over 1985–87 provided the Soviet Union with a new, powerful, advanced rocket capable of placing substantial payloads in a variety of orbits. By 1988 one pad was operational flying the SLX-16 — so identifiable because its payloads crossed the equator in a manner different from anything else flying out of Baikonour.

SPACE PLATFORMS

The summer of 1987 marked a peak of Soviet space achievement: the launch of Energia, an international Soviet–Syrian visit to the Mir complex (Soyuz TM3), and the beginnings of full-scale operation of the Kvant astrophysical module. Virtually unnoticed amidst this frenetic activity was the launching of a large remote sensing platform.

Cosmos 1870, launched on 25 July 1987, rode on a Proton out of Baikonour and soon settled in a near-Polar, 71.9 degrees orbit. An official announcement said Cosmos 1870 was dedicated to hydrology, cartography and meteorology, and that it carried a radar imaging system. It transmitted on frequencies hitherto used by Meteor and Intercosmos satellites, the Kvant module, and Star modules. Visual observations suggested the Cosmos was the same size and weight as the Star module, perhaps with a returnable capsule.

Table 4 – Cosmos 1870 Polar platform

Date	25 July 1987
Launcher	Proton
Orbit	71.9 degrees
Weight	Up to 21 tonnes

In a related development, the first of a new generation of Earth resources satellites was placed in a near-Polar orbit (82.6 degrees) on 26 December 1987. Cosmos 1906 carried advanced scanning equipment able to cover a million square kilometres in ten minutes taking multi-zonal pictures in visible and infrared wavebands.

These two missions demonstrated a new level of sophistication of Soviet space equipment. Indeed, Cosmos 1870, because of its size and the fact that it used frequencies normally associated with the manned spaceflight programme, was thought to be a prototype Polar 'man tended free flyer' an automatic space station to be visited by cosmonauts from time to time. Both the European Space Agency, ESA, and the American Space Agency, NASA, had planned such a free flier, but for not until the late 1990s.

11

Cosmos

The Cocos Islands are three tiny tropical islands off the coast of Malaysia and well out into the Indian Ocean. On 16 March 1983, one, two, three, then ten Soviet naval vessels appeared there, steaming over the horizon. One was a helicopter carrier. They idled off-shore, waiting. The crews relaxed in the sunshine. It was hot and white shirts and shorts were the order of the day.

The Australian Navy soon noticed the Soviet naval presence and from time to time sent over a Lockheed 'Orion' aircraft to swoop low above the ships to snap long-range pictures. Only the drone of its engines disturbed the near-silence of the sea lapping against the hulls of the naval force.

Eventually something happened. A sonic boom crashed out. On the ten ships, observers anxiously scanned the skies through long-range binoculars. Then they saw it — a tiny midge-like object in the distance. It was a glider. It straightened out its flight path, and evened out for a landing. A parachute slowed its final fall until, smack!, it splashed into the sea. Flotation bags ballooned out to stop it sinking. The Kamov 25 helicopter was now airborne and hovering over the glider. Its blades whipped up the sea and flung spray round about. Then the ship *Yamal* moved in, winched the glider out of the water, lashed it to the deck, and the flotilla sailed for home.

The Australian Navy had been there at the right time and had got the right pictures. The photographs snapped by the 'Orion' were rushed to Sydney and developed. Once they had been enlarged, no one had any doubt what they were looking at. It was the Soviet space shuttle — the long-awaited 'Kosmolyot' or spaceplane.

Tass reported the flight in the normal manner as Cosmos 1445 and stated that the mission had been accomplished in one orbit. All this was perfectly true — it was a 109-

minute flight out of Kapustin Yar — but gave no further indication as to its unusual nature. And the Australian photographs showed something that had never been identified by the West before on film. The Cosmos, when pictured lying on the *Yamal*'s real deck, was like a small, stubby, delta-winged airplane, its short wings tapering upwards and with a front cockpit designed for cosmonauts to fly.

Cosmos 1445 was not in fact the first flight of Kosmolyot, though it was the first one to be photographed. The first flight had taken place the previous summer, on 3 June 1982. Cosmos 1374 aroused interest quickly enough [1]. It was one of the few launches out of the little-used base of Kapustin Yar. It followed a flight path never before used. Cosmos 1374 headed due south, passed over southeast Asia and the south Pacific, and reached an orbit of 230 by 191 km. It came back over the USSR from the northwest, following an inclination of 50.7 degrees, different from Soyuz, but the same inclination as the one the Russians have long said they would use for their really big space stations. Retrofire was commanded by the old Yevpatoria Base in the Crimea as it flew overhead. Cosmos 1374 went into reentry, soaring over the Himalayas and India, and once its elevators came into play, performed a dog-leg manoeuvre of about 600 km and splashed down 560 km south of the Cocos Islands and 2250 km northwest of Australia. Upon touchdown, a 2.4 m cone ballooned out from behind the crew cabin, serving both as a visual and radar target.

Western experts knew that both Cosmos used a C-1 booster, whose maximum payload was 1.2 tonnes. The 'Orion' photographs revealed that neither spaceplanes were the real-life size of the spaceplane's final design, but a scaled-down model. Australian Navy analysis of the photographs, much facilitated by the presence around the craft of the men of the recovery crew (whose height could be fairly accurately guessed) gave measurements for Cosmos 1374 and 1445 of 4.6 m length, 6.1 m wingspan, and weight about 1000 kg.

The size of the recovery fleet, the fact that the test was repeated, both indicated that the Russians had attached considerable degree of importance to their shuttle programme. These first two tests were so successful that a third one was flown in late 1983, but with some significant differences. Cosmos 1517 went up on 27 December 1983. Instead of coming down in the Indian Ocean, its splashdown point was much nearer to home — in the Black Sea. One explanation for this was the Russian desire to conduct their operations free from the prying eyes of other peoples' navies. More important, though, was the fact that retrofire took place automatically, way out over the Atlantic. This indicated a growing sophistication in the test programme. The next step would be to fly a full-scale test model, first unmanned, and then with a crew, and to do so into an ordinary airfield landing.

For some, the mystery was not the existence of the Soviet shuttle, but the fact that it had not appeared earlier, and before the American shuttle which flew in 1981. The idea of a shuttle was not new to Soviet space design — it had been part of Soviet space thinking since the 1920s. And, second, there were some significant hardware tests carried out in 1976–78, which some interpreted as meaning a Soviet desire to beat the Americans into the air with a shuttle. These tests were known as Cosmos 881/882, Cosmos 997/998, and Cosmos 1100/1101 [2]. These were mysterious missions and have not been fully understood even to this day. They have generally been connected with Kosmolyot, though no one can be absolutely sure. The missions flew on 15 December 1976, 30 March 1978, and 22 May 1979.

These dual missions flew on a Proton booster at 51.6 degrees out of Baikonour up to an altitude of 210 km. The two payloads then deorbited after one revolution. Each Cosmos could have weighed therefore up to nine tonnes. This in itself was an unusual type of mission to fly – and no such missions were flown before or since – but more remarkable was the fact that all these flights were timed for about an hour and a half before dawn. So when they came down, the orbital path would have moved westwards, meaning that the craft would still come down in darkness. So why launch just before dawn if the landings are also to be made in the darkness was well?

Only one explanation seems possible – namely that the spacecraft landed somewhere else! – And somewhere to the east – and in a place where the Sun would have risen by the time the spacecraft would be coming in, lies a small sandy desert. It is just flat enough for a spacecraft to crashland and survive; unpopulated enough for it to do so without being noticed; and just within the range of an incoming Cosmos, but only if it had wings. A shuttle prototype, in other words.

The mathematics to support this explanation are quite favourable. The desert area is in east Kazakhstan and is called Peski Muyunkum. It is about 1000 km downrange from where a Cosmos could land if it had a winged, gliding capability. Such a gliding manoeuvre should not create any unusual problems, for the American shuttle has a gliding capability of 2040 km.

But why the timing, why the insistence of flying just before dawn? Early dawn is ideal for the study of reentry characteristics of any vehicle, winged or not: characteristics such as ionization, plumes, flames, heat resistance, radio blackout. These features show up well in the pre-dawn light of the upper atmosphere.

The use of two spacecraft rather than one is harder to explain. Perhaps one was a winged vehicle, perhaps the other was not, so as to give better comparative results. No one knows the exact answer to these mystery tests; but this one does seem to be consistent with the known facts.

So, by 1984, the USSR had, in all probability, tested out a winged spaceplane as many as six times. So where was it? The answer did not come out until the Moscow press conference of 12 December 1983, which welcomed cosmonauts Lyakhov and Alexandrov back to Earth. Cosmonaut Director Vladimir Shatalov volunteered the explanation that their shuttle programme had suffered problems. There were 'complications'. And as an official statement, that means serious trouble.

THE MiG BUREAU

In fact the Soviet space shuttle has had a longer history than these events might suggest. The concept of a space vehicles able to return to Earth like a plane first appeared in theoretical writings in the 1920s and 1930s. Even then the idea was grasped that if space stations were to function, they needed regular resupply, and that throwaway once-off rockets were an expensive way of doing that. Something was needed that could be used time and time again. And if it could land like an aircraft, be 'turned around' and readied quickly to fly again, some kind of spaceplane had obvious appeal.

The 1940s had seen this notion taken a stage further by Dr Eugene Sänger, the German rocket expert. He wanted to marry the new technology of rocketry with the more practised craft of aviation. He drew up plans for the launching of rocket planes on rails [3]. In 1947 Stalin sent his agents to the West to try persuade him to defect, but their mission was unsuccessful.

There things rested until 1962 when Nikita Khrushchev, attracted to the idea of space planes, ordered Artem Mikoyan to design one. He was the right man to ask, for he was chief designer of the MiG aircraft used as a jet fighter by the Red Air Force. If anyone knew about high-speed delta-wing planes that flew high, he did.

But the project never left the drawing board, and Khrushchev was gone in 1964. The Moon race commandeered all the existing resources. But two events contrived to revive the project. The first was the decision taken in 1969 to concentrate on space stations. Second, the Americans made the formal decision to design and build a shuttle in September 1969. Funds began to flow into the project the following year, and it had the full backing of President Nixon [4].

Both sides were now interested in the shuttle idea and for similar reasons. Both planned a space station that needed regular resupply, something for which neither Soyuz nor Apollo would be adequate. Both were conscious of criticisms of waste and the non-reuseability of their existing rockets. A shuttle solved both problems together.

Despite having the same starting point, the two programmes diverged. Despite President Nixon's go-ahead, and that of the Congress in 1972, neither he nor the Congress felt able to fund a space station. As a result, the shuttle would have nothing to shuttle to! So, instead, it became modified to be a cargo-carrier.

The Soviet problem in 1972 was quite the opposite: they had a space station. But, so long as Soyuz and Salyut flew, it was hard to get the resources to build a shuttle at the same time. Programme planners found it easier to stretch the Soyuz to the Soyuz T, rather than switch all resources to an unproven Kosmolyot. That might have meant no flights for several years, as the Americans found to their cost, for Apollo was grounded so that shuttle could be funded.

RAMJETS AND SCRAMJETS

So the pace of Kosmolyot's design was far from hectic. The design work was given to the TsAGI design bureau at Ramenskoye Airfield, in the southeastern outskirts of Moscow. They came up with a design of an orbiter similar to the American one, but with a winged, manned flyback booster. The launcher would bring the orbiter up to a speed of 8000 km/h at 30 km altitude, but would then disengage. Its two pilots would then fly it back to base. The whole system would be completely reuseable. By contrast, the American shuttle would drop its solid rocket boosters in the sea: they would be recovered and refurbished, but the external tank would be lost.

TsAGI was not the only design bureau involved. Others were asked to design a shuttle and to evaluate American designs as they appeared. These included the Korolov design bureau, the Glushko Design Bureau, the Moscow Aviation Institute, and one prominent aircraft design bureau (either MiG or Tupolev). TsAGI got the lead role because it had an airfield on hand and because it had wind-tunnel tested the Tu-144 supersonic jet aircraft.

The design institutes in fact went over every possible design and did not feel obliged to keep to the American framework. Design studies covered such esoteric possibilities as scramjets, ramjets, and vertical-take-off-and-landing rockets of the type that a young viewer of the *Adventures of Tin Tin* mught be familiar with. It seems they took their time over these studies and that they were not completed until late 1973.

Some kind of commitment to the building of a prototype seems to have been made in 1974. Even before that, altitude tests began of high-performance aircraft. Chief test pilot was Russia's second cosmonaut, Gherman Titov, who had publicly discussed the idea of a shuttle as far back as 1971. But 1974 was the latest possible lead-in time for the 1976 Cosmos tests and a number of other events reported around that time.

In June 1977 American reconnaissance satellites picked out a winged vehicle underneath a Tupolev-95 Bear aircraft at a remote airfield in Siberia. The Bear is a huge propeller plane and when it appeared in 1959 it could fly 220 passengers direct from Moscow to New York. Since retiring from civilian use, it has often tested military hardware, and would be the obvious candidate for testing a spaceplane.

Perhaps more significantly, spy satellites picked up signs of large amounts of earth-moving going on at Baikonour, north of the main pads. Work began after the spring thaw of 1979 and was largely complete three years later. By the summer of 1983 the runway appeared on photographs like a slash across the terrain. It was wide, and long and could only be a shuttle runway [5].

So, by 1979, three items of hardware had appeared: the Cosmos tests, a drop-test vehicle flying under a Bear, and runway work had started. What did the literature have to say?

The first appearance of the Soviet shuttle was in the Italian press review of the GDR technical press. It stated, somewhat incredulously, that *two* shuttles were under development – a vertical takeoff one and a conventional aircraft takeoff one, with a lower stage similar to the Tu-144. This was the first appearance of the two-shuttle theory.

The next instance was an interview that cosmonaut Pavel Popovich gave to the West German flight magazine, *Flug Revue*, also in the mid-1970s. He said the USSR was developing a two-stage, fully recoverable, shuttle whose upper stage would be a delta-shaped winged vehicle. The Glushko team were developing its high-pressure engines for use on the orbiter.

In a series of articles to commemorate the twenty-fifth anniversary of Sputnik 1 in October 1977, cosmonaut Gherman Titov referred almost as a matter of course to shuttles resupplying orbital stations [6]. But the most precise statement was to come when a listener asked a question to a listeners' programme on Radio Moscow's North American Service in English. The reply, on the crackly shortwave, was picked up by the BBC's monitoring service on 28 June 1978:

> The craft will resemble an airplane with delta wings and cigar fuselage. Its rear part will carry three powerful rocket engines. It will be 60 m long, with a 8 m diameter fuselage. The Soviet design calls for a specially designed launcher. [7]

America's shuttle orbiter is, by comparison, 64 m long and with a 38 m wing span. This 1978 information was corroborated by an address given by Soviet American Ambassador Anatoli Skripko to a group of students at Georgetown University in Washington DC at around the same time.

Before long, Western observers were coming round to the view that the Russians were developing a two-shuttle approach: a small craft on the lines of the Cosmos one-orbit tests, capable of ferrying crews up to orbital stations, and a larger super-shuttle for the 1990s. This consensus hardened. It was felt that the smaller Kosmolyot would appear first and go aloft on the back of a turbo-ramjet mother aircraft. Rumours and sources persisted in affirming this improbable airlaunching technique, and even gave an inservice launch date of 1988. The existence of a space shuttle project was not officially admitted until 8 April 1987 [8].

The super-shuttle was expected to come about five years later in 1993. It would be close in conceptual design to the American shuttle. The launch thrust would be something of the order of 2.7 m kg, able to launch a payload of about 60 tonnes — or twice the weight of the American shuttle.

The two-shuttle model was based, according to one Soviet writer, on a detailed traffic analysis of Earth-to-orbit needs of the 1990s. The super-shuttle would be needed about 8—10 times a year, and the Kosmolyot much more frequently and these were seen as two entirely different types of operation. The super-shuttle would carry large cargoes that would be components of orbital stations, while the Kosmolyot would carry crews of about six cosmonauts, and very little else. There seems some sense in this analysis. NASA had at one stage planned the shuttle to fly several times a month but found its cargo capability was more than adequate for the load required, and before long was scaling down this estimate to a launching every month — to the point that the shuttle's economics became highly questionable.

Even in December 1983, the Russians were still being very coy about their proposals and their current state-of-play. Roald Sagdeev, Director of the Soviet Institute for Space Research, responded to the question when asked by an interviewer:

Q.   Do you have plans to develop a space shuttle?
A.   We never advertise our programme in advance. But I should say that of the two kinds of transport — single use and multiple use, we are studying the latter as well. [9]

He had good reason to be cautious. In April 1983, the test model of the super-shuttle, flying on top of a Mya-4 bomber was damaged in a rough landing at Ramenskoye airfield. This setback was only one of several [10].

But one day the Kosmolyot, and then the super-shuttle, will soar heavenward in fulfilment of the prophecies of Tsander and others and will come in to land like any ordinary aircraft, and flights to and from orbit will become an everyday occurrence.

THE CITY IN THE SKY

'Kosmograd' or space city, is the name the Russians have given to their prime space objective in the twentieth century. It is central to the space tradition, from Tsiolkovsky down to Korolev and since. The early rendezvous manoeuvres of Nikolayev and Popovich above the Earth in August 1962 were but an early intimation of this. In a sense the Moon race was a diversion from this great target, the achievement of which was restored to its rightful place in January 1969.

Salyut, both in the form of a temporary station (1971—77) and a semi-permanent one (1977—84) laid the groundwork. But the prize was a larger station of at least a dozen or so cosmonauts and scientists, able to observe the Sun the stars and the Earth, manufacture special products, and serve as a stepping stone to the Moon and planets. This specific and precise objective was stated in the press releases of January 1969, but the suggestion goes back much futher. Gherman Titov put it in context in 1977 on the Sputnik anniversary:

> There will be increasing numbers of orbital stations with spacemen commuting to and fro. The size of the orbital station will grow, along with the number of people they can support. Shuttle spacecraft will improve in design so that their cargo-carrying capacity will continually increase. Near-Earth space will be a busy area in the coming decades.
>
> Looking further into the future, we see that space travel will probably follow this sequence: near-Earth orbital stations, bases on the moon, landings on Mars, the colonization of certain parts of the solar system, and finally travel to the stars [11].

In all this, the orbital station is the linchpin, the *sine qua non*. Statements about orbital stations abound in the Soviet press and no effort has been made other than to publicize them as an objective. Indeed, it is almost a ritual, and no space event is complete without a eulogy on their desirability.

The most comprehensive statement was made by Academician Georgi Petrov in *Pravda* on 3 September 1976. Stations with alternating crews of twenty to thirty would be constructed. They would carry telescopes, develop industrial technology, and make biological studies. Such stations would be assembled from specialized modules, and eventually a giant space city with 100 people would be constructed:

> The assembly would be done by a special flying assembly apparatus, a space crane, controlled either from Earth or from orbit. After completing its primary purpose it would correct the path of stations and make repairs. [12].

Cosmonauts would jet around in open space with rocket jets and pistols. Sometimes they would use small pressurized capsules.

For others, the possibilities of manufacture in space are exciting. Vladimir Dzanibekov, four-times veteran:

> I believe that the day is not far off when a mini-factory is put into orbit, with a long-period programme drawn up by the state planning committee. It will deal with alloys, semi-conductors, and pharmacy. [13]

The Soviet space programme for the years to 2000 is a relentlessly energetic one. By the late 1990s, cosmonauts and supplies will be taking off weekly from Baikonour. Most will head up to the main orbital space city, the Kosmograd. It will be the brightest object in the sky, a shining star visible to all below. As the Kosmolyot approaches it, spacemen and spacewomen will make out its living areas, research labs, and power supplies.

Tours of duty

The Kosmolyot will dock in one of four or five docking ports. Its crew will board, bringing food, supplies, equipment. Most of the cosmonauts will be scientists like meteorologists and astronomers and welding experts. Each will have a small but comfortable cabin. Each will work a normal day and a standard week, and the most popular form of recreation will be to watch the blue Earth spin silently below. At times, cosmonauts will spacewalk for repairs and inspections. At times, too, they will separate from the station in special laboratory modules to conduct unique experiments.

After every five or six months, the crew will return and fly down to Baikonour to the refreshing real air and breezes and smells of Earth. Such landings on the huge runway that was completed in 1982 will be routine and only families and relatives will turn up to watch them come in.

Other Kosmolyots will take off for smaller laboratories and stations. Some will be in polar orbit, so as to cover the whole Earth, and will have small permanent crews. Others will orbit at 81 degrees to watch ice and the polar pack in the Soviet Far North. Some will be astronomical platforms. Others will be experimental stations turning sunlight to electricity. Further out will be space stations in 24-hr orbit at 36 000 km: they will be communications complexes. A space tug will be used for these more distant outposts [14].

Spaceflight being more routine, the requirements for travel will be relaxed. A six-month training programme will suffice. Guest scientists from other countries — be they Finland, Sweden, Central America, Africa, and the type of countries represented at the Patrice Lumumba University in Moscow — will become commonplace. Before long, women will make up half the flight crews.

Eventually children will be born in space. The birth of human beings away from the Earth will be a step of enormous significance. One of the popular tabloids once claimed this was 'planned' for Salyut 6; but it was hotly denied. Quails and primates would come first, in the 1990s. But there was no denying it would happen.

All these developments would put the Soviet Union a quantum step ahead of the United States. By 1982 NASA was getting distinctly bad-tempered at the failure of the President and Congress to approve funding for an American space station. In 1983, several space station studies were made: interestingly all were based on the notion of assembling together modules the size of the European spacelab — in other words, the components had to be transportable in the shuttle's cargo bay.

The project was not approved until January 1984 and, even then, President Reagan's reelection campaign had something to do with it. Still, the earliest the NASA space station would fly was 1996 and the crew size would be limited to around 12. The shuttle was the only possible transporter. The USSR was already thinking of a cargo carrier ten times heavier.

Getting there

With the super-shuttle, Kosmolyot, Energia and the new medium-lift booster, the USSR will have, in the space of only a few years, replaced all its rocket technology with new equipment that will see it well into the twenty-first century.

There should be nothing surprising about this, for the present A-booster dates to 1955, Soyuz to 1962 and the Proton to 1963. To run 1990-type space cities on the technology of the 1950s is neither wise nor sensible. The literature confirms this. Academician Vasily Mishin wrote in 1980: 'Experts expect super-heavy rockets, able to put cargoes of hundreds of tonnes into low orbit, to be created along with existing carrier rockets' [15]. Roald Sagdeev confirmed this in 1983: 'The carrier we now use is less powerful than the American Saturn. It can carry about 20 tonnes, several times less than the Saturn. There are space problems that demand the launch of much heavier rockets. Our scientists are dreaming of a very big telescope in space, and sooner or later we will need carriers to solve such big problems' [16].

The CIA were so certain of these new rocket developments that in 1983 they let their data be used in a Pentagon publication called *Soviet Military Power* whose main purpose was to show growing Soviet military and technological strength. Two things they left out. First, they had information that work on a Soviet nuclear rocket was under way. According to CIA intelligence, it was crude but workable. Secondly, it left out the implications of these developments. One American commentator took the following view:

> The Russians are currently replacing all their existing space hardware and when they have done all this we may find that they have put together all the components they need for a flight to Mars or the planets. From our point of view we'll probably not realize this until it is too late: they'll have brought all the elements together and we'll be too late to catch them. [17]

So is Kosmograd a cover for a manned flight to Mars, to make it truly the 'Red Planet'?

THE MARS SCARE

It seems doubtful. The official view, again from Sagdeev, to a question:

Q. Are you planning interplanetary flight?
A. It would be a very expensive operation. I don't think it will happen this century. We are not even planning flights to the Moon. [18]

Earlier on, some public pronouncements were much more definite. Soon after the 18-day Soyuz 9 cosmonauts returned in 1970, Anatoli Blagonravov, then chairman of the Space Research Commission of the Academy of Sciences, said in an article in *New Time* that a flight to Mars by a crew of ten was a distant outcome of their mission. A virtually identical statement was made by cosmonaut Alexei Leonov at the same time. It was enough to prompt one British newspaper to report:

> Russia's spacemen may be blazing a trail to Mars that will lead to man's first landing on another planet, years ahead of America. Leonov's declaration is seen as another straw in the wind pointing to a daring Russian venture, to bypass the moon altogether and concentrate on pipping the Americans to a new winning post in space. [19]

There were other similar declarations at the same time but they receded in the late 1970s. So too did talk of putting a Salyut into lunar orbit, and using it for descent to the Moon by smaller craft. This was a repeated theme of Boris Petrov.

By 1988 both the literature and the hardware pointed to a lunar flight and a Mars mission as being some time off and into the new century. Statements from Sagdeev and others were unanimous that the Kosmograd would come first. The Moon race had been a hard lesson well learnt about racing to specific target by particular dates.

Such an approach would be more logical. From Tsiolkovsky to Korolov, space stations were stepping stones *en route* to the planets. Equipment, modules, landers and orbiters would be assembled in the relative security of Earth orbit. Faults could be located and instruments could be tested in real space conditions before committing them to longer journeys. The cosmonauts would then board their interplanetary vehicles from their space station.

There were other, perhaps more compelling reasons for waiting. Soviet unmanned missions to Mars had been for the most part unsuccessful, so much so that the unmanned Mars programme had been suspended in 1974. Eventually they conceded that the unmanned exploration of the planet had been neglected. Mikhail Chernyshev told Novosti in 1982:

> There has been little activity since the mid-1970s. The next step seems to be a lander similar to the lunar probes which brought back samples of soil from the Moon.
>
> But a flight back from Mars is a much more difficult task. . . The cost will be very high, but sooner or later it will be done. [20]

Once this is done, the long-awaited manned mission to Mars can begin, perhaps in the early twenty-first century. Cosmonauts will board their specially designed Mars ship in low Earth orbit, blast its engines, and swing out towards the dull red light that is Mars through a telescope. Their transit time will be a good eight months, and then their landing ship will touch down on its dry, rocky, deserts. Cosmonauts will fan out in space rovers, trucks, and caravans. They will spend a month there, collecting samples, testing the atmosphere, and setting up automatic weather stations.

They will then blast off for home. But the next expedition will not return during the 30-day period needed for a return to Earth during the same Mars return window. Instead, they will stay for the full cycle of the Martian year — 667 Mars days or 687 Earth days. The difference can be explained by the fact that the Martian day is 24 h 37 min, rather than our own of exactly 24 h.

The colony on Mars will be not unlike the present scientific stations in Antarctica. It will be a self-contained community working a normal Earth day. The colonists will take refuge indoors during the long sandstorms that can occasionally blow up. They will spend much time and effort learning how to grow their own food, recycle their air and water, and become independent. During the daylight hours, they will venture out in their rovers to map, study and investigate their world and select new sites for future settlements.

The Sun will not be as bright during the day as on our Earth. At night the skies will be clearer than anything anyone could imagine. They will watch little Deimos and Phobos, Mars' moons, track quickly across the sky. And above the far horizon will rise the blue-and-white globe of Earth.

Not long afterwards, other expeditions will set out for the asteroids. They will be mined for precious minerals. And, venturing further afield, spacecraft will land on the moons of Jupiter and Saturn. Colonists on such remote outposts will have a home with a view, for above them will spin the yellow-and-orange gaseous giants of our system. And one day a star ship will be constructed to venture into the unknown, into the galaxies beyond.

All this will be in pursuit of the vision of Tsiolkovsky in the nineteenth century and the great pioneers of the twentieth. The Soviet exploration of space has been characterized by a relentless pursuit of their dreams and ideals and ideas. The ultimate achievement of their goals has never been in doubt and has transcended the inevitable set-backs, disappointments and disasters that accompany any great undertaking. Instead they have added to the determination of designers, scientists and cosmonauts to see through one project after another. Konstantin Tsiolkovsky himself said it all:

The impossible of today will become the possible of tomorrow. [21]

References

CHAPTER 1

[1]   Evgeny Riabchikov: *Russians in space*, London, 1975, pp. 95 *et seq*.

[2]   Letter from K.E. Tsiolkovsky to B.N. Vorobyev, 15 August 1911. from: Tsiolkovsky memorial, USSR.

[3]   Karl Marx, 1848. From Edmund Wilson: *To the Finland Station*, London, 1942.

[4]   Wilfred Burchett & Anthony Purdy: *Cosmonaut Yuri Gagarin*, London, 1961, p. 21.

[5]   We shall fly to Mars! *Soviet Weekly*, 27 August 1977.

[6]   Lester E. Winnick: Birth of the Russian space programme, *Spaceflight*, **20**, May 1978, 168.

[7]   V.P. Glushko: *Rocket engines GDL-OKB*, Moscow, 1979.

[8]   For an appreciation of Stalin's position at this time, see Ian Grey: *Stalin: man of history*, London, 1982, p. 281.

[9]   Boris Belitsky: The early development of the Soviet space programme, Radio Moscow, 30 December 1987.

[10]   James E. Oberg: *Red Star in orbit*, London, 1981, p. 20.

[11]   Glushko, op. cit., p. 21.

[12]   Arthur C. Clarke (Ed.): *The coming of the space age*, London, 1967, p. 49.

[13]   Brian J. Ford: The rocket race, *History of the Second World War*, 1968, pp. 2837–2844.

[14]   Boris Belitsky: The German role in postwar Russian rocketry, Radio Moscow, 19 August 1987.

[15]   Hugo Young, Bryan Silcock & Peter Dunn: *Journey to Tranquility*, London, 1969, p. 14.
[16]   A. Romanov: *Spacecraft designer*, Moscow, 1976, p. 27.
[17]   Boris Belitsky: The rocket engines of Valentin Glushko, *Soviet Weekly*, 17 April 1976.

CHAPTER 2

[1]   Kenneth Gatland: Prelude to the space age, *Spaceflight,* **24**, November 1982, 386–392.
[2]   Martin Caidin: *Man into space*, New York, 1961, p. 171.
[3]   Article by V. Gubarev quoted in Kenneth Gatland (Ed.): *Illustrated encyclopedia of space technology*, London, 1981, p. 28.
[4]   Ibid. See also: *In Gagarin's trail*, Moscow, 1980, p. 8.
[5]   Alexei Leonov: *The Sun's wind*, Moscow, 1977.
[6]   Mikhail Chernyshev: The man who paved the way into space, *Soviet Weekly*, 29 May 1982.
[7]   James E. Oberg: *Red Star in orbit*, London, 1981, p. 25.
[8]   Ibid., p. 27.
[9]   Several sources give the date of this launching as August 21, owing to the manner of announcement on the flight. See Curtis Peebles: The early years: Soviet launch losses, *Spaceflight*, **29**, April 1987, p. 163.
[10]   Riabchikov: *Russians in space*, London, 1975, p. 146.
[11]   BBC Light Programme, 5 October 1957.
[12]   Hugo Young, Bryan Silcock & Peter Dunn: *Journey to Tranquility*, London, 1969, p. 68.
[13]   Riabchikov, op cit., p. 148.
[14]   Young, Silcock, Dunn, op. cit., p. 73.
[15]   *In Gagarin's trail*, p. 9.
[16]   Caidin, op cit., p. 119.

CHAPTER 3

[1]   Konstantin P. Feoktistov: Soviet manned spacecraft and orbital stations. From *New Research*, USSR Academy of Sciences, History of the USSR series, Vol. 5, Moscow, 1986, pp. 153 *et seq.*
[2]   A. Romanov: *Spacecraft designer*, Moscow, 1976, p. 41.
[3]   Ibid.
[4]   Wilfrid Burchitt & Anthony Purdy: *Cosmonaut Yuri Gagarin*, London, 1961, p. 86.
[5]   Yaroslav Golvanov: Cosmonaut number one, *Izvestia*, 2–6 April 1986.
[6]   Russia getting ready for man's first flight into space, *Irish Times*, 23 August 1960.
[7]   For a detailed description of this episode, see James E. Oberg: *Red Star in orbit*, London 1981, pp. 39–49; and Curtis Peebles: The early years: Soviet launch losses, *Spaceflight*, **29**, April 1987.

[8]   J.D. Ratcliff: Amateurs with their eyes on space, *Reader's Digest*, May 1965, 153.

[9]   For a detailed description of the Soviet Venus programme, see P.S. Clark: The Soviet Venera programme, *Journal of the British Interplanetary Society* (*JBIS* henceforth), **39**, February 1985, 74–94.

[10]   Evgeny Riabchikov: *Russians in space*, London, 1975, p. 19, *et seq.*

[11]   Obituary to Yuri Gagarin, *Daily Telegraph*, 29 March 1968.

[12]   Obituary to Yuri Gagarin, *The Times*, 29 March 1968.

[13]   Space man returns, *Irish Times*, 13 April 1961.

[14]   Hugo Young, Bryan Silcock, & Peter Dunn: *Journey to Tranquility*, London, 1969, p. 108.

CHAPTER 4

[1]   Hugo Young, Bryan Silcock & Peter Dunn. *Journey to Tranquility*, London, 1969, p. 110.

[2]   BBC Radio 4, *From here to infinity*, 4 October 1977.

[3]   Ibid.

[4]   Mstislav Keldysh (Ed.): *The creative legacy of Sergei Korolov*, Nauka publishers, Moscow, 1980. For the background issues of the Soyuz complex, see Phillip S. Clark & Ralph F. Gibbons: The evolution of the Soyuz programme, *JBIS*, **36**, 434–435.

[5]   Long trip likely by spaceman, *Sunday Times*, 12 August 1962.

[6]   Evgeny Riabchikov: *Russians in space*, London, 1975, p. 190.

[7]   Russians to reach for moon? *Irish Times*, 13 August 1962.

[8]   For Soviet launch failures in the period to 1965, see Curtis Peebles: The early years: Soviet launch losses, *Spaceflight*, **29**, April 1987.

[9]   Table of moon probes, *Sunday Telegraph*, 2 August 1964.

[10]   Soviet moon shot going well, *Irish Times*, 4 April 1963.

[11]   *Flight International*, 19 December 1987.

[12]   Spacewoman may join Vostok 5 in a day or two, *Sunday Times*, 16 June 1963.

[13]   Gordon Hooper: *The Soviet cosmonaut team*, Woodbridge, 1986, p. 279.

[14]   The Khrushchev–Korolov relationship is described in detail in James E. Oberg. Korolov, Khrushchev and Sputnik, *Spaceflight*, **20**, April 1978, 144–150.

[15]   Claude Wachtel: Design studies of the Vostok and Soyuz spacecraft, *JBIS*, **35**, 1982, 92–94.

[16]   Phillip S. Clark: The Polyot missions, *Spaceflight*, **22**, September/October 1980, 312–314.

[17]   Young, Silcock, Dunn, op. cit., pp. 204–205.

[18]   Ibid., p. 206.

[19]   Ibid.

[20]   Kenneth Gatland: *Manned spacecraft*, London, 1967, pp. 138–139. Philip Bono & Kenneth Gatland: *Frontiers of space*, London, 1969, p. 114.

[21]   U.S. likely to revise space plans. Russia withdraws from moon race. Mr. Kennedy faces attacks in Congress, *The Times*, 28 October 1963.

[22]   Correspondence, Sir Bernard Lovell to author, 29 June 1983.

[23] For a discussion on the different design institutes, see C. Wachtel: The chief designers of the Soviet space programme, *JBIS*, **38**, 1985, 562.

[24] C.P. Vick: The Soviet lunar landing programme booster, *JBIS*, 1985, 11–18.

CHAPTER 5

[1] *USSR probes space*, Moscow, undated (around 1968).

[2] Passenger service, *Newsweek*, 19 October 1964.

[3] Russian three man spaceship in orbit, *Daily Telegraph*, 13 October 1964.

[4] Evgeny Riabchikov: *Russians in space*, London, 1975, p. 209.

[5] Cosmonauts pleased by orientation fault, *Flight International*, 8 April 1965.

[6] James Oberg: Russia meant to win the space race, *Spaceflight*, May 1976, 167.

[7] Ibid.

[8] R.F. Gibbons & P.S. Clark. The evolution of the Vostok and Voskhod programmes, *JBIS*, **38**, 1985, 9.

[9] See Alan Bond & John Parfitt: The Proton launcher, *Spaceflight*, **27**, July/August 1985, pp. 318–320; Glavkosmos: *The Proton launcher*, Moscow, 1987; V.P. Glushko, *Rocket engines GDL-OKB*, Moscow, 1979; Valentin P. Glushko: *The development of rocketry and space technology in the USSR*, Moscow, 1973, p. 39; Christian Lardier & Boris Sternikov: Les secrets de la fusée Proton, *Orbite*, January 1986.

[10] Biggest boost, *Newsweek*, 2 August 1965.

[11] Oberg, op. cit., p. 167.

[12] James Oberg & Michael Cassutt: Phantom space crews, *Spaceflight*, **26**, June 1984, 277; Rex Hall: The Soviet cosmonaut team, 1960–71, *JBIS*, **36**, 468–473. *Transfer in orbit*, Moscow, 1969.

[13] Oberg, op. cit., p. 167.

[14] Russians admit moon failure, *The Times*, 9 October 1965.

[15] James E. Oberg: *Red Star in orbit*, London, 1981, p. 20.

[16] Radio Moscow, 2 February 1966.

[17] For an American appreciation of the role of Luna 10 and Soviet moon intentions at the time, see: Ring around the moon, *Newsweek*, 18 April 1966.

CHAPTER 6

[1] RTE Radio, 23 April 1967.

[2] The classic reexamination of the Soyuz 1 mission is to be found in James E. Oberg: Soyuz 1: Ten years after: new conclusions, *Spaceflight*, **19**, May 1977.

[3] It was learned twenty years later that chief designer Vasili Mishin (1966–74) had refused to authorize the Soyuz 1 launch documents, but had been overruled.

[4] Chapman Pincher: How much has Russia revealed?, *Daily Express*, 25 April 1967.

[5] Correcting the fatal flaws, *Newsweek*, 8 May 1967.

[6] Sven Grahn & Dieter Oslender: Cosmos 146 and Cosmos 154 – an analysis of two historically important missions, *Spaceflight*, **22**, March 1980.

[7] P.S. Clark: Soviet spacecraft masses for deep space missions, *JBIS*, **38**, 1985, 29;

R.D. Christy: Safety practices for Soyuz recoveries, *Spaceflight,* **23**, November 1981, 321–322.

[8]   For a more detailed discussion on Soviet developments during this period, see Phillip S. Clark: Launch failures on the Soviet space probe programme, *Spaceflight,* **19**, July/August 1977, 277.

[9]   Nicholas L. Johnson: Apollo and Zond – race around the moon?, *Spaceflight,* **20**, December 1978, 404.

[10] The full detailed report of that day was not published for nineteen years. See S. Belotserkovsky & A. Leonov: Im ne Kvatilo dvyuk sekyund, *Pravda*, 23 March 1987.

[11] Alexei Golikov: Valentina Gagarin tells of Yuri Gagarin's last day, *Sputnik*, January 1969, p. 19.

[12] James E. Oberg: *Red Star in orbit*, London, 1981, p. 117.

[13] Ralph Gibbons: Soviet man-around-the-moon programme: outline sequence of events, *Spaceflight,* **19**, November 1977, 388–389.

[14] Oberg, op. cit., p. 169.

[15] Angus McPherson: The riddle of Zond 6, *Daily Mail*, 18 November 1968.

[16] Kenneth Gatland: *Robot explorers*, London, 1972, pp. 142–144.

[17] Soviet moon shot postponed? *Newsweek*, 16 December 1968. Soviet moon shot that fizzled, *Newsweek*, 30 December 1968.

[18] Russia plans big space shot soon, *The Times*, 3 June 1969. Space rivals link up at Paris air show, *Daily Mail*, 3 June 1969.

[19] Russia races to land a man on the moon, *Daily Express*, 3 June 1969.

[20] See: Disaster at Tyuratam, *Time*, 28 November 1969. Kenneth Gatland: *Missiles and Rockets*, London, 1972, p. 193. Several sources give differing dates for these events. June 10 and July 4 are also cited.

[21] Russia puts up own moonship, *Daily Telegraph*, 14 July 1969.

[22] Moon mission ahead of schedule, *Irish Times*, 16 July 1969.

[23] Luna-15 destroyed in moon crash, *Irish Times*, 22 July 1969.

[24] Russia sees mission as realization of a dream, *Irish Times*, 22 July 1969.

[25] Pyotr Petrov: No mystery about Luna-15, *Soviet Weekly*, 27 July 1969.

[26] Correspondence with author, 29 June 1983.

[27] Ibid.

[28] See D.R. Woods: Lunar mission Cosmos satellites, *Spaceflight,* **19**, November 1977, 381–338.

CHAPTER 7

[1]   Portrait of Baikonour, *Flight International*, 12 June 1975.

[2]   Thomas Canby: A generation after Sputnik – are the Russians ahead in space? *National Geographic*, **170**, October 1986, pp. 422–423.

[3]   Col. M. Robov: Why pick Baikonour?, *Soviet Weekly*, 4 June 1983.

[4]   Nicholas L. Johnson: The Baikonour SS-6 space launch facilities, *Spaceflight,* **23**, April 1981, 109–116.

[5]   Details were first given in Nikolai Shestopalov: The soldier who builds, *New Times*, August 1987, 22. Yuri Zaitsev: Equipment of Plesetsk space launch complex described, *Krasnaya Zvezda*, 4, August 1987.

[6]   Phillip S. Clark: The Soviet space year of 1982, *JBIS*, **36**, 1983, 249–262.

[7]   Ralph F. Gibbons: Soviet launch vehicle designations, *Spaceflight*, **19**, February 1977, 54–60.

[8]   David Baker: Killer satellites, *Flight International*, 15 October 1977.

[9]   *Aviation Week and Space Technology*, 12 October 1987.

[10] G.E. Perry: Looking down on the middle east war, *Flight International*, 21 February 1974.

[11] G.E. Perry: Cosmos at 74, *Flight International*, 30 November 1972.

[12] For a more detailed discussion, see Yuri Dyemardian: *Structure and organizational principles of the USSR Remote sensing system*, Moscow, 1985.

[13] See *In Gagarin's trail*, Moscow, 1986.

[14] Radio Moscow, 21 August 1987, from BBC transcripts, SU/8665/D/3. Originally published in: Head of space complex testing commission discusses its activities, *Sovetskaya Rossiya*, 22 August 1987.

[15] Steven J. Zaloga: Soviet strategic missile development production, *Jane's defense weekly*, 30 May 1987, 1061–1064, 6 June 1987, 1119–1121.

[16] *Soviet aerospace*, 20 October 1986, p. 58.

CHAPTER 8

[1]   Moon race: Russia out to beat U.S., *Daily Express*, 17 January 1969.

[2]   *Peresadka na orbite*, Moscow, 1969, p. 99.

[3]   ibid. p. 135.

[4]   Latest achievement opens era of manned space laboratories, *Soviet News*, 21 January 1969, p. 26.

[5]   Philip Bono & Kenneth Gatland: *Frontiers of Space*, London, 1969, p. 117.

[6]   Manned space stations – the next step, *Soviet Weekly*, 27 September 1969.

[7]   Russia plans the first manned space laboratory, *Guardian*, 13 October 1969.

[8]   Moscow quiet as seven take to space, *Daily Express*, 14 October 1969. See also. Russians may put third ship in orbit, *Daily Telegraph*, 13 October 1969. See also. Soyuz 8 launch likely today, *Irish Times*, 13 October 1969.

[9]   Station in space, *Soviet Weekly*, 18 October 1969. Soyuz 6 carries extra fuel and equipment, *Soviet News*, 14 October 1969, 14.

[10] *Daily Mail*, 17 October 1969.

[11] *The Times*, 20 October 1969.

[12] Ibid.

[13] They've brought space down to earth! *Soviet Weekly*, 25 October 1969.

[14] Coming soon – a manned space station, *Soviet Weekly*, 15 November 1969.

[15] Ibid.

[16] 18-day flight completed, *Soviet Weekly*, 27 June 1970.

[17]   Ibid.

[18]   Evgeny Riabchikov: *Russians in space*, London, 1975, p. 282.

[19]   Russia plans first station in space, *Guardian*, 16 March 1971.

[20]   The space station flies on, *Soviet Weekly*, 1 May 1971.

[21]   Phillip S. Clark: Soyuz missions to Salyut stations, *Spaceflight,* **21**, June 1979, 262.

[22]   *Flight International*, 19 December 1987.

[23]   RTE Radio, 30 June 1971.

[24]   Radio Moscow, 30 June 1971.

[25]   Bleak outlook for man in space, *Guardian*, 1 July 1971.

[26]   New Salyut stations will be built, *Soviet Weekly*, 10 July 1971.

[27]   Death of cosmonauts: government commission reports, *Soviet Weekly*, 10 July 1971.

[28]   Radio Moscow, 7 June 1972.

[29]   Modifications delay Soyuz flight, *Flight International*, 2 November 1972.

[30]   David Baker: Countdown for new Russian space station, *Flight International*, 13 March 1975. Phillip S. Clark: The design of Salyut orbital stations, *Spaceflight,* **23**, October 1981. Nicholas L. Johnson: The military and civilian Salyut space station, *Spaceflight,* **21**, August–September 1979, 364–370.

[31]   Ben Bova: *The uses of space*, New York, 1965, pp. 31–33. For $1.5bn.: a new air force eye in the sky, *Newsweek*, 6 September 1965. US to launch manned space laboratory, *The Times*, 26 August 1965. Curtis Peebles: The manned orbiting laboratory, *Spaceflight,* **22**, April 1980 and June 1980.

[32]   Radio Moscow, 28 April 1973.

[33]   For a description of the Skylab missions, see Henry S.F. Cooper: *A house in space*, St. Albans, 1976.

[34]   US–USSR spacemen to orbit together, *Irish Times*, 25 May 1972.

[35]   For the American perspective on the joint mission, see Walter Froehlich: *Apollo–Soyuz*, NASA, Washington D.C., 1976.

[36]   See: Soyuz launch near? *Flight International*, 2 August 1973; and caption, *Flight International*, August 1973.

[37]   New visitors for space station, *Soviet Weekly*, 31 August 1974.

[38]   Kenneth Gatland (Ed.): *Illustrated encyclopaedia of space technology*, 1981, p. 184.

[39]   The great comeback, *Flight International*, 20 February 1975.

[40]   See James E. Oberg: *Red Star in space*, London 1981, pp. 135–136.

[41]   Spaceship: successful failure!, *Soviet Weekly*, 12 April 1975. This should be contrasted with: Mission misfire, *Time*, 12 April 1975.

[42]   More Soviet spacewalks?, *Flight International*, 22 January 1977. USSR launches fifth Salyut, *Flight International*, 3 July 1976.

CHAPTER 9

[1]   Pyotr Petrov: It's the decade of the space robot!, *Soviet Weekly*, 3 October 1970.

[2]   *The Times, Scotsman, Daily Mail*, 17 November 1970.

[3]   Radio Moscow, 9 October 1971.

[4]   Moon travellers may find water, *Soviet Weekly*, 16 January 1971.

[5]   Moon probe completes year in orbit, *Soviet Weekly*, 14 October 1972.

[6]   Radio Moscow, 7 March 1972.

[7]   Lunokhod 2, *Flight International*, 1 February 1973.

[8]   M. Shcherbakov: Step by step to the moon and planets, *Soviet Weekly*, 11 March 1973.

[9]   Radio Moscow, 25 March 1973.

[10]   More moon robots possible, *Soviet Weekly*, 21 April 1973.

[11]   Anatoli Blagonravov: Men and machines in space, *Soviet Weekly*, 2 June 1973.

[12]   Automatons study the moon. From *Soviet space studies*, Moscow, 1983.

[13]   *Spaceflight,* **20**, July 1978, 242.

[14]   Pyotr Petrov: It's the decade of the space robot!, *Soviet Weekly*, 3 October 1970.

[15]   For a detailed discussion of the Soviet Mars programme, see P.S. Clark: The Soviet Mars Programme, *JBIS* **39**, 1, 1986.

[16]   Two more visitors for Mars, *Soviet Weekly*, 23 March 1974.

[17]   Craig Covault: Soviets in Houston reveal new lunar, Mars, asteroid flights, *Aviation Week and Space Technology*, 1 April 1985.

[18]   Reported in: First pictures of Venus' surface, *Flight International*, 30 October 1975. See also: Venus is surprising, *Soviet Weekly*, 1 November 1975.

[19]   Reported in: Venus 9 and 10 round-up, *Flight International*, 13 November 1975.

[20]   V.L. Barsukov: *Basic results of Venus studies by Vega Landers*, Moscow, 1985.

[21]   Caption *Flight International*, 6 February 1982.

CHAPTER 10

[1]   For a detailed American assessment of these developments, see Congress of the United States, Office of Technology Assessment: *Salyut: Soviet steps towards permanent presence in space – a technical memorandum*, December 1983.

[2]   See *Salyut in orbit*, Moscow, 1975.

[3]   See: The Cosmos 929 enigma, *Flight International*, 17 September 1977; J. Oberg: The mystery of Cosmos 929, *Spaceflight,* **20**, February 1978; The Kettering group: Observations of 1977–66A. Cosmos 929, *Spaceflight,* **20**, September/ October 1978, 353–355.

[4]   Nicholas L. Johnson: The prospect of Soviet orbital construction in the summer of 1977, *Spaceflight,* **21**, December 1979, 518–520.

[5]   Gordon R. Hooper: Missions to Salyut 6, *Spaceflight,* **20**, June 1978, 229.

[6]   Ibid., p. 233.

[7]   Gordon R. Hooper: Missions to Salyut 6, *Spaceflight,* **20**, November 1978, 371.

[8]   Ibid., p. 379.

[9]   Kenneth Gatland (Ed.): *Illustrated encyclopaedia of space technology*, 1981, p. 225.

[10]   See James E. Oberg: *Red Star in orbit*, London, 1981, pp. 184–186.

[11]   Gordon R. Hooper: Missions to Salyut 6, *Spaceflight,* **21**, March 1979, 133.

[12]   Evgenia Alsats: The stellar house, *Soviet Weekly*, 29 November 1980.

[13]   Soyuz 33 aftermath: Russians plan new Soyuz–Salyut link-up, *Flight International*, 28 April 1979.

[14]   *Salyut takes over*, Moscow, 1983.

[15]   Yuri Glazhkov: Why no more women in space? *Soviet Weekly*, 8 March 1980. Women cosmonauts out, *Flight International*, 8 March 1973. For subsequent events see: Women demand equality in space, *Soviet Weekly*, 5 April 1980.

[16]   Neville Kidger: Salyut 6 mission report, *Spaceflight,* **24**, April 1982, 178.

[17]   For medical results of these missions see: A.I. Gigoriev *et al. Selected problems of psychological support of prolonged space flights*, Moscow, 1985.

[18]   Another step to space construction, *Soviet Weekly,* 11, 18 July 1981.

[19]   Salyut 6 says goodbye, *Soviet Weekly*, 7 August 1982.

[20]   This and subsequent extracts from Valentin Lebedev: Diary of a cosmomaut, *Soviet Weekly*, 10 September 1983.

[21]   French spaceman told to watch it, *Evening Press*, 23 June 1982.

[22]   In October 1987, Chief of the Yuri Gagarin Cosmonaut Training Centre, Vladimir Shatalov, strongly criticised his superiors for not following up this successful experiment. See *Shatalov sees lack of purposefulness in space research*, Transcripts of Soviet Press, SU/0022, D/1, 10 December 1987.

[23]   Soyuz blast escape, *Observer*, 2 October 1983. Cosmonauts – a scare in space, *Newsweek*, 31 October 1983. How emergency ejection system saved cosmonauts, *Krasnaya Zvezda*, 30 May 1987.

[24]   US ready for space swop, *Sunday Express*, 23 October 1983.

[25]   Cosmonauts confirm two space mishaps, *Irish Times*, 13 December 1983.

[26]   Ibid.

[27]   Basis laid for large space complexes, *Soviet Weekly*, 3 December 1983. Academician Boris Paton: Towards a permanent space station, *Soviet Weekly*, 4 February 1980. See also: Huge satellites are key to Soviet plan to transform Sun's energy, *International Herald Tribune*, 15 June 1987.

[28]   Vladimir Dzhanibekov: The rescue of Salyut 7, from: Man in space, *New Scientist*, 1986, 44–47.

[29]   *Mir orbital station – transfer to Salyut 7 by Kizim and Solovyov*, Moscow, 1986.

[30]   Rocket blasts off: new stage in space work. *Soviet Weekly*, 30 May 1987.

[31]   Soviet launch of shuttle rocket widens gap in superpower space race. *The Times*, 18 May 1987.

CHAPTER 11

[1]   Did USSR fly a shuttle?, *Flight International*, 19 June 1982.

[2]   Trevor Williams: Soviet reentry tests – a winged vehicle, *Spaceflight,* **22**, May 1980, 213–214.

[3]   See Philip Bono & Kenneth Gatland: *Frontiers of space*, London, 1969, p. 131–134.

[4]   The next giant step, *Time*, 22 June 1970.

[5]   Thomas Canby: A generation after Sputnik – are the Russians ahead in space? *National Geographic,* **170**, October 1986, pp. 422–423. The runway was officially confirmed in V. Golavachev: 200m from the Mir space station, *Trud*, 7 April 1987.

[6]   It's 20 years since Sputnik-1, *Soviet Weekly*, 1 October 1977.

[7]   Kenneth W. Gatland: A soviet space shuttle?, *Spaceflight,* **20**, September/October 1978, 325.

[8]   RTE Radio News, 8 April 1987.

[9]   A flight into space is not a stroll, *Newsweek*, 12 December 1983.

[10]   Other reports on the Soviet space shuttle can be found in the following: (i) Top topic in space research, *Soviet Weekly*, 24 November 1973. (ii) Soviet shuttle to fly this year?, *Flight International*, 4 June 1977. (iii) Craig Covault: Soviets build reuseable shuttle, *Aviation Week and Space Technology*, 20 March 1978, 14 (iv) *Spaceflight,* **25**, April 1983, 149–151. (v) *Spaceflight,* **26**, May 1984, 194–199. (vi) Peter Pesavento: Space shuttles – CCCP style, *Griffith Observer*, December 1984, 2–11. (vii) Art Bozlee & C.P. Vick: The Soviets' next step into space, *L5 News*, December 1985, 6–9. (viii) Soviet shuttle in 1988?, *Flight International*, 20 September 1986.

[11]   Cosmonaut Titov looks to the future, *Flight International*, 15 October 1977.

[12]   Gatland, op. cit.

[13]   Yuri Dokvuchayev: They were Gagarin's friends, *Soviet Weekly*, 17 April 1982. See also: Coming shortly – a factory in space?, *Soviet Weekly*, 4 August 1979.

[14]   Boris Belitsky: Science and engineering, *Radio Moscow*, 30 December 1987.

[15]   Academician Vasili Mishin: The future of earth-to-space transport, *Soviet Weekly*, 26 April 1980.

[16]   *Newsweek*, 12 December 1983, op. cit.

[17]   C.P. Vick, remarks addressed to the Technical Symposium (of the British Interplanetary Society) on the Soviet space programme, 3 June 1983.

[18]   *Newsweek*, 12 December 1983, op. cit.

[19]   Angus MacPherson: Mars by 1980? Russians shake the west, *Daily Mail*, 3 June 1970.

[20]   Mikhal Chernyshev: What next for Mars?, *Soviet Weekly*, 13 November 1982. See also: Man on Mars in about 20 years?, *Soviet Weekly*, 4 April 1981.

[21]   Kenneth Gatland (Ed.): *Illustrated encyclopaedia of space technology*, 1981, p. 234.

Appendix A
Some of the major events in the Soviet space programme

1927   Establishment of the Gas Dynamics Laboratory in Leningrad.
1933   Flight of the first modern liquid-fuelled rocket in the USSR: the '09', followed by the GIRD-X.
1947   Tests of the German wartime A-4 rocket at Volgograd station
1955   Construction of the Baikonour cosmodrome; final approval for the construction of an Earth satellite
1957   Sputnik 1 and Sputnik 2
1959   The first three Moon probes. Luna 2 hit the Moon and Luna 3 circled around the far side, taking pictures
1961   The first probe to Venus, Venera 1
       The first man in space: Yuri Gagarin
1962   Close approach flights in Earth orbit of cosmonauts Andrian Nikolayev on Vostok 3 and Pavel Popovich on Vostok 4
1963   First flight by a woman cosmonaut, Valentina Terreskhova
       Contradictory statements about Russia's withdrawal from the Moon race
1964   Flight of a three-man spaceship, Voskhod 1
1965   First spacewalk by Alexei Leonov from Voskhod 2
       Start of communication satellites – Moloynia 1
1966   Luna 9 soft-lands on the Moon; Luna 10 goes into Moon orbit
1967   Death of cosmonaut Vladimir Komarov on Soyuz 1
1968   Flights of Zond 5 and 6 around the Moon and recovery on Earth
1969   Luna 15 moon-scooper rivals the American landing on the Moon

1970   Recovery of samples from the Moon; the first moonrover
        Lunokhod 1 begins exploration of the Sea of Rains
1971   The first manned orbiting space station, Salyut 1
1975   Television pictures from the surface of the planet Venus
1977   Launch of the semi-permanent orbiting space station, Salyut 6
1980   Cosmonaut Valeri Ryumin spends a year in space on two missions.
1982   Venera 13 drills the rocks of Venus; new endurance record of 211 days is
        established by cosmonauts Berezovoi and Lebedev
1984   First woman spacewalker Svetlana Savitskaya carries out welding experiments
        outside the Salyut 7 orbital station
1987   Mir space station operational, with Kvant observatory module

Appendix B
Chronology of major events

YEAR	UNITED STATES		USSR
1957 Dec. 6	American attempt to launch Vanguard	Oct. 4	First Sputnik
		Nov. 3	Second Sputnik, with dog Laika
1958 Jan 31	First American satellite, Explorer 1	May 15	Sputnik 3
October	Setting up of National Aeronautics and Space Administration, NASA; approval of Project Mercury		
1959 April	Selection of Mercury astronauts	Sept. 14	Luna 2 impacts on the Moon
		Oct. 4	Luna 3 sent to fly around the Moon
1960		Aug. 19–20	Flight of space dogs Belka and Strelka
1961 May 5	First American astronaut, Alan Shepard	Feb. 12	First Venus probe
May 25	President Kennedy announces Project Apollo: target of man on the Moon	Apr. 12	First cosmonaut, Yuri Gagarin
		Aug. 6–7	Flight of Gherman Titov
1962 Feb. 20	John Glenn in orbit	Mar. 16	Start of Cosmos programme
Jul. 10	Telstar: the first comsat	Aug. 11–15	Vostok 3–4 joint flight
		Nov. 1	First Mars probe
1963 May 15–17	Sixth and last flight in Mercury programme	June 16	Valentina Terreskhova, first spacewoman
		October	Reports that USSR has withdrawn from Moon race
		Nov. 1	First flight of components of the Soyuz complex, Polyot 1
1964 Jul. 31	Ranger 7 reaches the Moon	Oct. 12	First three-man spaceship, Voskhod 1

YEAR	UNITED STATES		USSR	
1965	Mar. 23	Start of Gemini series	Mar. 18	First spacewalk: Alexei Leonov
	Dec. 15–16	Gemini 6 and 7 rendezvous	Jul. 16	First launch of Proton rocket
1966	Mar. 16	Gemini 8: first space docking	Feb. 2	Luna 9 soft-lands on the Moon
	Jun. 1	First American lunar soft-landing	Apr. 3	Luna 10 enters Moon orbit
	Aug. 14	First American lunar orbiter		
1967	Jan. 27	Pad fire kills Apollo 1 crew	Apr. 24	Death of cosmonaut Vladimir Komarov trying to land Soyuz 1
	Nov. 9	First launch of the Saturn 5	Oct. 30	Cosmos 186–188 dock automatically
1968	Oct. 11	Apollo flights resume (Apollo 7)	Mar. 27	Death of Yuri Gagarin
			Sep. 20	Zond 5 recovered after flight around the Moon
	Dec. 21–27	Apollo 8 flies to the Moon and back	Oct. 26	Soyuz flights resume (Soyuz 3)
			Nov. 16	Zond 6 recovered in southern USSR after flight around the Moon
1969	Jul. 20	Apollo 11 Moon landing	Jan 16	Soyuz 4–5 linkup
			Jul. 13	Luna 15 flies to the Moon
	Nov. 19	Second Moon landing, Apollo 12	Oct. 11–18	Joint flight by Soyuz 6, 7 and 8, with seven cosmonauts
1970	Apr. 11–17	Near-catastrophic mission of Apollo 13	Jun. 1–17	Record 18-day Soyuz 9 flight
			Sep. 24	Luna 16 samples return to the Earth
			Nov. 16	Lunokhod 1 rover arrives on the Moon
			Dec. 15	First soft-landing on Venus (Venera 7)

YEAR		UNITED STATES		USSR
1971	Jan. 31	Third Moon landing, Apollo 14	Apr. 19	First space station, Salyut
			Jun. 6–29	Three cosmonauts board and work on Salyut, but perish on return to Earth
	Jul. 26	Fourth Moon landing, Apollo 15	Dec. 2	Mars 3 reaches surface of Mars
1972	Jan. 5	President Nixon approves space shuttle		
	Apr. 16	Fifth Moon landing, Apollo 16		
	Dec. 19	Apollo 17 returns to the Earth – end of the Moon landing series		
1973	May 14	Launch of Skylab space station	Apr. 3	Salyut 2
			Sep. 27	Resumption of manned flights, Soyuz 12
1974			Jul. 4	Soyuz 14 crew boards Salyut 3
1975	Jul. 15–24	Apollo–Soyuz test project	Jul. 26	Soyuz 18B crew return after 63 days
			Oct. 20	Venera 9 photographs Venus's surface
1976	Jul. 20	Viking 1: first of two probes to soft-land on Mars	Jun. 22	Salyut 5
1977			Jul. 17	First Star module, Cosmos 929
			Sep. 29	Salyut 6
1978			Jan. 20	Introduction of Progress freighter
1979			Dec. 16	Introduction of Soyuz T

YEAR		UNITED STATES		USSR
1980			Apr. 9	Popov and Ryumin begin 185-day mission
1981	Apr. 12	First space shuttle, *Columbia*		
1982	Nov. 11–16	First operational shuttle flight with commercial cargo	Apr. 19	Salyut 7, followed by 211-day occupation by Berezovoi and Lebedev
1983	Apr. 4	Introduction of shuttle *Challenger*	Mar. 2	First operational Star module, Cosmos 1443
1984			Feb. 7	Start of 237-day mission by Kizim, Solovyov, Atkov
1985				
1986	Jan. 28	Loss of shuttle *Challenger*, with entire crew	Feb. 20	Launch of Mir space station
			May 21	Introduction of Soyuz TM
1987			Mar. 31	Launch of Kvant observatory to Mir
			May 15	Introduction of Energia super rocket
			Dec. 29	Yuri Romanenko returns after 326 days in space

Appendix C
Record of Soviet manned space missions

LAUNCH DATE	SPACECRAFT	CREW	MISSION
19610412	Vostok 1	Gagarin, Yuri	First man in Earth orbit
19610806	Vostok 2	Titov, Gherman	
19620811	Vostok 3	Nikolayev, Andrian	Dual flight with Vostok 4
19620812	Vostok 4	Popovich, Pavel	Dual flight with Vostok 3
19630614	Vostok 5	Bykovsky, Valeri	Dual flight with Vostok 6
19630616	Vostok 6	Terreskhova, Valentina	First woman in Earth orbit; dual flight with Vostok 5
19641012	Voskhod 1	Komarov, Vladimir; Yegorov, Boris; Feoktistov, Konstantin	First three-man spaceship
19650318	Voskhod 2	Belyayev, Pavel; Leonov, Alexei	First extra-vehicular activity (EVA) - by Leonov
19670423	Soyuz 1	Komarov, Vladimir	Komarov killed on re-entry
19681025	Soyuz 2	Unmanned	One of only four unmanned flights to carry the Soyuz designation. This spacecraft served as a target for Soyuz 3
19681026	Soyuz 3	Beregovoi, Georgi	Due to dock with unmanned Soyuz 2 but failed
19690114	Soyuz 4	Shatalov, Vladimir; Yeliseyev, Alexei; Khrunov, Yevgeni	First manned docking with another manned spacecraft; Yeliseyev and Khrunov from Soyuz 5 transferred to Soyuz 4
19690115	Soyuz 5	Volynov, Boris; (Yeliseyev, Alexei; Khrunov, Yevgeni)	Docked with Soyuz 4; Yeliseyev and Khrunov transferred to Soyuz 4
19691011	Soyuz 6	Shonin, Georgi; Kubasov, Valeri	Multiple rendezvous with Soyuz 7 & 8

LAUNCH DATE	SPACECRAFT	CREW	MISSION
19691012	Soyuz 7	Filipchenko, Anatoli; Volkov, Vladislav; Gorbatko, Viktor	Joint mission with Soyuz 6 & 8
19691013	Soyuz 8	Shatalov, Vladimir; Yeliseyev, Alexei	Joint mission with Soyuz 6 & 7
19700601	Soyuz 9	Nikolayev, Andrian; Sevastyanov, Vitally	18-day spaceflight
19710419	Salyut 1	See spacecraft	First space station (re-entered 19711011). Only visitors were Soyuz 10 and Soyuz 11
19710423	Soyuz 10	Shatalov, Vladimir; Yeliseyev, Alexei; Rukhavishnikov, Nikolai	Docked with Salyut 1, but no crew transfer
19710606	Soyuz 11	Dobrovolsky, Georgi; Volkov, Vladislav;	24-day spaceflight. Docked with Salyut 1 and crew transferred to space station, but all three cosmonauts killed on re-entry
19730403	Salyut 2	Never manned	First military space station. Vehicle suffered catastrophic explosion on 14 April which left it tumbling helplessly in low-Earth orbit from which it decayed on 28 May 1973
19730927	Soyuz 12	Lazarev, Vasili; Markarov, Oleg	(Soyuz spacecraft without solar panels)
19731218	Soyuz 13	Klimuk, Pyotr; Lebedev, Valentin	
19740625	Salyut 3	See spacecraft	Replacement space station for Salyut 2 which failed in orbit. The first operational military space station. Salyut 3 re-entered 19750124

LAUNCH DATE	SPACECRAFT	CREW	MISSION
19740703	Soyuz 14	Popovich, Pavel; Artyukhin, Yuri	Docked with Salyut 3
19740826	Soyuz 15	Sarafanov, Gennadi; Demin, Lev	Failed to dock with Salyut 3
19741202	Soyuz 16	Filipchenko, Anatoli; Rukhavishnikov, Nikolai	Test of docking mechanism for joint mission with USA – the ASTP (Apollo–Soyuz Test Project)
19741226	Salyut 4	See spacecraft	Visiting craft Soyuz 17, 18 and Soyuz 20 (unmanned test of Progress tanker). Re-entered on 19770203
19750111	Soyuz 17	Gubarev, Alexei; Grechko, Georgi	Docked with Salyut 4, scientific research space station
19750405	Soyuz 18 – 1	Lazarev, Vasili; Markarov, Oleg	Launch failure; Soyuz capsule ejected at 90 miles altitude; crew saved
19750524	Soyuz 18	Klimuk, Pyotr; Sevastianov, Vitally	Docked with Salyut 4
19750715	Soyuz 19	Leonov, Alexei; Kubasov, Valeri	First international space mission. Soyuz 19 was Soviet half of Apollo–Soyuz Test project
19751117	Soyuz 20	Unmanned	Test of Progress tanker vehicle; docked with Salyut 4
19760622	Salyut 5	See spacecraft	Visiting craft Soyuz 21, 23 and 24, although Soyuz 23 failed to dock. Re-entered on 19770808
19760706	Soyuz 21	Volynov, Boris; Zholobov, Vitally	Docked with Salyut 5. Flight ended with emergency evacuation, but crew saved
19760915	Soyuz 22	Bykovsky, Valeri; Aksyonov, Vladimir	Photographic survey
19761014	Soyuz 23	Zudov, Vyacheslav; Rozhdestvensky, Valeri	Failed to dock with Salyut 5. Soyuz capsule crashed at night in ice-filled lake but crew saved

LAUNCH DATE	SPACECRAFT	CREW	MISSION
19770207	Soyuz 24	Gorbatko, Viktor; Glazhkov, Yuri	Docked with Salyut 5 – military mission
19770929	Salyut 6	See spacecraft	Visiting craft Soyuz 25 to 40 inclusive, although Soyuz 25 and 33 failed to dock. Also visited by Progress tankers 1 to 12 inclusive, Cosmos 1267 (Star Module) and Soyuz T1 (Soyuz 34 & T1 were unmanned). Salyut 6 re-entered 19820728
19771009	Soyuz 25	Kovalyonok, Vladimir; Ryumin, Valeri	Failed to dock correctly with Salyut 6; Soyuz 25 brought home for an emergency landing
19771210	Soyuz 26	Romanenko, Yuri; Grechko, Georgi (crew landed in Soyuz 27)	Docked at secondary docking port of Salyut 6 as the primary port was thought to have been damaged by Soyuz 25; however, it was later shown to be undamaged. The crew received visitors from Soyuz 27, 28 and a new tanker called Progress. This 96-day flight beat the American endurance record set up by Skylab 4
19780110	Soyuz 27	Dzhanibekov, Vladimir; Markarov, Oleg (crew landed in Soyuz 26)	Visitors to Salyut 6; two ferry craft now docked with station
19780302	Soyuz 28	Gubarev, Alexei; Remek, Vladimir (Czech)	Docked with Salyut 6. First international crew launch and first non-Soviet cosmonaut (Czech) in a Soviet spacecraft
19780615	Soyuz 29	Kovalyonok, Vladimir; Ivanchenkov, Alexander (crew landed in Soyuz 31)	Docked with Salyut 6. Crew received visitors from Soyuz 30, 31 and three Progress tankers (2, 3, & 4). 140-day flight
19780627	Soyuz 30	Klimuk, Pyotr; Hermasziewski, Miroslaw (Polish)	Docked with Salyut 6

LAUNCH DATE	SPACECRAFT	CREW	MISSION
19780826	Soyuz 31	Bykovsky, Valeri; Jaehn, Sigmund (East German) (Crew landed in Soyuz 29)	Docked with Salyut 6
19790225	Soyuz 32	Lyakhov, Vladimir; Ryumin, Valeri (crew landed in unmanned Soyuz 34)	Docked with Salyut 6. Because later planned visits failed to materialize this long duration crew spent the entire mission on their own in this 175-day flight. Because of fears that Soyuz 32 had exceeded design life an unmanned Soyuz 34 brought the crew home
19790410	Soyuz 33	Rukhavishnikov, Nikolai; Ivanov, Georgi (Bulgarian)	Failed to dock with Salyut 6. Re-entry had to take place at over 15G, possibly the highest endured by spacemen in flight. Rukhavishnikov was first non-pilot to lead a multi-manned space mission
19790606	Soyuz 34	(Lyakhov, Vladimir; Ryumin, Valeri)	Launched unmanned, returned with crew of Soyuz 32
19791216	Soyuz T1	Unmanned	Final test of redesigned Soyuz, which docked with Salyut 6 on 19791219
19800409	Soyuz 35	Popov, Leonid; Ryumin, Valeri (crew landed in Soyuz 37)	Docked with Salyut 6. Crew received visitors from Soyuz 36, 37 and 38, the crew of a new craft Soyuz T2, and two Progress tanker vessels (9 & 10) in their 185-day flight. Ryumin, fresh from his 175-day flight, stepped in at the last minute to replace the injured flight engineer of Soyuz 35
19800526	Soyuz 36	Kubasov, Valeri; Farkas, Bertalan (Hungarian). (Crew landed in Soyuz 35)	Docked with Salyut 6

LAUNCH DATE	SPACECRAFT	CREW	MISSION
19800605	Soyuz T2	Malashev, Yuri; Aksyonov, Vladimir	New-style Soyuz able to make automatic docking with Salyut, but system failed and manual docking was carried out with Salyut 6. Crew wore new-style spacesuits
19800723	Soyuz 37	Gorbatko, Viktor; Tuan, Pham (North Vietnamese) (crew landed in Soyuz 36)	Docked with Salyut 6
19800918	Soyuz 38	Romanenko, Yuri; Mendez, Arnaldc (Cuban)	Docked with Salyut 6. Mendez was the first coloured spaceman; at thirteen years old he had been a shoe-shine boy
19801127	Soyuz T3	Kizim, Leonid; Markarov, Oleg; Strekalov, Gennadiy	Docked with Salyut 6. First three-man Soviet crew since June 1971. Crew carried out maintenance work on Salyut 6
19810312	Soyuz T4	Kovalyonok, Vladimir; Savinykh, Viktor	Docked with Salyut 6
19810322	Soyuz 39	Dzhanibekov, Vladimir; Gurragcha, Jugderdemidyin (Mongolian)	Docked with Salyut 6. Soon after return of this crew, on 25 April, Russia launched Cosmos 1267 (the first Star Module) which docked with Salyut 6 on 19 June and remained attached to it until July 1982 when the station re-entered
19810515	Soyuz 40	Popov, Leonid; Prunariu, Dimitru (Rumanian)	Last mission to Salyut 6 and final flight by old-style Soyuz spacecraft
19820419	Salyut 7	See spacecraft	Visited by Soyuz T5 to T12 inclusive, although Soyuz T8 failed to dock, Progress tankers 13 to 24 inclusive, Cosmos 1443 (the second Star Module),

LAUNCH DATE	SPACECRAFT	CREW	MISSION
19820419	Salyut 7 (continued)	See spacecraft	Cosmos 1686 and the crew of Soyuz T15 in May and June 1986. Unfortunately Salyut 7 suffered a number of catastrophic system failures and has been placed in a 'parking orbit', possibly for retrieval by the Soviet Shuttle in the 1990s
19820513	Soyuz T5	Berezovoi, Anatoli; Lebedev, Valentin (crew landed in Soyuz T7)	Docked with Salyut 7. Crew received visitors from Soyuz T6 and Soyuz T7 and four Progress tanker vehicles (13, 14, 15 & 16) during their record 211-day flight
19820624	Soyuz T6	Dzhanibekov, Vladimir; Ivanchenkov, Alexander; Chretien, Jean-Loup (French)	Docked with Salyut 7
19820819	Soyuz T7	Popov, Leonid; Serebrov, Alexander; Savitskaya, Svetlana (crew landed in Soyuz T5)	Docked with Salyut 7. Savitskaya was the second woman in space
19830302	Cosmos 1443	Unmanned	Second Star Module, which docked with Salyut 7 on 19830310 and re-entered on 19830919
19830420	Soyuz T8	Titov, Vladimir; Strekalov, Gennadiy; Serebrov, Alexander	Failed to dock with Salyut 7
19830627	Soyuz T9	Lyakhov, Vladimir; Alexandrov, Alexander	Docked with Salyut 7. Crew received no visiting cosmonauts as Soyuz T10-1 aborted on the launch pad, but they were visited by Progress tankers 17 and 18. The crew completed the first construction in space by adding new solar panels to the station during their 149-day flight

LAUNCH DATE	SPACECRAFT	CREW	MISSION
19830927	Soyuz T10-1	Titov, Vladimir; Strekalov, Gennadiy	First launch-pad explosion in manned spaceflight history but crew saved
19840208	Soyuz T10	Kizim, Leonid; Solovyov, Vladimir; Atkov, Oleg	Docked with Salyut 7. Crew received visitors from Soyuz T11 and T12, Progress 19 to 22 inclusive during their record breaking 237-day flight
19840403	Soyuz T11	Malashev, Yuri; Strekalov, Gennadiy; Sharma, Rakesh (Indian)	Docked with Salyut 7
19840717	Soyuz T12	Dzhanibekov, Vladimir; Savitskaya, Svetlana; Volk, Igor	Docked with Salyut 7. Savitskaya was the first woman to fly in space twice and to carry out an EVA
19850606	Soyuz T13	Dzanibekov, Vladimir; Savinykh, Viktor (Dzanibekov returned to Earth on 19850926 in Soyuz T13 with Georgi Grechko of Soyuz T14)	Docked with Salyut 7. Received visitors from Soyuz T14 and Progress tanker craft 23 to 24 inclusive. First crew rotation with Soyuz T14
19850917	Soyuz T14	Vasyutin, Vladimir; Volkov, Alexander; Grechko, Georgi (Grechko returned to Earth with Dzanibekov in Soyuz T13; Vasyutin, Volkov and Savinykh returned in Soyuz T14 on 19851121)	Docked with Salyut 7. Mission terminated abruptly when Commander Vasyutin became dangerously ill. He soon recovered on returning to Earth
19850927	Cosmos 1686	Unmanned	Large module carrying several tonnes of cargo to Salyut 7 and providing more workspace for the crew. It docked with Salyut 7 on 19851002
19860219	Mir	See spacecraft	New-generation orbital laboratory based on Salyut but with six docking ports. Visited by Soyuz T15

LAUNCH DATE	SPACECRAFT	CREW	MISSION
19860219	Mir (continued)		and Soyuz TM1 to TM4 inclusive and Progress tankers 25 to 35 inclusive, plus Kvant module. Still in orbit in May 1988
19860313	Soyuz T15	Kizim, Leonid; Solovyev, Vladimir (125 days in orbit)	Docked with Mir. On May 5th undocked from Mir/ Progress 26 complex and docked with Salyut 7/Cosmos 1686 combination on 6 May. On 25 June Soyuz T15 left Salyut 7 and docked with Mir; it returned to Earth on 16 July
19860319	Progress 25	Unmanned	Cargo vessel carrying 2 tons of supplies and research equipment docked with Mir on 19860321
19860423	Progress 26	Unmanned	Cargo vessel carrying 2 tons supplies and equipment docked with Mir on 19860426. On 4 May its engine was used to lower orbit of Mir prior to departure of Soyuz T15. Progress 26 left Mir on 22 June and re-entered atmosphere
19860521	Soyuz TM1	Unmanned	First test flight of an up-dated version of the Soyuz T. It docked with Mir on 19860523
19870116	Progress 27	Unmanned	Cargo vessel carrying 2 tons of equipment and supplies to Mir in readiness for long-stay crew aboard Soyuz TM2
19870205	Soyuz TM2	Romanenko, Yuri; Laveikin, Alexander	Docked with Mir
19870303	Progress 28	Unmanned	Cargo vessel carrying 2 tons of supplies and equip-ment to resident Mir crew

LAUNCH DATE	SPACECRAFT	CREW	MISSION
19870331	Kvant	Unmanned	20.6 tonne (take-off weight) add-on module for the Mir/Soyuz TM2 orbital laboratory, containing 40 cubic metres of workspace and a high-energy physics observatory
19870421	Progress 29	Unmanned	Cargo vessel carrying 2 tons equipment and supplies to resident crew
19870519	Progress 30	Unmanned	Cargo vessel carrying 2 tons of equipment and supplies to resident crew of Mir/Kvant
19870722	Soyuz TM3	Viktorenko, Alexander; Alexandrov, Alexander; Faris, Muhammad (Syrian). Viktorenko and Faris returned to Earth on 30 July with Laveikin of Soyuz TM2 crew leaving Alexandrov aboard with Romanenko. Alexandrov and Romanenko returned to Earth on 19871229 in Soyuz TM3 with Levchenko of Soyuz TM4 crew. Romanenko had completed a record-breaking 326-day flight and Alexandrov (who replaced Laveikin) made a 160-day flight	Docked with Mir
19870803	Progress 31	Unmanned	Cargo vessel carrying 2 tons of equipment and supplies to resident crew. Docked with Mir/Kvant on 19870806
19870924	Progress 32	Unmanned	Cargo vessel with 2 tons of equipment and supplies for the resident crew. Docked with Mir/Kvant on 19870926

LAUNCH DATE	SPACECRAFT	CREW	MISSION
19871120	Progress 33	Unmanned	Cargo vessel carrying 2 tons of equipment and supplies to resident crew. Docked with Mir/Kvant on 19871123
19871221	Soyuz TM4	Titov, Vladimir; Manarov, Musakhi; Levchenko Anatoli (Levchenko departed on 29 December with Romanenko and Alexandrov aboard Soyuz TM2)	Docked with Mir/Kvant on 23 December, 6 days before departure of Soyuz TM3 forming a space complex consisting of Mir, Kvant and two Soyuz craft with 5 cosmonauts working on board
19880120	Progress 34	Unmanned	Cargo vessel carrying 2 tons of supplies and equipment to crew of Mir/Kvant
19880323	Progress 35	Unmanned	Cargo vessel carrying 2 tonnes of equipment and supplies to resident crew of Mir/Kvant

Appendix D: Maps

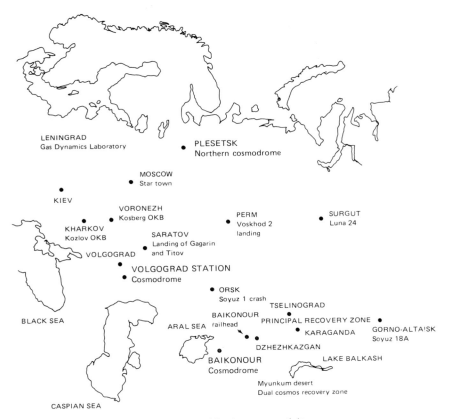

LENINGRAD
Gas Dynamics Laboratory

● PLESETSK
Northern cosmodrome

MOSCOW
● Star town

●
KIEV

VORONEZH
● Kosberg OKB

PERM
Voskhod 2
landing

● SURGUT
Luna 24

●
KHARKOV
Kozlov OKB

SARATOV
Landing of Gagarin
and Titov

● VOLGOGRAD

● VOLGOGRAD STATION
● Cosmodrome

● ORSK
Soyuz 1 crash

TSELINOGRAD

BLACK SEA

ARAL SEA

BAIKONOUR
railhead

PRINCIPAL RECOVERY ZONE ●

● KARAGANDA

GORNO-ALTAISK
Soyuz 18A

● DZHEZHKAZGAN

BAIKONOUR
Cosmodrome

LAKE BALKASH

Myunkum desert
Dual cosmos recovery zone

CASPIAN SEA

Principal centres of Soviet space activity.

Cosmodromes
PLESETSK 62° 43′N, 40°18 E
BAIKONOUR/TYURATAM 45.6°N, 63.4°E
VOLGOGRAD STATION 125 miles SE of Stalingrad

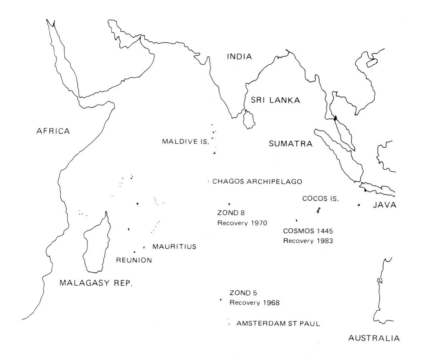

Indian Ocean recovery sites.

Recovery zones
45.5°N to 52.5°N, 61.0°E to 72.5°E

Exceptions: Luna 24, Surgut, Siberia
               Cosmos 1887, Mirny, Yakutia
               Soyuz 18A, Gorno-Altaisk
               Soyuz 1, Orsk
               Voskhod 2, Perm, Urals
               Vostok 1 and 2, Saratov

Indian ocean zone: Zond 5, 8
                      Cosmos 1374, 1445 kosmolyot
Myunkum desert: Dual cosmos

Index